D1541521

STORIES PARENTS
SELDOM HEAR

STORIES PARENTS SELDOM HEAR

College Students Write About
Their Lives and Families

HARRIET HARVEY
Introduction by Robert Coles

A Merloyd Lawrence Book
DELACORTE PRESS/SEYMOUR LAWRENCE

A MERLOYD LAWRENCE BOOK
Published by
Delacorte Press/Seymour Lawrence
1 Dag Hammarskjold Plaza
New York, N.Y. 10017

Manufactured in the United States of America
First printing

Designed by Rhea Braunstein

LIBRARY OF CONGRESS CATALOGING IN PUBLICATION DATA
Main entry under title:

Stories parents seldom hear.

"A Merloyd Lawrence book."
1. College students—United States—Attitudes—Ad-
dresses, essays, lectures.   2. College students—United
States—Family relationships—Addresses, essays,
lectures.   I. Harvey, Harriet.
LA229.S65   378'.198'0973   82–2538
ISBN 0–440–07661–7   AACR2
ISBN 0–440–58262–8 (pbk.)

To my students
who had the courage to look at their lives
and write about them honestly.

CONTENTS

APPRECIATION

MANY people helped in the creation of this book. First and foremost, my students gave invaluable advice, whether or not their stories were included. From this group I'd like to thank particularly Debra Hermon, Ann Kennedy, Phyllis Orrick, Timothy Kenslea (who gave up a week of his vacation to help me edit) and my son, Alexander Gibney, who was at Yale during this period (but did *not* take my course).

My thanks also to Professor Gaddis Smith, who as head of the Hall Seminars at Yale encouraged me in my teaching; Professor R.W.B. Lewis, formerly master of Calhoun College, who initiated my seminar; Eustace Theodore, Dean of Calhoun, who made my administrative duties simple; Katherine Pollak, who helped me read papers and meet with students in the semester during which, in addition to other duties, I was teaching two seminars simultaneously.

For my writing and editing period I want to thank my friend Deane Lord, who provided the title; the psychiatrist and author Price Cobbs, who gave me a deeper perspective on the black student issues in the sixties and seventies. Then there were those good

APPRECIATION

friends who offered me hospitable shelter during the peripatetic period when I was writing the book: Philip Zaeder and Sylvia Thayer of Andover, Massachusetts; Rita and Len Sperry and Licia Hayden of Belvedere, California; Millicent Tomkins of San Francisco; Jack and Hope Patterson and Nora and Farwell Smith of Washington, D.C.; and Marc and Bea Simont of New York. The patience award must go to my mother, who, even when she visited me, accepted my preoccupation; and to Cynthia Cadua, who typed endless drafts with good humor and had the magical ability to read my handwriting.

Finally, there are those wonderful people who, as well as giving sound advice, provide support at those moments when you feel everything should be tossed into the wastebasket: Arthur Deikman of Mill Valley, California; Larry Daressa of California Newsreel; and my editor, Merloyd Lawrence, who, in addition to providing editorial wisdom, gave of her monumental patience and understanding.

INTRODUCTION
BY ROBERT COLES

*Y*OUNG men and women who attend colleges such as Yale have not suffered a lack of public notice in recent decades. If anything, our newspapers and magazines and television journalists have concentrated their attention rather excessively on the preferences and inclinations—and not rarely, the passing postures—of students enrolled in Yale or Harvard or Princeton. Why do we spend so much time being interested in, let alone worried by, the various fluctuations in mood or ideation of these young men and women—in contrast to the millions of others their age in this country who don't get writers and social taxonomists and political or psychological theorists eyeing their every whim or fancy? I remember the powerfully stated and strongly felt words of a twenty-year-old Cambridge factory worker I came to know in 1969 and 1970, when the Harvard Yard was alive with all sorts of slogans: "They sneeze over there in those college buildings and everyone comes running over, saying what's going on, what's going on. People like us could scream and scream, or we could say the smartest things since Jesus Christ came, and no one would give a damn. Once you get into an Ivy League school, you're part of a big investment the country has—in itself, I guess. I walk to Harvard Square, on my way to work, and I see kids who aren't so different from me. They're not snobs or lazy bums living off some rich ancestor; they're kids from ordinary homes, you can tell, and they're learning to become high on themselves. That's how I see it; they're from *Harvard*, and even if their old man works in a factory, and their old lady does, it's going to be different for a Harvard graduate—so I guess all the attention those students get, the talk in the papers and on television, is what they're going to have now and forever after. The higher you go, the more people you'll have looking at you. But when they talk on the television news programs about *the young*, meaning kids from places like Harvard, a lot of the time, I ask myself what about all the people my age out there working, or going to a plain college, with no big airs attached to it? And if I can ask that question, you'd think some of these news people and experts could!"

His expectations of others, especially those last ones mentioned, were rather higher, alas, than ought to have been the case. One need not be a backwater anti-intellectual to notice the special attention given a relative handful of America's college youth—not those attending community colleges all over this nation, or universities located in the South or the Northwest. It is important to consider the destructive possibilities that disparity holds—for Yale students, say. It is no great boon, necessarily, to have one's egoism constantly boosted by a public regard that is, finally, unearned. After all, the interest so many of us have in Harvard and Yale has to do, not rarely, with our nervous worries about our own situation. Where do we stand? How are we doing? Who is moving along faster or slower than us? What can we do to hold our position, or improve it? Those inevitable questions of the anxious, frightened snob are asked by many American men and women who harbor a perennial, eager affection for places such as Yale. And those questions do not go unheeded by students lucky enough to be told yes by certain admissions committees. To quote yet again the young factory worker from Cambridge: "I see those kids, and I wonder if they feel *themselves*, or if they just enjoy being big-deal Harvards. That's what they become, as soon as they get here. No matter if they come to Cambridge for the first time on the subway, rather than a limousine—

it's all the same: the stamp of Harvard on them! Everyone 'out there' is watching and drooling and holding their breath! Some want them to climb as high as the ladder goes, and some are waiting for them to fall on their faces!"

Not a bad summary of the peculiar psychological burdens of Harvard people—or of those that befall the extraordinarily privileged young men and women who get called Yalies from eighteen or so until the last breath. In this book we become privy to some of those Yalies—their personal and intellectual lives; and the nearer we move toward them, the more ridiculous a number of sociological generalizations turn out to be—including a few from working-class youths or their sometimes self-appointed spokesmen. If working-class youths have a right to be disgusted by some of the awe commanded by their Ivy League age-mates and fellow citizens, those latter men and women have a right to scratch their heads and wonder what some of the fuss is all about—given the distinct heterogeneity of the present-day Yale undergraduate population. As the students we get to know in these pages make clear, there are all sorts and conditions of human beings in those various Gothic New Haven colleges that make up, collectively, one of the nation's leading centers of higher learning. And for many of these young Americans, as for others of their generation, the struggle to become part of one or another institutional life, as against the wish to be one's very own self, at least to a degree, ranks as a major, if occasionally veiled, preoccupation. Even as a Cambridge factory worker can tell a visitor that he wonders sometimes where he begins and his life in the General Electric plant ends, these Yale students stand perplexed and apprehensive as well as rather bravely (innocently?) sure of themselves as they negotiate in microcosm the corridors of today's American knowledge—and power.

When I first skimmed Harriet Harvey's manuscript, I worried about the problem of self-centeredness in her students—that sin of sins, pride. None of us is spared it. No combination of social reform and psychological scrutiny will spare any of us the more than occasional lapse into what George Eliot wonderfully called "unreflecting egoism." But young people at leisure to learn (and learn about themselves) are perhaps specially vulnerable to that temptation. They are not yet compelled to take account of others as strenuously as they one day will be—as husbands or wives, as parents, as members of this or that "group," "company," "department," "firm." They have been given a kind of sanction: the leeway to read and read and read, and experiment in laboratories and play sports and party —in sum, a "period" in their lives, a moment enviable to others not able to claim such permission for themselves. But it is not all learning —or pleasure. And for some, the price of admission to the club, as it were, has ended up being exceedingly high—the rote of compliance in classrooms becomes an inner, psychological rote of devastating proportions.

Yet, it is possible to turn one's back on that rote. One need not search for resentful, truculent (and arguably, envious) members of the "working class" for a strenuous criticism of certain aspects of Ivy League life. In that Ivy League one can meet those who have said *basta!* to multiple-choice tests and the seemingly endless, pointless, and amoral factuality of premedical or prelegal education. One can listen to one's students—"fieldwork" done, for instance, right in the Harvard teacher's office: "What am I supposed to do—join a commune, wherever there's one that lasts longer than a year? Or drop out and get a job in a factory or an office—like my father, who's on the assembly line at eight every morning, or my mother, who sits in an insurance office all day, shuffling cards and sticking them into computers? I'm their only hope! I haven't got the money to worry about 'the environment,' and the troubles in countries five or ten thousand miles from here. I haven't got the time to take the chic courses. I'm here to try to get just a little better deal—to become a member of 'the black bourgeoisie.' I hear these rich, liberal whites sneer at the expression. They can sneer. They have the money to sit back and sneer. They can sneer at the teachers, too; they can say we're all becoming 'mechanical learners,' and we memorize and memorize, and we're not 'original' and 'creative,' just 'grade hungry.' I'll tell you—I'm not only 'grade hungry'; I've heard my parents talk about being hungry for food.

"My grandfather was a sharecropper in Alabama. What am I supposed to do—go and fight with these professors? People turn on the students of the seventies; but it's the professors who keep giving us these stupid, nitpicking tests. Let's have some criticism of them. You know what they'll say, though? They'll say it's not their fault;

it's the fault of 'the whole society.' Like my mamma used to say: everyone turns and points the finger at everyone else. And everyone says they'd like the world to be much different, but what can *they* do? Like I heard a preacher say: 'Everyone wants to go to heaven, but no one wants to die.' Now, there are some who've got a lot behind them; so they can drop out, or tell a place like Harvard off, or go travel someplace for a year. That's nice for them. They can look down at me, and call me a grade-grubbing conformist. I'm here on a scholarship. If I leave, it's back to the ghetto! Who's going to support me there, while I sit and ridicule Ivy League education for not being 'open' or for stepping on the 'individuality' of the young?"

Why should an educational critic be troubled by that line of argument—one that can be rather easily labeled, I fear, as "defensive" in the ever-ready, convenient, and banal language of contemporary psychology? Is it not best that "we" who consider ourselves "above" such comments (and the desperate self-justifications implicit in them) continue to press our point of view upon others, even if we have to set up "alternative" courses or curricula or entire schools and colleges? Such questions are, to an extent, rhetorical—or, of course, fiercely polemical. Still, they ought be kept in mind—and particularly remembered when an interesting and valuable book such as this one appears. In her own way Harriet Harvey wanted to challenge the educational status quo—even as many of us, teachers and students, have surrendered to it. She has not wanted to settle for the demanding, exhausting, frustrating if not enraging "reality" that young factory workers or certain Ivy League students have keenly in mind as they prepare themselves for the long haul of "adulthood"—a given life, with all its strains and limits. She has wanted to stand and look hard at what seems inevitable; and ask students to do likewise—learn to speak their minds, a necessary start in the development of a critical posture. She has helped at least a few students to listen to themselves and learn a little of what they fancy. She has gently but persistently nudged her self-selected students toward—themselves.

Not a pedagogy of narcissism, though. One begins her book afraid of that—worried that what some might regard as a brazen luxury, the autobiographical statement, will also turn out to be a self-indulgent one. When does legitimate self-scrutiny end and a wanton, bragging self-preoccupation begin? Is it true that if people of any age but "express" themselves, then a lot of wonderful truths will be showered upon them—and us? Or was Flannery O'Connor right when—told that a lot of would-be writers for one reason or another get discouraged and don't pursue a career as storyteller or novelist —she observed wryly that *not enough* such people were, in fact, being diverted from their ambition? Moreover, do we really need to ask college students to get more "in touch" with their "feelings," their "emotions"—we who live in a country cursed by "sensitivity groups," "encounter groups," things called "est" or "actualization experiences"? Those questions, like the comments of skeptics of various races and classes, ought to haunt us when told that an Ivy League class has spent weeks coming to terms with memories, moments of personal triumph or failure, long squelched reflections or daydreams that have ruled a particular mind, but never got told to anyone.

This book wonderfully and triumphantly faces down the issues I have (somewhat crankily) dragged into this introduction. These are strong, compelling stories—the harvest of a very special kind of teacher. Not that they are all uplifting stories. Quite the contrary, some are sad, even morally suspect—personal accounts of what T. S. Eliot summarized so well as "compromise, complacency, and confusion." But these are writers who have been taught. They haven't been allowed to pour out their "emotions"—the more the better, and no matter the sloppiness or dreariness. Someone with a sensible eye and ear has kept track of their language, their assumptions, their narrative manner, the logic of their claims on themselves or others. Someone has pronounced them "messy" or repetitive or all too self-absorbed. Someone has tried to push or pull them, tap them on the shoulder, point a direction, ask a series of questions, make a suggestion or two. The result is a series of testimonies that have in them, often enough if not always, pacing and surprise and humor and dramatic twists or turns: what Flannery O'Connor called "the truthfulness of the essential that creates movement."

Nor is it inappropriate to summon once more that stern, tough, often disapproving Georgian storyteller, with us so terribly short a time. In a lecture she used this suggestive phrase: "the mystery of our position on earth." It is in our nature as human beings to come up against that mystery. Language is the vehicle, of course, that enables the sense of such mystery. Language lends itself to questions and more questions, and to answers galore. Young college people are especially prone to do the asking, to find the replies (in various books, theories, ideological postures). It is condescending and reductionist in the extreme for any of us to "explain" such inquiry, be it youthful or otherwise, as prima facie evidence of a psychological "problem." We are not only driven by Oedipus complexes; we are not only anxious to obtain an "identity." We are the creatures whose nature it is to know what Paul Tillich kept calling "finitude." That there will be a last breath is a discovery children make; from that moment on, the "mystery" Flannery O'Connor mentions, a central ("existential") mystery, won't let go of us—even if we use a million ruses to "forget," thereby remembering all too well our flight. Give a person four years, and introduce him or her (wonderfully) to George Eliot or Fëdor Dostoevski or William Faulkner or John Butler Yeats or Dante or Shakespeare, or from another direction, Newton and Pascal and Gödel and Bohr and Einstein—and no wonder there is plenty of "soul searching" on our campuses. And if that tendency connects with the ingredients of one life, then another, are we to suggest a need for more psychiatric facilities, or for more psychological theories about "adolescence" from the many (too many?) social scientists who find work in our contemporary universities?

True, these are stories parents seldom hear; but they are, many at least, stories that the tellers themselves would not have thought to tell. A teacher wanted to hear the voices of a few members of a certain community. She made clear that interest. She was heard—and rewarded. She received responses—the humdrum, the pitiable, the surprising, the amusing and entertaining, the thoroughly idiosyncratic and the conventional. She helped give those responses coherence and vitality. It is for us, the readers, to register our affection or dismay—that students can be so forthcoming and sincere and decent and thoughtful, or that, alternately, they can be so boldly selfish, so ruthlessly ambitious, so cold and calculating in their social, political, and economic approximations.

These are not members of a generation "greened"; they are the familiar ones of human history, the children of light and the children of darkness. I hope the various social and psychological theorists who can't let anyone breathe, let alone speak or write, without coming up with an interpretation, a conclusion, will stop long enough to consider the amplitude of these stories—the range of voices, the breadth of interests as well as backgrounds, the depth and intensity of speculation and bewilderment and (occasionally) ethical conflict. The final worth of this book may well be determined by its capacity to resist the ambitious inroads of those theorists. Stories are either *sui generis* or—alas—they become illustrative polemical tracts, case histories, asides in this or that proposition, argument. One hopes that Harriet Harvey and her willing, even ardent, narrators will be spared that kind of intrusion, if not degradation—will send off signals that, in effect, tell us all to say a quite particular hello and good-bye to each of these youths, whose opinions or allegiances may not please us, but whose anecdotes, observations, evocations of the past and present have been told in such a way that we ought attend as any raconteur would wish, with eyes widened and ears quite open.

STORIES PARENTS SELDOM HEAR

FLESH IN THE INKPOT

> Part of the pleasure of writing, as well as the pain, is involved in pouring into that thing which is being created all of what [the author] cannot understand and cannot say and cannot deal with or cannot even admit in any other way. The artifact is the completion of personality . . .—Ralph Ellison in *The Writer's Craft*

The tales in this book are personal stories from the lives of eleven college students. They are views into that tumultuous passage from childhood to adulthood—the identity crisis, if you wish—that youth of all ages and all nations must pass through to gain their independence and their adult role in society.

Each story is strikingly different from the next because each person's life is so different, reflecting the enormously varied backgrounds—economic, religious, social and personal—of the college population of today. Elías Aguilar, a Puerto Rican Catholic who, as a small boy, was deserted by his father and with his mother emigrated from a Puerto Rican *barrio* to a Harlem slum, obviously has a tale different from that of Helen Billinger, the Episcopalian great-

1

granddaughter of an American coal baron, who spent her girlhood years at a posh New York private school or on the tennis courts and sailboats of the exclusive family estate at Southport. Bob Simmons, a Kansas City public high school kid whose father worked as a machinist for a Minute Man missile plant and whose mother deserted him when he was nine, lived several worlds away from Al-Noor Hirji, an Ismaili Moslem of Indian descent, who grew up beneath the jasmine and baobab trees of Dar-es-Salaam and served in the all-black army of the newly independent state of Tanzania before coming to college in America. Beyond all that, of course, is the unique thumbprint of each personality, not one of which, as James Agee says ". . . is ever quite to be duplicated, nor replaced, nor has it ever quite had precedent: but each is a new and incommunicably tender life . . ."

These are also contemporary tales because they touch on many personal and social problems that young people are facing today. All the young authors in this book were in grade school, high school, and college in the sixties and seventies—those years of explosive social change that brought Vietnam, the sexual revolution, and the Black Power and Women's Liberation movements. During this period, the young developed a radically new and outspoken voice that can be heard clearly in these stories and that sets the stage for the personal and sexual style of many of today's college students. All the young authors are just now beginning their struggles to establish careers in the economically uncertain eighties.

Their stories were all written for a special undergraduate seminar I taught at Yale in the seventies, called in some semesters Experience and Expression, a Writing Workshop—and in others, Writing from Yourself. Gradually, during the five years I taught, I came to see the stories as those "parents seldom hear." Not because their children didn't want to tell them. Quite the contrary. Most of, if not all, the stories in this book were, I believe, written—consciously or unconsciously—*for* parents. Or for someone who, in that generation, the authors hoped would understand an old agony, a puppy love, a doubt, a secret episode—something they had not wanted to talk about before. Sometimes it was an experience they felt was shameful, like Lynne Hall's drug peddling; sometimes it was a confusing political upheaval, like Al-Noor Hirji's search for a national

2

identity; sometimes it was a struggle to find an independent position within an old family structure, like Helen Billinger's family ghosts. The authors were, just as Ralph Ellison describes, "pouring into that thing which was being created" all of what they could not understand or could not say or could not deal with or could not even admit in any other way.

But both the stage of life—youth (when the search for an independent identity seems to demand the monosyllabic "yeah" and "no" response to elders)—and a superrational education usually keep these stories underground. They seldom surface in composition classes because they are too confusing, if not too exposing, to formulate easily. They are created from the stuff discussed now and then in late-night bull sessions with peers or penned into journals at private moments. And yet these stories sit at the center of the writers' lives—as all good stories do.

In Front of the Fireplace

In order to help students focus on some of this elusive material, I designed my course in a special way. Each semester, I admitted sixteen students to the seminar, not on their already acquired ability to write but on their desire to learn how. I urged them not to compete with one another and assured them they would not be graded in relationship to anyone else but only on their improvement. This meant I always had, in addition to literature majors and budding writers, a sprinkling of math and science majors, who usually had a terror of writing. One of my favorite students, a computer-science major, when applying for admission to the course, wrote: "I can't write anything without numbers in between. If you are honest when you say you will grade people on how much they get better, I feel I could pass the course because I could improve by 75 percent."

There was only one central requirement for the course: students were to find an important experience from their lives and write about it in a chapter-length story—thirty to forty pages. The first draft was due two thirds of the way through the semester, and in the final four weeks everyone was given that unenviable task that students rarely experience but professional writers know only too well: rewriting, rearranging, cutting, editing, and reediting—sometimes as many as five times. Because writing is lonely and difficult, I encouraged the students to help each other and to seek out advice from other teachers and students in the university whenever they wished.

I conducted my weekly class in front of the fireplace in my living room from nine to eleven at night because I wanted to remove the students as much as possible from the academic atmosphere, where they were used to competing with one another and to dissecting critically everything from the common crayfish to Camus. I wanted them to put their analytic intellects aside and touch base with what John Hersey calls "the dark womb of the mind"—the unconscious or preconscious or whatever those deep wellsprings of past experience and emotion are that bubble up, presenting a new idea—a different way of looking at things. I was determined to shake up their rational thought patterning and draw out their feelings and memories. Conrad had said ". . . the artist descends within himself, and in that lonely region of stress and strife, if he be deserving and fortunate, he finds the terms of his appeal."

Rediscovering "I"

I knew that most of these young people had mastered the art of getting good grades—on SAT's, on exams, on papers—and that, in the highly competitive race for admission to college, most of them had become all too competent in what John Holt calls "writing in the third remove"—what you *think* the teacher would like to have you say about the battle of 1812 or the literary style of Proust or the religious symbolism in T. S. Eliot. In the process, most of them had lost faith in the pronoun "I" and had embraced instead that disembodied pronoun "one," as if they had no right to voice an opinion of their own. "Truth" somehow lay outside the self; it was something that somebody else—like Einstein or Shakespeare or Sartre—had discovered. Their own experiences and points of view seemed too silly or trivial to write about and their personal thoughts and feelings petty, immature. The poet Kenneth Koch, when teaching poetry to the elderly, discovered the same hesitancy. "People," he writes, "usually think best of themselves for making general statements and those also seem safest. . . . How did they know they wouldn't be

4

thought foolish if they talked about playing with their dog or what color their babyhood pajamas were? I gave them examples from my life . . . I encouraged them to say the first thing that came to mind. I liked students talking about something strong and emotional that might seem silly to others. . . ."

In the first class, I always read the students an article by the novelist (and Yale man), John Knowles:

> Yet if education is a friend up to a point, it can also be an enemy. . . . Several years after graduation from Yale, I decided the time had come to write a novel. So I withdrew to the island of Ischia and began to work out the symbolic pattern of my book, and naturally the metaphysical paradoxes, the underlying myth and the levels . . .

> I actually completed this work and called it *Descent to Proselito,* my name for Ischia. . . . I sailed proudly back to America with the manuscript and laid it before Thornton Wilder, who had been very kindly reading and criticizing my work. "Knowles," his comment ran, "I'm on page 151 and can't go on. You're not interested in this."

Interested, interested? Did I have to be interested?

> . . . So I withdrew *Descent to Proselito* from the publisher, who rather reluctantly thought he might bring it out, and began to write about things that interested me, and involved not just my observation and my mind but my temperament and my feelings. I had failed because I had received more education than I could digest. I needed to go back to an earlier and simpler approach where I knew how to function.

That was just what I wanted to do: take the students back to a simpler place where they could speak out with their own authority.

The Jaundiced Notebooks

Because I wanted my students to think of their writings not just as college papers—on which they might get a grade and a few comments and which they could then lay aside—but as "real" stories they might submit for publication, I had instituted a system of putting their weekly papers in a large yellow loose-leaf binder in the library on closed reserve, where they could check it out like any other reserve book. By this method I felt they might gain a certain distance from their own material and read it as if their ideas had been proposed by someone else. I was also eager for them to read about each other's experiences—an opportunity I felt was extremely important in helping them understand one another and their tremendously varied backgrounds. Any student who didn't want his story read by the others could put an X on the paper and I would not put it in the notebooks. Usually, in the early weeks, quite a few X's appeared, but very soon most class members came to trust one another enough not to feel embarrassed by what they were writing in either content or style. Because they all read what the others were writing, and talked over their personal experiences in class, the students in each seminar soon developed a close rapport with one another and I, too, came to know them well and value their friendship. On one occasion, Charlie Musser, a student who'd just returned from a vacation from the outer banks of North Carolina, brought us a huge sack of fresh oysters and we all sat around eating oysters and telling stories from our lives. On another night, we all took a half hour off to visit a class member in the infirmary who'd been hospitalized with a knee operation. I was often touched by the lengths to which the students would go to help each other—not only with their writing but also in their daily lives.

About three weeks into the course, the library notebooks would suddenly burst into life. On the inside cover of the yellow binder, I always pasted, in large type, the advice of Catherine Drinker Bowen: "Get your story down on paper. Cover the pages right or wrong. Never mind how scared you are or how exposed you feel." Bowen's mandate seemed to liberate the students and all hell would break loose. The emotional floodgates would open suddenly and my students would be pouring out pages and pages of passionate, undigested material—childhood reminiscences, adolescent musings, snatches of poetry, notebook agonizings, letters—about their families and personal lives. The initial single binder would spill over into two and then threaten to become three. I also heard that the class members were having a hard time getting access to the notebooks because the student librarians were pouring over them, fascinated with the "soap operas" that were unfolding there. This attention flattered the authors as well as making them nervous. One year during this process, my students dubbed their collected works "The Jaundiced Notebooks."

Flesh in the Inkpot

In the early weeks of the course, I was insistent about the need to find just the *right* story—before worrying about syntax or style. "Look in thy heart and write means just that," said Nancy Hale. I told them that the real feelings that surround an experience are often hidden behind a tangle of personal defenses, fears, and rationalizations; and to pry out the real story could be a painful job, like digging for a sliver. "One ought only to write," said Tolstoy, "when one leaves a piece of flesh in the inkpot each time one dips one's pen."

Above all, I said, I didn't want anyone imitating another writer's style—no matter how much they might admire Proust or Anaïs Nin or Norman Mailer. Style was a matter of discovering one's own voice, one's own thumbprint, one's own personality. If ever I waxed melodramatic, it was on this point. I would quote Virginia Woolf with passion: "So long as you write what you wish to write, that is all that matters; and whether it matters for ages or for hours, nobody can say. But to sacrifice a hair of the head of your vision, a shade of its color, in deference to some Headmaster with a silver pot in his hand or a professor with a measuring-rod up his sleeve, is the most abject treachery. . . ."

A Window on the Past

Before I began teaching, I had assumed that the students would write mostly for and about peers. After all, these were people with whom they seemed totally involved. Very soon, however, I discovered that few students chose to write about contemporary scenes and fewer still about peer relationships—even from high school days or earlier. Childhood and family matters—particularly parental relationships—took center stage. As the mother of teen-agers myself, I must have been led astray by the uncommunicative stance of adolescence. The last thing in the world I felt they were concerned about was their childhood and their relationship to me or to anyone in the adult world.

So whenever I sat in my study reading papers, I couldn't help wondering how many of the parents of my students had any idea of the long and agonizing hours their children were devoting to writing about their brothers, their sisters, their mothers, their fathers. I imagined my students home on Christmas vacation, sleeping more than half the day, and, when not asleep, off with their friends at a rock concert or a local hangout. Had the parents any idea how much time their child was spending describing the early years in the small family grocery store on a corner in Bedford-Stuyvesant, or the Valentine's Day when a brother was killed in a car crash, or the winter afternoon Dad picked his daughter up at boarding school because she was thrown out for smoking pot?

The students had a strong drive to understand these earlier events and relationships—to cut loose from the family past and at the same time to become reconciled with it. The drive to complete childhood was as impelling as the desire to leap into something new. It was as if the authors couldn't step confidently into adulthood without integrating what had gone before.

I noticed that the need to understand an experience was particularly strong in those students who had suffered a severe crisis or family tragedy. Phyllis Orrick, a student from Baltimore, comes to terms with her brother's death in *From a Spiral Notebook*. In *Letters to my Grandfather,* Ann Kennedy entertains her grandfather with amusing tales from her childhood while grappling with painful feelings over his impending death.

Some students had experienced personal traumas that were simply too difficult to absorb. Such experiences take many years to assimilate—if, indeed, that is ever possible. Ellen Talbot, a sophomore from Oregon who had rarely mentioned her family life, one night told us—almost in a whisper—about her mother's suicide. She was eleven at the time and the only child still living at home. She said she had never before discussed the event with anyone—including her family, which had fallen apart following her mother's death. After much self-debate, Ellen decided she'd try to write about the tragedy. As she worked on her narrative, it became a letter to her

8

older sister, who had been overseas at the time of the tragedy. It was an angry letter, but at the same time it reached out for further understanding from her sister about the event and their relationship. As a story, it was powerful and worked well. But it did not satisfy Ellen and she never mailed it. When I telephoned her about the possibility of including it in the book and then sent her a copy of the manuscript for her to review, she wrote back that it had taken her three weeks to open the envelope that she knew contained the story, and said: "It's painful for me to read it. It's not yet an experience I have absorbed . . . and until that's done, it's a private account. I'm being disingenuous—I question if it will ever cease to be private."

Declarations of Independence

Throughout the many tales, one underlying message seemed to predominate. Not surprisingly for this age group, it was a declaration of independence and a request for a redefined relationship with their parents. It was as if they were saying *Please know me and accept me as I really am.* Helen Billinger at the end of her story, *The Billinger Ghosts,* delivers her message in a single sentence. Because she has a long family tradition, more prescriptive than most, she addresses her remarks to Edward Augustus Billinger, her imposing but long-deceased great-grandfather, the family patriarch. "I want," she writes, "to be able to face him as an individual and say, 'Here I am, your great-granddaughter Billinger. But first let me be Helen. Then let's be friends.' "

For some, the desire for independence is opposed by an equally strong desire to cling to the safety of childhood, where no independent decisions nor commitments are required. Obviously this conflict can manifest itself in many forms—some socially acceptable and some not. One contemporary option is to sign up with a cult in which a self-appointed evangelist or guru can give devotees *all* the answers. So long as the faithful follow the rigid edicts of the cult, they can be "born again" as a fundamentalist, a Moonie, or a Krishna. In her story *Dorothy and Hare Krishna,* Michele Lewis describes the seductiveness of such father figures and substitute families and her sister's tendency to surrender to them.

Similarly, a criminal "gang" can also create a close, if rivalrous, "family." Defined by the rejection of others, such a negative identity can be impelling. Lynne Hall in *The Questionnaire* describes how she came close to being swept into such a life and how she swapped this option for another.

Delivering the Message

Over the years, I began to hear that after the stories were finished they often found their way—weeks, months, or sometimes years, later—into parental or some familial hands. They became a vehicle for opening up an intergenerational dialogue on difficult or embarrassing matters and, as such, often functioned as instruments of reconciliation and deeper understanding. Often a former student would telephone me out of the blue or buttonhole me on campus to tell me about it. They were almost always surprised by their parents' reactions. As one student put it: "You know that story I wrote. I showed it to my parents. They didn't think it was such bullshit. As a matter of fact, the old man cried."

This sense of surprise seems to hold true for professional writers as well. John Updike reports that "it's harder to shock my parents than I might have thought." Erica Jong's mother, after reading her book, said simply, "Why don't you be more like Graham Greene, dear?" She also remarked, however, that her father and grandfather began to talk more openly with her and reveal secrets of their own. On reading *A Separate Peace,* John Knowles's mother said to him, "If I'd known you were so unhappy at Exeter, I'd never have let you stay there." Not surprisingly, any art form is frequently threaded with a yearning to draw closer to someone. Jane Fonda says she persuaded her father to act with her in *On Golden Pond* because she felt it would smooth some of the rough edges of the relationship between them. "Working within the script," she said, "I could tell him things and show my feelings in a way I couldn't quite bring myself to do otherwise. Face to face, it wouldn't come out right. After making that film we understood each other a lot better."

For some, however, delivering the message is an impossible task. Franz Kafka provides a famous example of this in his *A Letter to My*

10

Father. Kafka had struggled most of his life to break free from the outrageously harsh view his father held of him. As much as he felt overwhelmed by his father's demands, he was even more dominated by his father's belittling image of him. Although he was up against a father more autocratic and unreasonable than most, he nevertheless tried to set the record straight and reorder their relationship to a balance point where they might find some sort of reconciliation. He must have spent weeks, if not months, writing *A Letter to My Father,* in which he describes how difficult it was to value himself in the face of his father's scorn. "You only encourage me in anything," he writes, "when you yourself are involved in it, when what is at stake is your own sense of self-importance. . . . What I needed was a little encouragement, a little friendliness, a little keeping open of *my* road, instead of which you blocked it for me, though of course with the good intention of making me go another road." Undoubtedly feeling it was useless to try to mend the relationship, Kafka never sent the letter and he never broke free of his father's image of him. Even for those who have more supportive parents, it's a hard job *not* to interpret ourselves in terms of our parents' perceptions of us. To do so effectively can take years and, at best, is never fully realized.

Like Kafka's, not every student's story was delivered, but fortunately not for the reasons that confronted Kafka. Sometimes the students wanted to protect their parents, sometimes the enterprise seemed too risky or too embarrassing, sometimes the student was just plain shy. When Al-Noor Hirji told me he had never shown his mother or brothers his story, he blushed and said: "My family are merchants—practical. I can't be talking about such things."

The momentous psychological task of youth, says the psychoanalyst Erik Erikson, is to establish an identity separate and apart from parents and their parents' generation. The narratives in this book are small pieces of that process—exploring a past mistake; making peace with a childhood loss; reconciling, if possible, with the past and with one's parents; and then establishing an independent identity. The different authors wrote them during different years in their college experiences and at different stages in their search for independence.

11

Finding Your Own Voice

But the task is, of course, not just a personal one of establishing a new relationship with one's parents. It is also deeply connected to finding a fruitful place for oneself within the larger family—society itself. And society, if it is not to stagnate or suppress what is most vital in it, must nurture the new ideas of each new generation.

In light of this, I am apprehensive about the diminishing options open to students in the eighties—a period where the student is under more and more pressure to "tool up" quickly for a job in a highly technological society. Increasingly, both parents and their children seem to be looking at college solely as an investment for future vocations, often defined in terms of a narrow specialty or the "hottest opportunity" in an advancing technology. Yet, as early as 1960, in *The Uncommitted,* the sociologist Kenneth Kenniston cautioned: "What our society lacks is a vision of itself and of man that transcends technology. It exacts a heavy human toll not because technology exists, but because we allow technology to reign. . . . It is a society that too often discourages human wholeness and integrity, too frequently divides men from the best parts of themselves, too rarely provides objects worthy of commitment."

To "make it," students in the eighties apparently, have little time just to hang out or involve themselves in extracurricular activities like informal art or musical groups, theater, or the college newspaper. They must keep their noses buried in their texts to get the A's and B's requisite for the "good job" or graduate school. In a recent AP article about "Straightlaced College Freshmen," a Brown senior was quoted as saying, "When I was a freshman, we studied hard too. But when we came back from the library late at night, we would talk about politics and important things. Now the freshmen just stay up late typing. I haven't heard one political discussion this year . . ." The registrar at Tufts reported that "more and more kids are dropping courses when there is even a remote chance they will get a C. We had a girl drop out of an economics course this fall, with approval from her parents, after she got a B-minus on a test."

Nor do students seem to involve themselves in the ideas they've memorized. Recently, one of my friends—also a teacher—told me he had met a student who was reading Paul Tillich's *The Courage to Be.* He asked her how she felt about the issues raised by Tillich. "I started to think about that," she replied "but I had an exam coming up and I didn't want to be sidetracked by becoming personally involved."

In a stage of life—and a period of history—when it's vital to try out new ideas, to consider radically new approaches to a nuclear era none of us can understand, students ironically have less time to experiment and play—less time to mature. They have less leeway to risk, to make mistakes and learn from failure—a process that has often been more productive than success. Only infrequently are they allowed the invaluable time-out—what Erikson calls "the adolescent moratorium"—in which to integrate their subjective experiences with their objective education and learn how to make their own choices, to become their own authorities, to exercise their own creative potentials. "It is not learning or the learning process which matures men," said the psychoanalyst Lawrence Kubie some years ago, "it is maturity, however won, which makes it possible for learning to be creative."

The creative process—that art of synthesis that pulls together diverse and often contradictory material into a new whole—is invaluable learning in the adolescent years. It becomes even more urgent to teach it in a technological world, which, if we are to survive, must be subsumed under a more deeply human and moral purpose. Unlike analysis, which breaks down a whole into small parts, the creative process—whether in art, the humanities, or in that part of science Lewis Thomas calls "questioning bewilderment" —has the power to cast off outmoded assumptions and create a whole new way of perceiving things. It can transform our view of the world, not just rearrange the furniture within it. However problematic the product—the poem, the story, the statue, the dance composition—the creative process itself can, at its best, help students integrate their past experiences and give form to their feelings. If my courses succeeded for students, it was not because of the product—the stories themselves (though they were pleased with these). It allowed them time and space to investigate their very human endeavors and desires. By digging deep into personal material, each author attempted—with enormous energy and enthusiasm —to express what was most vulnerable and most valuable in themselves and to speak out with an authentic voice.

The spirit in which these stories are offered to the reader also suggests the beginning of a new kind of radical openness and trust that Jean-Paul Sartre speaks of when he says: "A man's existence must be entirely visible to his neighbor, whose own existence must in turn be entirely visible to him, in order for true social harmony to be established. This cannot be realized today, but I think that it will be, once there has been a change in the economic, cultural, and affective relations among men . . . I can quite well imagine the day when two men no longer have secrets from each other, because no one will have any more secrets from anyone, because subjective life, as well as objective life, will be completely offered up, given."

The student stories in this book are small attempts at just that: secrets out in the open, the subjective life offered up in hopes of a deeper communion with themselves, with their parents, and now with others.

PORTRAIT OF ANN

ANN Kennedy entered Yale with the second class that admitted women. Although (to put it mildly) most of Yale's first women were not overly pleased with Yale's friendly-but-patronizing stance toward women in the early coeducational years, Ann was neither surprised nor intimidated by it. Indeed, she hardly noticed it. Ivy League types were familiar to her, and their special prides and defenses were qualities she knew how to handle without thinking about it. Many of her acquaintances attended Ivy League colleges, and her father had gone not only to Princeton as an undergraduate but to Harvard Business School and Yale Law School as well.

Ann was, moreover, a "preppie"; her high-school years had been spent at Emma Willard, where she was an honors student and president of the school government. Troy was not that geographically distant—nor Emma Willard that atmospherically different—from New Haven. Unlike many of her classmates, she was treading on an intellectual and cultural terrain that was known and comfortable. On paper, a description of her read like a Hollywood version of just what a Yale woman should be.

15

Nor would she have been the least disappointing on camera. She was tall—with a lovely figure—and appropriately athletic. She had a delicately chiseled face with high cheekbones, brown eyes, and fair, fair skin. But it was her hair that was utterly extraordinary. For me it came to symbolize the independent streak that set her apart from any stereotype. An afro as kinky as any black's, it was blond—ash blond—and more often than not asserted an askew stubbornness all its own. So distinctive was it, in fact, that, after she had been persuaded to be a princess in Omaha's fashionable Aksarben Ball, the dance committee insisted that she have it straightened for the occasion. Ann complied reluctantly while Omaha hairdressers "smashed, rolled, pulled, stretched, electrified" it into flat submission. She wasn't happy again until she washed out the "proper" curls the next morning and it resumed its wiry, upward thrust. (Few people have been as shortsighted as the Aksarben dance committee. An artist friend of mine paints another portrait of Ann almost every time he runs across her in New York or near his home in Cornwall, Connecticut; and few professional photographers will let her pass by without running for their cameras.)

I met Ann when she was a sophomore and joined my initial seminar—the first occasion on which I had taught anything at all except Girl Scout fire building. As a neophyte, I was not without my terrors, but whenever Ann bounced into class, I always felt better. She exuded a contagious energy and optimism that made all of us assume no undertaking was impossible. Her humor was effervescent, and at moments flashed out with a biting Irish wit. Through her direct manner—and the open sharing of her own vulnerabilities— she could put all of us at ease, and if the occasion called for it, pull the group into action. I was very grateful to her. She wore responsibility and leadership as naturally as the old silk scarf she knotted casually around her neck.

Ann was the eldest of five children from a close-knit and prosperous family in Omaha, Nebraska. She saw herself as responsible for carrying forward much of the family tradition—both feminine and masculine. In this she was not atypical of many of Yale's first women; a large proportion of them were firstborn and had assumed fairly early in their lives that they would seek and succeed at professional careers. In the class notebooks she described herself somewhat nar-rowly as "a compulsive oldest child, always responsible for reserving the tennis courts, organizing the anniversary party, and mediating in potential crises. Our family led a somewhat self-contained exis-tence, so I had plenty of time to practice. Whatever traits evolved from this were later recognized by my peers, as I always seemed to become the president of the French club, of the class, or of the school."

Tennis courts and anniversaries were very much the fabric of Ann's big family life. She was surrounded by energetic and athletic brothers, sisters, and cousins and frequently went off to visit one or another of them at their various schools and colleges. Through the years she had received many of the advantages of affluence with few of its disadvantages: family relationships were close and balanced; money was no worry but well planned for; Catholicism was binding but not oppressive (at least within the family); success at school was assumed but not pressured. Once a year her paternal grandfather would whisk everyone off for a summer holiday at Aspen or Cape Cod to ride, play tennis, swim, and sail. All this was to stand Ann in good stead in a time of tragic loss to come.

In the year I taught her, Ann was concerned with two things—Catholicism and her grandfather—and they were not unconnected. Ann had always been doted on by her extraordinary grandfather, who at ninety-five was still practicing law. As the first child of the grandfather's youngest child and only surviving son, she appeared in his life at just the moment when the rest of his children and grand-children had grown up and moved away. "I overheard someone saying," she wrote in the notebooks, "that I thereby gave him a renewed reason to live. He absolutely spoiled me to death, and because of him I always had—or thought I had—the very best. And because he told me so all the time, I considered myself smarter, prettier, and quicker than anyone else in the world."

In the summer before her sophomore year, Dad—as the grandfa-ther was called by the whole family—suffered a heart attack and everyone believed he would die shortly. Ann was frightened and confused. For the first time in her life someone in her family was seriously ill and she was facing the possibility of losing a person she

17

loved dearly. This brought her straight up against her conflicting feelings about Catholicism. In her early school years she'd undergone a rigorous religious training at Omaha's Duchesne Academy of the Sacred Heart. By her senior year at Emma Willard, she'd given it all up. Now she found herself torn. "The fact that my grandfather is dying," she wrote in the notebooks, "has raised indescribable trauma as far as the Church is concerned." (This kind of sentence construction was a hallmark of Ann's early writing.) "I now find myself attending services compulsively every day and wishing I were still very, very Catholic. At the same time, I'm frightened that my religious training is so ingrained that it is permanently embedded and that I wouldn't be able to let it go if I wanted to."

Ann worried, too, about her ability to write creatively. She told me she was well used to turning out "the usual term papers of literary criticism," but she'd previously reserved her personal thoughts and feelings for her journal or letters to friends. She doubted she could write anything that would be interesting to a general audience. "I'm a letter writer," she told the class, "of the six-typewritten-single-spaced-pages variety, and all about things no stranger would be interested in. I have no characters or plots in my head and I don't know how to get started. . . . I have little inspiration about form or genre."

I suggested to Ann that, for her long piece, she write a series of letters to her grandfather. Although she was well aware that letter writing was a traditional literary form as valid as any other, she couldn't quite believe that a teacher would allow her to write letters for course credit.

"I could do *that*?" she asked, and was delighted when I reassured her that I felt it was by far the best thing for her to do—for herself, for her grandfather, and for her writing.

She leapt into her first two letters with enthusiasm and received a great deal of support from other members of the class who faced similar losses or felt they would soon. Bob Schloss, an Orthodox Jew who also came from a close-knit religious family, wrote in the class notebooks: "Ann, all the time I was reading your letter, I was thinking about my grandfather and how, in a few years, I will face the same thing. . . . I wonder if I'll have the nerve to express myself so openly."

It was a struggle for Ann to write her grandfather things she'd never talked about before. She wasn't sure at all that the beloved but reserved old man would accept either her tales or her strong feelings. Moreover, she worried about confronting him with all this when he was ill and perhaps dying. Yet before he died she wanted to say— straight out—how much she loved him and how much she would miss him. In doing this she wanted to meet him not as the little girl she'd been but as the independent woman she was becoming. She didn't have much time left.

After the first two letters were finished, Ann was reluctant to send them. On top of her other reservations she felt they might not be grammatically correct enough for the stately and exacting old man. They still needed editing. Tentatively, at midterm, she mailed off a noncontroversial but amusing letter about heaven, and her grandfather sent an affectionate reply. She delayed sending others. Her grandfather's health seemed to be improving, and that would give her time to perfect them. In the meantime, she kept pouring them out on paper.

Some of the writing was messy. She was a master at using "I guess," "actually," "at one point," dangling clauses, pronouns without antecedents, and inverted sentences. However, as Ann became more confident in her point of view, her prose automatically grew better. Her problem lay not in her lack of grammatical knowledge (Emma Willard had done pretty well by her) but in thinking she had no right to take a position without citing an authority. When there was no expert to quote, she hedged behind clauses and qualifiers. Gradually she began to discover her own position and to gather the nerve to affirm it with a simple declarative sentence.

Ann redrafted her letters three times and was still not satisfied with the results. So after the class was over, we sat down together and she edited them more. Luckily enough, while we were engaged in this lengthy editorial activity, her grandfather's health was improving and he was back on his feet again—if a bit shakily.

In July, Ann left New Haven for a trip to Greece and asked me to mail the series of letters (now thoroughly edited) to her mother after her departure. Her mother would decide if any passage should be omitted (only one brief one about smoking dope was censored) and then give them to her grandfather at the most appropriate time. She was still queasy about how he would receive her renegade opinions about Catholicism and her attempts to reach through his formality to his heart. Being halfway around the world made it all seem safer.

*L*ETTERS TO MY GRANDFATHER
by Ann Kennedy,
Omaha, Nebraska

September 15, 1971

Dear Dad,

I guess you don't know how you're ripping me apart. I can't imagine living my life without you around. I can't imagine you lying in a box. Yet there you sit, ninety-five years old and fifteen hundred miles away in Omaha; and here I sit in New Haven with so much to say to you before you die.

Ever since you were so sick at the end of August, every little sorrow, hurt, or suffering that I see around me wrenches my soul. I think that it was harder for me to see you suffer than it would have been to see you die. It would have been so much better if you had just dropped of a heart attack, so much easier for you and for us. In the hospital you were so weak that you could barely negotiate the distance between the tray and your mouth, so weak that I had to turn the pages of the scrapbook for you. It was so painful for me to watch a man as proud and independent as you rendered suddenly, painfully, helpless. What a change it must be for you, who have prided

21

yourself on your independence for ninety years, to be forced suddenly to have to live on your savings. (What? Spend money without making it?) What a change for one who has always been so active, physically and mentally, to be confined to bed and cursed with an abbreviated attention span. I love you, Dad, and I don't know how to cope with your leaving.

The day you almost died I was in San Francisco playing with friends. While we were dressing to go out for the evening, something kept nagging me to call home. I could think of no real reason to call, but the nag was persistent enough so that I finally did and the moment I heard Mom's voice on the line I knew that something was very wrong.

"Intensive care? I'll be home tomorrow. . . . Ma? Why didn't you call and tell me about it?"

So Dad, you didn't want to send for the kids. You didn't want to call me home. I know, I know. Travel is educational and therefore good for me, and besides, what could I have done? Maybe suffering and dying are things that cannot be shared; maybe they have to be weathered alone or only with very special people. It's learning when to share that's the hard lesson.

All the way home on that silver United 727 I clenched my fists and tried to gather my strength for what I thought would be one of the hardest things I had ever had to bear. "Ann, you've got to be strong. Got to be strong. Got to. Be strong," I kept telling myself. But then I realized that I had nothing to give me strength. I had never had to be strong before. I had never had to deal with anything quite as overwhelming as your dying, so that when I tried to draw on strength that I had just assumed was inside me someplace, to my surprise I discovered that I had nothing there. Tanned and healthy, I left behind the blue Pacific and then the gray peaks of the Rockies. The sun was setting behind the jet as it moved above the familiar lush green summer plains. I was distracted. Everything seemed distorted, illusory.

Daddy met me at the airport, which was melting in the oppressive heat of early evening Omaha. We drove directly to the hospital and the moment I saw that ugly, monstrous building appear over the brink of the hill, I had to start trying not to cry. I could feel your hatred for the hospital as soon as I saw it. Your disgust at having to be there oozed out of every crack in the enormous wings of dirty brown brick.

We had promised you that you would never have to go to the hospital; and yet there I was walking into a huge smelly antiseptic warehouse. We all know now (and knew then) that you wanted to be at home, and for a long time afterward I felt they should have let you die in your room that afternoon, so you wouldn't have suffered. I have not seen enough of you recently to know whether the months of extra time have been worth the pain. Is it best to be snatched from life at its peak and not to suffer the decline? Or is part of life accepting and living out its waning?

As Daddy guided me through the hallways, I became aware of him saying from someplace ". . . the best care." I was also vaguely aware of nurses who were taking note of my lime green dress, as a signal of my not belonging, of my novelty. Everything else was a clean dirty-white—the walls, the floor, the ceiling, the Formica counter-tops. We passed through corridor after corridor, oblivious to pass-ersby and the rooms on either side of us. Finally we pushed through a set of swinging doors marked Intensive Care/Cardiac Division/ Authorized Personnel Only. Your room was on the left, a tiny dark gaping hole. The door was ajar and I could distinguish only gray shadows; I couldn't see your bed at all. Outside the door I stood sweating nervous smelly sweat—my arms clutching each other tightly together by the elbow, my foot tapping, my eyes blinking very fast. All I could think of were the "perfectly splendid" rooms you provided for us in Santa Barbara and Sun Valley and Bermuda, rooms with lovely porches where we sat enjoying the cool evening breeze, watching the sun set over the ocean or behind the moun-tains. Spacious, open, airy, light rooms, "high up, with a view." We would sit there in the lovely evenings—you in your navy suit and soft French cuffs, Cath and I in our white dresses and cardigans— waiting until it was time to go down to dinner.

A nurse's voice filtered through the memories. I tried to be nice to her so she would take even better care of you; she tried to distract me by telling me the story of your arrival. So, Dad, the first thing

23

you did was order them to turn the bed around so you could see out the window. I smiled because it sounded so much like you.

While Daddy went into your room, my eyes suddenly caught sight of your heartbeat tracing and retracing itself across the machine on the nurse's desk. I felt it was God's fingernail drawing that line. Then I heard your normally dry, precise voice sounding wet and clogged as you said you wouldn't see me. In an instant I understood why, but understanding didn't help me accept it. I knew you couldn't let me see you helpless on your back, attached to all those machines, without enough energy to be strong or to crack a joke. I could see Daddy's profile as he stood at the end of your bed watching you try to live. I sensed him slipping into a reverie as I slipped into my own, and I wondered at all the years he had lived in your shadow. I'm not sure how long we stood in our own little worlds before, startled, I heard him say beside me, "He's asleep, Annie. You can tiptoe in and look."

I knew that he was preparing me and he knew that I knew, for tomorrow I would have to look you in the eye and not flinch at the machines and at what had become of you. We exchanged places. Daddy stood in the hall watching the heartbeat and I stood at the foot of your bed. It was much worse than I had expected: the oxygen tent, the automatic functioning of the machines, needles, and tubes, the immense labor of your raspy desperate breathing, and you— unconscious of me standing there. You, who like to sleep hampered only by sheet and nightshirt, could now not even turn over at will. I stuffed my hand in my mouth so I wouldn't have enough air to sob.

The next week and a half passed in a daze. Every day was the same: get up and go to the hospital for a fifteen or twenty minute visit; come home and search for something—a scrapbook, a photograph album, a story—to amuse you during my next visit; return to the hospital a little after noon for half an hour; then back home to search again; and then back to the hospital before dinner. Even after you moved out from under the mechanical eyes of the Intensive Care Unit and into a different section of the hospital, I still assumed that within a week I would be attending your funeral.

That new room (with the amazing grotto in the corner) came to mean to me only that you were strong enough to be affronted by the gross inefficiencies of the hospital. Thank God you kept your sense of humor, because I was in anguish, knowing how much you despise ineptitude and waste. And these seem so much more awful in a hospital. God, it was painful to watch you subjected to the callousness and mediocrity! Every day, you demanded that the doctor name the date you could go home; every day, he hedged.

One day I stayed longer than usual. We watched the tennis matches on TV all afternoon, and Michael delighted you with stories of how with great skill he, a mere thirteen-year-old, had foiled the hospital attendants and gained access to your patrolled floor. Just as the tournament ended, an aide brought in your dinner—cold and late, as usual, and not what you ordered. "You know, kids, every day I approach these meals with the theory that they are warm, and every day I'm surprised." We basked in your twinkly eyes. But the nurse had forgotten to cut the meat. The fact that you were unable to do it yourself upset you so much that the fragile atmosphere of the afternoon was destroyed. I cut the meat and we were all embarrassed. Michael and I left, sensing that your frustration was approaching the point where it had to be suffered alone. You didn't want us to see how difficult it was for you to eat. Or so I thought.

The next morning Mom told me at breakfast that I was not going to the hospital. She said Dad had gone on strike; that he had thrown his pills across the room, yelled at the orderlies, and pushed away the dinner I had so meticulously cut. He had refused his breakfast, and would not eat or cooperate in any way whatsoever until he could go home.

So you got home!

Do you remember the conversation we had not long afterwards? It was a cooler day than usual and I was sitting on the windowsill with my feet propped up on your bed. It was so much easier seeing you in that familiar book-lined room filled with sunlight. There were still some incongruities, an overbearing oxygen tank sitting behind your right shoulder, a persistent nurse flitting in and out, and the simple fact that you were sitting in bed at ten o'clock in the morning. At that hour, on any day of the seventy years preceding, you would have been hard at work at your desk downtown.

"Hey, Dad?"

25

"Yah?"

"Do you remember when we used to talk about Washington earlier this summer?"

"What?" You were curt, impatient with your waning hearing.

"Washington, D.C., when people tried to shut down the city to stop the war. You know, they blocked roads and bridges and stuff, refusing to cooperate."

You nodded.

"Hmm. . . . Well, Dad, remember how you got out of the hospital?"

Your hands, which had started their familiar upward motion to rub your bald head, halted momentarily in midair before continuing more slowly.

"Well . . . you went on strike and refused to do what they told you so that you could get out."

There was an extended pause. With your hands folded on top, you tipped your head way back and opened your mouth a little. I was growing pretty nervous about the whole conversation. Slowly, you brought your face down again. And thank God . . . there was a smile on it.

"Yes," you said, nodding. "Yes. . . . Yah. . . . Okay, sweetheart, call for my tea."

Our eyes met and we were both smiling.

I'm glad I tweek your mind a little. Sometimes I feel a little cocky, but most of the time our conversation forces me to think things out and keeps you from becoming a little too set and inflexible in your ideas. Last summer, all the hours we spent talking about civil disobedience—you pointing out the evils, and I, the merits—were good for both of us, I think. You can be pretty strong-willed, you know.

But there are some things I don't dare mention to you. For instance, what would the rigid lawyer in you say to my smoking dope? I know that for some reason never clear to me you didn't speak to one of your own daughters for many years. Would you stop talking to me? Refuse to see me? Although part of me would like to talk about this with you, I couldn't tell you for fear it would hurt both of us too much. I couldn't bear to displease you or to damage our relationship.

26

October 5, 1971

Dad—

I've been thinking a lot about my last letter to you and about my reaction to your being sick.

You know, there was more to my pain last summer than just seeing you suffer. It seemed as if everything I had believed in and depended upon was suddenly unstable, demanding examination and reevaluation. Things that had once brought me strength just weren't what they had been; they failed me when I needed them.

At the beginning of the summer when I was home working downtown, I used to drive way out into the country almost every night. Whenever I was depressed by my job, or by too many people around me, or by boredom, or loneliness, I would drive—either by myself or with friends—for hours on the back country roads under the pink and orange cavernous sky. About nine we'd stop the car and sit beside a wheatfield to smoke dope and watch the sunset reach its climax and fade into navy blue night. It was beautiful and peaceful. The breeze ruffled the corn and wheat, sweeping whole fields and hillsides. The air smelled of cattle, fertile black earth, sprouting greens and wildflowers. Lying flat on our backs in the fields, we lost ourselves in the all-encompassing sky and the plains that stretched unbroken from us to the huge circumference of the horizon. Nightly, my optimistic view of the world was reinforced. Everything seemed ordered and as it should be. I believed that whoever controlled this beauty, whatever god or spirit permeated (and I believed there was something that did), was good—just, calm, and essentially good.

When you were in the hospital in August, I went out to the country as I used to but it no longer brought peace. The trees that had been graceful and calming were suddenly filled with dark, grotesque little faces. The breeze became their voices, shrill and taunting: "It's all a joke, Ann. It's not all good and beautiful and calm and strong. It's a frame-up—a false image. God, whoever He is, is jealous, mean, frivolous." I hated God. No God could be good if He made people suffer like you were suffering—debased them to such an extent. I hated Him. He was Zeus, amusing Himself with little puppets on strings. I couldn't go to the country anymore because it

27

was more painful there than staying home. My feelings were so exposed, so overwhelmingly unexplored, that no one could come near me. I couldn't relate to people, couldn't talk about what I was feeling. Everything was pressing against me relentlessly, everything became painful. Now I again go for long walks in the woods or whatever country I can find, and I find some peace and calm. But I know that when I really need the strength again, the country is not where I will find it.

And Dad, I won't find it in religion either. It didn't help me last summer. You see, I no longer believe in Catholicism. It is so awful, but I just don't believe. I don't, I don't. And yet, I don't even know what I don't believe. What does it mean to be Catholic? After eleven years in a convent, I don't have any of the basic theological guts of Catholicism. I only know the fringe, the stuff with which they inculcate little kids in grade school. I know only what they wanted me to know; enough to keep me quiet, practicing, and devout. And I haven't the time or the interest to be bothered investigating further. Right now, I feel that Catholicism has done so many bad things to my mind and that whatever good there is in it is so buried beneath bureaucracy and stupidity that I just can't be bothered with it. Last August, however, I found myself wishing that I were still Catholic; wishing that I still believed what the nuns had taught me: everyone dies, but the good people all meet again later in heaven anyway . . . so everything's all right, really. Dad, it's so much easier to believe that.

That's the only way the nuns taught me to cope with death. Our religion books had many full-page pictures of all the people who ever lived sitting in flowing robes in a field on Judgment Day while God sat enthroned at the front of the multitude, judging. Dad, do you really believe that you'll join your wife again in heaven? That you'll see me in fifty years up there? *Shit*, Dad. Who's kidding whom?

Nevertheless, the fact that I only know the bullshit part of Catholicism doesn't seem to make the ties any looser. I thought that I had —outgrown is the only word I can think of—the Church because I never went to mass or confession and never felt guilty about it. Until you got sick. Then suddenly I found myself going to church every day—compulsively. At home I went to the side chapel in the cathedral, the one with the stained-glass window and chandelier. In

28

New Haven I don't go to the Catholic church. Yale's Catholic chapel is too light, too airy; the ceiling is too low. Instead, I go to the Protestant university chapel, which is huge, dark, and cavernous. I sneak in early in the mornings, after lunch, or in the late afternoon, and just sit by myself. Sometimes an organist is there, practicing up in the loft. Sundays I go to services, telling myself that the reason I'm going is to hear Bill Coffin preach. But I hear very little; I sit there becoming more and more depressed. I can't get up and leave, although I sometimes become almost physically sick, watching all those people invoking "our help in ages past, our hope for years to come." What help? What hope? "The dead shall be raised." Dad, do you really believe that? I'm fascinated by people who are able to open themselves to all the experiences life has to offer, accepting the harshness, pain, and tragedy without becoming callous or without withdrawing. Because of some elusive, sustaining quality they call faith, they seem to retain their sensitivity, their impressionability, their humor, their humanity, and find strength to continue to fight for what they believe in, in spite of insults or attacks. I am intrigued, seduced, skeptical.

When I think of you and Catholicism, I picture you sitting at your mother's knee by the potbellied, woodburning stove, learning catechism. And here I am two generations later, questioning, rejecting. I believe that this Catholic education you wanted me to have has strange effects on people. Education is what? Third on your list of priorities? Next to health and thrift. My education has been a combination of things, a sort of gradual exposure to non-Catholicism. From a strict cloistered convent, I moved to a parochial junior high and then to a sheltered (but non-Catholic) girls' prep school, and now to Yale, struggling in its first years of coeducation. Finally this fall, I resolved a question I have been mulling over for a long time. If I ever have a child of my own, I definitely will not raise him or her as a Catholic. But if I were struck by a car this afternoon, I think I might ask for the last rites. Is that contradictory? The roots of my Catholicism are deeply embedded, I guess—planted not as much by the family (I don't think that you and Daddy are particularly strict Catholics) as by Duchesne Academy of the Sacred Heart.

My earliest memory of life in the convent is of my first day, when, holding on to Mom's hand, I climbed the steep stone steps that led up the long hill to the front door (or, as I soon learned to call it, the main foyer). I was four and a half and Mom and Daddy decided that it was time I went to school. I was so excited and curious that I allowed myself to be led down a dark high-ceilinged corridor by the mistress general, without even giving Mom a backward glance. Because of the many afternoons you had spent reading to me, I already knew my ABC's and was just about to read. This made my first years at school boring; but I was confident! I knew I would love school, and if anything ever went the least bit awry, I needed only to crawl through the hedge and cross the street to your house.

How convenient it was that you lived catty-corner to Duchesne! Remember those early years when I spent the night with you? With my bookbag over my shoulder, I would trudge up the steep hill along the edge of the campus where on Sunday afternoons the nuns took walks. Then I'd push through the tough bushes that kept the world away from Duchesne Academy. Dinner was served to just the two of us! (A far cry from the table for seven at home. I didn't even have to set the table!) I sat on the sofa and you sat across from me in your large chair, a card table between us. After our meal, I curled up at the end of your bed or sat at Aunt Ami's desk and did my homework while you read. In the morning, I would hear you check on me before you went to work. You stood at the door of Ami's pink room (it was mine when she wasn't there) and watched me. I might sneak a peek at you, but always feigned sleep, knowing that you were looking at me. Then I followed your creaky step going down the stairs, out the front door and down the cement, on the first leg of your long walk to work downtown. A little later I would get up and walk to school.

For me those evenings were fantasies become real. Whenever I thought my family was picking on me, I had daydreams of moving in with you. One summer evening when I was about six or seven, I got mad at Cathy. This was not at all out of the ordinary except that on this particular occasion our fight was more painful than usual. Because she had short, straight hair like Mom and Daddy, I was becoming increasingly sure that she was Daddy's favorite. After our fight I decided to run away to your house forever. I found a huge dumpy brown suitcase and began to pack all my material possessions except the clothes I hated. (I knew you said you liked them only because you didn't want to offend Mom, who had picked them out. I knew that secretly you hated them as much as I did.) I was dramatically unhappy. While packing, I kept going over and over in my mind the route to your house. Although I had a few vague thoughts about how little girls were not supposed to go out alone at night because of masked robbers and other assorted crooks, I just assumed everything would work out. My only threat, I thought, would be a policeman who might pick me up and return me home. I decided that I would need to be alert, prepared to secrete myself behind a tree or in some bush the instant I spotted a patrol car.

When I arrived at your house, I would somehow get inside. I don't remember whether I planned to take the key out of the flower pot and manage to open the huge oak door (I knew all the motions from watching you do it many times) or whether I planned to wait on the porch until you came out to get the morning paper at six o'clock. I do remember that I planned to avoid Thora by hiding behind the red velvet curtains between the front hall and the living room. When she was safely in the kitchen, I would sneak upstairs. I assumed, of course, that you would never divulge my whereabouts to anyone, even though Mom and Daddy would be very worried. When they came for dinner on Sunday night, my plan was to hide underneath the bed in Ami's room (which you would give to me) and calmly watch their feet and ankles from my secure hiding place.

After I had finished packing and had hidden the suitcase under my bed, I went down to the living room and plopped myself on the couch with a book, which I pretended to read. It was midafternoon; I had a long wait until everyone went to sleep. In the meantime, I remained soberly sad and slightly nervous that Cathy might find the suitcase. Almost immediately Mom asked me just what was the matter, honey. Was I sick? Was something bothering me?

"No, nothing, nothing at all." I pouted and looked at my book. I don't know how long I held out, but finally I asked her if she really wanted to see what was wrong. Solemnly I led her up to my room, where she reviewed the suitcase and assured me that everyone loved me very much. But I never told her, or you, where I was planning to go.

October 14, 1971

Dear Dad,

I've just finished Mary McCarthy's *Memories of a Catholic Girl-hood.* Her experiences were very different from mine; the book made me decide that nothing was quite like Duchesne Academy of the Sacred Heart.

In my first four years there, Duchesne was, as you will remember, in its finest period. In the lower school, we thought we were chosen by God—especially privileged to attend the convent. There were so many students that each day at mass the lower classes were squished six or seven into pews meant for four or five. The incense, together with the heat generated by hundreds of chanting, worshiping bodies, frequently took its toll. I remember one or another of us fainting and being held upright by the pressure of our neighbor's shoulders. Religious fervor and "true vocations" inspired our souls; we all wanted to join the strictest and most cloistered order possible.

We did, however, have our pranks. Whenever we went to chapel, all of us—from preschool to twelfth grade—wore waist-length clean white veils which were fastened securely with bobby pins that dug into our scalps. Occasionally we would decide to knot together all the ends of the veils on the girls sitting in the row in front of us. Because we all stood, sat, and knelt together on signal, the victims usually remained ignorant of their situation until Communion. Then the first girl, full of piety and grace, would rise and haul an entire row of bobby-pinned heads after her. No one tattled; that wasn't cool. Instead, the victims shuffled tightly together in the long Communion line, surreptitiously trying to disengage their veils before reaching the Communion rail.

Generally, however, I was much too frightened of hovering nuns to pull any pranks at academy mass. I had my own special opportunities in the early morning before most of my classmates arrived. Classes, as you remember, started at 8:30, and most girls didn't arrive until 8:10 or so. Mary Kevin and I, however, were usually dropped off before 7:30 by our parents on their way downtown. We would approach the entry in those dark freezing mornings, our feet crunching beneath us on the frozen snow. We would struggle with the huge oak door, climb the flight of steps, and walk hesitantly down the long dark hall to the academy library, where we had been assigned seats on which we were to sit in silence until classes began. From further down the main hall we could hear the high wailing sound of the nuns singing their morning office.

With time we became bored, and this led to dares. At first we dared each other to walk to the door of the library, then, a few days later, to the end of the short hall, and then, soon after, to take ten big steps down the main hall that led to Reverend Mother's office and the academy chapel, where the nuns were chanting.

One day we laid a plan to investigate a small hole (an inch and a half in diameter) in the pine floor just outside Reverend Mother's office. After reading *A Secret Garden* (remember that book?), I had become convinced that dead nuns were buried in a vault somewhere underneath the convent. Although I realized that they probably weren't just beneath the main hall—especially because the cafeteria and kitchen were located on the floor below—I still felt that strange mysteries lurked in the shadows under the pine floor. We planned carefully.

On the appointed day we arrived earlier than usual, each with a Mattel flashlight purchased by mail for twenty-five cents and four Kellogg's Frosted Flakes boxtops. We went to the library first and then, making sure the coast was clear, started down the main hall. It took us ten minutes to make fifteen yards; we hid behind every velvet curtain, every large chair, and every saint's statue on the way down. We remained undetected, and we could hear in the distance that the chanting nuns were only halfway through their office.

Trembling, we knelt down on either side of the hole. I magnanimously let Mary go first. She took her time peeking until, impatient and a little nervous, I jabbed her in the shoulder. It was my turn. After several minutes of searching the dark shadows beneath the floorboards, I felt a sudden jab on my shoulder.

"Just a minute," I whispered shrilly. But the jab came again, this time more insistently. "What do you want?" I looked up. It took my eyes only a few moments before, to my horror, they focused upon a pair of very large shiny black shoes. I followed the long black habit up and up past the suspended crucifix to the face. Reverend Mother! We couldn't run; she knew who we were, and besides, the shock had rendered us completely immobile. We scrambled to our feet, drop-

33

ping deep curtsies and stammering repeatedly, "Good morning, Reverend Mother."

"Anything down there?"

"Uh, uh . . . nnnno . . . Mmmmmmmother."

My problem was acute. Daddy was on her Development Board, and I was sure she would tell him that I had been bad. I lived in terror for two weeks until the next board meeting had passed and no paternal comments were forthcoming.

After this, as you can imagine, Mary and I were exceedingly good. We remained seated in silence in the library every morning for months. On another winter morning, however, the devil again tempted and conquered our guardian angels.

On that morning, we took a new bottle of Skrip's (luckily) Washable Black Ink off the library desk and dumped it into the holy water font in the chapel. To do this, Mary and I undertook the same procedure as in our hole exploration. We sneaked from chair to statue down the long hall, listening carefully to the chanting in the chapel so we could be certain just how far the nuns had proceeded in their office. We had put on our veils with the requisite two bobby pins because we knew everyone must wear veils whenever they entered chapel—even the vestibule, which was our destination.

As we entered we could just make out the backs of nuns' heads as they knelt at prayer with the gray winter morning light barely filtering through the stained-glass windows. In the vestibule there was almost total darkness, so we kept bumping into each other, and as we dumped the ink, we didn't experience the joy (horror?) of seeing the pure holy water cloud up in black billows. We rushed back down that long corridor, arriving at the library door completely out of breath. Luckily, no one else had arrived yet, and we stood and stared at each other as we realized the finality of our act. Neither of us doubted that we would be expelled and condemned to hell for the mortal sin of sacrilege in desecrating God's Blessed Holy Water.

When at 7:45 the lights were turned on in the hall and the nuns emerged from chapel, we were standing behind the library door, watching. Not all of them had a gray mark on their foreheads; only those who had made a hasty sign of the cross. The others' marks evidently had landed on the strip of black habit that covered half their foreheads. However, not a single nun escaped without at least

34

two blue-gray fingertips. I was sure that I was going to throw up and give us both away, but both Mary and I managed to maintain our cool, criminal demeanor. Infusing our voices with innocence, we complained to the library mistress that we couldn't find any ink to practice our chancery.

On the next few mornings we heard members of the upper school talking about the incident and, later on, the middle-schoolers. But I guess no one ever suspected two innocent seven-year-olds. We were, for heaven's sake, preparing for our First Confession!

I never confessed it; I never even mentioned it until quite a few years afterward.

October 20, 1971

Dear Dad,

I've been wondering what you believe about death. Do you really believe in heaven? Does thinking that you'll go directly to heaven make you comfortable? I doubt that you even consider purgatory, and I suppose that when you do catch yourself questioning an after-life, it's worrying if there really is a heaven after all.

I don't know what to think about heaven now, but I used to believe in the whole idea without question. When I was in third and fourth grades, heaven was a huge golden medieval castle nestled on a pillow of fluffy clouds. For a time I thought it just floated around directly overhead, but after a while I couldn't really picture heaven above Omaha, with all the jets of the Strategic Air Command buzzing around. So, in my mind, heaven became fixed directly above the north pole. An aerial shot of the earth would show a shimmering little castle with lots of turrets hovering over it. Whenever someone asked me where heaven was, I responded not by pointing straight up but by trying to figure out which way north was and pointing in that direction. (The fact that Daddy was mildly displeased whenever we didn't know the direction in which our house faced, or the car was headed, may have had something to do with my concern over the proper direction.) I pictured very graphic images of people all over the earth simultaneously sticking their index fingers straight up into space so that, from an aerial view, the earth looked something like an orange with cloves stuck in it, or like a porcupine with his spikes up. If everyone had pointed due north, I figured, the world would look more pressed and organized, like cat's fur or velveteen smoothed in the right direction. As it was, I was the only one who pointed in the right direction.

From a distance, the image of my castle-heaven was a combination of the cover picture on a *Camelot* record album and Sleeping Beauty's castle that I saw weekly at the beginning of the Walt Disney show. If, however, one zoomed (supported by guardian angels) from the earth through outer space to a close-up, heaven underwent a radical change. The castle disappeared and only the inside of it became important. It looked like a Holiday Inn. There were different degrees of happiness up there, because of course those who had just barely managed to get in after thousands of years of cleansing and redeeming in purgatory could not possibly be as happy as Moses and all the martyrs. So the better the individual was on earth, the happier he would be in heaven. I believed every little mistake I made counted against me; perfection was the goal. Every time I told the tiniest fib or was the least bit unkind to my brothers and sisters, my degree of future happiness moved down a slot, just as whenever I missed a question on a test at Duchesne, my grade point average dropped a little bit further away from a perfect 100 percent.

In the plush and carpeted Holiday Inn heaven, the ranking system was in perfect order. On the top floor lived God. His faithful lived on the floors beneath Him; increasing goodness brought you closer to the hallowed top floor. Because, naturally, I was among the happiest (you told me continually that I was the smartest, the prettiest, and the best girl), my room was on the second highest floor and my roommate was the Blessed Virgin Mary. For a while I toyed with the idea of having Saint Theresa of the Little Flowers as my roommate, but I guess I realized that she just was not the very best. So I decided on God's favorite, Mary of the Immaculate Conception. We had identical twin beds and a huge bookshelf in our room and our own bathroom. Being best friends, we spent most of our time together.

"Good morning, Blessed Virgin," I said in my fantasies. "Would you like some orange juice?"

On good days, the Blessed Virgin and I were allowed to go upstairs and visit our Holy Father. (In my real life, "good days" were those days I could visit you in your top floor office where you kept Hershey bars in your desk drawer.)

God had his penthouse floor all to Himself, and it was completely open—no partitions, just one huge room. One wall was covered from floor to ceiling with shelves of neatly organized record albums containing recordings of everybody's every thought, word, and deed. He had a lot of room on His shelves, because there were an awful lot of people He had to keep track of. (The nuns taught us that God is everywhere always and keeps with Him a complete record of everyone to use on the Day of Judgment in deciding who is going to heaven, purgatory, or hell.) The opposite wall was covered with a huge curtain. God would walk over to the wall and pull back the curtain, revealing a panoramic view of the universe that looked very much like the cover of my fourth-grade geography book. It was a deep blue-black space dotted here and there with planets that looked like meatballs and sprinkled throughout with sparkling stars. The earth was the closest object and it was placed in the very center of the screen. With a huge camera, God could, at will, zero in on any place He wanted to, on any scene, on any person or any person's thoughts. I think I must have acquired this whole image when we saw *The Swiss Family Robinson*. (Remember that?) Warner Bros. opened the movie with a great shot focusing on the earth from some three miles out in space. Through this image and pompous music, the camera somehow managed to convey the immensity of the earth and the speed of its turning. Those ten seconds left me with a dizzy, awesome feeling of the earth's bigness and my own smallness. (Do you remember how tightly I held your hand after that?) From this shot of the turning world, the camera zoomed in, sweeping through a long tunnel (in my mind, a combination of our metal clothes chute and the fire escape at Duchesne Academy), to a deserted Africa, where the unfortunate Swiss family was confronted with the unpleasant necessity of eating bananas. At the time I really felt sorry for them, because I could understand that, at first taste, a banana must be a lot like a rotten pear.

That, I figured, was how God checked up on me and everyone

else. His mind was specially stretched, so that He could focus on everybody and everything all the time, even when He was talking to the Blessed Virgin and me.

October 28, 1971

Dear Dad,

I want to talk to you about your dying, but I'm afraid to. You seem so calm and unworried. What right do I have to upset you? I have a feeling that you think about death abstractly, not in terms of personal relationships drawing to a close. It might upset you to know that someone was thinking about putting relationships in order by saying things that need to be said before it's too late. It might worry you to know that I was sad and distressed. But how *do* you say good-bye to someone you love?

Is it Catholicism that enables you to be so calm? You never appeared to be terribly religious—you didn't go to daily mass, you didn't have holy books or crucifixes around the house, you didn't even talk much about religion—yet you claim to be orthodox and devout. I gather your faith is deep. But if you do believe so deeply, why didn't you make confession when you were in intensive care last summer? Every Sunday, you joined us for mass and Communion, but you never joined us for confession. Was it really your poor hearing that prevented you? Did you feel that you had no sins to confess? Or did you think the practice was meaningless? When you first returned from the hospital, I used to imagine that when you were about to die I would be the only one with you. At that time, my first inclination would have been to call the cathedral for a priest. But now I don't know whether I would—whether you would want me to.

I guess I am asking some of these questions because I am still concerned about my own loss of faith. I didn't stop believing all at once; nor was it a steady continuous process. It was like a graph tracing the ups and downs of a gradually declining stock.

Do you remember my first confession and Communion? I was holy, but not nearly as holy as I thought I should be. There were months and months of preparation. From the first week of second grade, all our actions were directed toward receiving Jesus Christ

38

Our Savior into our souls. We were supposed to sweep out the cobwebs from our souls and polish their surfaces. The Most Perfect Guest in the World was about to visit. "Welcome, Holy God," I practiced, "and welcome to Your Beloved Son My Sweet Savior. Right this way to my soul. Oh yes, thank you. My walls are clean and shiny—I have been preparing for your visit for weeks." In my imagination, I led God and Jesus through the gleaming gold and white hallways of my soul, and as They passed, stately and unhurried in Their long white robes, They made whooshing noises like Reverend Mother.

We made our first confession only a week before Communion so that our souls would remain as unblemished and lily white as possible. At the end of that fateful day I was suddenly disappointed. All our catechism and "how to" books had told us that we would feel a great change in ourselves, a sense of peaceful forgiveness; a new beginning would overwhelm our souls. As I emerged from the little wooden confessional, absolved, I realized that I didn't feel any holier than I had before. I did notice a devout and trancelike expression in the eyes of several classmates but felt no jealousy; I figured they were just faking it.

First Holy Communion turned out to be much the same. I was aggravated but also a little pleased that all our weeks of practicing, processionals, and novenas had failed to elicit a perfect performance. The communicants, if you remember, knelt on a specially constructed semicircular platform, draped in white and placed between the regular pews and the Communion rail. Our special communicant chairs were about four feet behind us. Unfortunately, when at last the time came to sit down, one kid on each side sat on the wrong chair and the two of us who were kneeling in the center were left chairless. Like perfect little martyrs, we continued to kneel until, at the prompting of a nun whispering and gesticulating crazily from the vestibule, my partner's row suddenly shifted chairs, giving her a place to sit down. My row was not so obliging. To my horror, I was left alone out in front, kneeling for the rest of the offertory. Unfortunately, those were the days of exceedingly long offertories.

Afterward, you told me that the other girls had been stupid and that I had been smart, pretty, and graceful. And Daddy said that he felt sorry for me having to kneel during the whole mass. In the excitement of Communion brunch that followed, I soon forgot about my embarrassment altogether. There were blessed candles, scrambled eggs served by the sisters, and gifts and holy cards from each nun to each one of the communicants. As I read the inscriptions on the backs of the holy cards, I imagined the nuns staying up all the night before to write each of us a personalized card. I supposed they wrote the same baby talk on each card, whether they knew the kid or not. When it was time to go, I left reluctantly, clutching my treasures, the grandest of which was a white, blessed-by-the-bishop, First Communicant candle that I planned to keep for my wedding day. (I think it was lost two years later when we moved to our new house.) I wanted to do the whole thing over again!

After that, Communion was a big deal every Sunday. You had given me a beautiful sable-and-alligator missal with six ribbons. My initials were emblazoned upon it in gold. I carried it proudly and stuffed it with a collection of holy cards, the current vogue among us seven-year-olds. (We even cut pictures of the Holy Family off Christmas cards to supplement our collections, and I was always a little upset because our family didn't receive many Christmas cards with holy scenes of the Nativity and Holy Family.) I also carried my First Communion silver rosary with my initials engraved on the back of the crucifix. As the whole family marched from our second or third row seats in the cathedral to the Communion rail each Sunday, I felt very holy, stately, and important. I was the perfect granddaughter in my navy blue double-breasted coat and white gloves.

In third grade we were introduced to sacrifice—defined as a pain which you didn't have to endure but which you chose to endure joyfully because He suffered for you. The saints whipped themselves, wore horsehair shirts, ate only bread and water, and got stigmata. We sat bolt upright without even touching the backs of our chairs, gave our portions of candy or dessert to a brother or sister, or knelt throughout an entire mass without moving a muscle.

In fourth grade I found my vocation: I would be a nun. The only books I read in fifth and sixth grades were the lives of saints.

In seventh grade, however, I began reading "dirty books" in the sacred-reading hours during retreats. I covered *Gone with the Wind* with a brown paper bag and inscribed it *St. Theresa of the Little Flowers;* my best friend was reading *Wuthering Heights,* alias *St.*

40

Francis of Assisi. This was a far cry from the winter before, when in religious ecstasy I wept, "Jesus died, He suffered and died, for sinners like me!"

But it was not until our ninth-grade retreat that I had my first conscious doubts about religion. Outfitted in our long veils, we were all sitting on the hard pews, and the incense from benediction hung in the hot air. For this retreat a special priest had been called in for freshmen and sophomores.

"A mortal sin!" he shouted, pounding out each word. "Do you realize, my children, what a mortal sin is? Do you have any conception of its magnitude? An eternity of suffering, of fire and *hell*. An eternity without God!" He went on and on describing the lurid details of hell's pains and horrors. We were growing nervous and hungry. He continued, "And understand, my dear young ladies, that any attempt on your part to purposefully arouse your boyfriends is a MORTAL SIN. As is masturbation. Yes! YES!! Mortal sins—both of them!" At this point, two sophomores ran from the chapel in tears.

I wasn't that upset, but I really didn't see what was so evil about masturbation, and I didn't understand how women were supposed to change their conduct completely on the day of their marriage. Turn *off* your boyfriend, turn *on* your husband? That was the first time I remember really rebelling. Since then, I've made a conscious effort to rid myself of a lot of these rigid, inculcated attitudes when I recognize them cropping up. Unfortunately, they are deeply rooted. "Men only want to use you, you know," the little voices still whisper to me.

I think that Catholicism gave me an inhuman model to emulate. It was too much like a statue of pure white marble—unfeeling, undemonstrative, unemotional. On second thought, the model would have had to feel something, or she would not have had the opportunity to endure suffering by repressing her feelings. A very unjoyful, inhuman, ungrowing way to live, I think.

Two days from now I'm coming home to see you. A surprise for your birthday and for Halloween. I'm excited and happy, but I'm also nervous. On the phone, Mom and Daddy glide over my questions about you too easily, too quickly. I'm not sure they are telling me the truth about your condition, for fear of upsetting me. They don't know I'm coming, either, but the surprise is really for you. And for me. I want to talk to you about life and about dying.

November 7, 1971

Dear Dad,

I'm still not sure what impulse sent me home for your birthday. I liked surprising you, although you didn't seem to be surprised at all. No one except Ami knew I was coming, and she only because my miserly tendencies got the better of me: I decided I couldn't afford the taxi from the airport to your house, so I asked her to pick me up. She had told you only that you had a visitor coming that afternoon. But because you rarely have visitors and always know beforehand who they will be, you must have been suspicious.

When I walked into your room, you sat at your desk all dressed, working. At the sound of my voice, you wheeled around in your chair and after a moment said, "Well, hello there, sweetheart." You were beaming, but registered no incredulity like Mom and Daddy did when I went home later. On the other hand, you did keep asking me over and over again what I was doing there. Feeling I had to justify myself, I finally replied, "Well, I'm not coming home for Thanksgiving." You simply couldn't believe that I had come all the way from New Haven just for your birthday. You kept testing me, trying to send me away to see my brother and sister, to play tennis, to visit friends, to talk with Mom. I had to keep reassuring you that I had come home to be with you.

At home, it felt strange to be almost an only child. Cath and Jim were away at school, Mike and Jeannie in school most of the time. I did see friends; I did study a little; but most of all, it was nice to see for myself that what Mom and Daddy had been telling me was true. You were much better, spiritually as well as physically. Death seemed much further away, much less imminent. The August crisis made your death immediate. Last week the immediacy was gone, leaving only the mass of emotions to be worked out.

The first time I saw death it was a fairly simple affair—terrifying, but uncomplicated. I was uninvolved. It had the air of something mysterious and frightening, but like a horror movie, somewhat intriguing.

Sister Sophie was the first dead person I ever saw. She had been a very old arthritic tiny nun at Duchesne Academy who barely spoke English and who dished out our daily rations in the cafeteria (half a hot dog and a beet). Her death brought a terse announcement from the mistress general, extended wails in the early morning when the nuns sang their office, even fewer lights in the main hall, and a quiet pallor over the whole convent. The nuns wore long, mournful faces, and the more holy students followed suit.

A special service in our chapel was planned so that the academy could honor her on the afternoon before the funeral. For this occasion, the two smallest girls were chosen to keep watch during the requiem. They were to kneel without moving on either side of her coffin, like guardian angels keeping vigil over the tomb of Jesus. Liz Kelly was one of them.

At the appointed time the youngest children silently marched into the chapel in strict ranks. Our white-gloved hands were folded at our waists, our veils were pulled across our faces, our steps were measured. We were very much aware of the mistress general standing above us in the choir loft, where, like God, she could see instantly if anyone was the least bit out of line. We filed down the long aisle to the casket and there, six at a time, paid our last respects by saying a short prayer for Sister Sophie's repose. As I passed the casket, I saw only a single focused, vivid image of my first dead person. At a signal we turned away and marched to our pews.

As I knelt resolutely in my third row seat, I resigned myself to a very long service. The entire middle and upper schools had to follow us—six at a time—and the line of chanting students still stretched the length of the chapel, down the long front hall, and up the stairs to the study halls. I could hear the faint clicks of the wooden clackers belonging to the study hall mistresses. These were little hand-sized, brown-hinged boxes which the nuns snapped for any number of situations: to bring immediate silence, to start or stop the ranks, to signal that someone was out of line or behaving poorly. They were all-purpose instruments, expressing every emotion except approval, and each had a personality of its own. You could see, for instance, a picture of Jesus exposing His Sacred Heart if you were quick enough to peek inside a clacker between clicks. Sometimes a nun would stand between the ranks clicking softly and rhythmically to

43

keep things moving, creating a somewhat secure, supportive effect; most of the time she clacked loudly for silence. On this particular afternoon, three or four nuns clicking at once kept the tensions just at the proper level for paying respect to a dead nun. Suddenly, in the midst of this rhythmic clacking, I heard a high-pitched metallic sound. It took me a moment before I realized it was Liz—laughing hysterically. The minute I looked at her beside the coffin I knew why. I, too, had seen the huge hairy wart on Sister Sophie's face.

Liz was whisked quickly out the side door by a guardian nun, and another nun slipped in to kneel in her place of honor behind the rows of candles lining the open casket. It was a nice picture: on one side, a nun, on the other, Liz's little partner, who I'm sure never flinched. And that was all there was to death. It was dull and scary, but not without a macabre thrill.

Now it is more complicated. Death is happening to people I love. It is shaking my whole being, although I'm calmer and more centered now than I was when you first got sick. My mourning has become more subdued; it churns and burns quietly inside, hidden below the surface. Now it is fired only occasionally, when I hear a symphony, or notice your picture on my bulletin board, or see a proud old man on the street. Then the tears don't flow but they well up, quietly stinging and burning.

The birthday visit was good but it's hard to say good-bye twice to someone you love. And harder than ever because it was I, not you, who was optimistic this time. You looked very well, but I'm afraid that if I let myself count on seeing you again, I won't be able to.

The evening of your birthday was a little eerie. Your eyes never left me for an instant, and I was frightened. It was as if you were trying to take me all in, draw strength from the little curly-haired blond granddaughter who had become this tall, educated stranger, familiar but different. Although at our parting you said hard and reassuringly, "Christmas," you didn't mean it. I could feel the trembling hesitation. Are you getting scared again? When you were in the hospital, there were moments when I sensed despair and loneliness and I sense it in you again now. Dependency is a hard lesson to learn and in spite of yourself it is now you who are the dependent one.

Andrew, a good friend in my college, says that I want you to fight more, that I want you not to accept death passively. I think he's right; that's why I brought you Dylan Thomas's poem "Do not go gentle into that good night." I wanted to know why you weren't fighting more. It took four days for me to work up enough guts to show it to you. And when on the last day I finally did, it was painfully simple. Painful because you accepted it so easily, responded so quickly and effortlessly that I was ashamed at my hesitation. I wondered about the many times I have held back from saying or showing something for fear of offending or upsetting you or others.

Your response to the poem was very simple, very rational: "If the man were younger, I would see the need for him to struggle." I think I can understand now. When a man reaches a certain stage, he is ready for death, another stage. "Sweetheart," you said, "when you're tortured by what it might have been, remember sometimes how good it was."

But your explanation doesn't really help me to accept your death or to live without you. Your complacency upsets me because I want you to feel pain at having to leave me. If you are feeling that way, you certainly don't show it. I love you. It's so hard to see you dying.

December 8, 1971

Dear Dad,

In my calmness now, I am sifting through my mind to sort out what just happened. Two days ago I had a tremendous shock, and although the worst is now past, I still feel unbalanced. A friend of mine committed suicide. It was Ginny Stokes, my roommate from boarding school, the girl I was staying with in San Francisco when you got sick last summer.

Talking about it helps me, but there are disappointingly few people with whom I can talk. No one here at Yale knew Ginny. She comes from a different part of my life and her death isn't real to them. They can listen and put their arms around me and talk about friends of theirs who died, but they can't feel the intensity of having to come to grips with Ginny's not being alive anymore. I need to put my feelings into some form so that they can be understood by someone else. Perhaps, if I order the experience sequentially, it will be easier for me to grasp and eventually accept. So I write to you,

45

Dad. I'm not sure why, unless perhaps, as with you last summer, I must accept the death of someone close to me.

Tom, a mutual friend of Ginny's and mine, called me Monday afternoon. "Annie," he said, "do you know about Ginny?"

"Ginny? Ginny Stokes. . . . No." My mind raced to think of something about Ginny that would account for his strained voice.

"Jane didn't tell you about Ginny?" He was caught by surprise. He had assumed that I already had the news, and had called to comfort me.

"No," I said. "What's wrong?" For an instant, it occurred to me that she might be dead, but I discarded the idea as ridiculous and tried hard to think of some other possibility.

"Ginny committed suicide last Monday. She jumped off the Golden Gate Bridge."

A static silence hissed on the telephone line. I felt as if the wind had been knocked out of me. Tom told me in just the way books say one ought to convey a shock. He was direct, matter of fact, trying to satisfy that strange need one has to know all the details of a tragedy, and at the same time trying to keep up a steady murmur of talk as the first impact of death sank in. I didn't cry; I bit my knuckles; my head felt as if it would burst. I thought of Ginny and her extreme swings of mood—her joyous, lively days and her sad, depressive states. I thought of her parents and friends and our idyllic days together in San Francisco last summer.

As memories flooded my head, Tom talked on—slowly, quietly—painting the picture of her death more and more graphically. It's strange, the need one has to be able to picture the circumstances as clearly as possible. I guess description makes tragedy easier to accept . . . or more difficult not to accept. The details pin it down, make it real.

When I hung up the receiver, I was mechanical. I had five minutes to get to Commons to meet Andrew for dinner, so I carefully gathered up my coat, my room key, meal and ID cards, books, pen, umbrella. I don't remember walking over, although I do remember waiting by the door, because Andrew was late.

That was the worst meal I have ever eaten. I should have realized that it was an awful mistake to go to Commons, and perhaps that it was a mistake to go with Andrew. On the best of days, the dining

46

room can be difficult—nearly a thousand people pushing and shoving, shoveling food into their mouths, jabbering to be heard over the clatter of china plates, trays, and silver. When I'm feeling good, it's no problem. But on Monday it was a catastrophe. I told Andrew about Ginny as we walked in. I blurted it out: "You know the girl I stayed with in California last summer? I just found out that she committed suicide." My voice was mechanical; I gave no details. He told me later that I had said it in such a way that he forgot about it immediately. But, Dad, I don't know any other way to share something like that!

Andrew was in a feisty mood, insensitive to my feelings, which, for my part, I was not good at communicating. After we sat down, he rattled on about pettiness and superficiality at Yale, made biting comments about my friends with whom we were sitting, about my being superficial. I was so hypersensitive that everything he said was disproportionately painful. I was detached, shocked, preoccupied. I remember struggling to keep a grasp on the conversation. Then, suddenly, Andrew announced that he had a meeting and ran off into the night while I was still in the middle of my coffee.

Confused and upset, I walked back to my room, thinking about the three papers I had to write, the letters I needed to answer, and how different they would all be now than they would have been if I had written them earlier that afternoon. When I reached my room, I realized I had to telephone Emily at Radcliffe and talk to her about Ginny. Whether this was for her sake or my sake or both, I didn't know, but I had to call. In the last eighteen months, Emily had lost two close friends; Ginny would be the third. I wasn't sure whether Emily had yet heard the news, although it had been Emily's parents who had told Tom. I sensed that her parents might not have told her, but I didn't want to be the one to tell Emily either. For some reason, I felt it was their job.

So I called Emily's parents at home and discovered they were in New York staying at the Biltmore. Then I called the Biltmore to find they were out and not expected back until eleven o'clock. Yes, they would have my message to call as soon as they came in, but I was afraid that by that time it might be too late to call Emily, and I really wanted to talk to her. I needed to.

My frustration built up and anger set in full force. I stared at the walls of my room and, hallucinating, saw huge cracks suddenly tear through the concrete. Anger had never been my reaction to death before, but now it was exploding—and directed full force at Andrew. My head throbbed with imagined invective hurled at him and at the walls, and I screamed out loud. But even in my anger, I realized painfully that I am still so good at hiding my feelings that even my closest friends can't know when I am upset.

My evening was broken into short, restless periods of trying to keep occupied. I told myself there was nothing I could do for the time being. So why don't you work, Ann? I'd work for fifteen minutes and then get furious at Andrew for not calling or coming over. Perhaps he thought this was something I had to go through by myself, but he could at least call me and say so. Intermittently, I telephoned the Biltmore to see if Emily's parents had returned. Then I tried studying again. I finally resolved that, if they hadn't called by eleven, I would call Emily anyway. At 10:55 I sat down on my bed, put the phone next to me, and stared at it. It rang. Emily was on the line. "Sit down, Ekker," she said, using the name she had given me, "I have some really bad news to tell you." Her voice was close to that laughter which follows on the heels of a shocking absurdity like "Ginny killed herself last Monday," so I knew that she had just heard the news and was still in shock.

"It's okay, Em," I said. "I already know."

She was surprised, and asked who had told me. My relief at not having to give her the news was quickly replaced by confusion as I realized that it had not been her parents who had called her, but another friend. (Dad, I simply can't understand people who use this kind of avoidance. In the end, it is so hurtful to those close to them.)

Emily didn't know much about the facts of Ginny's death. So, as Tom had done for me, I repeated every detail as clearly as I could for as long as I could. She needed the time, the details, and the support to stop wallowing in the absurdity and shock, and begin to accept the reality, the finality. We speculated and rationalized: Ginny hadn't been crazy; the notes she left proved that (didn't they?); no, it wouldn't have made any difference if you had answered her letter. You can't think like that.

When no more words came, we sat in silence, glad of each other's company. The subject changed, and in a sudden guilty silence we

48

realized that we had been laughing. The pause was painful until Emily said quietly, "Hey, Ek, remember the night Kim died?" Kim was her best friend, who died in a car accident just before graduation. On the night we learned about the accident, Emily, Ginny, and I were talking, and suddenly caught ourselves laughing. We sat, shocked at ourselves, until Ginny said, "Come on, you-all, you have to laugh. It's okay."

"Yes, Em," I said. "I remember. I guess she'd want us to laugh now too."

After we hung up, my restless anger returned and I decided to go across the courtyard to see Andrew. Anger and agony at high pitch, I walked through the halls half-crazed and dizzy; I was running when I finally reached his floor. I threw myself against the door only to confront a recently activated suite lock. It was a good reality check, I guess; my head was suddenly much clearer, as if someone had slapped me across the face. It was 12:30. I couldn't pound on the door and wake up all the occupants of the suite. So I stood there in the hallway for a while, shaking hard and laughing quietly, and then walked back to my room. I finally went to bed at 2:30. I still hadn't cried.

The next morning I woke up thinking I was okay, but gradually the oppressiveness of the previous night returned. I felt exquisitely fragile, like a fine glass goblet that might shatter at a sound. I sat through music class blinking back tears. After class I went to the post office, where I found a letter from Meg, an Omaha friend. The letter was sad and caught me completely off balance, because the last time I had heard from her she seemed fine. The thought that she was unhappy suddenly brought everything flooding to the surface. I stood in front of my silly Yale Station mailbox and pressed my hand over my mouth to keep from crying in the middle of the milling crowd. Then, clutching the letter in my fist, I glued my eyes to the ground and headed for my room, determined not to cry until I reached it.

I only made it as far as Elm Street. There the red metal of a fire hydrant I happened to pass suddenly brought before me the picture of Ginny's suicide that Tom had drawn so clearly, and tears flooded my eyes. I could see her poised on the rust-colored steel bars of the bridge, her body rocking slightly, first backward toward the harsh concrete, then forward toward the black night void of San Francisco Bay in the rainy season. I saw her hurtling through space and then breaking through the churning surface of the bay. Everything became vivid: the finality, the parents, the note in the car, and the poor kid on the bike who tried to stop her. I heard her amazing laugh, which sounded more like a seal's bark than anything else. You couldn't believe there was enough wind in her skinny small body to produce an energetic noise like that.

As I walked on, I suddenly confronted a pair of wet track shoes, dirty and probably smelly. They seemed absurd on the snowy awkward cobblestones between Hungry Charley's and Mory's. I knew I couldn't avoid bumping into the owner of the shoes, but I wasn't sure I could cope with conversation.

"Annie, how are you?" When I looked up I found a jaunty Bob Warren in jeans and parka.

"Not too good."

His smile faded, his face was immediately concerned.

"What happened?"

"I have a friend who committed suicide."

"Oh, no, Annie." He hauled me and my huge pile of books close to his down parka, and held me. What a funny way to word it, I thought, "I have a friend who committed suicide." With my recorder stuck in his rib cage, he held me close while I cried and like a fool thought of the people walking by and wondered if he was bored, or put off, or in a hurry. His embrace was strong and steady, however, and he didn't seem to mind that I was trying to absorb some of his calm and strength into my own body.

When we went our separate ways, I felt calm at last. Finally, I felt as if I could cry and cry hard. In that moment, I think I regained all the faith that I had lost when you were sick. Everything wasn't suddenly, completely resolved. I was still upset and sad and still needed to cry, but suddenly it seemed worth it. It's necessary to suffer, necessary to struggle, but there is some pervasive spirit, some being whose nature is calm and good in which I want to share. It's a struggle to share it, but I believe now that it's a good and necessary struggle.

Where that leaves me with Catholicism is hard to say. I can't participate in the "mass every week," "the pill is a no-no," "repress

50

your feelings" part of it. I can't be a part of a church that tolerates
—no, encourages—such harmful teachings. Perhaps I'll try going to
hear Coffin again. Perhaps I'll try meditation. There are a lot of
things that I can try, but in the meantime, it's nice to have regained
a basic faith in a goodness and coherence in the universe.

The moment I got back to my room, however, the old chaos
returned: anger, frustration, and hurt from the night before, and the
pain and sadness of the morning after. I wanted to rip my room apart
—the blue-green curtains, the blue-green sheets, my lamp, my bedspread, the poster, and my notebook. I wanted to heave all the blues
and greens out my window and replace them with warm pinks, reds,
and oranges. As it was, I had to settle for open windows, an open
door, music. But this didn't work. I reread Meg's letter. I began to
cry and cry and cry. I cried so hard that I almost blacked out.

Afterward, I looked as if I'd been bludgeoned. My face and eyes
were swollen and splotched. Because I was going to meet a friend
for lunch, I had to remedy the situation quickly. I used the very cold
washrag trick that Mom had taught me once on a sultry Saturday
afternoon when you were coming to visit. I saw your taxi pull up in
front of the house, and I was terrified that you would see that I had
been crying. Now, as I applied the washcloth again, I couldn't help
smiling at the memory of that day. Here was the same face in the
same splotchy condition looking again into the mirror—fifteen years
later.

In the Morse College dining room, Kathy and I picked a table
hidden behind a pillar in the farthest corner and agreed that if
anyone came over we would ask to be left alone. We talked, mostly
about our friends and vacations, and I was impressed once again by
my ability to hide my feelings—even from my best friend. When I
finally told Kathy about Ginny's death, we both cried quietly.

When we left each other after lunch, I was calmer and very
grateful to Kathy. I found a tiny cubicle in the Cross Campus
Library and tried to write my psychology paper, but all I could think
about was how much I wanted a back rub. Gradually I began to write
in my journal, trying to sift through what I had learned in those past
twenty-four hours: how I had dealt with death in a way that I would
never have thought possible.

Since then, I stand wary, expecting the gnawing pain of Ginny's death to return to haunt me. But in spite of my uncertainty, my calm remains relatively unruffled. I'm sad sometimes, but the knot inside is softening—I'm beginning to accept her death.

Because of Ginny, will I cope differently—or better—with your dying? I feel calmer about the possibility of your death than I felt four months ago or even a week ago. I've learned a lot. It is because this faith has come back, I think, that I'm more accepting. Your dying will still hurt, though. I'll miss you so much.

I love you, Dad.

ANN–BUSINESSWOMAN

*W*HEN Ann returned from Greece at the end of the summer, she still had no idea what her grandfather thought of her letters. Ann's mother, in a note thanking me for mailing the letters, had written, "I feel as if I'd had a look into Ann's very soul. . . . As much as you love your children, you really never know them completely nor can you shelter and protect them from life." But Dad—that was another question altogether.

On her first afternoon home, she approached his house with some trepidation. She found him in his sickroom—abed—but lively and alert. During their visit he said not a word about the letters, but she knew from the "way his eyes followed me around the room" that all was well. "I was exhilarated . . . released," she told me later. "I had spoken about things we'd never spoken about before and he had accepted them. From then on, we were closer than ever."

After she returned to Yale, she received an official acknowledgment:

Dear Ann,

I have read your brochure of letters to your grandfather. They are completely splendid in expressive thought and breadth of accomplishment.

I favor Religion; the world needs it badly. I believe the Catholic Church came down from Peter, but I dislike its continuing administrative faults. And I do not believe in auricular confessions.

I would eliminate four-letter words; it is a passing fad and not too elegant.

Generally, we seem to think alike.

Love,
Dad

Several months later, I, too, was to receive his blessing. On Christmas Eve, when I answered our doorbell, the florist handed me a large basket of flowers. The card inside read simply, "With very best wishes, JAC Kennedy."

I hadn't been aware that he knew anything about me or my involvement in the letters, and I was quite overwhelmed. For me, this gesture—made to a stranger months after he'd received the letters—said more about his feelings for his granddaughter than the letter he'd sent Ann, which I found sounded a bit too much like a note he might have sent a colleague who'd just published an article in *Forbes*. But if Ann had been the least disappointed, she never showed it. It may have been that simply declaring her own independence from authority (as well as her love) was a sufficient reward in itself. For me, the astonishing fact was that someone so young could take her first stand with so much tenderness.

Somewhere within this period (perhaps while working on the letters themselves) Ann sorted out her feelings about Catholicism. Thereafter, whenever problems arose in her life, she continued to consult her old friend, Yale's Protestant associate chaplain, Phil Zaeder, but their talks were more secular than religious. I never heard her mention Catholicism again—not even in the heartbreaking months that were to come.

For a shocking twist of fate suddenly brought not Dad's death but that of Ann's father. During the summer of 1973, what at first had looked like a manageable leukemia accelerated into an acute form.

His health disintegrated throughout the fall and he died just after Christmas. Ann, who was now in the second semester of her senior year, was plunged into grief. She kept mostly to herself, seldom leaving the rambling Victorian house not far from the campus which she shared with her friend, Geof—a Yale law student—and six other students. She sat in her room crying and trying to read for her classes, which she couldn't bring herself to attend. She fought a respiratory infection and low-grade fever that wouldn't clear up; she found she couldn't talk to anyone outside the small group in the house. After spring vacation, she was able to pull herself together enough to complete her courses, but it wasn't until after she had graduated and spent a healing summer of travel and a Rocky Mountain pack trip with Geof that some of her old energy began to return.

During her period of mourning, the letters she'd written to her grandfather served Ann well. By writing them, she told me she'd come to know many of the chaotic feelings involved in the loss of someone she loved. Although the months following her father's death were very painful, they weren't altogether foreign territory. She had learned not to push away feelings but ride the emotional roller coaster; she'd learned how to grieve.

Ann had always wanted to "take a trip around the world" after graduation and had planned to get a good job, save money, and go when she had enough. Her grandfather now offered her the trip— "with special concentration on Japan, China, Russia, and Germany" —and advised her that if she didn't go now before she became involved with a job she might never go and would always regret it. Ann was worried about leaving her mother and her brothers and sisters, but by fall—with great mutual support—they all seemed to be weathering the tragedy well. "My mother told me I'd better not be hanging around on her account. She said she was ready to be alone and that she was planning a trip of her own to Austria with her brother and sister-in-law." Ann decided to be off.

Her grandfather, who had been devastated by his son's death, now began to take pleasure in helping Ann plan her year's trip. He set to work studying travel guides and suggesting itineraries. He would have liked to persuade her to take several shorter trips so that she'd be home in between (especially for Christmas), but Ann yearned for one long journey. "Although I wasn't aware of it at the time," Ann told me later, "I guess I wanted a real break from the emotional oppression of the last years—Omaha, family, death, worry, sorrow, pain. I wanted to be free." As for leaving Geof, who had graduated and was now working in a Houston law firm, she had ambivalent feelings. She felt strongly that the trip was something she had to do alone even if he'd been able to come along. Yet she felt she couldn't commit herself to him and then leave for a year. She hoped he wouldn't abandon her while she was away.

After Ann had settled on her route, she collected a series of *National Geographics* about the places she would visit and put them all in order for her grandfather to read. She bought a huge map for his wall and traced her route with a Magic Marker so he could follow her progress by placing a new glass tack along the Magic Marker trail whenever he received a postcard from her. Then, in October 1974, she flew off to Tokyo.

Her trip was everything she'd hoped for. With her pack on her back and one duffel bag, she flew, hiked, and bused her way through the urban and rural areas of Japan, Korea, Taiwan, Hong Kong, Southeast Asia, India, Nepal, Russia, and western Europe. "Never before had I been able to do whatever I felt like, whenever I felt like it. If I met other travelers, I could decide on the spur of the moment to go off—say—for a two weeks' hiking tour through the remote villages of northern Thailand to see the Laos tribes. This we did Christmas week. It was great." Very faithfully on every alternate day, Ann sent off a postcard to her mother or grandfather so that the old man could follow each step and each tale of her journey.

All along the route, Ann kept bumping into former Yale students, who, of course, always recognized her. One day on the streets of Katmandu she ran across an "old upper classman, a giant, a black with a huge Afro." Ann herself was no shorty by Nepalese standards, and her hair, which was now "about as wild as it's ever been," hadn't gone unnoticed even on the streets of New York. In Nepal they'd never seen anything like it. The striking pair, together with two young German women, decided to set out on a two-week hike through the Himalayan foothills. Since Ann and Tom walked faster than the Germans, they would arrive in a village ahead of the others, only to find themselves immediately surrounded by a whole town of astonished villagers. "I was awfully glad he was with me," said Ann.

"There were two of us and that made me feel like much less of a geek."

When she returned to Omaha in June, she found her grandfather in good spirits but older and frailer. A few weeks later, he died suddenly when the whole family was east for the high-school and college graduations of Ann's two brothers. "We were all very very sad, and numb from so much death, but I wanted to think of it as he would have—as a passing of the torch to the new graduates." JAC Kennedy died just four months short of his one-hundredth birthday.

During her trip Ann had thought about living abroad for a while and finding a job with the diplomatic corps or with the foreign bureau of a newspaper. But along the way she had come to the conclusion that home, community, and friends were too important to her and "impossible to maintain with constant transfers." She returned home determined to be a writer/reporter on the home front but not necessarily in Houston, where there were few jobs outside the gas and oil business.

Ann, like many of her women colleagues, felt that her first priority was to establish her own independent career. If the best opportunity happened to present itself in the same place where your "good friend" was living, that was just an extra bonus, but one that often had to be carefully explained to one's peers. No one wanted to be considered—and last of all consider oneself—"a camp follower." Career, independence, and self-sufficiency must be established first.

As luck would have it, through an earlier chance meeting with a *Time* correspondent, Ann was offered a good job in Houston on a temporary project with *National Geographic Magazine*. She moved in with Geof. During the next two years she worked at an assortment of free-lance writing jobs, coauthored a travel guide *(Houston, Supercity of the Southwest)*, and for six months moved to Houston to be a legislative assistant to Houston's state representative. She commuted weekends to see Geof. While in Austin, Ann decided that "business—not government—was where the big decisions were made" and so she took a job in the public relations department of the multinational engineering firm of Pullman Kellogg and moved back to Houston.

During this period, she and Geof had found a "dumpy" two-story house in an old section of Houston with ceiling fans that might have been taken off the set of Casa Blanca, and a backyard full of bamboo, banana and fig trees, and an enormous palm. They paid for it jointly, just as they jointly shared all their expenses.

Fifteen months after they bought the house—in the spring of 1978—Ann and Geof were married by a Protestant minister in a lovely backyard ceremony beside the banana tree. Friends and family poured in from around the country, and Ann's mother arrived early to paint their living and dining rooms, wall-paper their bathrooms, and then to cook some of her best recipes for the occasion. Monday, Ann and Geof returned to work.

Like many of the "live together" couples of their generation, they had contemplated and discussed marriage for many years before they married but Ann had been leery of falling into the "just a wife" role, both in her own eyes and in the eyes of others. "While I knew I loved Geoffrey and couldn't imagine not being with him forever, the idea of marriage was very threatening. The image I associated with it was of a huge suffocating white sheet." Living together openly was not a major problem in Houston, although in many ways it is a socially conservative city. In retrospect, Ann feels there may have been some friends and colleagues who disapproved, but no one talked about it openly. Ann's mother, however, like many mothers in her generation, was not at all comfortable with Ann's domestic arrangements —though she, too, never said anything, and Ann admired her for her restraint. When Ann and Geof finally married, her mother was overjoyed and immediately began mailing off her letters to "Mrs. Geoffrey Walker" with delight. Later she sent Ann a large box of the finest stationery embossed "Ann Walker."

Ann, however, had staunchly retained her maiden name, and whether her mother failed to understand this fully or chose to overlook it in her joy Ann is not completely sure to this day.

The dilemma now facing Ann and Geof was still one of careers. Ann felt trapped in the bureaucratic structure of Pullman Kellogg. She needed more of a challenge and began to realize she wasn't going to get it without further training. Geof, on the other hand, was happily situated. He liked Houston, liked his law firm and his particular job—corporate securities—at which he was fast becoming an expert. He suffered, however, from his own conscientiousness and

58

the work overload thrust on junior lawyers. He stayed glued to his desk long after hours and on most weekends. He was exhausted most of the time; his nerves jangled; his time with Ann and his other friends was sparse to the point of starvation. But he couldn't let up.

Although Ann was not immune to the success drive herself and sympathized with Geof, she didn't want to give short shrift to their personal life. "It was crazy," said Ann matter-of-factly. "I didn't marry him *never* to see him. I was hurt, felt abandoned, and thought our relationship was on the rocks. I also felt he was really hurting himself." Ann quit Pullman Kellogg—"a great relief"—and flew off for a vacation on the east coast to gain some perspective. From a Maine island she wrote Geof a long letter saying she loved him but didn't want to live with an absent partner. When she returned to Houston, the climate changed significantly. By luck, another securities lawyer had joined Geof's section, relieving him of some of his pressures, and he had also done some heavy thinking on his own.

Shortly after, the tables reversed themselves. Ann decided to apply to business school, and it would now be Geof who would come to her support with his understanding of work pressures. Both were trying hard to establish a balance between their careers and their personal life.

In the winter of 1980 Ann took her qualifying exams and sent out her applications to business schools. Rice was only a few blocks from home, but Harvard and Stanford were more challenging—"the best," as her grandfather would have said. She decided to aim high —so she "would never have to wonder if I could have gotten in but hadn't tried." She would postpone the difficult decision of whether or not she would be willing to go as far away as Palo Alto or Cambridge until she was accepted—which she didn't quite believe possible.

When in April she received a yes from Harvard, she was thrown into conflict. Geof did not want to leave Houston. Did she want to leave Geof for the better part of two years? Advice came from many quarters—none of it neutral. Her mother and some of Ann's friends were shocked that she would even consider it. Others felt she would be crazy not to accept the opportunity. Geof was particularly insistent that she do what she wanted most. "For my sake," he said, "I hope there's a way you can justify staying here, but if you don't go, at every professional setback you have in the next forty years you'll think, 'If only I'd gone to Harvard.' " They could meet on weekends in New York, Cambridge, or Houston; the flights were good, and they could afford them. The decision was hers. In May, still unde- cided, Ann attended a weekend open house at Harvard Business School, designed mainly, I suspect, to woo students like Ann who had been accepted by other schools as well and were still on the fence. Harvard won, and Ann found a Cambridge apartment. Al- though the two years would be an expensive proposition in tuition and rent, they decided not to scrimp on the phone calls or airfares and to meet on alternate weekends.

Because I was living on the west coast, I was out of touch with Ann for most of the school year and so was eager to find how her first year had gone. I called her in Houston in early July.

"It was awful—terrible. The work was relentless." She spoke with passion. "You get up at six o'clock every morning and go to bed between midnight and two A.M., and in between you just study. I studied straight through the weekend. I didn't see Geof. I took a break to run every day and that was it. I learned a lot of new concepts and I'm much more analytical. I'm the first to say the program's effective, but for someone with a soft background like me—no college math, accounting, engineering, economics, marketing—it's just awful to go through. They don't need to terrify people. They're needlessly—for lack of a better word—sadistic. The implication, I guess, is that's what it's like in the 'real world.' Theoretically, you're subjected to the pressure an executive is subjected to and you've got to learn how to handle it. And it's certainly true you get better at handling it, but it is terrifying. In every subject, the professor auto- matically fails ten to fifteen percent—no matter what. And, if you flunk four courses, you're out.

"I wouldn't have survived at all if it hadn't been for Geof and a few other people who supported me. Geof was a saint. In my mind it was really touch and go whether I'd pass, but Geoffrey believed all along that I'd make it. We talked on the phone for a half hour every evening while I was cooking and eating and he was winding up his day in Houston. We saw each other alternate weekends as we'd planned, but he did most of the traveling. In the end, my mother was very supportive too."

In her summer respite from Harvard, Ann was working with a Houston land development company. All her male colleagues turned out to be Harvard Business School graduates (evidently some 10 percent of last year's HBS class took jobs in Dallas or Houston). "A lot of them are married to professional women. It's great. They treat me like I'm an intelligent human being and can understand what's going on—which was not the case at Pullman Kellogg at all. And working hours are a dream—nine to six. When I first got home from Harvard, the idea of being free from 7:00 P.M. on took some getting used to. I hardly knew what to do with myself. To be able to sleep until 7:30 in the morning—incredible!"

For the first time since I've known her, Ann raised the question of having children, which for Ann means that some decision is not too far off. Like many other young professional women nearing thirty, Ann thinks a lot about just when and how she can break into her career without losing too much professional momentum in the process. Ann is now twenty-nine and has another year of business school to go. "I guess," she said, "the bottom line is there will never be a good time. You just decide you want to do it and make it work out. But I haven't figured out yet just how much time I want to take off to have a kid—three weeks, a couple of years, or part time for six years? Taking time out is a big problem.

"I'm setting myself up as best I can. If I have a Harvard degree they can't say I'm dumb; they can't say I can't handle a good job. On the other hand, what kind of projects will they give me? How am I going to be penalized for wanting flexibility? As time goes on, women will design their own work so they'll have the flexibility they want. Now the whole structure is built on an eight-to-six business day and on hours billed. From start to finish, the professional world is not set up for having children."

I asked her how many children she was thinking of having.

"At first I'd say two just because that's what you're supposed to have for population control and all that. But then I think of how much I love my family, how great it is to have four brothers and sisters, how they're your best friends. They used to call me at Harvard and tell me I could make it and that Mom loved me." Her voice was wistful now. "Then I think maybe I'll have three or four."

61

PORTRAIT OF LYNNE

LYNNE Hall (pseudonym) almost never spoke in class. Each week she would slip into the room quietly, find a cushion or a chair in an unobtrusive spot, and watch. She was an acute observer. Very little escaped her notice and everyone knew it.

Lynne was lovely to look at—tall, with shoulder-length black hair and soft brown skin—but her face revealed no clues to what she might be thinking. The only black and the only freshman in my first class, she held a certain clout from her silent stance and her different status. Although shy, she was not altogether unaware of her power and she would speak up when she felt she needed to reassure others that she was not indifferent or hostile. At the same time, she remained wary of the rest of us and hid her real concerns under academic generalizations.

I had admitted Lynne to my class because, among other reasons, her course application showed me she wrote in simple declarative sentences—a rarity among Yale students. She also had written with extraordinary honesty about the type of things she wanted to write about and her difficulties in doing so. This was in direct contrast to

63

the vague statements she used to express herself in class on the rare occasions that she spoke at all. What I didn't realize until much later was how much of this posture was the result of her need to maintain a solidarity with the other blacks at Yale. Black codes on how to deal with whites were very strict in this period, and you didn't talk with whites very much—let alone expose yourself. Whereas the Puerto Rican student, Elías Aguilar, whose story appears later, hid behind dramatic rhetoric, Lynne—with her innate shyness—hid behind silence and vagueness.

At first none of us had any hint of her past life. She told us that she came from Waterbury, that her mother and father were divorced, and that, on a special full-tuition scholarship, she had attended a fancy girls' prep school as a day student. In the beginning she was the only black in the school. From her early papers we knew that Lynne planned to become a psychologist to help her fellow blacks "get their heads together." Many of life's problems for blacks as well as whites, she felt, came from breakdowns in the relationships between men and women. We had no clues to her own personal experience in this arena, although she had said in the first class that she had started keeping journals because people never understood what she said. "I would like the time," she said, "to write down things I can't talk about."

But weeks passed and Lynne had trouble getting anything on paper. When I suggested that she write letters to make her writing come more easily, she wrote a letter to her boyfriend about trivia: a paragraph about searching the attic to find her journal; remarks about her father not liking to stay home if the TV were broken. But now and then a reference cropped up that piqued my curiosity. When I asked her about the sentence "I'm sure Dad feels as we all do that there was something he could have done to prevent Dawn from going off," I discovered that Dawn was a sister who had committed suicide the year before. She had jumped off a Charles River bridge in Cambridge after months of being involuntarily committed to a series of state mental hospitals. In the same letter there was a sentence that read, "I tried to recall what could've been going on in my head at this time; then I remembered that this was the period when I was at the height of my criminal career." What

64

criminal career? Was this hyperbole? A romantic turn of phrase? Or
had she really had a "criminal career"?

I didn't want to pry into her life, and yet I wanted her to get
beyond the boring trivia. But in spite of these hints of deeper
experience, she persisted in the old way. If she handed in a paper
at all, it was apt to be a high-school dialogue about nothing:

> She stepped out of her clothes and left them where they landed—
> for the time being, of course. She was a very tidy and orderly person;
> one would almost think that she was mechanical. . . . The phone
> rang. . . .
> "Hello." Her heart pounded heavily.
> "How are you?"
> "Fine. How are you?"
> "Okay. Would you like to go to the store with me?"
> "Oh, that new store that just opened. Well—yeah, but I'm in my
> pajamas."
> "You're kidding! It's only six thirty."

. . . and on and on, ending with a sentence like "She dropped the
receiver with shaky hands."

This, when she'd had a sister who committed suicide? And perhaps a criminal career before eighteen? Why?

I recalled her earlier statement that she wanted to write about
things she couldn't talk about. I reread her initial application to the
course. (The application almost always reveals more than either the
student or the teacher is initially aware of.) In one paragraph she
said, "I get discouraged when I put my whole self into a piece, think
it's really good, then have somebody come along and say it's lousy,
or just read it and not take a second look at it. . . . I never know how
much of myself to reveal through writing. I wonder how much
people can take before they pass a value judgment."

As much as she wanted to write, Lynne, I suspected, didn't trust
anyone to read what she had to say—particularly whites. I also
suspected that her fear was not unfounded.

One sunny fall day as we sat on my back porch, she told me that
she really wanted to write about Greg, her psychotic high-school

boyfriend, and about their criminal career together. "But," she said, "I have never told anyone this story except for Mac [her current boyfriend]. If I did, it might jeopardize my scholarship position at Yale. Besides, I don't think my mother or father would like it." She also wondered how other people in the class would receive such a tale. She talked about her fears matter-of-factly, just as she recounted matter-of-factly—almost in deadpan—some of the terrifying episodes with Greg. She spoke as if she felt these events were inevitable in her life but were not to be revealed lest someone penalize her for them. I knew her assessment might well be right.

I urged her not to write the story unless she wanted to, but I could promise her that it would never be read by anyone but myself—if that was what she wanted. She then said that, when she was applying to Yale, she had been tempted to answer the second half of her Yale admissions application with this story; indeed, she felt her drug experience with Greg was the real reason why she should be admitted. It had matured her, given her an understanding of criminality and a direction for her life.

Together we decided that she should live out her fantasy and write a story in answer to Yale's Questionnaire Number 2. The result was dramatic. From that afternoon onward—with the exception of a few awkward words and misplaced clauses—Lynne wrote a clean and unflinchingly objective prose that was a thumbprint of herself.

When she finished, she showed it to the class. Her classmates were stunned by the story and the way in which she told it. Ann Kennedy wrote in the notebooks, "Oh—Lynne, this is the most incredible thing I've ever read. I sit here filled with sorrow and anger that such a thing should happen to you. . . . You've taught me a new writing tone, a new attitude of detachment yet involvement that I think is necessary to write something that is as close as yours is. I appreciate that and the fact that you let me read it. Thanks. Ann. P.S. How do you keep your writing so clean? Mine goes crazy when I get involved."

Lynne is now willing—with a pseudonym and a few other name changes—to let a wider audience read it. "If it works right," she says, "it should help them understand a few things."

THE QUESTIONNAIRE
by Lynne Hall,
Waterbury, Connecticut

**Yale University
Application Form**

2. Personal Commentary

Instructions:

This is the part of your application that belongs to you. Use it in any way you wish to enable us to get to know you as a person, not as a statistic. . . . If you submit a sample of your work, we will have it examined and evaluated by a Yale faculty member knowledgeable in the particular area. . . .

We are most interested in anything of importance to you that will help us better understand you, your abilities, your interests, your reasons for wanting to attend college, and why you feel that your attending Yale will be a mutually beneficial experience. . . .

White people are always asking this sort of question and then making judgments against a person if he or she gives them the truth. They think they won't but they do.

I believe that the experiences I shall relate not only describe who I am but have given me a strong motivation to go to college, to finish it, and to use my education to help people less fortunate than myself. I don't know which of your professors is "knowledgeable in the particular area" of my essay, but I leave that up to you. I hope that all of you who read my essay will agree that what I have learned from my experience will make my attending Yale a "mutually beneficial" experience.

I learned most about myself and other people between the ages of thirteen and sixteen, when my boyfriend and I hung around the streets of our city. If it hadn't been for Greg, I probably would not have come in contact with the people and the experiences that I did.

Looking back, it's hard for me to understand why I went along with Greg and why I stayed with him as long as I did. At the time I was extremely shy and passive, and Greg was the only person with whom I had any relationship at all. I needed him, I think, to make contact with the world I was too timid to approach on my own. I just went along with anything he did.

I lived with my mother and five sisters in a two-family house on a pleasant street not far from a district that contained five hospitals and nursing homes. A large park was just two blocks away. Although we lived on the edge of a black district, we were the only black family on our particular street. My mother and father were separated, and although my father owned the house in which we lived, he lived in an apartment on the other side of town, where he was the reading specialist for a local elementary school.

My mother, my sisters, and I occupied both sides of the two-family house, and we had knocked an opening through the wall between two upstairs bedrooms in order to join the two sides of the house together. On the ground floor, however, there was no passage between the two sides, and we had to go upstairs to reach the other side of the house. I lived alone, in the unused ground-floor living room and kitchen on one side, which meant I had both a front and back door exit of my own. This arrangement made it possible for Greg to come and go without anyone in the house—especially my mother—knowing anything about it.

During this period, as I look back on it, my mother was unhappy and worried, and she didn't approve of much of anything my sisters and I did. So we just went our individual ways, not paying too much attention to one another and not telling anything to my mother. My oldest sister worked in an insurance company and my mother as a secretary to a doctor. The rest of us went to school.

Greg lived a block and a half away. We first started going together when I was thirteen and he was fourteen and we were both in eighth grade. He was quite short, light-skinned, and had short hair. I began going out with him, I suppose, because I was competing with my girlfriend for his attention. At first Greg did everything he could to heighten the competition between us, but later I won him over and just the two of us hung around together.

From the very beginning, my mother didn't like him. She thought his mother was a phony and she didn't like his father because he ran around with other women. When my mother first saw Greg with me, she warned him not to hang around me, so I was careful that she didn't see us together. Greg's own mother and father didn't like him much either. When he was sixteen and had grown bigger, he beat them up and they would throw him out of the house.

We'd been going together for about three months when our juvenile delinquency started at the hospital gift shop, quite by accident. Because it was closer than the nearest store, Greg and I went to the hospital often to get snacks and Cokes from the vending machines and Life Savers and potato chips from the gift shop. The shop was usually tended by a single woman volunteer. One day, as the volunteer turned her back to us to get the potato chips we'd asked for, Greg snatched a pair of earrings off the rotating stand on the counter and stuffed them into his pocket. The old lady didn't see us—nor, I think, did she suspect us. Having discovered that we could get away with lifting earrings, we visited the gift shop often and devised tricks to get the lady to turn her back on us. We would change our minds about whether we wanted potato chips or potato sticks and stage fake fights to divert her attention. Then we would slip the earrings into our pockets. When we weren't wearing clothes with pockets, we would stuff them into our mouths or half-filled Coke cups. In less than two months we had "liberated" more than $125 worth of earrings. I was very proud of my collection and kept it in a jewelry box made just for earrings that one of my eighth-grade classmates had given me. The box itself I hid under my mattress so my ten-year-old sister wouldn't help herself to a few.

After this start we expanded our operations by discovering a way to break into the local recreation center. The center, which was run by the parks department, sat in a small playground midway between Greg's house and mine. In spring and summer it offered outdoor recreation such as basketball and handball for older kids and swings and sandboxes for younger ones. In winter and fall the building itself was opened, offering indoor basketball, Ping-Pong, pool. Throughout the year the director ran competitions in the various sports, and the winner usually won prizes of candy. On weekends, however, the center was not open and the building was locked tight. A set of double doors at the back were fastened together by a chain that ran through the handles. Greg and I discovered that these doors could be forced open just wide enough for a skinny person to squeeze through an opening at the top. Greg would give me a boost to the top of the doors, I would wiggle through and then run down the hall and unlock the side door for Greg. So we spent our Saturdays and Sundays playing pool or basketball and trying to find a way to unlock the cellar door to get at the prize candy in the center's refrigerator. This was an exciting enterprise. We had to be very quick and secretive so that the neighbors and their kids wouldn't become suspicious and call the police. On Saturday nights we'd put everything back in its proper place and lock the center up again.

One day some neighborhood kids heard us inside and we had to let them in so they wouldn't tell on us. They of course soon told their friends, and before long the activity inside the center was just as great on weekends as it was during the week, when the center was open. As time went on, it became more and more difficult to cover everybody's tracks; eventually some little kids told the director and he put new locks on the doors. Greg and I were never caught, because after a while there were so many of us that the little kids didn't know who was responsible for opening the doors. Others had learned the trick.

With the recreation center closed to us, we looked for new enterprises. One day we broke into the local junior high school, which was Greg's school and also the school where my father taught. We went

70

to the homemaking room, stole all the edible food, and stored it at my house. On another day, when we were on our way home from our early morning paper route, we broke into a candy wagon parked at a gas station for the night. Greg broke a window and opened the door from inside. We filled our paper-route bags and our pockets with all the candy we could carry. We hid the candy in my room at home and opened up what turned out to be an unprofitable business. At first we tried to sell the candy, but because most of the kids had no money, we were forced to take IOUs. These were never paid, so we soon accepted the inevitable and just gave the candy to our friends or ate it ourselves. Eventually my little sister discovered our business and, in spite of being bribed on many different occasions, told my mother. At least I was fortunate in that I was leaving for camp in a few days and all I had to do was pack the candy with my clothes and tell my mother I had gotten rid of it.

That summer, ironically enough, I had been hired as a junior counselor for nine weeks at an overnight camp for ghetto children. It was located in the Connecticut hills and had formerly been a Jewish resort hotel. Although drab and ugly, it was well equipped, with a swimming pool, fields for archery and baseball, and an arts and crafts room. There were woods nearby for nature walks. All thirty-two girl campers and four girl counselors lived in one large building; the forty or so boys in two others.

I was the counselor for the seven- and eight-year-old girls, who came for two-week sessions and were usually frightened and homesick for the first week. Most of them were black or Puerto Rican, and some of the Puerto Rican girls could hardly speak any English. The counselors were very young—all under eighteen—but at fourteen I was the youngest. It was my first time away from home and my first experience in communal living with people my own age. I was to learn a lot from it.

Until I went to camp, I had difficulty talking to people I didn't know very well. At camp I was forced to come out of my shell in order to take care of the little girls and to work with the other counselors and kitchen help. I was impressed by these people: they weren't flawless, but they were down to earth, and they were trying very hard to make something out of their lives. They were all struggling hard to survive the inhuman conditions that had been forced

71

on them by the sick urban ghettoes in which they had grown up. It was the first time I had seen people make a real effort to overcome their difficulties. After camp was over, I was to learn that some of these new friends of mine had succeeded in their struggle to survive while others had been pulled down and defeated. The dishwasher, Mike (who was nice but looked like a thug), had been sent to camp as an alternative to reform school, where he had been sentenced for assault and burglary. After camp he was caught taking LSD and was returned to reform school. George, a counselor for eight- to ten-year-old boys, was tall, skinny, and comical. He kept us all laughing. He had a drug habit which he tried hard to lick at camp, and if he took anything at camp, I never knew about it. After he left, he was caught in the LSD episode with Mike and sent to prison. I never heard what became of Bill. A dishwasher like Mike, he was vulgar, dirty, and nasty, and all the other girl counselors and I hated him. Although he was only twenty, he had already been married, but his marriage had broken up. Some say this breakup was the cause of his bisexuality, but I suspect that sexuality had been a problem for him all his life. In any case he made constant passes at the girl counselors, and Mike, his roommate, caught him having sexual relations with a cat on one occasion and with a small boy camper on another. Although Alan, the director of the camp, was later arrested in Ohio for abusing a young boy sexually, at camp he was straight.

On the other hand, there was Ann, the counselor of the ten- to twelve-year-old girls. She married the next winter and is living happily with her husband and their baby girl. Curtis, the counselor of the eight- to ten-year-old boys, has joined the army, and John is now at divinity school. Two other counselors, Sandy and Dianne, have gone on to college. I spent a lot of time with Dianne. She came from Virginia, where she had been sheltered and brought up strictly. Although she was only seventeen, she seemed older and wiser, and I found her nice to be with. My favorite person at camp, however, was the cook, Mac. He was handsome, and I had a girlish crush on him from the first moment I saw him. Much older—twenty-two— he had been married but was separated from his wife. At first I would just sit and stare at him, not daring to show him I liked him. But he was so nice to me that I gradually started talking to him, and he looked after me. He gave me extra food and taught me how to swim. One night, Mac and all the counselors went on a hike in the woods, trying to follow the north star. We lost our way, had a cookout, and came back to camp in the early dawn. For the first time in my life, I was having fun. So when Greg turned up to visit one day, I wasn't happy to see him at all. I just introduced him around, and after a few hours he left—but not before threatening to beat up Charlie, whom he erroneously suspected of being my boyfriend.

From all these people I began to gain an understanding of why people—myself included—behave the way they do. I also was learning to handle difficult situations, particularly personal confrontations from people who were messed up. For the first time, I had begun to learn to deal with people on my own without Greg or anyone else acting as intermediary. For the next year, however, much of what I learned that summer lay dormant within me while my delinquent life expanded.

A few days after I returned home, Greg returned from another camp, where he had been a camper. While I came back with a new appreciation of people, Greg came back with a new appreciation of marijuana, hashish, speed, LSD, cocaine, and who knows what else. In spite of my camp experiences, I was still very much under Greg's influence. I had not yet found any goal for my life nor formed any judgments about what activities were good or bad for me. In a desultory sort of way, I was antiestablishment. I had no strong feelings against taking drugs and told myself I should at least have some knowledge of what it was I wasn't supposed to be doing.

And so I began. I spent New Year's Eve with Greg at a pot party. Someone has said that whatever you do on New Year's Eve you will do for the rest of the year. That was true for me—almost completely.

For the better part of the next year I played with drugs. I used marijuana, hash, speed, and cocaine frequently. I experimented with LSD, DMT, and downs. I watched people shoot up, turn on, and freak out. Through Greg I met an an assortment of hippies, drug pushers, black militants, street corner artists—many of whom were simply passing back and forth from Boston to New York. On street corners and in alleyways and little stores, I saw many business transactions and watched the arrival and distribution of large shipments of drugs. This was different from the year before, when our activities were restricted to our own neighborhood and just to young kids like ourselves.

All this scared me. (If I saw someone with a rubber strap around his arm about to shoot heroin, I would have to leave the room.) At most times, I was a passive tagalong, just following Greg and watching mindlessly, not considering the consequences nor really feeling much of anything at all.

In fact, I didn't particularly like drugs. And internally I must have resisted quite strongly, because I never freaked out; all the time I was under, I would concentrate on keeping control. The one time I took LSD Greg told me it was something else; if I had known that he was giving me LSD, I would have refused. When I found out, I fought the drug and sat still, simply controlling myself and waiting for the trip to be over.

The same was not true of Greg. He liked to take drugs and to peddle them as well—a thing I could not bring myself to do. Experimenting with drugs on myself was one thing; pushing them on other people was, for me, another thing altogether. It was true that I would sometimes go with Greg when he dealt nickel bags of pot at the evening concerts in the park. Because policemen couldn't shake down girls without first bringing them to the police station, it was safer if I carried the bags in my pocketbook and handed him one when he made a sale. But I did this only to reduce the chances of Greg's being arrested. I never went with him when he made other transactions or peddled stronger stuff. On one of these occasions, in April, he was arrested for selling LSD and speed to an undercover agent. He was in jail for about a month, and I visited him there once. When he came to trial, he was convicted but given a suspended sentence, because it was his first offense and he was only sixteen. He was put on probation. On the day he was released from jail, he returned to his usual activities, making no attempt to give up drugs or to stop selling them.

It didn't take me long to realize that Greg was hooked and had a serious problem. Slowly, during that year, he had turned weird. He would frequently imagine that people and objects were trying to harm him. At night he'd lie in bed, afraid that his overhead light was plotting to explode, emitting gaseous fumes that would kill him.

School authorities had enrolled him in a drug rehabilitation program, and he told me, rather proudly, that the psychiatrists there had said that he was "a paranoid schizophrenic" and was "psychologically addicted to drugs." I, too, felt that his persecution feelings caused him to seek refuge in drugs. When he was high, he seemed oblivious to the things he normally saw as threats, and could be quite gentle. Although he would frequently promise me he was going to swear off, he attended the rehabilitation clinic only sporadically and then usually when he was high. To reduce his paranoia the clinic gave him tranquilizers, but he would take overdoses of these in order to get high again. He was proud of deceiving people and would spend his time thinking of new ways to "blow people's minds" or "psych them out."

He was also violent. Whenever he was in his paranoid state, he would beat me for some imagined wrong—usually that I was going out with someone else. I grew to dislike him, but I was afraid to leave him because he threatened to kill me if I did. On rare occasions when he wasn't having a fight with his family, he lived at home, but mostly he stayed wherever he could find a bed. Sometimes he stayed with me.

Meanwhile, I lived a schizophrenic life of my own. After I graduated from junior high school, I had been given a full scholarship to an elite private girls' day school in the suburbs. The rules were strict: knee-length skirts and saddle shoes were required; bare legs were forbidden—they must be covered with stockings or knee socks; makeup was outlawed; and of course no one was to have a thought about swearing or drinking. The catchphrase was "ladylike behavior" and along with it went a set of unspoken rules that I sometimes had difficulty figuring out. "Polished" was another word frequently laid on us.

And so, by day, I wandered politely over green lawns in my knee socks, studied French, and mingled with middle- and upper-middle-class white girls in a New England prep school. My first year I was the only black in my class and one of six in the whole school. A few more blacks were added in subsequent classes, and in my senior year, when our school merged with a private boys' school, there were over twenty. On the playgrounds or between classes, the other girls talked mostly about school, but gradually, as I became somewhat friendly with them, I described to them—in very general terms—another kind of life, where people used drugs and had different ideas about sex and money. (You can be sure I gave no hint of being connected with these people in any way. I was the "sociological observer.") They had never met any black people before except their maids, and they never accepted the fact that I was different from them, or to be more accurate, they never admitted it openly. I don't know if they let themselves learn anything from me. I didn't belong to any of the cliques, and most of the time I felt as if I was just part of the furniture. At one of the school dances the girls met Greg and flocked around him—fascinated and vying for his attention. On this occasion, I felt even more like an inanimate object and silently resented them all. Of course I told them nothing about our nighttime activities.

Academically the school was good for me and taught me a great deal more than I could have learned in the public high school in our neighborhood. I was fortunate to find an understanding English teacher who realized the position I was in and encouraged me to speak from my own point of view, and write from my own experience. She did a lot for all the black students. I was active in sports and played on the hockey, lacrosse, baseball, and basketball teams.

Each day, I'd return home from school about five o'clock, work at my chores around the house, do a little homework, and pick up what I could to eat. My mother hated to cook and so never prepared any real dinner. About ten, I would put on my pajamas, go upstairs, pass through the door that connected us with the other side of the house, and continue on to the bathroom. En route, I'd stop in my sisters' and mother's rooms to find out what time each one needed to get up in the morning. It was my job to wake everyone up. Then I'd say my good-nights and, returning to my room, would turn out the lights, get dressed again, and wait long enough for my mother and sisters to think I was asleep. When enough time had elapsed, I would sneak out the front door on my side of the house.

Greg would usually be waiting for me at the corner. We'd walk through the park and across town to Charlie's Drug Store—"the dope dealer's haven." Out front, middlemen would be standing in little groups; inside, buyers, sellers, and middlemen would be milling around trying to negotiate without looking suspicious. When a seller located a buyer, they'd go outside to score. Inside, the game was to see how many cigarettes, papers, pipes, magazines, and other small items could be liberated without rousing Charlie's attention. After midnight, the place was so full of weird-looking people that it was like a circus. At Charlie's, Greg and I would say hello to our friends, and after a while Greg would wander outside to do whatever business he had in mind. We would hang around there for a bit and then make our way to the dairy, where products for the next day's delivery would be set out on the loading ramps behind the factory. There we would pick up a couple of gallons of chocolate milk, some cream cheese, and some eggs, and proceed to the People's Pad.

The People's Pad was a five-room apartment located in one of a long line of apartment buildings near the milk factory. The area was known for its many busts, and many young kids and dope dealers lived in the apartments there. I never knew exactly who rented the People's Pad, but it was open all night to anyone who wanted to go there and smoke dope, take drugs, or just hang around. Anyone who had no other place to sleep could always spend the night there.

After arriving, Greg and I would fill up the refrigerator with our haul, have something to eat, and sit around and listen to music from a record player. All night, people came in and out of the apartment; they'd sit down for a while, pass around a couple of joints, and talk about the places they'd been and the things they'd seen. Greg and I would sit and listen to their tales or catch a few catnaps until about four, when we would go back to my house. Sometimes Greg would stay with me, but mostly he went off to wherever he was staying that week. At 6:45 I'd be up and ready to catch my school bus. No one ever knew that I had left my house the night before or suspected that I was using drugs.

Sometime in the spring term, a few of my girl friends at school started smoking pot. They were obvious and foolish. They would come to school visibly stoned, their eyes red and their hair and breath smelling like reefers. Or during class hours they would sneak out behind the school buildings and get stoned on campus. Occasionally they experimented with LSD and speed, but they smoked pot almost continuously. I never joined them. Even cigarette smoking meant automatic suspension, but I wasn't worried about that; as the only black in my class, I knew they wouldn't suspend me. It was

77

just that I felt that school was not an appropriate place for pot and that the girls behaved stupidly when they smoked. Everyone else at school knew what they were doing—even the administration, who simply pretended that the situation didn't exist. My guess is that the headmistress didn't want to take the chance of having a pot scandal. Occasionally she would talk to me, always very guardedly and in general terms, about pot and other drugs. I think she felt that I, as a black, understood the world of dope and might be able to give her advice on how she could handle the situation. Speaking in a saccharine voice, she was always falling over herself to "understand blacks," but she wasn't sincere.

In the spring of that year, when I was fifteen, I began to look at myself and the people around me. I realized that the way I was living was stagnant. I wasn't doing anything that I could actually call "something." I was just sitting around wasting time, and not even enjoying that. I wasn't taking advantage of the educational opportunities in front of me, nor was I doing anything to help the less fortunate people who would have liked to have the scholarship I had. I decided that I would stop playing at being into drugs, and fighting the establishment, and give up all my strong opinions on things I really knew nothing about. I thought that I would just give up my night life and start taking school seriously.

After making this decision, I discovered that I was pregnant. I couldn't tell my parents, so I was dependent on Greg for all the financial and moral support I was to get. Marriage to Greg was out of the question, and more than anything else I wanted to finish high school; so we agreed that I should get an abortion. Greg knew a chemist at an airplane manufacturing company who performed illegal abortions on the side. Earlier in his life he had been rejected by medical school and so took up abortions both as a moneymaking enterprise and as a vendetta against the medical profession. He charged two hundred dollars, so Greg and I planned to make the money over the summer. Time was the only cause for concern. In two weeks I had to leave to be a camp counselor for the second year. I would be gone for two months, so it was absolutely essential that we have the money and all the arrangements made before the end of August and be able to proceed with the abortion on the day I came home.

78

That summer was taxing. I worked very hard with my girls, trying to make an impression on their lives and to teach them to live with each other. I was in charge of eleven- and twelve-year-olds, and the cultural and language differences caused more conflicts than I had had with the younger ones. In my care were three black girls, one white girl, and two Puerto Ricans, one of whom spoke no English at all. In addition, we had a new camp director who was a slavedriver. He ran the camp like a military training camp, insisting that each camper and counselor participate in some organized activity all day long. I was the exercise teacher and my job, apart from counseling the girls, was to lead the campers and counselors in exercises for a half hour every morning in the blazing sun. I began to gain weight and had to fight against morning sickness. Throughout the day I made what seemed a superhuman effort to stay awake to play baseball or basketball, when all I wanted to do was crawl into bed and sleep.

All summer I successfully hid the fact that I was pregnant, but I couldn't wipe out my own fears. I was beset by fantasies: I would be deserted by Greg; I wouldn't be able to have the abortion; I would be found out by my parents.

Greg came to see me once that summer, just three weeks before the end of the season. He told me that he hadn't any money but assured me that he could raise it in less than two weeks dealing dope.

When I returned home three weeks later, Greg was nowhere to be seen. For the next week I sat around waiting for him to show up and trying not to believe what I knew was true: when the chips were down, Greg didn't want to know me. He didn't care what happened to me. Just at this point, Mac called me from out of town, asking if he could come see me on my birthday. (I had seen him only once since my first year at camp; he hadn't been cooking there the second summer.) I spent the day with him, and just before he left I told him about my pregnancy and Greg's disappearance. We discussed the problem and agreed that the most sensible thing to do would be to tell my parents. Since Greg obviously was not concerned with my well-being, we decided that if he should show up, I wouldn't proceed with his abortionist. He, too, might turn out to be a fake—or worse. The matter, we concluded, should be taken out of Greg's hands altogether except for whatever financial aid he could contribute.

So on my sixteenth birthday I came home about seven, went to my mother's room, and I told her I was pregnant. At first she didn't believe me, but when she realized that I wasn't joking, she took it calmly. The next day she told my father. Both my parents said they would go along with the abortion as long as I was sure that was what I wanted. Through friends they were put in touch with a retired doctor in New York City, and the appointment was set for two weeks later. It would cost five hundred dollars. A week later, Greg showed up, penniless.

My father wanted to break Greg's neck and my mother wanted to have him thrown in jail. They didn't act on their feelings, however, because they needed whatever money he could produce; instead, he was warned against ever again setting foot on my parents' property. Before two weeks passed, Greg had come up with $180. I still had $120 of my summer earnings and my father had been able to raise another $200.

When the day arrived, I was outwardly calm, but inside I was scared. I took a bus to Bridgeport, where I met my parents. My father had been working and living there for a couple of years and my mother was attending a two-day Masonic convention and staying at a hotel. The moment I saw her in her hotel room, I knew my mother was frightened. She told me that on the previous night she had dreamed that I had died. Some of her friends had told her that she shouldn't let me have an abortion, because if anything went wrong she and my father could get into a lot of trouble. She told me that I could go away somewhere and have the baby and come back in a year or so. She had already concocted a story we could tell our relatives about my absence. But I had made up my mind to go through with it. School was going to start in four days and I was determined not to miss a day. So as soon as my father turned up, we got into his car and started for New York. All during the trip my mother and father discussed possible alternatives to the abortion.

In New York we first went to the house of a woman who was acting as intermediary and, I surmise, a check against police investigation. She sat us all down, offered us some coffee, and then interviewed us about my age, physical condition, and length of pregnancy. After she had finished taking my history, she went into the next room and called the doctor. When she returned, she told us the doctor had been reluctant to proceed when he found out I was only sixteen and was three and a half months pregnant. But because I was in good health and had come so far, he had finally decided it would be all right to go ahead. None of this made my mother a bit happier.

The woman gave us the doctor's address on 125th Street and told us to leave the car and go there by cab an hour later at eight o'clock. To kill time we went to a small store around the corner and ate some pickles and, after what seemed like a long time, proceeded to the doctor's address as advised. The doctor lived above a small variety store, and the hallway off the street was narrow and dark. We walked up two flights of stairs, passing garbage cans crowded around the apartment doors on each floor. The walls of the stairwell were dirty brown and the paint was peeling. The whole place smelled of garbage.

When we knocked on the appointed door, we were admitted by the doctor himself. He was a small man with snow-white hair and a full snow-white beard. Against his very dark skin his hair looked even whiter than it was. He looked about eighty, but was still spry and had a pleasant face. He was dressed in a dingy white doctor's jacket and black pants. He greeted us and led us into an office where there was a scale, two medicine chests, a stool, two chairs, a table with medical instruments on it, and an examining table. Everything in the room, except for some colored pills and the steel instruments, was the same dingy white as the doctor's jacket. Plaques and medical certificates—from Vienna, London, Stockholm—hung on the walls. The doctor was such a friendly little old man that I felt at home.

The doctor told us that I would have to stay there two days, which surprised us all and made my mother and father more uneasy than they already were. He patiently explained that the operation took time and that it was necessary for me to remain twenty-four hours after it was over so that he could watch over me to be sure there were no complications. He reassured my parents that everything would be all right and told them to go home and stop worrying. They could call at midnight if they wanted a progress report. Because it was the policy to pay in advance, my father, looking terrified, took out the money and gave it to the doctor. Then he gave me some money to come home on the train. They paused for a moment, looking at me as if it were the last time they would see me, and left.

Their look made me feel eerie for a moment. But, for myself, I was no longer frightened. I had made up my mind that everything was going to be all right. I had too much to live for. I was going to finish school and go on to college in order to study psychology. I wanted to do something for people whose minds had been messed up—people who no longer believed they had any worth or purpose. I was going to help these people regain their self-esteem by showing them that they were victims of a system devised to keep them down. Then I was going to get married and have a large family. I had talked all this over with Mac before I had come to New York, and he told me he had faith in me and that everything would be all right. I knew he expected me to be brave, so I had promised myself that for him I would take it all like a woman.

After the doctor's wife had searched about and found an old nightgown, many sizes too big, the doctor put me on the examining table and gave me a knockout shot. I must have wanted very much to stay conscious because I fought the medication even after a second shot. I could not tell exactly what the doctor was doing to me but it felt as if he were pulling my insides out, piece by piece. I wanted to scream or cry or jump off the table, but I remembered that I was supposed to be brave, and the doctor scolded me every time I moved a muscle. At midnight, when my parents called to check on me, the doctor told them I was fine. He continued to work on me until, about an hour later, the water broke—something I knew happened to women before they went into labor. His wife brought me a dry nightgown and I heard the doctor mumbling something about how strange it was and how he had never seen anything quite like this before. He then took me into a small bedroom next to his office and I fell asleep.

When I woke up, it was morning, and the doctor's wife gave me breakfast in the kitchen. After breakfast the doctor asked me to remove a tube he had put in me the night before, and when nothing happened, he looked worried. He then gave me a large black pill and told me to lie down and rest.

Late in the afternoon I began having terrible pains in my abdomen and could feel something moving around inside of me. When I called for the doctor, he told me I was going into labor and that I should walk around the room to reduce the pain and hasten the process. He warned me not to make any noise, because another patient would soon be arriving in the next room. He left me a pail and told me to use it. I paced for another few hours before I fully understood what I was to use it for.

That night, all alone, I aborted. It was a boy. I called the doctor, and he examined me. Because I had lost a lot of blood, he gave me a variety of iron pills and I fell asleep again. The next morning I drank tea and soup, and by midafternoon I was up and dressed. My clothes were falling off me; I had lost seven pounds from Friday night to Sunday afternoon. The doctor gave me instructions about more medication and advised me not to get into any more trouble. He and his wife then walked me around the apartment twice to be sure I was steady. They told me how to get to the train station, gave me their address, and said good-bye.

I arrived home all right, and after answering my mother's questions, fell into bed, exhausted. The next day I went to school to buy books. I was offered a ride by some of my classmates, but it was no joyride; they had chosen this day to tell their favorite jokes about abortions and knitting needles. For the rest of the week I attended school, but by the following Monday I was feeling too weak to move from my bed. I had tried to do too much too soon. I rested for a week and after that I was fine.

All during that week I saw the little boy in my mind's eye, and over and over again I thought what a waste it had all been. I felt that I had deprived him of his chance to make something of his life. When I stopped thinking, I hated myself and I hated Greg. I decided I wouldn't see him anymore. When I told him what happened and how I felt about the baby, he shrugged it off. He laughed and said I'd get over it—he'd known lots of girls who'd been through it. When I told him I didn't want to see him anymore, he beat me.

For the next year I tried to get away from him, and for a year he beat me. I didn't dare not see him when he came around because I thought he would kill me if I didn't. He threatened many times to do so and I believed that he was capable of it. I couldn't tell my mother because I wasn't supposed to be seeing him, and besides, I couldn't see what she could do to prevent his coming. If I brought up the subject of our breaking up, he'd beat me. If I tried to give him the cold shoulder, he'd beat me. If I tried to avoid him completely, he'd beat me. Every day he would wait for me along the route I took coming home from school. When I changed routes, he'd wait for me in the small yard beside our house, where he could hide in the bushes if my mother came along. If, when I arrived, I didn't let him in, he would threaten to kill me. Sometimes he wouldn't be waiting for me in the afternoon but would come later, at night. If I turned off the light and pretended I wasn't there, he would bang so loud at the door or the window that I would open it in fear my mother would hear him. Sometimes I would move upstairs with one of my sisters for a few days, but it was so crowded that I had no room to study and barely room enough to sleep.

All this time I was looking for some large guy who could walk home with me from the school bus stop and confront Greg. I thought that when Greg saw I was serious about seeing other people he would realize he was wasting his time and would no longer force me to go out with him. Especially if the guy was bigger than he was. Mac was working in another city, but he too was trying to find someone whom he trusted and who could stand up to Greg. Then, one day, Larry, a school friend, offered to walk me home. He knew nothing about the situation, and I couldn't bring myself to tell him. But he was bigger than Greg, and I thought Greg would back off when he saw him.

As usual, Greg was waiting for me at the corner of my street. He was shocked but he didn't hesitate to walk right up to us.

"Who's that guy with you?" he asked in a growly voice. I explained that he was a good friend of mine. "And just what does that mean?" he asked. I answered as I had many times before—that it meant that we were no longer going steady and that I didn't want to see him anymore. The next thing I knew, quick as lightning, he struck me across the face. Larry stepped between us and they started arguing. Greg asked for his ring, and when I handed it to him, he jumped around Larry and slapped me again. I dropped the ring on the sidewalk. Larry took my arm and said, "Let's get out of here." We left Greg on his knees looking for the ring in the dark.

When I arrived home, I was so angry I told my mother what had happened and we went down to the police station and filed a warrant for Greg's arrest. For a long time the police took no action. But when I told Greg what I'd done, he no longer tried to meet me on the street or at the house. He did, however, phone almost every night to harass me. He wasn't served with the warrant until four months after we first filed it. Then he was jailed for two weeks, but when his case came to court, he was freed because I failed to give testimony against him. Too much time had elapsed for my anger to be hot. After the warrant, he made no attempt to contact me.

In October my mother and sisters moved to Middlebury. I stayed behind so that I could graduate from my prep school in the spring. I live in an upstairs apartment in our house; the rest of it has been rented to another family.

Each evening now I spend filling out the long application forms for college, and like all personal questionnaires they force me to reflect. More and more, I feel my experiences have helped me shape many of the values and ideas I hold. I hope you too will realize the value of my experiences and decide to admit me to your university. I am a responsible and stable person.

LYNNE –
CLINICAL PSYCHOLOGIST

I was eager to find out what Lynne had done since graduating from Yale. Was she out helping "people less fortunate" than herself, as she had vowed when she was a freshman? Or had she changed direction as so many of us do at that age?

During her later college years I'd run across her here and there on campus, but I'd never had a long chat with her. Whenever we did meet, she was, as always, uncommunicative—almost monosyllabic. She was growing livelier and prettier, but she continued to maintain her distance, especially from whites.

In 1979, when I tried to locate her, I couldn't find her anywhere. The Yale Alumni/ae Association and the Calhoun College dean's office had only old addresses that led to dead ends. In desperation, I put a reporter from the *Yale Daily News* on her track; he found her a few days later at the University of Pennsylvania, where she was working for her doctorate in applied clinical psychology. Lynne telephoned me the next day—just as the sun was coming up in California and I was not quite conscious. A rush of exuberant words broke through my early morning fog. "Wow!" she said. "I never

86

thought I'd hear from you again! How are you? . . . Watcha' doin'?
. . . I couldn't believe it when this fella from the *Yalie Daily* called
last night. . . . You know, you could have found me through the
student loan office—they always seem to know how to find me." She
laughed. "Still paying off the loans, y'know. Suppose I'll be doing
that for the rest of my life. Gee! It's great to talk to you." Lynne
had changed! It was now I who was speechless.

We met a few months later at a friend's apartment in New York,
and she was more beautiful than ever. We talked nonstop from early
afternoon until late into the night, and she was alternately ebullient
and quietly self-reflective. In the intervening years she had learned
a lot and was hard at work in her profession. In her personal life she'd
had some further harrowing experiences with men and was struggling to become less dependent on them, to speak up for herself, to
draw her own limits. Again, I saw Lynne's extraordinary talent for
honesty, her ability to evaluate her experiences without defensive-
ness or self-pity.

"I wish I'd had it to do all over again," she said of Yale, "because
I pretty much maintained the same stance all through college—I
was a quiet observer of everything. I was going through the changes
that I hadn't absorbed in the previous years. When I entered Yale,
my sister had committed suicide just two months before and I really
hadn't had time to stop and think about that or any of the other
crises I'd gone through in the past three years. I think I used your
course to do that through writing . . . 'cause if you recall [and I did
recall!], the things I wrote about were all my life experiences. After
your course I didn't do any more. I just put all the writing aside. I
wanted to get out of Yale as fast as I could."

"You became a grind?"

"No—not then—not till my junior year. In my sophomore year
I went through a reaction to having been in an all-white setting most
of my life. At Yale there was a Black Students' Alliance. They said
good things about blacks getting together and I went into a period
where I didn't speak to white people unless I absolutely had to. That
meant only to my dean and to my professors and that was it. I had
a black roommate, so I didn't have to have anything to do with white
students. I missed the whole interchange of ideas with other people
in my classes because my classes were predominantly white."

87

In the latter part of her sophomore year, Mac—the cook from summer camp who'd been her boyfriend since she had split up with Greg—moved to town to work for a graduate degree at the University of New Haven. She no longer needed to commute weekends to see him in Waterbury, which she'd been doing since she'd come to Yale. But with Mac in New Haven, she spent even less time at Yale. She now became a part of New Haven's black community, where she worked part time as a counselor. "In the community," she told me, "I didn't know how to handle being an elite person, you know . . . of being a Yale student. The sentiments—at least towards blacks —were that if you were a Yalie they didn't want to have anything to do with you; that meant you were not black. So I wasn't proud of the fact that I went to Yale, and I sought out a lot of activities in the community."

At the end of her sophomore year Lynne decided she was getting too deeply in debt, accumulating more student loans than she could handle. She moved to her own apartment off campus and, a few months later, moved in with Mac. She accelerated, taking seven courses in the last half of her junior year, and by her senior year needed only two more courses to graduate. As a senior, she worked full time, first at a group home for delinquent adolescents and then in an alcoholism rehabilitation center. She prepared for her courses at night.

"I only went to Yale to go to classes," she said, "and from there I went to work and back home. I don't think I spent one weekend at Yale all the time I was there. I'm sorry about that now. I wish I'd been more involved, but I just didn't know how."

I asked her what she meant by that. She looked reflective and her voice became very quiet.

"I've thought a lot about not participating at Yale," she said. "You know, we don't really consider enough where a student comes from and how she adjusts to college. We just assume everybody can. I'd come from a private girls' school where the largest class I'd ever attended was twelve people. In class you were automatically pulled into the discussion, or at least you knew your teacher. When I got to Yale, I was sitting in a class of three hundred people and I didn't know what to do. I didn't know I could seek out a rapport with a professor or get to know his work. Approaching a white male, even to ask a question, was a "no-no" for me and most of the black women. Even when I saw all the eager beavers going after the professor, all I felt I could do was be quiet, fall asleep, or avoid the situation altogether by not going to class.

"At prep school I was the black model—I was there to teach white students about black people. I was given a full scholarship and was grateful for that. But I wanted to be a member of the class—to really belong—and I never felt I did—though I repressed any feelings I had about that when I was there. When I came to Yale, I was reacting to that with anger. The most contact I had with any whites was in your class. So part of being quiet and removing myself was feeling I had nothing worthwhile to say—the old self-esteem bit—and part was having been spoon-fed at prep school and simply not knowing how to be an active participant in my own education. And part, of course, was my black anger."

Lynne graduated in the spring of 1975 and continued to work in the alcoholism center throughout the summer. In September she went directly to graduate school at the University of Pennsylvania and commuted on weekends to New Haven to see Mac. During the week she lived with Mac's sister in Philadelphia. About this time, Lynne began to realize that her relationship with Mac was taking on perilous similarities to her earlier relationship with Greg. There had been some stormy scenes before she'd left New Haven. He'd complained about her going so far away, but when she offered to attend graduate school in New York instead, he didn't want to make concessions of his own. "We were engaged and he wanted me totally committed," she said, "and I wanted to be totally committed—I'm basically a homebody. But I wanted him to be totally committed too. And he wanted to run around with other women; to do whatever he wanted to do. If I didn't like something he was doing he'd just say 'too bad,' and I was still so passive or dependent or whatever, I'd tolerate it. Basically, I went through the same things with Mac that I did with Greg—the man I wrote about in my story."

"But at least you weren't into crime, and Mac had a good job."

"Yes—but my behavior was basically the same. You see, when I first met Mac at camp I was only fifteen. I was this little dependent thing. I was still passive. I still needed somebody to follow and somebody to talk for me. I don't think I really started talking until

89

I got the job in the alcoholism program in my senior year. Suddenly I had a lot of responsibility. I felt I'd better talk. I *had* to talk."

"One day you just started talking?"

"No—it was new to me and I was awkward at first, but as I began to talk, I started feeling like I wasn't as dependent as I'd been before. I could do a few things on my own. Come to think of it, it was then that friction started between me and Mac. I wasn't ready yet to *really* stand up for myself, but every once in a while I did."

It was going to be another three years before Lynne could walk away from Mac. In the meantime, Mac gave up his job as a district sales manager for a baked goods company and moved to Baltimore to open a seafood restaurant in a partnership with a friend. But the promised financing never materialized and Mac became depressed. So, in her second year of graduate school, Lynne studied Monday through Thursday and then, after her 10:00 P.M. class, drove from Philadelphia to Baltimore to spend the weekend with Mac. In Baltimore, Mac put her under increasing pressure to get a job and contribute toward their living expenses while he got his "restaurant package" together. By the end of that semester she was exhausted and "couldn't go on like that."

She decided to move to Baltimore for a year and take her psychology internship there at an outpatient clinic for emotionally disturbed and learning-disabled children. Meanwhile, to help make ends meet during the summer months, she took a job as a waitress in "a sleazy diner with sleazy people coming through."

"I wasn't used to being around men who'd make sexual advances at me all the time. I'd always worked with men, but I was always in a job where I could say 'Look, I'm attached' and people understood and wouldn't press the issue. In the diner, men came through all day, saying 'Hey, baby.' I wasn't used to dealing with that, so being my nice self, I'd say 'Hi, how are you?' They took that to mean they could pick me up after work. It was tough dealing with that."

Lynne began to develop an ulcer; every day when she came from work, her stomach was in knots. And Mac was no help. Depressed and uncommunicative, he was absorbed in his own desperate attempts to get the restaurant under way.

In September, Lynne started her internship at the Baltimore clinic, which was also undergoing a difficult transition. Formerly a private institution in a predominantly upper-middle-class Jewish community, it had become a public clinic and its clientele—but not its staff—also changed drastically. "The Jews had moved out and the blacks had moved in and the staff hadn't changed at all. They didn't like the new population and had all the negative stereotypes of blacks you could think of; they thought all blacks were ego-deficient. I was one of the only two blacks on staff. The other was an Uncle Tom who just grinned and bowed and scraped. I was doing therapy with the kids, running parents' groups—some marital therapy, some family therapy. The black adults had been totally turned off; the clinic had a difficult time keeping the parents in any kind of treatment. They started coming to my group and it was the best turnout the center had ever had. I was beginning to feel effective."

Lynne and I talked for a while about male resistance to women entering the business and professional world. "Unlike white women," said Lynne, "black women have found it's been okay—and usually necessary—to work and bring in money for food and clothing and that sort of thing. But most black men don't like it at all if their women hold jobs with more responsibility or make more money than they do. Mac's that type. He resented anything I accomplished away from him, and when we were in a group together, he had to make sure he was Mr. Personality and I was this nothing in the background. But the only thing that saved me in this period *was* my profession."

By May, Mac had obtained funding, renovated a restaurant that had two bars and a banquet room. He was in business at last! He began to pressure Lynne to help out, and she soon found herself working from nine to five at the clinic and then, after a short rest and a change of clothes, from eight to two at the restaurant, which she did for no pay. There she was frequently required to play hostess, a job which, with her shyness, she disliked intensely. "I'd get so uptight about it," she said, "that I'd break out in a rash."

Her life with Mac continued to disintegrate. He was obsessed with his restaurant and felt Lynne should devote all her time to it too. In spite of his protests, in September she moved back to the university in Philadelphia, but still commuted on some weekends and helped him out during the Christmas holidays.

Toward the end of the holidays, Lynne left for Stamford, Connecticut, to see her father and, while there, met up with an old Yale friend—"as good a friend as I was able to make at Yale"—who treated her with warmth and kindness. That did it. She returned to Baltimore, packed up her things in the back of her ancient Chevy, gave Mac her engagement ring, and left. But not before a rather terrifying scene in which Mac—alternately hostile and pleading—first threatened to ruin her life and then, on his knees, begged her to stay. The restaurant was folding, he said; he was facing bankruptcy; his life was falling apart; how could he do without her? As she drove away he threatened suicide, but when, in great concern, she called him from the turnpike an hour later, he was his Mr. Personality self again and having a good time with his pals at the restaurant.

"That's quite a soap opera," I said, feeling utterly foolish as I said it. "And a pretty painful one."

Lynne laughed and then turned reflective again. "Yeah, I suppose it is. But I asked for it in so many ways. I didn't need to hang in with Mac all those years. I wasn't doing anything for myself. I was revolving completely around Mac, saying *he* was my future. I really kick myself when I think of the time I wasted convincing myself that I had something that was completely different from what I actually had."

"Do you think that experience is in any way unique to black women?"

"No, not a bit. It has to do with someone's early family relationships—your own psychological needs. There is, of course, a common stereotype of a macho narcissistic black dude acting tough and pushing women around, but there are just as many white men like that. And I guess just as many white women put up with it. Poverty doesn't help, of course. The interesting thing is why people like me are attracted to men like that in the first place and then let them run all over us, lowering our self-esteem even further.

"I think Steve—my old friend from Yale—is a completely different type of person. At least I hope so. And we have a completely different kind of relationship. Different from anything I've known before. I've had to readjust my whole way of doing things. Some of the ways I developed to deal with Mac I still use with Steve, though they're completely inappropriate."

92

"Like what?"

Lynne paused for a long time. "Well," she said at last, "I'm not used to anyone trying to work out a conflict with me, because Mac's tactic was to ignore it, go silent. If there was a problem or a fight, there was no discussion. I never learned how to resolve a conflict through talking about it and working out a solution."

"And, at the same time, in your clinical work, you were trying to encourage other couples to do this."

"Yeah, I know," she said. "I could tell them how to do it and I know how to do it intellectually. But to do it myself when I'm emotionally involved, I need practice."

Lynne was also reestablishing ties with her own family—who had not gotten along with Mac. "I had never really related to my family," she said, "not ever. My father was in and out of the house since I was five and left permanently when I was fourteen; and my mother viewed me as her psychologist whenever she talked to me. Now, however, I'm on a better footing with both of them and stay a lot with my father when I'm in Stamford."

"That must make you feel good."

"Yeah, it does. I guess it's easier to relate to your family when you get your own self-esteem built up." She looked pensive. "You know," she said, "self-esteem is a complex issue for both blacks and whites. You can have a high sense of self-esteem in one setting and feel like zero in the next. For blacks, we may think that we can do certain things in a black community that fit the norms there but that we'd be lost in a white culture. So we say to ourselves there's no point in going out of our community and trying anything. We don't take action."

"But you've done a great deal—in spite of all the discombobulations in your life," I said. "When push comes to shove, you always seem to take the right turn."

"I suppose. In my work life this seems to be true—with a few ups and downs. I've always thought I could do okay at school, the intellectual part."

I asked her what made her feel so confident in school, when she seemed to feel so unsure of herself in other ways.

"When I was just a young kid in primary school, I got tracked into the accelerated class when I was in third grade and so I got special

93

attention at an early age and was placed on an honors track all the way through. Also, my father was in the school system—first as a teacher and then as an administrator—so I was aware of schools in a way other black kids weren't. Then, when my mother read about the prep school scholarships in a local newspaper, I applied and got in. That status meant a lot to her. And even though I didn't do that well at prep school—that's when I was running around with Greg —I somehow had confidence that I could if I tried. So much so that when my guidance counselor told me not to bother applying to Yale I did so anyway."

"Your counselor told you not to apply?" I asked.

"Yeah, and in a way she was right. I was below the average of other kids who'd applied and were having a hard time getting accepted, and she just thought I couldn't make it. But I just got rebellious and said to myself 'Oh, yeah?' She didn't know that those were the days when being black helped."

"Do you think being black helped you get into Yale?"

"I know it did. My admissions interviewer was looking for blacks. He liked me a little better because I was a black and also a woman. The expectations for blacks were so much lower that, just given the fact that I had *survived* in a school for intellectual white students, he figured I must be something special."

"And what do you think of your Yale experience now?"

"In retrospect, I got a lot more out of it than I thought at the time. I was exposed to a lot of ideas, to a lot of thinking people— even though I was only an observer."

In the year since that evening, I've touched base with Lynne whenever I was near Philadelphia or New York. For a while she lived very happily with Steve in New York while simultaneously pursuing her graduate studies. Then, a few months ago, she decided it was time for her to live by herself. She moved back to Philadelphia, where she now has her own apartment.

"That doesn't scare you as it did the last time?" I asked.

"No. Not at all. I need time with myself now. Besides, I'm very involved in my dissertation—preparing for that—and being a teaching assistant. I love what I'm doing, even though it doesn't pay anything." She laughed again—that wonderful new-Lynne laugh!

She went on to tell me she had changed the direction of her studies, from alcoholism to studying the impact of separation and divorce on adults, "particularly on the subjective experience of stressful life events and the ability to master them." I couldn't help remembering that spring day long ago when she was sitting on my back porch in New Haven and had said that she wanted to write about a "stressful life event" from her own experience.

I asked her if she would eventually go into private practice after she got her degree.

"Well," she said, "I might, part time, but no more than that. A lot of people go into psychology just so they can make seventy-five dollars an hour, but I can't do that. I like material things, but I have to do something I think is worthwhile—help people who can't normally get help. I want to see a few other people make it."

PORTRAIT OF TIM

*T*HERE are those Irishmen you know can write just by looking at them. Tim Kenslea was one. His rather pudgy smooth-skinned face reflected the writer's authority that I always imagined graced the faces of Brendan Behan and Dylan Thomas. Whenever I glanced at him in class, I had a vision of him sitting in an Irish pub, chewing on a worn-out pipe, and discussing in immaculate sentences the latest twist in contemporary fiction. He had a passion and respect for good writing and very few doubts that he, too, could write.

In class he spoke infrequently, but when he did he was so articulate and so on target that all the rest of us listened carefully. Moreover, we had all been impressed by his weekly pieces in the notebooks, which were usually gems—often very funny and always well crafted.

Nor was Tim in the slightest smug about his ability; his sense of humor would not allow for it. He was simply in command of what he was doing and, as a freshman, was just beginning to realize it. In the summer after the course was over, he wrote me a long letter about the seminar, in which he said, "In reading the works of my

97

peers, I came to realize how thorough my own command of the language and narrative form was. This gave me confidence; I can no longer stop writing with the excuse that it would be no good anyway, or that nobody would be interested. I have to look elsewhere to justify my unproductivity." That was Tim—one problem solved, on to the next.

The best thing I, as a teacher, could do for Tim was to give him the space and time to write whatever he wanted. "For a four-month period," he wrote me in the same letter, "at a critical time in my life, the seminar gave me not only the occasion but the obligation to write. Writing was no longer time stolen from schoolwork; it *was* schoolwork."

And what did Tim write about? He had already passed through that somehow inevitable phase of weaving romantic fantasies about people and places never seen and never experienced—a tendency not altogether relinquished by some of my other students. Even in college, the mythical idea somehow persisted that "creative writing" could only be "creative" if you invented everything from whole cloth —without a thread of your own personal experience or passion in it. Tim was a shoo-in when he wrote in his course application:

> When I started writing fiction—at the age of seven—I was taken with the sensationalistic: wildly improbable and historically impossible story lines, heroic deaths, invaders from other planets. All the subtlety of a small sledgehammer marked all my "works." This violent period lasted until I was about fourteen, when I began to write, using a first-person narrator, about the things that actually happened to me.

So Tim wrote about those momentous events that stirred the childhood of so many of us who grew up on the blocks of American middle-class towns or suburbs: being banned from backyard baseball games because you were a "little kid"; stealing your first kiss behind the shrubbery, in the certain knowledge that the lady next door had seen you; being scared to death of your third-grade teacher. Under Tim's pen, such scenes sprung to a new life—helped along, perhaps, by the fact that he was one of six boys in a close-knit Roman Catholic family in Newton, Massachusetts. In that community one knew exactly what was right and what was wrong. The things that grew bigger than life there were backyard baseball, the Boston Red Sox, and nuns. Especially the Red Sox and the nuns.

Of the Red Sox, Tim wrote in agony of the 1973 strike, "Poor, poor baseball. If the season ever starts, the Red Sox will have on their roster only three of the forty men who carried them to the pennant just four and a half years ago. *Sic transit gloria mundi.*" Of nuns, he poured out a whole series of wonderful stories—one of which I include here because it describes his life much better than I can.

I'm sure Sister Laurinda always had it in for me. I had heard tales of her tyrannical rule over her first-grade section from my big brother and his friends, and hoped and prayed that I'd be placed in another section. For in addition to these terrible rumors, I had a firsthand encounter of my own with Sister Laurinda, which convinced me that it would be no fun to have her as a first-grade teacher.

I was almost five at the time. Tom must have been three and a half. Gerry, at one year give or take a few months, was just learning to walk on his own. Dan was a serious first-grader, and Matt, at the other end of the spectrum, had just been born a month or two earlier. We three big kids plunked ourselves down on the back seat of the Plymouth to go to nine o'clock mass one Sunday morning. Gerry was strapped into his plastic driver's seat in the middle of the front seat, and Mom held Matt securely in her lap.

As Dad drove us by the church with the white steeple and the four clocks, next to the library, I asked, as I did every Sunday, why we didn't go to that church. Mom gave her usual rational but somehow inadequate explanation about Protestantism and different churches for different people. This answer never completely satisfied me. It was Dan, on whose shoulders the awesome weight of academic responsibility had only recently been placed, who came up with the most satisfying response: "I bet we go to Our Lady's because it's right near school, right, Mommy?" This at least was a good enough answer for me.

As always, we were late for mass, so we couldn't get an entire pew to ourselves. Dad and Mom, each with an armful of baby, split up; Dad and Dan moved into a pew a short way up the aisle, while Mom, Tom, and I squeezed into the last one on the middle aisle.

It usually took me twenty minutes or so to get really bored with a mass and fall asleep. But then, I usually wasn't seated next to Tom. Today we were side by side in the back pew, with a mother we knew to be powerless against us because of her own intense interest in the mass and the month-old baby she had to hold on to. So in about ten minutes Tom and I started to explore our surroundings.

Of course we never left our pew; we knew that was forbidden. We did, however, stand up on it and face the back of the church to examine the row of grim nuns' faces, each surrounded in drab black and white, lined up against the back wall. One or two of the younger ones smiled at us, but most, if they paid any attention at all, tried to stare us down and make us feel shame for misbehaving in God's house. Eventually, Mom's whispered command, a real shock to us both, brought us back to our proper positions.

We simmered in silence. I wondered how Dan, looking so pious and attentive two pews ahead of us, could stand it, but then again the nuns would be watching him, especially whichever one was Sister Laurinda. If he looked bored at mass, she would probably give him a bad mark on his report card.

I don't know when the bells started ringing—they rang so often during the mass back then—but by the second or third ring Tom and I both had the same thought. At the next tinkling of the chimes we slid together on the hard wooden seat, turned and kissed each other loudly, then slid apart. This went on through the entire offertory and into the canon. Whenever the altar boy rang the bells to call the congregation's attention to whatever important was happening on the altar, Tom and I moved together, kissed, and separated.

Mom whispered to us to cut it out, but we knew she had no place to put Matt down long enough to effect an actual separation. At the last bell before the consecration, one of the nuns—a small elderly woman with a severe gray countenance—had apparently had enough. She stepped up to the back of our pew and pushed the two of us away from each other, firmly. My mother slid over on her kneeler and placed herself between us to ensure that there would be no repeat performance. I looked over at Tom, confused, and then looked up at the woman who would become in but a year my tormentor. She was

100

staring down at my mother, who was beet red with embarrassment but clearly on the verge of laughter. I turned back toward the altar, but focused my attention instead on the back of Dan's solemn crew-cut head. I was asleep in no time.

As confident as Tim was about his writing, he was not as sure of himself in relationship to girls. Or as Tim would put it, "girls . . . women . . . girls." References to this hesitancy sprouted every once in a while in his pieces: "I developed the most magnificent dream existences. I wonder if any of those girls knew of the wonderful lives I had dreamed up for them. Probably some of them were on to me, had me figured out by the rather shy, abstracted manner in which I always conducted myself in their presence. But that neither helped nor hurt. I had only myself to stand on, and who really gave a shit about this naïve, frightened little boy with a double chin?"

When it came time for Tim to write his long story, he floundered for a while trying to write something too complex—a story within a story with a few too many philosophical overtones. He'd forgotten his earlier resolve, and he also suffered occasionally from the dread fear of committing what many imaginative students consider to be the cardinal sin—stating the obvious. When that fear was running high, everyone's papers could become awfully obscure.

Then on Holy Saturday—("I'd always had a vague suspicion that this day doesn't really exist—that we all enter a temporal vacuum for thirty-six hours or so. Nothing can happen")—he decided to sit down and write everything he could remember about his summers at his family's cottage on the Massachusetts seashore: "bonfires at sunset the night before the Fourth," "red nylon bathing suits," "gooey orange Popsicles dripping down chubby-boy fingers," and the gang of kids, "Humphrey, Mike, Fuzzy, Dave . . ." From this spill-out of memory, Tim gradually shaped "Incoming Tide" as a farewell to the idyllic summers of childhood and to childhood itself.

But for Tim the story was more than that. In a letter he wrote me later, he said that "the story became a communication, a demand for answers from the two people who had most mystified my adolescence"—my father and my teenage goddess of summer, Paula. Even when I wrote in applying to the course that 'I am sitting on a wealth of experience which I have not yet had the time or strength to record,' I did not realize how heavily the experience of the previous four years had been weighing on me."

It was to his father that the challenge was most forceful. He had heard tales from his mother's life but seldom any from his father's —and he knew little of how his father felt, especially about the beloved summer home, which his father was now threatening to sell. The story is "a demand that my father produce some kind of past, some tradition." Timmy, writing as a fictional character, can ask his father the questions he could never ask to his face. Moreover, said Tim, the fact of writing this story was in itself a challenge to his father. "I wanted to say, 'Here's my story, Dad. Now, please, what's yours?' "

*I*NCOMING TIDE
by Timothy J. Kenslea,
Newton, Massachusetts

"*W*ELL, you better enjoy this summer down here, 'cause it's going to be your last." The words are my father's, spoken at least once a week every summer for five years. A typical instance: he has just come home from work, he is still wearing his seersucker suit, he has loosened his tie; he is seated at the dining room table, opening some bill that came in the day's mail or pondering the week's grocery list; a bottle of beer sits on the table before him, leaving wet rings on the red and white checked tablecloth. Whichever kids happen to be in the house at the time listen with somber, emotionless faces, then run off to join in whatever is happening outside—for something is always happening outside—and forget the warning.

Almost. It's really impossible to forget so big a threat to our world as this one my father keeps making. We cannot argue with him, for he has economics on his side. The house on Tenth Road is too costly for us, too costly for his sister and her family, who use it during the second half of the summer; there is too much money tied up in it for his brother and other sister, who each own a quarter of the house but never use it.

So we heard the first warnings. We chose to ignore them for the time being. No, we said; we laughed off the threat. No, Dad, you can't sell the house. It must mean as much to you as it does to us.

My father's father built the house fifty years ago in Penfield, a small middle-class resort town, about halfway between Boston and Cape Cod, that some might consider the poor man's Cape. I never did, for whenever I was in Penfield life was rich: rich with friends, with things to do, with seashells, with lucky rocks with rings around them.

The year we heard Dad's first warning was also the year the Hagertys rented out their cottage for the entire month of July. Since Fuzzy Hagerty was the only kid who still liked to play off-the-steps with me (for we were all twelve, thirteen, fourteen years old now, too old for baseball, the others would say), I had to find something else to occupy myself that summer. I had to do what the other kids were doing. That usually turned out to be loafing in the hot sand behind the Lawsons' garage, reading the *True Confessions* and *Secret Love* magazines that older kids had stockpiled, and trading dirty jokes.

One day Mighty Mike Lawson, the oldest kid in our group, told a story about a girl from his school who had set up a show in her garage. She'd charge people a quarter to get in and then take off all her clothes. Some weeks she could make seven or eight dollars.

I was confused. "But so what, really. I mean there's this naked girl standing in her garage. What's the big deal?"

Mike's reply was condescending. "You'll see."

"What? What possible good is it for a girl to be naked?"

"Well, jeez, you can spit at her and everything!"

"Spit at her?"

"Sure! See who's the first one to hit her crack."

"Naw!" I was incredulous. What a stupid thing to do. I wished there was someone to play baseball with me.

The next summer we began hanging out at the public staircase on the seawall at Ninth Road. Such public staircases had been built along the entire length of the wall at every odd-numbered road. A stretch of rocky, dirty sand extended from the end of each of these roads to a huge concrete stairway that led up to the top of the seawall. Daytime bathers stopped after climbing the stairs and stood for a while on the wall to look out at the ocean before going down the stairs on the other side to the beach. Summer nights the walls and stairways were gathering places for the vast numbers of kids in their early teens who spent their summers in Penfield. An older group had held the Ninth Road wall the two preceding years, but they got cars and licenses and moved on. Now it was ours. We would sit there each evening from seven thirty on, waiting for something to happen. As a rule, nothing did.

A few girls decided that we should call the wall home and declare ourselves one big happy family. Everyone was given a role: father, mother, aunt, uncle, cousin, brother, sister, husband, wife, son, or daughter. Originally I was married to a good-looking girl named Donna, whom I didn't like much. Nevertheless, the arrangement rather pleased me, until my older brother Dan decided that he wanted to be married to her. He spoke to the mother, a pleasant, chubby girl named Kathy, and arranged for my demotion to family dog. In my new position I was dubbed Max. For a while it was debated whether I should be the dog or Uncle Max, visiting from California, but dog seemed a more permanent position, so I settled for it. Danny and my ex-wife were given a lovely young daughter named Paula, the only girl I ever knew who wore braces well.

Toward the end of the summer, after Dan had been married three weeks, he wanted to go out with his wife; so he asked her.

Going out has specific connotations in Penfield. Beaching was our parents' word for it, when they did it or talked about it years ago, though I've never heard my father use the term. It involves a precise ritual whose exact nature has always been mysterious to me. A boy makes a proposal to a girl, usually in a casual, oh-by-the-way manner, and they disappear from the public staircase down onto the beach for a few hours. They walk a way, chatting I suppose, until they are out of the sight and hearing of those left behind on the wall. Then they do whatever they're inclined to do—not everything, never everything—and come back. I'd heard some interesting variations that certain people had developed, such as the couple who went at it under the overturned hull of the Corcorans' boat down between Sixth and Seventh roads, and the girl who, after suggesting skinny-dipping to the guy accompanying her, removed her blouse and bra and said, "Well, maybe we don't have to go swimming after all."

One night, in the glow of the electric spotlights the people with oceanfront cottages trained on the seawall to keep passing teenagers in line, Dan decided it was time to ask Donna to go out with him. He asked her, and she said no.

Mike, who had been near Dan and Donna on the wall, later told me the whole story. "Danny says, 'Hey, Donna, wanna, uh, go for a walk on the beach?' y'know, an' she looks up at him kinda funny, like are you kiddin' me, you schnook? and shakes her head an' says 'No, I don't think so.' I don't think so! Can you believe that? She didn' wanna!" Mike was more offended by her mistreatment of my brother than was I. Dan was his best friend in Penfield, but even more importantly, as he saw it, it was wrong for any girl to turn down any boy's offer. For my part, I felt it served him right, stealing my wife like that.

The next summer, my father's warnings about selling the cottage became more frequent. Idle threats, I told myself. He's been saying that so long, this is the third summer now, but he hasn't done anything. He wouldn't. I knew it.

The first of our five weeks in Penfield that summer was utter hell for me. I had come down there for one reason only. I had to get a girl. At fourteen I had just finished my first year of high school, and the more I collected stories of friends' adventures with girls, the more convinced I became that this was the thing for me. By the end of the first week, however, I was angry, tired, and disgusted. I might as well have stayed home, I thought, and got a job somewhere. Then at least I wouldn't have to watch other people having fun all the time. Friday night, as I sat on the public staircase and looked down at the band of rocks, about thirty feet wide, that stretched for miles along the beach against the crumbling seawall, I felt an almost irresistible desire to pick up each rock and smash it against the others until they were nothing but billions of chips of stone that would cut the feet of anyone trying to cross to the sandy beach.

I spent a weekend feeling sorry for myself and by Tuesday was reconciled to the idea of spending another month at the beach. I wouldn't have anything to look forward to, but I wouldn't have anything to worry about, either.

That afternoon I was standing on the seawall, thinking of nothing,

106

more or less at peace with myself, when, stepping suddenly to one side, I found myself tumbling toward the ground eight feet below. Somehow I managed to land on my feet, splitting my big toe open on a piece of broken bottle. There was no other damage except for a large rip in the sleeve of my favorite yellow shirt. I looked up at the kids on the public staircase, who were laughing, applauding, and saying "Do it again." Peering down at me was Paula, the girl who had been dubbed Dan's daughter in the family the year before. She shook her head. "That was stupid, Timmy." Then she smiled.

I had known Paula for about as long as either of us could remember. We both lived in Newton in the winter, but far enough away so that we rarely saw each other there; still, we had seen each other every summer since her family bought the little white house with red trim on Ninth Road. But there was something in her look and smile that day, braces gleaming in the sun, something that said, we will come to know each other better. You cannot ever turn away now; we've got you, say the eyes, so be prepared for captivity. Even as I write this, the eyes are still looking at me and the mouth is smiling at me from high above, as I stand in the high grass with blood on my toes and sand on my face.

I smiled back.

That night we built a fire against the seawall. I was sitting alone on the wall above the fire, warming my wounded foot, while a few yards away Dan, Mike, and some friends sat on the staircase, lying about girls they had known or perhaps never known, waiting to see if they could pick up any of the ones walking by on the beach as they had the week before. Bump, Fuzzy Hagerty's ten-year-old brother, ran up the stairs and down onto the beach. He sauntered over to the fire, clutching a piece of driftwood and proudly displaying the gray sweatshirt he wore, several sizes too big for him, with Everett Football printed across the chest. Bump poked at the dying fire with his driftwood and looked up at me.

"Hey, Humphrey," he grinned. Some older kids had given me the name when I was six or seven, in honor of my total lack of coordination and athletic ability. I don't know why, but it seemed to them an appropriate name. Fortunately, I only had to hear it for a month or so out of every year, here among my old friends.

Bump continued. "Whatcha doin', waitin' for some chick to come by so's ya can grab her, some nice honey?"

"No, I don't think so, Bump."

"Why not? I am. I'm gonna get Paula, y'know. Grab her and say, hey, you wanna come for a walk on the beach? I'm gonna get her this week."

I was amused but I couldn't help feeling a bit threatened. "Yeah, sure, Bump. What if she doesn't want to go with you?"

"She will."

"But what if she doesn't?"

"Then I'll grab her and I'll make her come with me. After we get down there, she'll be glad she came."

"Okay, Bump. Yeah, sure. This I hafta see."

Bump was suddenly silent. Four girls were walking up the public staircase from the street. They stopped to talk with the guys who were sitting on the stairs. After a few minutes one of them came over and sat down next to me. It was Paula. I tried to look nonchalant. Bump climbed up on the wall and started to perform. "What, 'dja come over here to sit next to Humphrey? Paula and Humphrey! All you Newton people stick together. Newton sucks!"

I was shocked to hear him use that word in front of Paula. Ordinarily it would have been time for a witty comeback, but I decided that a "Sure, Bump" would do. Now he was strutting back and forth on the wall like a little field marshal. "Yeah, Newton really sucks." He paused. "Humphrey's got his green shirt on. All the fellas from Newton wear green shirts? Ooooho! Green shirts!" I could see that he was running out of material fast. "Paula sittin' here next to Humphrey. Paula, you like Humphrey? Paula likes Humphrey!"

"He's better than you, Bump." Her reply silenced him momentarily.

"Oh, yeah, sure!" He wouldn't give up. "Okay, if you Newton people wanna all stick together. Boy, Newton really sucks!"

Fortunately, Mr. Hagerty had just come down to the end of the street to call Bump home. Giving us a final mocking laugh, he swaggered off down the staircase. When he was gone, Paula and I laughed at how stupid he was.

Then we talked, and wasn't it a nice fire, yes, little things like that, yeah, my green shirt, I put it on 'cause I ripped the yellow one,

108

remember, yeah, that was funny. Pretty soon it was ten o'clock and she had to go home, and then I went home, even though it wasn't ten thirty yet. As I walked down Tenth Road I said yes, write this day down, July first, remember it always, Timothy. I couldn't sleep at all that night. I pulled up the shade at four thirty and lay in the bottom bunk and watched the sun rise over the ocean.

The next day I saw Paula at the beach. Her bathing suit was patterned with orange, yellow, and brown flower petals that made me think of summer turning into fall. With her skin lightly tanned by the sun, just enough to complement this flurry of orange, her whole body seemed to say, I am the goddess of summer. I couldn't imagine her in winter, I couldn't imagine her more than a few hundred yards from the ocean. She would have to wither away and die, I told myself, for she is so alive now; life, like summer, is temporary. Only death and winter are permanent.

Every year on the eve of the Fourth of July there is an informal bonfire contest among the roads. Kids spend a week or so collecting scrap wood from houses along their road. The woodpiles against the seawall get bigger by the day. Occasionally, acts of sabotage are performed against the early favorites—one year a mattress on the Ninth Road pile was set aflame on July first. But everyone survives until the night of the third, when after the kids have finished collecting wood and then stacked it on the beach around a twenty-foot pole with an old jockstrap or beach towel flying atop as a flag, the men of the street pour kerosene on the pile and ignite it. For years we kids have complained that after we do all the work, the men get all the fun of lighting the fire. They say they're doing it for our safety, but I think they just get a thrill out of it.

The whole thing is quite a spectacle—almost a hundred fires along a stretch of beach about five miles long, flaring up just after sundown, usually hitting their peaks just before nine, and glowing on late into the night. The next morning each road declares itself the winner and spends the day planning next year's defense of the title.

That year, for the first time, I was not looking forward to the bonfire. On that night the seawall would belong to old people and little kids; they would move in on our territory. On that night I could not hang out at the stairs with my friends. I would not have a chance to speak to Paula of my feeling for her, as I had so carefully planned it. The approach had to be cool, offhand, not revealing any sloppy or overbearing sentimentality, yet never underestimating the seriousness of the matter at hand. Still, this invasion of the generations was a blessing as well as a curse, for I had not yet thought of a satisfactory line that would achieve this effect. "Wanna go for a walk on the beach?" was passé; I knew I could come up with something so classy, so cool that she couldn't turn it down. Not that I was expecting her to, but then, what if? Naw, don't even think that, I told myself. It just won't happen.

All right then, what would I do once I had convinced her to come down on the beach with me? I'd never done anything like that before. What if I couldn't figure out what to do next? Well, that's ridiculous. It would come to me, I said. I'd think of something.

All this passed through my mind as I sat on the crowded seawall. The people around me were watching bonfires or fireworks. I was the only one who watched the girl standing a few yards away from Ninth Road's bonfire, spinning a coathanger with a flaming steel wool pad attached to the end. Sparks flew from the steel wool; it sputtered, looking as if it were about to go out, so she flung it high into the air. It flared up in midair, then landed on the flat, wet stretch of beach the low tide had uncovered, and burned out. Paula turned away from the fire and looked in my direction but did not see me.

The night of the Fourth of July is always anticlimactic in Penfield. Dan and I stayed at the stairs until about eight thirty. Nothing was happening, so I decided to go home. Nothing was happening there either, so at about nine thirty I went back down to the wall. There were only a few people there, among them Paula and her cousin, who was visiting her for the day. I sat down on the wall. Paula moved from where she was sitting to come over and sit next to me. We chatted meaninglessly, there goes a police car, yeah, they always keep me awake, who's down at that little fire on the beach? Oh, that's Mike and some girl.

I stood up. I pondered lines. Wanna go down and sit by the fire? Wanna go for a walk? Wanna go down and test the water, see if it'll be good for swimming tomorrow? Now there was a good one.

It stuck in my throat.

I opened my mouth, looked at Paula, moved away. What about her cousin? She can't just leave her here when she doesn't know her way around. And what if she doesn't want to? Then I've exposed myself, I'm vulnerable; to what I don't know, but it's bad, it must be. So I didn't speak. Instead I flashed a sudden-brainstorm look and dashed down the stairs, across the vast beach now fully exposed by the low tide, to test the water alone. Deep inside me I expected her to join me, but she didn't. I went back a few minutes later to report to an uninterested group that the water would be warm the next day. Then I went home.

Dammit, I thought, don't kid yourself. You can't even talk naturally to your friends when there's no pressure on. How do you think you're going to pull this off?

When I woke up the next day, I heard my mother talking excitedly to Mrs. Hagerty in the yard. Bob, Fuzzy's oldest brother, had been in a car crash. Two kids had been killed. Three or four more were in poor condition at Mass General. Bob was injured but he had been conscious enough to identify the bodies of his friends, kids who had held the Ninth Road stairway before us. Bob had a bandage on his head that looked like a turban. He was walking with a cane. Everyone talked to him that day but no one said anything about the crash.

A few of us sat on the seawall later that morning, feeling helpless. Rain was threatening, so swimming was out of the question. Paula told us that her brother had been driving another carload of kids, but originally he'd been in the car that got hit. In the seat of one of the kids who died.

Someone said they would probably never want to get into a car again.

There was nothing else to do, so we played football on the beach until the rain started.

The next night Mike introduced us all to the girl who'd been with him on the beach earlier in the week. Her name was Lois, she was from New Orleans, visiting relatives on Ninth Road for the month. She was gorgeous, almost as beautiful as Paula. After she had to go home, Mike told us that he'd watched her undressing every night that week, he could see through her window from his backyard.

"And she doesn't pull down the shade?"

"Naw, she knows I'm there, she does it on purpose."

"Yeah, sure. I don't believe it."

But one night he took Dan with him, and Dan watched, and told me it was true, and she had to be quite a piece. I can't figure some people.

I had several political discussions with Lois on the beach that week. "You Boston people just don't know how awful nigras really are," she told me. Her New Orleans boyfriend's initials were penciled on the inner thigh of her white levis. This amused me, but no one else thought it was funny.

One night that week a guy named Steve, who usually hung around at the Thirteenth Road staircase, came down to Ninth. After talking with a few people for a while, he asked the girl who had earned fame in the to-skinny-dip-or-not-to-skinny-dip incident to take a walk on the beach with him. They slipped off quietly.

Twenty minutes later they were back. The girl stayed around for a minute or so, looking uncomfortable; then she left. Steve was interrogated. Whatcha do? Whatcha get?

He looked about in pain, then began to shake his head slowly. "Nothing." He raised his hands in a helpless gesture. "I couldn't get nothing. I mean, I just couldn't get started. I mean, shit, I just couldn't do anything. So after a few minutes she says let's go back, so here I am. Shit."

I didn't even consider trying to approach Paula for the rest of that week.

Thursday another kid who'd been in the crash died. The only one that I knew well. When I was in second or third grade, and he was maybe in fifth, he used to play along with Dan and me at a game we had, three slugs to anyone who mentioned school during summer vacation.

Saturday it rained again. I painted the back porch anyway, because it had to be done before we went home. Two more weeks, I might as well do it on a rainy afternoon when there was nothing else to do.

Later I went down to the beach and played Frisbee with Paula and her best friend Linda. When they left for dinner I asked, casually, "You gonna be up at the wall tonight?"

"Yeah, I suppose so," Linda replied. "That's all we ever do is sit at the wall and wait for something to happen."

I was perplexed. I had come to regard being at the wall as what happened. It didn't occur to me that there could be anything else so interesting and so consistent as hanging around the public staircase. It was an end in itself.

That night I sat on the wall alone, facing the ocean. Fog surrounded me. I cursed the woman whose damned spotlight was aimed at the Ninth Road staircase. I sat in awe of the ocean. Not fifty feet away, the waves pounded with a noise that was distant and huge, as if someone had dragged my ocean far away and hidden it, but could not keep its persistent, powerful noises hushed up.

Paula and Donna came to the foot of the stairs. "Who's up there?" Paula asked.

"Just me."

"Who?"

"Timmy."

"Whatcha doing?"

"Oh, just listening to the ocean."

Now Donna spoke. "Oh, yeah?" She seemed to think this was funny.

She and Paula turned away and went home.

Yes, I thought, sitting in the thick fog, not seeing the ocean but hearing its noises and smelling its smells stronger than they ordinarily were; yes, I thought, as a raindrop, soon joined by others, splashed against my glasses; I would love to die in the ocean. To drown, to drift away, to sink to the bottom somewhere and never be recovered, forever in union with the great ocean. No one could point to one spot and say, this is where Tim is buried. The whole ocean would be my monument, indestructible, eternal.

Dan first went out with Lois the next night. For some reason I'll never understand, my mother liked Lois enormously.

A couple of days later Lois and I had another big political argument. "Why aren't you home watching the moon launch?" she asked me as I stood on the seawall, looking at the beach in the midmorning light.

"I'm watching the ocean. It's better. Why aren't you?"

"Well, I'm going right home to."

"Whatta we need to send some guys to the moon for anyway? Why don't we save all that money? We could feed everyone in the country for a month at least."

"You don't understand anything. It's for scientific and political advantages. I suppose you think we should be spending it all on nigras!"

"That's right! And on anyone else who needs it."

"Oh, you're impossible."

That afternoon Sandra, one of Paula's friends from home, came down for the day. She had borrowed the orange flowered bathing suit Paula usually wore. This seemed to me nothing short of sacrilege. For weeks I had spent my afternoons lying on the beach, carefully studying this bathing suit and the body that filled it. It was perfect, one of a kind. It was presumptuous of anyone else to wear the suit. Nonetheless, I let her get away with it.

Paula, Sandra, and I borrowed a fiberglass rowboat and took it out. Sandra sat on the prow, Paula and I sat in the seat across the stern. I had an oar and was paddling now and then. The other oar lay in the bottom of the boat. Neither of them wanted to use it. I stopped paddling for a minute or so, distracted by the whole situation, my entire left side covered with goosebumps not so much from the cool seabreeze as from such close contact with Paula. "Timmy dear," she finally complained, "will you row please?"

"Well, will one of you take the other row and oar the other—I mean take the other oar and row the other side?" We all laughed (what did she call me, I thought frantically), Sandra took the other oar, and we paddled around in circles for half an hour or so, laughing, until it was time for Sandra to go. We paddled in to the shore. Paula said good-bye, and Sandra said good-bye, and Paula led Sandra back to her cottage, and I sat down on the beach in a daze.

The next day Paula and I discovered the beginnings of a sandcastle that some little kid had abandoned. Paula, once again in her rightful orange suit, suggested that we finish it. We knelt on the beach and packed and dribbled wet sand around the base until we had a rounded conical structure, about a foot high, the most primitive form of sandcastle. We realized but refused to admit that our work was a battle against the incoming tide, which would eventually sweep it away.

That night at around nine someone came down for a late night swim. We all went down to the water's edge to cheer him on. I turned toward Paula. This is the time, I told myself. You've waited long enough. I opened my mouth. Again no words came. We all went back to the seawall and stood around for a while, looking bored. Again I began to turn toward Paula. My right hand twitched. For a third time my mouth opened without emitting a sound.

After Paula went home at ten, I walked along the beach for a while. In the moonlight it seemed strange, not at all the same place it was in the daytime. Tiny phosphorescent sparks filled the impressions my feet left in the wet sand. I wondered if such sparks were there during the day, just waiting to be noticed. Probably not. The daytime beach is less mysterious. On a sunny July afternoon the beach is always full of people who make it a place for simple, relaxed fun. Little kids running around in red nylon bathing suits that dry so fast in the warm sea breeze, clutching orange Popsicles that melt and drip down chubby fingers; young fathers teaching young children how to bodysurf; a small group beginning a game of Frisbee or run-the-bases; a baby confronting a horseshoe crab. As I walked on the dark beach, I could mark the spot where, three years ago, Mike had stood, grinning, eyes sparkling intently, as he stared at the enormous breasts of an older girl who lay propped up on her elbows. Once again I felt the same embarrassment I had felt three years ago. I saw myself grinning along with Mike, gawking along with Mike, not knowing what was so funny. What a child I was then, I thought. But my embarrassment now seemed more agonizing, more permanent. Still, no matter how embarrassed I felt, I had to speak to Paula. Even though I knew it was all useless, all over before it began, I just couldn't let it float away.

I went home. I went into the bathroom to wash my feet. By the bright, harsh light I looked at myself in the mirror, at my flushed red face, and said, Yes Timothy you're hopeless, you're all through. You might as well give up.

I spent another weekend feeling sorry for myself. Sunday night a man walked on the moon. Monday night a group of us went rollerskating. According to Mike, rollerskating rinks are almost as good as dance halls for picking up girls, the only difficulty being that there are so many little kids.

Midway through the evening Paula and Linda skated by me, then stopped to talk. "Oh, Timmy, what can I do?" Paula was speaking. "There's this boy, and I want him to ask me to skate around with him, but I don't think he will."

"Go ask him yourself."

"Oh, but I can't."

"Well, who is he?"

She pointed to a kid in a paisley shirt with rolled-up sleeves. "That's the one there." Oh, well, so much for that.

"What can I do about it?"

Linda pitched in her suggestion. "You could go up and tell him that she wanted—"

I cut her off. "It wouldn't work. It wouldn't be right, really. And I don't think I could pull it off."

"Oh, thanks a lot, Timmy."

They went off to ask Mike's brother Dave and Linda's brother Greg to do the job. A few minutes later I saw Dave talking with the kid. At the next "couples only" skate he was with Paula. Dave came over to tell me what he had done, and pointed them out.

"I know, Dave. I saw them. She asked me to tell him first."

"Why dintcha?"

"Well, ya see—" I paused too long.

"Oh." Dave realized what was going on. "Why don't you go cut in on her?"

"No, I couldn't do that."

"Wamme to cut in on her and bring her around to you here?"

"No! Well . . . maybe. Wouldja do . . . naw, Dave, that's no good either."

"Sure it is. I'll go get her."

"No, Dave!" I knew it was too late to stop him. "No, please don't!" He caught up with them and asked if he could cut in. The guy recognized him and gave him a confused look, but obliged. Paula looked at him with burning malevolence. When they came around to the corner of the rink where Dave had left me, he could not find me and looked bewildered. He finished skating with her through one

116

song, and I slipped back to the corner. When they stopped, Paula began to chew him out, but he explained his motives to her. I attempted to slip by them out onto the rink, but Dave called me and I could not ignore him. Paula glared at me.

"Is that true what he says? Timmy, did you—"

"I told him not to . . . to bother."

"Oh, thanks a lot, Timmy you creep. Thanks a lot."

"But I told him not to. I wanted to, but I—"

She skated away. I didn't have enough energy left to finish the sentence. Not only did she not love me, now she hated me.

The last song of the night, right after the Hokey Pokey, was another "couples only." The paisley shirt was nowhere to be seen, Paula was skating with Linda's brother, and I was standing back in my corner. Paula spoke a few words to Greg and he skated off toward the snack bar. She skated over to where I was standing, looked at me, took my hand, and asked me to skate with her. As we went around and around, I grew more uncomfortable. An ocean of sweat filled my palm. The song ended; we went home in different cars.

When I got home, my mother was waiting up for me. "So how was it?" she asked.

"Pretty good, I guess."

"You didn't get into any trouble?"

"No, of course not, how could I get into any trouble?" I shut the bedroom door behind me.

Dan was awake in the bottom bunk. "But I know one thing you'd like to get into." Even in the dark I could feel his grin. "Paula, huh?"

"Well," I lied, "you know me. I'll take anything I can get."

"Yeah, sure, but it just so happens that Paula isn't anything you can get."

"Oh, I don't know about that, really."

"You don't, huh? Everybody else does."

"Well, we shall see." (What does everybody else know? I've told no one.) I slept late the next morning.

Later that week, even though she knew, and I knew she knew, I still could not speak to Paula. We acted as if nothing had happened.

Wednesday morning the sky was overcast, so there was no point in swimming. I was sitting in someone's backyard, watching some little kids play whiffle ball, when suddenly I saw a green and yellow

117

kite rising above the houses on Tenth Road; then, further down, another kite, this one blue and red. They rose and fell, swooped and glided in the wind, like demented birds. I dashed out to the street to see my two youngest brothers, surrounded by a horde of their little friends, clutching reels of kite string, slowly letting more string out, then yanking it back to make the kite bob up and down. I hadn't seen a kite all year, hadn't flown one myself for several years. "Hey, Matt!" I shouted at my brother. "Lemme try it!"

"No! It's mine!"

"Aw, c'mon, just for a minute!"

Grudgingly, realizing my size and strength advantage, he handed over the reel. I let out more string, sending the kite higher up into the sky until it was just a greenish spot against the gray clouds. Then slowly, carefully, I began to rewind the string, drawing the kite closer and closer to earth. I held it at about sixty feet and called Matt to take it back.

As I placed the reel in his hand, the kite broke loose from its string and flew off into the air. It rushed down the street; we rushed after it, Matt screaming at the top of his lungs. It darted up, down, left, right, but always away from us, always toward the beach and the freedom of the ocean. We rounded the corner of Tenth Road and dashed across a field to the Ninth Road stairs, up the stairs, and down to the beach, but the kite was out over the ocean, irretrievable now.

"You bum! You gotta get me a new one!"

"Yeah." I didn't feel like listening to Matt now. "When we get home." I watched the kite, now no longer herky-jerky in its flight, obviously more sure of itself, as it drifted farther and farther away from the beach, high above the choppy sea.

We got back to Newton Saturday. Paula would not be back for a week. I sat down and wrote her a letter, apologizing for my conduct at the rollerskating rink, baring my inmost feelings to her and asking her to meet me on the day she got back at a shopping center not far from her house. I did not sign the letter. Saturday, after it was dark, I walked down to the street corner to mail it. Sunday morning I contemplated going down to the mailbox and asking the mailman who did the morning pickup to give it back, but I decided that I really had to know this year; there was no way I could wait till next summer.

On the following Saturday, even though I had to go caddying first, I put on my best plaid shorts and the green shirt that had impressed Bump so much just a month earlier. I tucked my lunchbag into my belt and headed for the golf course, which was just a few blocks away from the appointed meeting place.

As I walked down the fifth hole on my morning loop, my lunchbag chafed against my hip. Would she be there? What would I do, what would I say if she was? I almost began to hope she wouldn't show up.

After a few moments I began to feel uncomfortable. I looked at my leg and saw an embarrassing wet spot developing. I soon discovered the reason: my hip had been bumping against a bad spot on a peach, which had begun to ooze its juice through the brown paper bag onto my pants. I took the peach out of the bag and threw it away, but the damage was done.

That afternoon I volunteered to make a second loop. Even though I hated caddying, I needed something to keep my mind off the approaching appointment. It didn't work; I lost three golf balls and only got a quarter tip. I couldn't stop thinking of Paula.

By five thirty the spot was dry and almost unnoticeable. I headed toward the shopping center, several times almost turning back, telling myself, why bother, she won't be there; but I had to find out for sure. I was ten minutes late when I got there. I was sure everyone in the parking lot was watching me, ready to burst out laughing. I peeped hurriedly through the window of the ice cream parlor where I'd asked her to wait for me. I couldn't see her. I felt a strange sort of relief, and left quickly.

Later that week we went down to Penfield to visit our cousins. By this time I'd invented all sorts of excuses—she didn't get the letter, her family stayed in Penfield an extra week—but they proved untrue. Their house was occupied by renters, and as for the lost-in-the-mail theory, my brother Tom told me that Bump Hagerty had told him what Paula said about my letter.

"Bump Hagerty?" I couldn't believe it. That she would tell *any-one* was bad enough, but she had a lot of goddam gall to tell Bump

119

Hagerty of all people. I could just see her sitting on the seawall, laughing, telling whoever came by, hey, did you hear this one about Timmy? I was furious.

I went home to Newton and survived the winter.

The day we opened up the cottage for the next summer, my father again talked about selling it. Sick and tired of this nonsense, I challenged him. "You wouldn't really sell it, would you? I mean—" Suddenly I couldn't think of a single argument that would convince him. What is the cottage to him? I don't know, I never will, except that it's been in the family a long time. And really, what's it to me? Memories are just as good wherever one experiences them, perhaps memories of Penfield will be better if I don't have to confront the unpleasant realities of Penfield today. But no, we have to hold onto this, there is something magical even now in Penfield. "I mean, what about the little kids? We got the whole experience, the beach, the friends, the games, when we were little. You can't really take that away from them, you've got to wait at least until they're older."

"Well, I know what you mean, Tim, but we've got to be realistic. We can't afford it, we've got everybody else's money tied up in it that they could be using for something else—do you think my brother couldn't use the four or five thousand bucks he'd get if we sold this house?"

"So let's buy out his share!"

"We can't afford that, either. Dan's going to be in college in a year, then before you know it, you will; we don't have money to throw around." He paused. "Now I mean this, Tim; I don't think you realize what money really is. I stay at the office most days eleven, twelve hours. Do you think I do that because I like it there? Do you think I don't want to come home and have free time with your mother and you kids? Believe me, kid, I'm the world's first hippie. I'd love to spend my days just breezing around the world without my shoes on, doing nothing, walking along the beach. Only problem is, I have six kids who've got the goddam lousy filthy habit of eating."

Dan was staying home alone that summer, working for the Newton Street Department. Next summer, I realized, I'd have to do the same thing, but I saw no point in worrying about that yet.

Every Saturday night there was a dance at the Rexicana Ballroom, three or four blocks away. I had never gone to dances at the Rex, as they seemed too expensive and I had not liked what little dancing I had done in the past. Anyway, there had been a small group of people who would not or could not go to the dances, so there was always someone to hang around with down at the wall. As I sat on the wall at around seven thirty one Saturday early in July, waiting to see who would come up and what would happen, Paula, Linda, and a few of Linda's cousins climbed the stairs.

"Hi!" they all said at once.

"You going to the dance, Timmy?" Linda asked me.

"Naw, I don't think so. You?"

"Oh, yeah." It was Paula speaking. "Oh, yeah, we are. You should go, Timmy. It's good."

"How do you know?" I snapped at her. "You ever been to one?" She was taken aback. "Well, no, but it should be good. I mean . . . Oh, well, you should come."

"Well, I don't think so."

I went to the dance every Saturday night for the rest of the summer.

Since Dan was at home in Newton and the Hagertys were again renting out their cottage, I spent most of my time talking to Mike Lawson. He told me stories about all the times he got drunk or stoned and all the girls he had almost laid. All of the latter had the same ending: "An' I woulda fucked her but"—he holds his right hand beside his ear, snaps his fingers and pulls the hand down toward his chest—"but I had no rubber!"

I never believed Mike really meant that. "You wouldna really fucked her, wouldja, Mike? I mean, jeez, I dunno if—I don't think I could bring myself to do that to a girl."

"Wait till you're older. Wait till you're in that situation. You'll see."

Once he told me of the night the summer before that he'd been sleeping in the family tent-trailer out in his driveway. "It's about three o'clock an' I hear this noise outside so I open up the tent flap an' it's Lois, so I says 'Come on in' an' she gets in an' takes off all her clothes an' I says 'Jeez, if my mother comes out here an' finds you I'm gonna get screwed' an' she says 'I got news for you, Mike, I'm gonna get screwed even if she doesn't come out.' An' I coulda

121

fucked her but"—there was the snap of the fingers, I could have called out the next words with him—"no rubber! Wouldja believe it!"

"Jeez, Mike, I dunno. Lois did that?"

"No shit. Really."

"Who woulda thought?"

Then Mike told me about the time he and Mad Dog Huntington had gone into Hubbard's to buy rubbers. "The little ol' man says 'Whattya wannem for?' an' Mad Dog says, "Whattya think? They're raincoats for Jesse!' Jeez, that kid's a hòt shit. I couldn't believe it. You shoulda seen the guy!"

"Didja get the rubbers?"

"Oh, yeah, we got 'em."

"Jeez, I dunno."

Paula changed her hair that summer, parting it down the middle, and she never wore the orange bathing suit of the year before, but the sight of her still made me glow and tremble and lose track of my thoughts. Although she was always polite to me, I noticed a trace of condescension in her manner. It seemed to me that we could not avoid reaching some kind of conclusion to last year's bumblings, that she would have to say something that would either put me off once and for all or renew my hope. I was wrong, of course; we never spoke of the preceding summer. I suppose that in itself was some sort of conclusion.

One night I was sitting on the seawall talking to Linda. Everyone else had gone in. I figured if anyone knew Paula, she did, so I asked her if she had any insight into the ways of Paula's heart.

"Oh, Timmy, why do boys always worry about things like that? Paula and I just want to be friends with all you guys. Why do you have to bring romance and sex into everything?"

I felt very cheap, and did not answer except to thank her for telling me. It seemed quite reasonable that Paula should feel that way. Because of it, I loved her even more.

One night in the last week of July, a guy who lived on Eleventh Road told me that he was going to get Paula. I might have treated this as I had Bump's similar claim of a year earlier, but Billy Randall was as old as Paula and me, and not a bad-looking guy. "I'm gonna take her down on the beach, and she's gonna love it, and then the next day she'll come back for more and I'll tell her, no thanks, honey, tough luck. She'll learn."

"You wouldn't really do that, would you?" Somehow the end of his plan caused me to panic. "I mean if you have to take her out, you wouldn't just dump her like that, would you? How could you do that to a person?"

"Easy. I'll just say so long, see me when ya get your braces off, or something like that."

Later in the evening I heard Billy counsel a friend who had been pursuing a certain girl for three weeks: "Hey, that's no good, you gotta forget her, you can find someone else. No one's worth waitin' three weeks."

"Oh, you don't think so?" I asked him. "You must know some pretty sick girls."

"Why, how long would you wait for a girl?"

"Would you believe I have been waiting for one girl for over a year?"

"A year! Who's that?"

"Well I guess that's my business, isn't it."

"A year! You gotta be kiddin' me!"

I decided I was better off sitting home than hanging around with this crowd, so I went home.

The next day about ten of us played a game of football on the beach at low tide in a thunderstorm. Wet and tired, I was about to go home when I saw Paula, Linda, and one of Linda's cousins a few hundred yards away at the top of the Ninth Road stairs. I noticed immediately that Paula had once again parted her hair over on the left side of her head and that she was wearing the orange bathing suit that she hadn't worn for a year now. Behind them the sun was just beginning to set, and the air around them, still moist from the rain, seemed to shimmer red-gold. I stood in the middle of our football field with my mouth open and stared at this vision from out of my past. The three of them started toward the water, then stopped, consulted each other momentarily, and decided against swimming. They picked up their towels and left the beach.

Friday was our last night at the beach for a year. That afternoon

I had been sitting on the beach talking to Mike. "Shit, I don't wanna leave yet. I mean this has been one shitty summer. I can't leave like this."

"Didn't get anything, right? I know. Well, there must be some girls you can get here. At least make your last night worthwhile."

"I dunno, Mike."

"Sure there are. You're not so bad-looking. You're a hot shit. Lookit," he said, looking up and down the beach, finally fixing his gaze on the top of the Ninth Road stairs and nodding at Linda, who was standing there alone. "Take Linda. You could get Linda. Go ahead, try tonight. I mean, it's worth a try."

"Linda? Naw, Mike, I don't think so. I don't even think I'd want to. I mean, I like Linda, but not that way. And I don't think she'd want to, either."

"Don'tcha? Sure she would. I betcha she would."

"Well, I don't think so, Mike. I guess I just won't bother."

"Jeez, whattya want? Well, if that's the way ya feel about it, okay, but I think you're bein' kinda dumb about it. At least try."

"Naw."

That night on the stairway I said almost nothing. I decided to stand on my head, my feet braced against the concrete barrier that surrounded the landing. Linda came over and asked me why I was feeling so unhappy.

"Why shouldn't I be unhappy? It's what I do best in life. Besides, what's to be happy about?"

"Plenty of things. Just look around you."

"I've been looking around for years and it didn't work. Why should it now?"

"Timmy, how can you say that? There's so much that's beautiful around."

I had no inclination to respond—the only thing that takes the fun out of being unhappy is talking about it to someone who's happy. Linda was silent for a long time. Then she said, "I think I'd better let you read my book."

"Your what?"

"You'll see." She dashed down the stairs and ran home. In a few minutes she was back, carrying a little yellow memo book. The cover looked ready to fall off. "Here," she said. "Read this tonight. It's all the beautiful little things I've read or heard and copied down to remember. Whenever I need something to make me smile or feel good I just open it up and read something and remember when I wrote it down. It's really nice to cheer you up."

I was touched. I took the book home and read it that night; I really don't remember any particular things that were in it, but after I finished I was overwhelmed by the very idea that anyone could find so many little things that could make her so happy. Some of the quotes she had were silly, some trite, but some were beautiful, and all of them were just so nice, so sincere, and it was clear that Linda truly loved them all. I knew that I had to find myself a part of this happiness, had to ally myself with anyone who found happiness so easy and obvious. Although it was almost midnight, I grabbed a few sheets of paper and a pen. I wrote a short letter telling Linda that she had to write to me through the winter months, to tell me more of these beautiful things, to keep me alive. Then I began to jot down a few favorite lines of my own, from songs, poems, books, and movies. When I finished I had filled six large pages, and I could have gone on. I stopped, folded the pages, and put them in the back of her memo book. Then, at one thirty in the morning, I ran down to the beach. I stood on the sand, then moved into the water, wading out until the tiny waves lapped against my thighs and wet my blue shorts. I stood still. Yes, I thought, someday I will die, and I will have to die at sea. It's the only place for it.

The next morning I gave Linda back her book with my letter inside, saying nothing but "Thanks." That afternoon we went home to Newton and she went back to her home town, somewhere in New York.

Linda and I exchanged many magnificent letters during that winter. I told her I was once again happy, and it was true. Every time I read one of her letters, I was happy. Every time I wrote her a letter, I was happy. One time even, Linda was unhappy and asked me to cheer her up. I did so without a second thought. Reading her letters and writing back were the only things in life I looked forward to.

At Easter, Linda and her family were near Boston visiting relatives. She called me from her cousins' house. I had just finished dinner and was expected next door to babysit, so I asked her to give me the number and I'd call her back.

An hour later I fished the number out of my pocket. I dialed it and asked for Linda.

"Who?"

"Linda."

"There's no Linda here."

"Linda Howard?"

"No, I toldja."

"Is this 555-7741?"

"Yeah."

"Are you sure?"

When I hung up, I looked again at the number, then dialed a few that sounded like it. I didn't find her. Later in the week I wrote her a letter explaining what had happened. She claimed to believe it, but I'm sure she didn't. I wouldn't, I know, under the same circumstances.

The next summer I was working at a day camp in Boston. Weekends I planned either to ride my bike down to Penfield or to pick up a ride with my father. The first weekend I spent at Penfield was Fourth of July weekend. There were no bonfires; a new air pollution ordinance had outlawed them.

Linda and I were very happy to see each other. Some of her cousins whom I hadn't met before were renting the Hagertys' cottage for all of July. Linda, Paula (who had had her braces removed), some of Linda's cousins, and I sat on the porch of the rented house the night I got down, laughing and playing cards and chatting with Linda's grandmother.

Dances that summer were held on Sunday rather than Saturday nights, for the owners of the Rex had opened a cocktail lounge in a nearby building and needed all the parking space they could spare on Saturdays. At the first dance of the season I picked up a chubby little girl named Maureen who held on to me like a pair of pliers. She lived on Ninth Road. I walked her home along the beach. Between Thirteenth and Eleventh roads we stopped and kissed for a long time. I could taste the green beans she'd had for dinner. My hands slid slowly up the sides of her body toward her breasts, but she clamped her arms tight by her sides. We walked together as far as the Ninth Road staircase, but I refused to escort her to her door. The next day I ignored her.

Linda was disgusted with me. "Oh, Timmy, how can you do that? That's real nice, ignoring her like that. If you don't like her, you shouldn't have gone out with her in the first place." I was horrified at what I had done, not so much in abandoning Maureen as in turning Linda against me. I was glad to be going back to Boston the next day. I'd give the situation a week or so to cool down.

That Friday I drove down to Penfield with my father. He talked about contacting real estate men to keep an eye out for people who might be interested in the house. He didn't want to put a For Sale sign up, but he was ready to sell if he could get a good price.

That evening, while my father was driving the little kids up to the rollerskating rink, I talked to my mother about this new development.

"Dad's really serious about selling the house this time, isn't he?"

"He has been all along."

"I'll really hate to see it go. I don't see why he has to—I mean, it means so much to all of us—to me."

"Don't you think it does to him, too? Don't you think it has happy memories for him? It'll be hard for him to sell this house, but it has to be done."

I thought, but could not say aloud, Does it really hold memories for him? Tell me, does he have memories? Can he have memories like mine? Why, then, why don't I know about them? If it's a wonderful place for him, why doesn't he tell us about it? What are his stories?

I have heard all your stories, mother: of your drunken uncle's interminable phone calls (collect); of your Aunt Lizzy with the speech impediment, who smiled as she called herself "Liddy"; of struggling to make do during the Depression; of six kids studying late nights around the big dining room table; of your brothers in the army; of your father's conversion to Catholicism; of your mother, whom I never met but probably know better than any of my other grandparents. All these stories I have heard. I have seen no pictures, visited none of the places where all this took place, but your past is real to me, I know that you have been living since the beginning of your life.

But with you, Dad, it's different. I have seen the pictures, I have visited the places countless times, but I know none of the stories. I have met several of your childhood friends at the beach. They are all, like you, boisterous, beer-drinking, successful men who sit up nights and argue politics, sports, business, anything, all through their vacations. None of you ever talk about yourselves or your own pasts.

I have seen pictures of the house in the thirties, with your mother, looking young and severe, and your father, straightbacked and expressionless, not knowing he had but a few years to live, surrounded by four shy, grinning children who all look like your own youngest son. I have seen pictures of the house in the forties, you just back from the war, in your army uniform, chatting with one of the friends of your youth, a man I hear even now discussing the defense budget with you into the early morning hours, or teaching my little brothers quick tricks to mastering the multiplication tables. I have seen pictures of the house in the fifties: your mother, my grandmother, now noticeably old, sitting on the front steps with Nippy Fred, the dog who had to be put to sleep for some reason; you and the green '54 Mercury you were so proud of, outside the garage that has since been torn down to lower the property tax assessment. I have seen all the pictures, but I have never heard the stories behind them. Still, there must be stories, Dad. You cannot sell your key to all those stories, you cannot possibly sell this house and leave it all behind.

I went down to the Ninth Road stairs and looked out at the ocean. It was just after sunset. The tide was out so far it looked like it planned never to come back in. I wanted to go for a swim but decided against it. I walked onto the beach, down to the water's edge. I remembered another low tide, many years ago. I had seen some small fish swimming about in the shallow water and had decided to catch them. I had found an old rod and held it out over the water, letting the tangled nylon line float on the rising crests of the tiny waves, then snapped it back over my head, then out over the water again. I hadn't caught any fish, but before long I had myself wrapped in fishing line. Even at the time it had struck me funny.

When I climbed the stairs again, I grinned hello to Caroline, one of Linda's cousins from the family that was renting the Hagertys' cottage. From the first she had struck me as a crazy fourteen-year-old, dumb and sentimental, but with a unique sense of humor. She

128

had been brilliantly funny cheering on Miss Lebanon (who eventually won) as we watched the Miss Universe pageant on TV.

Sunday Caroline was down at the seawall singing from her repertoire of crazy songs, and I taught her two of my own favorites, "Does Your Chewing Gum Lose Its Flavor on the Bedpost Overnight?" and "My Heart's in a Shambles, I Can't Eat My Scrambles, My Eggs Don't Taste the Same Without You." She loved the latter, was sure she'd heard the former somewhere before. She has countless brothers and sisters; I think there are nine or ten in all. It was their first summer in Penfield, and their mother was considering buying a beach house so the family could spend every summer with their relatives and new friends.

The Saturday they were going home was also our last Saturday at the beach. While her brothers were packing the family cars, Caroline came up on the front porch to talk to me. She spoke absentmindedly. Finally she started to cry. She didn't want to leave, she said. She loved the beach, all the people here, so much, she couldn't leave them now for an entire year.

Go ahead and cry, Caroline, I thought. You will be back next year, for the whole summer; your time is ahead of you, but crying now will do you good. Cry before it's too late. I know I will not be back next summer, I will never really come back to Penfield, and yet I cannot cry. Once I could cry: the last time I cried, I remember, was the night I stood in the harsh glare of the bathroom light, washing my feet and cursing myself for being unable to speak my inmost feelings. I cannot cry now.

One Saturday in August we came down to Penfield to visit our cousins. This involved an obligatory half hour or so at the house to lend legitimacy to the visit. After that we were pretty much on our own.

I was surprised to discover that Paula and her family were down for the week. I sat on the wall, bullshitting with Fuzzy and a few of his friends, who were all drunk. One of them offered me a can of beer, but I told him I didn't drink. They all started singing "Ninety-nine Bottles of Beer on the Wall."

Dave Lawson came up the stairs. The moment I saw him I started to smile, thinking for some reason of the day he and my brother Tom had played a fifty-seven-inning game of off-the-steps before Dave finally scored and won. At any rate, I was glad to have sober company.

"Timmy!" he said. "What you doing here?"

"Same as always," I replied.

He grinned. "Still tryin' to get some, huh? Hey, you know what, you see who's here this week? Paula. Timmy, you should try an' get her. I remember you used to like her. You should try it. Go ahead if she comes up."

"Naw, Dave, I don't think so. It wouldn't work, y'know."

"Sure it would. Just try it. Go ahead an'—"

"Hey, Dave, wouldja keep it down, huh?" I saw Paula coming up the steps. She said hello, we talked for a few minutes. She stood over by the corner of the landing and looked out at the ocean.

One of Fuzzy's friends came over to her and started to talk to her in a loud, empty voice. Then, suddenly but gently, he touched her arm and turned her around until she faced him. He kissed her for a long time, roughly forever. I could not take my eyes from them. A short while after it finally ended she said, "I have to go home," and left. A few minutes later I did the same.

At a party at home the following week I got roaring miserable drunk for the first time in my life. Two days later I saw Paula again. She was working behind the counter of the ice cream parlor I had chosen for our meeting two years earlier. We talked for a long time, about drinking beer and things like that. She asked me if I knew where she could get a ride to Penfield before the end of the week; she had to see her boyfriend—"you know, Larry, Fuzzy's friend"— before he went back home to Virginia. I honestly wished I could help her, but I couldn't.

Linda's letters started coming again around the end of August. I wrote to her that I was worried about our relationship, that we were not as close as we should have been over the summer, as the nature of our correspondence seemed to imply we should be. She wrote back a simple answer: we expected too much of each other. In time we would begin to know each other better. We must keep writing.

I agreed that we must keep writing. I did not tell her so, but I disagree on her other point. I do not believe that we will ever know each other better than we do now.

In September I saw a girl on the trolley. She was no older than thirteen. She had braces. She dressed well. Her eyes and her smile reminded me of Paula. She sat across from me. Her eyes met mine, she smiled and looked away, at the roof of the car. Slowly she brought her eyes back down until they met mine again. For the barest fraction of a second she stared straight at me and smiled.

I smiled back.

She got off two stops ahead of me. I knew I would never see her again, but there was something about the whole incident that left me curiously satisfied.

A small colony of men with whom my father grew up, among them his younger brother, had bought year-round houses near the beach in Penfield. In November one of these men died. A large, red-haired, red-faced man, he was the owl man, because, when we were little, he would take my brothers and me to a farm near his house to see a caged owl. For hours the owl man would pretend to be engaged in learned conversation with the bird. When I was in my early teens, the farm was sold and the owl disappeared from our lives, but we still talked about him whenever the owl man came to visit.

My parents went down to Penfield for his funeral. Unwilling or unable to make the return trip to Newton that night, they spent the rest of the day and night with my uncle, at his home on the beach about three miles from Tenth Road.

My mother told me a few weeks later how they had spent the Saturday afternoon after the funeral. "We were down on the beach walking, and Dad was watching seagulls as if he'd never seen them before. I swear, he could have just stood and watched them for hours. He was so fascinated with the way they flew so effortlessly, the way they could glide along for the longest time without even moving their wings, the way they'd just swoop straight down and all of a sudden poke their bills into the water, come up with a fish to eat and then just fly away as if nothing had happened. I'd never seen him watch anything as closely as that before."

Over the winter Linda and I again exchanged magnificent letters. In February she wrote to tell me that Paula's family had sold their cottage. I don't know why, but I felt relieved.

One Friday afternoon late in March Linda called. She was in Boston again for Easter. We talked for about five minutes. I told her that our cottage was now on the open market and a deal seemed imminent. She told me she had to go off and see her relatives, but she gave me the number and asked me to call back later.

I called her at about eight that evening. We had a bad connection, so after a few minutes I had to hang up and dial again. Still the same problem.

Linda said she'd try to call back the next afternoon. She was planning to go into downtown Boston with one of her cousins, meet Paula in there, go shopping and all that. She'd call me, maybe I could go in and meet them afterward, maybe we'd just talk on the telephone, but she said she'd call. She didn't.

The next day, Easter Sunday, I decided to go down to Penfield by myself. After I dropped my little brother off at Little League tryouts in Newton, telling him I was going to spend the afternoon at the library, I drove down. I parked in the driveway of our cottage. I knew where the key was hidden, but I didn't want to go into the house. I looked up Ninth Road and noticed that whoever had bought Paula's cottage had painted it olive drab.

I walked down the beach about a mile, looking up at each public staircase, at each name chipped into the seawall by some kid with a stone who yearned for immortality. There were too many public staircases to count. Over the years, dozens of names have been patiently inscribed at each of these. I had never felt any particular desire to put my own name up there, and now it was really too late. This summer, I thought, some new group of kids will probably hang out at the Ninth Road staircase. Well, they're welcome to it.

TIM — EDITOR

TIM showed his father the story almost as soon as it was written. "When he read it for the first time," Tim wrote me that summer, "his major objection was, to my surprise, not the smattering of profanity but my description of his own father as 'expressionless.' He immediately rattled off three stories about his father—stories I'd never heard before. It worked. He'd still rather tell about Billy Squirrel or toss off a good pun, but even he occasionally has to scratch the autobiographical itch. The summer house is sold now, but, at last, piecemeal, my father's story is emerging."

It took longer to give the story to Paula. By chance, he ran into her the next summer, swimming at a public lake in Newton. "We spoke briefly, haltingly, about summers, about school, about Linda, about the heat, whatever came to mind, everything, nothing." He went home and sent Paula a copy of the story that night. He got no response.

"Two jaded years later," he wrote to me, "I was sleeping late one morning (I was working a night shift that summer) when one of my brothers came into my room and dropped an envelope on my pillow.

133

Handwritten. No return address. A mystery. I waited a few minutes before opening it. I cut open the envelope. Fancy stationery, lacy borders. 'Dear Tim,' I read. (No one called me Tim. Timothy or Timmy.) I read on. 'This letter should have been written two years ago. I'm sorry for its delay. I just feel that I have to tell you that your story is beautiful. I remember the first time I read it . . . I sat there and cried.' The triumph of art! It was all worthwhile! 'Whenever I read it'—she does so often?—'my summers are brought back to life.' And so on . . . 'I will always cherish those memories and in them I will carry the memory of you, Timmy.' (That's more like it. "Timmy.")

"The last line of the letter, before 'Luv, Paula,' (she must share my aversion to that four-letter word) is 'I wish you luck and happiness in everything you do.' My roommate once read that and grinned, 'She doesn't sound as if she expects to see you again real soon.' True. And she still hasn't told me, will never tell me, whether I dreamed up her attraction to me that summer or whether there was something real that I detected there, even if it did die too soon. But then, how could she?"

I caught up with Tim again in 1979 in his beloved Boston. The previous summer he had joined the College Division of Little, Brown and Company (he is now an editor) after spending two postgraduate "apprentice" years working for a Christian education publisher in Connecticut. He was overjoyed to be back in Red Sox country and was already active as an umpire for the Little League on weeknights and Saturdays on Boston Common.

He had also found himself a studio apartment on St. Botolph Street—"in a very trendy area on the edge of the South End—the new South End." Modern adaptations of old gas streetlamps had been installed along the tree-lined street and it all looked very Boston indeed. He was delighted to be within walking distance of everything—"supermarkets, restaurants, theaters, cinemas, museums, symphony halls, public library, train station, the Charles River . . . and the office." But most particularly he was glad to be near the public library and Boston's Haymarket—where he bought "everything fresh" and then cooked "vegetarian inventions," baked ("chocolate! chocolate!"), and concocted "wild poultry sauces and fish stuffings." Tim was in Boston and all was right with the world. His only complaint was that, although he loved his studio apartment, he had to make his bed before he could have anyone to dinner.

The bed was made when I was invited to one of his special Haymarket dinners, which was delicious. His apartment exuded Tim: A well-thumbed *Oxford English Dictionary* (magnifying glass edition) sat prominently on the floor beside an impressive record collection. His father's old cherry colonial desk was piled with papers, pipes, and letters; a reproduction of a Wyeth watercolor hung on the exposed brick wall. The old sofa was one to sink into and ruminate. We talked a lot that night.

His beginning publishing years had been useful but crazy-making. "Writing and editing Christian education stuff almost made me lose my faith. I decided I couldn't *be* a Christian and pour out Christian flotsam and jetsam for profit at the same time. Also, half the time I had no idea what I was doing. I had a lot of things to learn." He had written a number of thirty-two-page children's paperbacks, like *How the World Began*, based on the early chapters of Genesis; *The Family That Wanted a Home*, about the wanderings of Abraham; and *The Shepherds Find a King*, a Christmas story. But a child's view of Christianity was not for Tim. He was now very glad to be working at Little, Brown. And his faith, which was reawakened during a brief flirtation with the Episcopalians in New Haven, had now returned to its original roots. He was a member of St. Paul's Catholic Church near Harvard Square in Cambridge, where "they have Catholics who actually seem happy to be in church—and the best music anywhere around."

But Tim was also in love—deeply in love—with Julie, a devout Jew. And this was cause for concern.

Tim and Julie deeply respected each other's faith. Indeed, they appreciated each other more because they both took religion seriously. They frequently talked of marrying. But therein lay the rub. Neither could imagine bringing up children in any but his or her own faith. This dilemma so wracked Tim that he published a blistering letter in response to an article in *Christian Century* that he felt trivialized the problems of mixed marriage.

I am a devout Roman Catholic. The woman I love is a devout Jew. We love and respect each other as neither has ever before loved and respected another. This has been the case for some time now. We respect and try to understand each other's religious tradition, . . . and it would seem that we have every reason to marry, and every reason to hope that our union would be happy, fruitful, prosperous.

The problem . . . is the children. For a devout adherent of any religion, its tenets must be the most important thing in life, the yardstick against which all else is measured. The passing on of the articles of faith and of the attitude of love and worship of God must be the primary concern in the upbringing of children. How are two people who agree that faith is the most important thing in life, but who do not hold the same faith, ever to pass anything on to the next generation? No one has come up with an answer that is not foggy or platitudinous. Even Dr. Samuel fudges this one; after pointing out that it is the most difficult issue, he mentions that he knows parents who claim to have raised children in both religious traditions. Where are these parents? How did they do it? What do the children believe now? . . .

I am indeed confused. . . . I know that my salvation is to be found nowhere save in the faith imbued by the spirit of the crucified and risen Christ; that the world's salvation, too, is to be found nowhere else. Still . . . I am left to confront paradox, which the reason of this world cannot undo. And I am left to shake my head in bewilderment and anger at those who would try to simplify the issue, as though religious faith were no more than one person's race or another's temperament. The issue of mixed marriage has nothing to do with either of these and should be of little concern to the nonreligious, whether their ancestors were Jews or gentiles. But to those who endeavor to love God as He has revealed Himself to them, it is a most painful, complex, and heartrending issue, and it must not be dismissed or trivialized.

In the end Tim and Julie decided they could not resolve their religious dilemma. Julie, who was unhappy with her graduate studies in anthropology at Harvard, switched to Johns Hopkins.

This morning—a bright San Francisco day in April—I called Tim in Boston and found him busy at his desk at Little, Brown. He'd just had a promotion, and although he finds his new administrative duties somewhat "strange," he still loves editing and had received a bigger raise than he expected.

Tim is, however, angry with Massachusetts voters for adopting Proposition 2½. "In Boston they're laying off everybody—firemen, policemen, librarians, schoolteachers—they may even close the schools by early May. Library hours and services are cut. It's depressing. Even the Red Sox are depressing."

"And are you in love again?" I asked.

"Yes—you might say so. I'm seeing someone pretty steadily."

"Is she Catholic?" I asked.

He laughed.

"Yes," he said, hesitantly, "she just happens to be."

Tim also said he was developing a wanderlust and had checked out a lot of travel books from the library—to look for good vacation spots "anywhere near an ocean beach."

"And have you been back to *the* beach?"

"It's funny you should ask," he replied. "I was just there ten days ago for the first time in years. We stopped by on a drive to the Cape and walked down to the Ninth Road stairs. Someone had painted them a horrible luminous paint; it should be illegal.

"Then we walked down Ninth Road, and I saw that Paula's house had burned down. It must have happened recently. Her family hadn't owned it for a few years, but it gave me a twinge.

"Burned to the ground."

PORTRAIT OF HELEN

HELEN Billinger (pseudonym) was convinced that she came across to others as a prim, uptight WASP—a Miss Goody Two Shoes—and she didn't like the effect at all. More than anything else, she wanted to be spontaneous—to dance on tabletops and make people laugh. *Spontaneous* and *creative* were the two words she used most often to describe what she felt she was lacking. Somewhere along the line since the days when she was the nursery school cutup and had tried to lock little Billy Price in the school bathroom so the fire department would have to come and rescue him, she'd lost the old verve. Her writing, too, she felt had lost "its spark, its passion, its color" and become "gray and lifeless." She'd applied to my course to bring her writing back to life. She was, of course, overstating the case, but that didn't mean she didn't worry. And that worry was to become the central theme of her story.

There was no question but that Helen was a WASP—an Episcopalian of German descent, a New Yorker with a family summer estate edging Long Island Sound in Southport, a preppie (Brearley), an accomplished tennis player and skier, a good and hard-working student, well endowed with the puritan ethic. In some ways, she could have been a character straight out of the pages of J. P. Marquand or Louis Auchincloss. Whenever she talked of her life, I imagined turn-of-the-century scenes—tea parties on immaculate green lawns sloping to The Sound, croquet matches, ladies in wicker chairs with parasols and white gloves; gentlemen sauntering off the family tennis court in white ducks. All very Victorian and polite. In reality, I'm sure it was much more contemporary, but somehow her descriptions always had a period flavor—perhaps because she had spent so many childhood summer afternoons with her grandmother.

Like Ann Kennedy, Helen was at home in the Yale milieu. Her father and uncles were all graduates. She was, however, the first Billinger woman to attend (one sister was to follow her) and she felt the responsibility of that position. Even more, as the eldest child in a family of three girls, she felt the responsibility of carrying on the exacting family tradition—what she calls the Billinger Ethic—which had evolved down the years from her formidable and puritanical great-grandfather, Edward Augustus Billinger, who had amassed enormous wealth as a coal baron. Although maintaining the tradition had always been the job of the men in the family in earlier generations, Helen had no brothers and had taken on this duty from earliest childhood—carefully studying how her father and grandfather behaved. This left her with a dilemma, because the Billinger men were very different from the Billinger women. The women were warm, gay, and sociable; the men "reserved, stern, and proud." Although she never for a moment resented doing what she felt was her "duty and privilege," she longed to let go and be more frivolously adventurous.

Helen was shy rather than stern or reserved, but she did have the slightly "other-worldly" air of an earlier generation. It was not that she looked the least out of character in blue jeans and an old sweater, the uniform of the times. It was just that when you looked at her, you had no difficulty imagining her in white gloves, having tea with the vicar. She was tall and thin, with shoulder-length straight ash-blond hair and delicately chiseled small features—lovely to look at. At the beginning of each class period she was apt to be diffident, talking quietly and politely. As she was drawn into the class discussion, she grew lively and deeply involved in the tales and problems

140

of other class members. There was a special caring quality—a gentleness and earnest concern—about her that I rarely saw in others. She was also, like her Billinger ancestors, astute and tenacious. If she were wrangling with a problem she wanted to solve, nothing would stop her. She would sit on the edge of her chair, knitting up her face with the intense concentration of a scientist about to make a discovery.

Such was her stance one rainy March night when she was describing to the class how—try as hard as she might—she couldn't break free of the hovering and stern Billinger ghosts.

"They're running my life. I just can't seem to break out of the mold. I've lost all my creativity. I envy you all . . . you can do wild things . . . be spontaneous . . . warm. The people in my family never really hug or kiss each other—not spontaneously." Her voice was wistful.

Joseph Snell, a black and a fine jazz pianist from the Bronx, looked startled. "Oh, my family's spontaneous all right," he said. "When I go home everybody rolls around on the bed together—nothing sexual—just having fun. But I envy *you*. I don't have the slightest idea who my grandfather is. For many years, my father tried to locate his father but he never could. . . . And so I don't have any ancestors, not even a grandfather, and no civilization I can really attach to."

Joe had just spent a "really wonderful" summer in Germany, where he'd been deeply impressed by German culture, the Gütenberg Bible and all it represented in scholarship and hard work, German family life, and German heritage. He told Helen he wished he'd had some of her German background. "Oh, I like the spontaneity of my family and other blacks—all right—but I wonder if they're not too easygoing, too spontaneous to build a strong culture. We need more discipline. Paternalism can be valuable—I've seen it in Germany—we blacks could use more of it."

I sat, stunned. I never thought I'd live to see the day a black American would praise German discipline. I mumbled something about Hitler and discipline for just what purpose.

As much as Helen kept protesting her "straightness," she had a romantic spirit, sometimes touched with a fine ironic wit that showed up in her writing. In one story she wrote of a summer

141

romance she'd had with a fellow counselor at a tennis camp who
turned out to be a devout member of the fundamentalist Campus
Crusade for Christ—"The God Squad":

> I began to suspect something out of the ordinary that night when
> Bob told me his affection for me was guided by the Lord. Nothing
> was further from my infatuated mind than the Lord! Moreover, his
> outlook was alarming; it brought to my mind snatches of past sermons
> and Sunday school lessons, whose flavor conflicted uncomfortably
> with the flavor of my adolescent passion. I did listen to him carefully
> as he explained that I would be forever lost if I didn't replace my
> "ego" with Jesus Christ on "the throne of my soul." . . . My relation-
> ship with Bob, I'm afraid, was much more important to me that
> summer than my relationship with Jesus.

Nor was Helen so conservative that she didn't break out of her
traditional family framework and live almost all of her four years of
college in the room of Andy, her friend and classmate.

In this period many of the Yale women lived under such long-
term arrangements. It was the style and, in the early years of coeducation when men outnumbered women so heavily, almost necessary
as a protective measure. In tone and practice this arrangement was
quite different from a state university, where if a couple lived together they usually did so off campus. Those dorms and sororities
and fraternities—whatever their sexual practices—were not places
for live-together arrangements. Although a number of upperclassmen lived off campus at Yale, it was also quite usual for a couple to
move in together in one or the other's room in the colleges (in rather
squashed quarters, I might add), frequently keeping the second room
as storage space and as a decoy for parents who might have raised
some objections. Generally, parents were aware of the arrangement
but they were loath to discuss it openly or allow it within their own
homes, where the couple almost always slept apart when they visited.
This practice elicited an unspoken—but sometimes awkward—truce
between the generations, which no one wanted to disturb.

Helen's relationship was particularly domestic. "In terms of life-
style, we were married as married could be. I had all my meals in
his college, and all my friends were there too."

Helen worked hard on her story through most of the semester. Because she knew so many tales that would illustrate "the spirit" of her family and how it functioned, she had trouble bringing all the material within a manageable framework. She decided to focus on incidents from the beloved family summer estate in Southport— Valhaven.

Then, with her usual devotion and tenacity, she cut and pasted, cut and pasted, and produced a story of how she shook off the heavier strictures of the Billinger ghosts and began to kick up her own "two shoes" with a new élan.

*T*HE BILLINGER GHOSTS
by Helen Billinger,
New York, New York

I live with a ghost—a whole collection of ghosts in fact. They all have grand old names like Cornelia, Abigail, Louise, and Hector. But they also have one name in common—Billinger.

I've always known that this long line of genteel Victorian ancestors hovered in my background, making my life different from others. But it was only recently that I realized that these ghosts were haunting me. Over the years they had worked their way into my daily life. They were now infiltrating everything—my college themes, my travels, my friendships, my judgments. I realized I wasn't Helen, a person in my own right; I was only a look-alike leaf on the great Billinger tree. Somewhere I had lost myself.

About two years ago, this began to trouble me enough to make me want to do something to get these ghosts out of my system, or at least loosen their strong grip on me. I started investigating in the microfilm of Yale's Sterling Library. I searched out the obituary of Edward Augustus Billinger, my great-grandfather. I found thirteen paragraphs in *The New York Times* of April 20, 1910:

"Edward Augustus Billinger, president of the Billinger Coal Company, died yesterday afternoon at Valhaven, his country home at Southport, Connecticut, after an ineffectual attempt had been made to sustain his life by the administration of oxygen. His condition had been satisfactory, according to Hector Billinger, his son, up to noon."

In the quiet darkness of the library, I read on. "Edward A. Billinger . . . devoted himself with great persistence to business and gained success from the start . . . the fighting qualities which were among the prominent characteristics of the 'Coal Baron,' as Billinger was called . . . The war of the Billinger Coal Co. against the Leightons . . . entered upon that contest with all the enthusiasm of a schoolboy . . . He had met other competitors and had vanquished them. . . . long struggle and the expenditure of great sums before the Billinger Coal Co. and the Leightons called a truce. Billinger Coal was the victor. . . . The Leightons were credited with heavy losses."

I turned the film further. "The closeness with which Edward A. Billinger attended to business did not prevent his taking a deep interest in other matters. . . . fond of country life, and took pride in different country homes . . . His residence was one of the most richly furnished in the city. . . . Metropolitan Museum of Art . . . American Fine Arts Society . . ."

And then came the names of the other ghosts: "Mr. Billinger married Cornelia Ross. They had four children, Abigail, Louise, Sarah, and Hector."

As I turned the microfilm, I realized for the first time that in the business world Edward Billinger had been a tyrant. I had always known that he had been scrupulously correct in his actions and had demanded the same high standards from his family and friends. What I hadn't known was that he possessed this ruthless fighting spirit as well as the strict puritan ethic which all Billingers were meant to emulate. He was not someone whose grip would be easily loosened.

Edward had implanted his ethic in the character and life-style of his son, my grandfather, just as it had been handed down to him by his father and just as Grandfather had handed it down to my father. In each generation there had been at least one male heir who took over and passed on the Billinger Ethic, much as a king reigns and passes on his title.

But in my immediate family there are no sons. I am the eldest of four girls. Perhaps because I was the eldest girl, I felt it was my duty to fulfill all those responsibilities that my father's male heir would have carried out had he existed. Perhaps it was because I had spent so much time with my grandfather as a young child. Whatever the reason, from a very early age I saw myself as the person responsible for continuing the family tradition, and as such, I took a special interest in the Billinger Ethic. In childhood I was completely and happily possessed by it. I believed that by following it I would be directed to an upright and productive life.

Had there been a son in the family I would have grown up differently. In our family the women are very different from the men. The women are warm, talkative, and responsive while the men remain reserved and stern—proud bearers of the Billinger respectability. But because my father had no son, I jumped in to fill the gap.

It was always in the summer that I felt the strongest sense of attachment to the Billinger Ethic. Summer was a great gathering time for the Billingers. The whole family—all the aunts, uncles, cousins, and grandparents—spent it together in Southport. I will never forget the feeling that took hold of me each June when we returned there after a long winter away. As the family car took the final turn off Beech Lane and entered Valhaven, I was flooded with a certain reverent exuberance. I was reminded of this annual home-coming when I saw the movie *Rebecca*. The bend of a long drive-way, a burst of symphonic music, a vast and immaculate lawn, and a majestic mansion appeared. Manderley! And so it was for me on seeing my own home for the first time each summer.

When Dad stopped the car at the gate, I would jump out and run across the lawn, bounding like a puppy just freed from a leash. I would run by Grandmother's house shouting "Hello" and head for the four giant beech trees. From there I could see the water. I would stop still, breathe in the salt air, and know I was in heaven.

Perhaps Edward Billinger felt the same rush of freedom when he set foot on the land for the first time in 1890. When I try to picture that moment, I imagine a stern, dark-suited businessman stepping out of a carriage and extending his hand to his wife, Cornelia, dressed in long flowing skirts and a wide-brimmed hat. This would become his summer retreat from the dusty, sweaty coal company, from the endless struggles in the courts over the antitrust laws. It would also be his retreat from people, with whom he was usually uncomfortable. In Southport he would be alone with his beloved family and an occasional fellow sportsman. He would be near his longtime friend and comforter, the sea. He would ride and sail to release the frustrations that were pent up in his strongbox mind in the city. He would find peace.

Over the years the family grew and gathered together in Southport. After Edward's death in 1910, Grandfather decided to make his land more of a self-sufficient compound. Houses were built, along with stables and barns. Cows and horses were purchased and a large vegetable garden staked out. Grandfather named it Valhaven. Whether he had Valhalla in mind when he named it, I don't know. But the parallel has always struck me as fitting.

By the time I was born, the idea of a farm had been abandoned. I suppose Grandfather had found farming burdensome. But the buildings remained and new houses were added as each of Grandfather's three children married and had a family. When I was seven, we built our house on a green stretch of lawn not far from my grandparents'.

We lived at the tip of a peninsula jutting out into Long Island Sound. A row of tall pines separated us from the adjoining estate. In our oasis we couldn't see any houses except our own. For rainy days, the old barn had been made into a gym, and other abandoned farm buildings were used for clubhouses, shops, anything we could think of. We never had to leave Valhaven to have a good time.

It was a big, happy, close-knit family. "Family," in fact, was the unspoken password for admission through the gates to Valhaven. In the Billinger mind there was always a strong distinction between family members and outsiders. Dad told me one night over dinner that, because of an inexplicable feeling he had, he never wanted to invite his school friends out to Southport for the weekend. I think he was afraid to; it might have upset Grandfather's schedule or made him feel ill at ease.

In this way the Billinger men isolated themselves from the outside world each summer, and they did so because they felt most comfortable with each other. Among strangers they lacked social ease; they weren't interested in small talk. Then there was another quality. It

147

certainly wasn't snobbery in the usual sense. It was a feeling of moral superiority. The Billinger values were puritan in the most literal sense of the word, excessively strict in matters of morals and religion. Every Billinger worked hard, was punctual, and lived a healthy life. Grandmother never wore makeup or earrings; Grandfather was seldom seen out of a dark suit and was never late for an appointment.

So, when we spent our summers at Valhaven, cut off from the diluting influences of the outside world, we were free to express our Billinger nature in its purest form. But it was never something we did consciously; it was more as if the Billinger spirit hovered in the air, mixed with the seagull's cry and the cricket's song, and filled our souls with its force and direction.

My best friend and constant companion in Southport was Grandmother. We were best friends because we were so suited to each other. We both felt alone in Southport. She lost her husband when I was four and lived in the big white house by herself. I had no one to play with; my cousins were too old and my sisters were too young and frivolous. They played with dolls, which I had never done. Grandmother, on the other hand, was adult, refined, and queenly— but her manner was gay. She was perfect, I thought.

Grandmother's life-style was best reflected in her paintings, a group of Impressionist works collected by her parents-in-law before Impressionism had come into vogue. They were scenes of the leisurely, carefree life of the nineteenth-century French aristocracy, scenes of plump, pale-skinned women in full-flowing pastel skirts sipping tea on green lawns, and of tawny sportsmen rowing lady friends down canals. The expressions on their faces were warm and the atmosphere sunny. Such had been Grandmother's world—first as Miss Emily Ann Winslow, who spent her young days chatting on green lawns, and then as Mrs. Hector Billinger, whose charming monologue over the dinner table kept the austere house from freezing up in silence. I loved Grandmother for her infectious warmth, particularly since I couldn't seem to produce one bit of it on my own. She had the same warming effect on me as her paintings did. Whenever I despaired of having a sense of humor, I had only to think of the giggles we shared in order to be reassured. I suppose her warmth was part of the reason Grandfather loved her so. Stern and reserved as he was, he must have needed the cheerful aura that surrounded his gay wife. In return, she idolized him for exactly those qualities that were so different from her own. The attraction of opposites had been a Billinger pattern which had mirrored itself down the generations, even to my mother and father.

Grandmother and I spent many hours roaming the grounds together. Since Grandfather's death, she had assumed responsibility for seeing that the land was properly maintained. Hand in hand, we would walk to the four beeches to check for dead branches. So thick was their leafy spread that a wholly different world had grown up beneath them; the ground was covered with moist moss, the light was dim, and the air was cool and damp. Bulbs and roots twisted around each other, forming pockets in which water collected. Every time it rained, Grandmother and I would bail out the pockets with clam shells so that mosquitoes would not hatch in them.

After inspecting the beeches, we would walk over to the water to look for crabs or to have stone-throwing contests. We tried to see who could throw a stone across to Mr. Steele's island. Although her throws were longer than mine at first, Grandmother never made it. As I grew older, her throws became shorter and mine longer, finally reaching Mr. Steele's lawn. When we were tired of throwing, we sat on the bulkhead and she told me stories about the Billingers. They all had the sea in their blood, she said, and would never be happy for long away from it. She told me about the brisk autumn day before she was married when she went sailing with Grandfather. To keep warm she'd put on her scarlet coat, but when she arrived at the dock she could see from Grandfather's face that something was wrong. "Take that thing off!" Grandfather snapped. She did and had the coldest sail of her life. But she had learned her lesson; scarlet was not an appropriate color for a lady.

I told Grandmother I was very glad I never had to sail with Grandfather, for even before I heard her story, Dad had told me that sailing with Grandfather was always fraught with tension. From his earliest childhood, Dad had been his father's crew in the Long Island Sound races. One foggy day when he was still very small, he was sent forward to sight the racing buoy, but he could see no buoy anywhere. Boats were sailing in all directions. The fog grew thicker. "George," shouted Grandfather, "for God's sake, are we on the right course?"

The little boy had no idea, but he knew if he didn't give a definite

149

answer, his father would explode. "Yes," he shouted, and for the next ten minutes lived through hell, wondering if they were sailing hopelessly out to sea. Then, by some miracle, he sighted the buoy in the distance and shouted to his father. They won the race; they had been the only ones on the right course. Grandfather didn't say a word to his son. Dad had saved the day, but, after all, it was expected of him. (Even if Grandfather approved of what his son did, he rarely, if ever, expressed it.)

On rainy days when Grandmother and I couldn't explore outside, we played at her house. After breakfast I would run barefoot through the soft grass, carrying bits of it into the hall, for which I always got a dirty look from the housekeeper. When I entered the living room, I felt I had entered the innermost sanctuary of Grandmother's special world. Everything in her house was precious to Grandmother and, taken together, told the story of her life. There was the familiar musty antique smell, the soft light which was dimmed to protect the paintings, the untouchable quality of the furniture. One very tired-looking needlepoint sofa had a rope hanging between its arms to keep unsuspecting visitors from sitting on it. There were vases of bright-colored flowers from the garden. There were mementos from family and friends—a bust of Nefertiti, a tinfoil star made "For Great-Grandmother with love from Randy." And everywhere there were photos, in big frames, in small frames, in leather frames, in silver frames. They filled her tables and she loved them; they kept her company when she was lonely.

Photographs had always been important to Grandmother, and to Grandfather too. By tradition the whole family gathered every ten years to be photographed by Henry Foster. After some research, Grandfather had discovered Mr. Foster. Then the family tried him, liked him, and gave him its trust, with the mutual understanding that he had just entered into an unwritten contract to take care of the photographic needs of the Billingers. In this way Mr. Foster became a tradition much like Harvey, the gardener, Fred Slagle, the gas station owner in Southport, and the family accountant, Lawrence Farley. I remember seeing these men and their wives at every family wedding. At my cousin Anna's wedding, I saw Mrs. Slagle go up to my aunt and say, with tears in her eyes, "We are so grateful you included us," as if this were an honor she would always remember.

A Mr. Foster photograph was taken when I was thirteen and had a crush on one of my older cousins. Mom made me wear a hand-me-down dress from my Davis cousins because she wanted Aunt Catherine to know that we used the dresses she gave us each year. (Mom is a Billinger-in-law and Aunt Catherine is a Billinger, which meant that for a long while Mom was a little in awe of Aunt Catherine.) I hated the dress. It had puffed sleeves and made me look too young. At least I was wearing stockings.

While I was having my problems, my sister Abby was having hers. She was crying under a nearby tree because Mom had made her pull her long bangs back with a hairband. Dad was growing more and more impatient with the problems of assembling his daughters and putting them together with thirty other members of the family. He was gritting his teeth and jangling the coins in his pocket.

We all gathered at the customary hedge and Mr. Foster and his assistants erected their huge giraffe of a camera. Grandmother positioned her family around her; her two sons and their families on either side of her, her daughter and her family seated in front. I was glad to be near Grandmother. We held hands and played squeeze games while Mr. Foster darted around endlessly, fixing up rows of Billingers. In her other hand Grandmother held the photograph Mr. Foster had taken ten years before. It was custom that the older photo always be shown in the newer one.

Later that summer, when the photograph arrived, Grandmother invited me over to look at it with her. She was pleased. "Isn't it a handsome family?" she said. "When people compliment me on it, I always tell them, 'Well, that shouldn't be surprising, their grandfather was a handsome man and I'm not so bad myself!' " I had heard her say this many times before, but both Grandmother and I were a little sad at that moment, because Grandfather was missing from the photograph for the first time.

I found that if I looked closely enough at the new photograph, I could see not only the photo Grandmother was holding in her hand, but the photo within that photo. It was a little eerie seeing the past recorded like that, almost like seeing a mirror's image in a mirror.

But, as I think about it now, I realize how fitting that custom is for our family, because in so many ways each generation has been a mirror image of the one before it.

Still thinking about Grandfather, Grandmother picked up the silver frame that held the photograph Mr. Foster had taken ten years earlier.

"Look at the resemblance between Grandfather and his two sons," she said proudly. I saw it. They were all dressed in their dark suits and stiff white shirts and looked handsome, upstanding, and stern. "You look like them too, dear," Grandmother continued. She might well have added, "and you act like them." It was as if my great-grandfather had discovered that the secret of immortality lay in raising his son in the image of himself. So, too, Grandfather had raised his son and so, apparently, Dad had raised me. But if he did so, he did it unconsciously. Dad, like his father and grandfather before him, preferred women like my mother, his mother, or his grandmother. It was as if the male image had descended on me by the accident that my father had no sons.

Grandmother and I were soon deep in pictures of all sorts. We had carried six boxes of them down from the wooden chest in the attic, and sat on the porch listening to the rain and reliving the past. "Look at Great-Grandmother Cornelia," she said. "Now, there was an outstanding woman. She devoted all her time to raising her children. Only when they were all grown did she take on any outside interests." She paused to make sure I was receiving her message. "Then," she continued, "she began to fight for women's suffrage. Once, she went to jail for protesting in the capital. Her son had to go down and bail her out!" Grandmother chuckled.

We found another picture of Cornelia, which I remembered seeing in a book about suffragettes. She was dressed in a long satin dress that was stiff enough to stand up by itself. Beside her was Edward in a dark coat and trousers, looking cold and formidable. Unless caught off guard, all Billinger men look formidable in photographs. Formal occasions demand a certain demeanor—an impenetrable, impeccable reserve—and for Billingers, almost every occasion is formal.

I was surprised, therefore, to come across a picture of Grandfather with his head thrown back in laughter. Dressed in white tie and tails, he was standing beside a marquee and holding his sides as if to keep from exploding. But as I thought about it, I realized that explosions like that were also characteristic of Billinger men. If such a facade of reserve must be preserved so tenaciously, the bottled-up emotions must burst forth now and then. I have always loved to see my father explode with laughter and I have hated his explosions of anger. When he can no longer restrain his anger, his face turns red, his veins bulge, he jangles coins in his pocket. My aunt calls this rage the *cou rouge*.

As I sat with Grandmother that afternoon, I felt the full weight of the inheritance I had been born into. I felt completely and happily consumed by it, as if its spirit had made its way into the empty cavity of my heart and had taken possession of it. If I was to carry on the Billinger tradition, that spirit was a necessary and welcome support. I felt stronger when the Billinger ghosts surrounded me.

Even after he had died, I often felt my grandfather's presence. I was never frightened when I walked home from Grandmother's house in the dark because I was so preoccupied with the thought of him. Often late at night in bed, especially after a day with Grandmother, I would relive the very few real memories I had of him: holding his arms open wide so I could rush into them; pulling out his gold pocket watch so I could play with the alarm. I also remember being frightened when I saw the doctor's puffy black car in the driveway. I knew that whenever the car was there I wouldn't be allowed to see Grandfather. And although Grandfather looked well enough to me, I sensed there was something ominous about the doctor's regular visits. What I didn't know was that Grandfather had angina and was frequently in pain. As his suffering increased with the years, he withdrew from most people and grew closer to those select few he would admit to his presence. In the last summer of his life, my father, mother, and I lived with him and Grandmother, at his request. Knowing he hadn't long to live, he wanted to make sure my father absorbed his business experience. Dad was just beginning his career in the coal business. We were the only ones who saw much of him that summer. The bond between us grew very strong, and although he died when I was four, it has not yet lost its intensity.

Fourteen years after his death, on my eighteenth birthday, I was to feel the strength of his presence again. My father approached me

153

after breakfast. "Helen," he said, "your grandmother has something for you. She has asked us to go over to her house at two this afternoon." He spoke in his usual businesslike manner, and a certain finality in his tone told me he wouldn't explain further. Since I saw Grandmother all the time, I was curious about the formality of this visit. I was not going to receive an ordinary birthday present. I knew that. Whatever it was, the occasion would involve a family matter, because Dad had been asked to come along.

That afternoon we walked along the lawn to Grandmother's house in silence. It wasn't an awkward silence; it was a silence we both understood, marking a close bond of kinship. Understanding through silence was always the way we expressed this bond. I knew that we were different from other people in this way. All my life I had seen fathers and their children hugging and kissing, chattering and telling jokes. None of this went on in my home, and at the time I was proud of our differences. After all, as Grandfather always said, "Those who talk the most say the least."

As we opened the door, a voice greeted us from within: "Hello, darling. Happy Birthday." We found Grandmother in the sunroom leaning on the two canes she needed to use since breaking her hip two years before. I kissed her soft wrinkled cheek and enjoyed the clean, familiar smell of her skin. She was the only relative I ever kissed. We walked with her slowly to her special chair. I sat on a sofa beside it. My father found a chair across the room from us. He was going to let Grandmother handle this occasion by herself; he had come only because the importance of the occasion demanded a man's presence. I soon forgot about him altogether.

Grandmother picked up a box from the table beside her. Her movements were slow and delicate with the slight tentativeness that arthritis had given them. "Now that you are eighteen, dear," she said, "I want to give you a present your grandfather bought for you when you were very little. He wanted you to have it when you were eighteen, but he knew he wouldn't live to see you reach that age." She handed me a box. I unwrapped it slowly, feeling the terrible loneliness that comes when someone special to you is gone forever. Inside the box I came upon a little note and I noticed Grandmother start. "I didn't know he had written anything," she said, her eyes filling with tears. I read the note silently. "To Nini with much love

154

from Grandfather," it said. I could hear his voice speaking to me across the years and I wanted very much to speak back. Busying myself with the white tissue wrapping, I fought back the emotions whose expression would be unseemly before my stoic father. I uncovered a spade-shaped brooch with diamonds set in it. I don't remember exactly what it looked like. All I could think of was Grandfather on one day long ago walking out in New York to buy a token of love for a tiny child which would be given to her fourteen years later when he was gone. I could see from the box that he had gone to his friend Raymond Yard, the jeweler. He must have discussed it all very carefully with him. I gave the brooch to Dad because I knew it should be put away for safekeeping; it was enough for me to know that Grandfather had thought of me. Then Grandmother repeated what I had already heard many times before. "You know he loved you so. Just before his death, he said, 'I regret so that I shall not live to see her grow up.'"

Although he was dead, I still believed Grandfather was watching me grow. Whenever I did something I knew he wouldn't like, I felt his disapproval as strongly as if he had been present. And when I did something I knew he would approve of, I could feel the warmth of his smile. Acts of generosity like the gift of the brooch strengthened the iron bond between us. I knew, too, that all his values were embodied in his son, my father, and I tried to imitate Dad as closely as I could. Unswerving, I kept to the Billinger path. I had not so much as a momentary desire to turn my head to either side to see where other paths might take me. The Billinger way, I believed, was leading me to all I could ever want both in my home and out of it, just as it had led my father and grandfather before me.

As I grew older, my world at Valhaven expanded only as far as the Southport Beach and Tennis Club. My sisters and I would go there to take part in the tennis, swimming, and track competitions. Even there, Grandfather's ghost was with us. It was he who had established the club many years before as a gift to the community. Each summer the club sponsored a tennis competition for contestants from throughout Fairfield County for the Billinger Cup, and at the end of each season the Billinger Trophy was awarded to the junior club member who had that summer demonstrated the best leadership and sportsmanship.

At the club, as everywhere, I felt I had to live up to the Billinger standard. This drew a sharp line between me and the teen-agers who played and partied together. One side of me envied their carefree gaiety, their late-night campfires on the beach, their illicit smoking and drinking. But another part of me took pride in maintaining the ethic. I told myself it was more important for people to respect me than to like me. I had been taught that I would earn respect if I controlled any "hedonistic" or "unchristian" impulses and kept a fair-minded objectivity at all times. In this respect I disapproved of my sister Louise. She was frivolous and uninhibited; she never thought before speaking or acting. One day she told me that she was sad that I was losing my youth so rapidly. I, on the other hand, thought that was something to be proud of and said so. Nevertheless I worried; I was aware that I was socially ill at ease.

One day when I was fifteen, I did make a brief foray into the teen-age social world. That summer Wayne, a friendly local boy, worked behind the lunch counter at the club. I was aware that he was interested in me because I could feel him watching me whenever I was in the room. He was nineteen, and I was impressed. I found myself visiting the lunch counter more frequently than usual. It was midsummer, however, before Wayne mustered up enough nerve to ask me out. One day when I was at the counter buying a soda, he asked me out to a movie. I was terrified. I felt awkward and silly and couldn't think of a thing to say.

"What's the movie?" I finally blurted out.

"*Grand Prix,*" he said.

"Er—ah—well, what time does it begin?" I asked, hoping to find some words.

"Ten o'clock." By this time he, too, was feeling awkward.

"Well, all right," I said, trying somehow to be casual, "I'll come." He said he would pick me up at home shortly before ten. Unable to find anything else to say, I picked up my soda and walked away from the lunch counter.

That night he was late arriving. Although he had lived in Southport all his life, he had never before been in Valhaven and he lost his way. After wandering around for some fifteen minutes, he turned up at Grandmother's service entrance, and from there was referred to the correct driveway. When he arrived, he looked shaken and ill at ease. But he was no shakier than I. Before he came, my mother had given me a lecture about proper etiquette on dates, especially on dates with older boys. To make matters worse, she gave me a strict midnight curfew, which I knew I couldn't keep because the movie wouldn't be over until twelve. What if Wayne wanted to go to Carvel for ice cream afterwards? What would I say then? I wondered why I had even agreed to go.

As we drove to the movie, conversation was slow—something about long driveways, tennis, and orange sodas. Indeed, conversation was slow all evening. I was very thankful for the movie, even if it was about car racing; it meant we didn't have to talk. The high point of the evening occurred in the middle of the feature when there was an explosion in the men's room. The door burst open, belching clouds of smoke and steam into the theater. I felt a surge of relief. Suddenly, we had something to talk about.

"What happened?" I asked.

"That's the gents'. Must be some sort of explosion in the pipes. Lucky I went to the gents' earlier!" he laughed.

What a weird way of saying men's room, I said to myself. To Wayne I said, "Yes, I guess so."

"Happened once before at school."

"It's the first explosion I've ever heard," I said.

The movie ended without further incident and he took me home. No complications, no invitations to Carvel. In retrospect, I don't wonder.

The next day at the club, a girl who played tennis with me and was friendly with Wayne approached me.

"Wayne said you acted very mature last night," she said. I was pleased; I didn't have the sense to realize that was hardly a compliment. To me "mature" was a golden word. Wayne never asked me out again.

I was more successful in the club's sports. When I was thirteen I won the tennis championship for girls eighteen and under. After that, my name went up on the plaque year after year. In swimming competitions I raced girls who swam indoors with the AAU all winter, and somehow I always managed to pull out ahead and win. This made Mom think I might eventually become an Olympic racer. She was very proud of me and her support meant a lot to me. But it was not *her* approval that I longed for. It was my father's. He was the person I was trying to live up to. He was the one who had been president of his school, captain of Yale's tennis team, commander-in-chief of the Army and Navy ROTC at Yale, the recipient of the John Dickens Award for citizenship. He was the one who was first at everything he tried. His life was difficult to emulate, but I tried very hard, and at times it seemed as if I was succeeding. Even so, I could not seem to gain my father's approval.

At the dinner table in the evenings, I frequently talked about the day's competitions. My mother would beam and praise me, but my father would stare off into space, looking uncomfortable. Mom told me not to worry about Dad's lack of interest in my achievements. His father, she said, had never praised him, fearing that his many successes would go to his head. (I remembered his sail with Grandfather.) I knew that public recognition of any sort was something that no Billinger should seek or pay heed to. Humility was one of the primary Christian virtues.

Dad admired success, but his heart went out to those who needed support and reassurance. He seemed drawn to my younger sisters. They didn't excel as much as I and seemed to need more guidance and encouragement. I would feel his warm response whenever he asked Louise why she was looking so sad and then invited her to play a game with him, or when he joked with Abby on the tennis court and made her feel special. Perhaps he thought it was important to counterbalance my achievements by giving my sisters as much attention as he could. But also—to my sadness—he simply seemed to like them more. They were more like my mother, warm and feminine. Mother often said that Dad had a huge soft heart; I began to feel that there was no place in a soft heart for a person like me. My sisters, who didn't even attempt to be competitors or achievers in the Billinger tradition, felt loved and secure in our family and easily accepted by our father. Although I sought my father's approval with a desperate intensity, I failed to gain it. Or at least I felt that I failed. I, who looked so successful and self-assured, was up against a great obstacle in developing a sense of self-confidence.

It was my father who first forced me to take a new look at the Billinger Ethic. Because he seemed to take so little pleasure in my progress through life, I was beginning to wonder if I was going wrong somewhere. I agonized over this problem for two long years until I was sixteen, when it occurred to me that my father himself was not happy with all aspects of the Billinger mold—especially the part of it that had given him such extreme social reserve and isolated him in the narrow world of the coal company. While I was busily and diligently cementing myself into the rigid and stern demeanor of a Billinger patriarch, he was trying to break out of it. To him, I must have been a daily and painful reminder of his own entrapped spirit.

One night at dinner he informed us all that he and Uncle Hector were leaving the coal business. We were stunned. Billinger meant coal. The coal business had been an integral part of the family since Edward Billinger's grandfather went into it. Edward had been referred to publicly as the Coal Baron, the rest of us as coal heirs. Coal was part of our lineage. The move was drastic. The coal dynasty was ending.

Gradually, Dad's life changed and he along with it. He immersed himself in social philanthropy. He became a member of our church's vestry and organized projects to help the community; he joined the board of trustees of a number of schools; he volunteered as a fund raiser for Mayor Lindsay's campaign. Because his new occupations brought him into contact with new people, he and Mom went out more frequently and had people to our home more often. He didn't grind his teeth as much; he laughed and joked with guests. He seemed to be enjoying life.

At first I was distressed and confused by the change in my father, because he seemed so different from himself and from all the Billinger men I'd ever known. I turned to Grandmother for support and found in her a source of stability and an implicit reassurance that the old Billinger manner was still valuable. At the same time a part of me was growing restless with the old way. I envied the new pleasures my father was experiencing, his fast-growing ability to relax and enjoy life. It was the same part of me that had envied the parties and beach bonfires of my peers.

One day that summer I put aside the old rules of morality and propriety for the first time and made my first foray into "hedonism." I had surprised my sister Abby in the act of assembling her "vice kit." She was visibly frightened by my intrusion into her room at this delicate moment, but I was feeling restless and disgruntled, and so, in that instant, I decided to join her.

"Are you kidding?" she asked. "You?"

"No, it might be fun," I said a little defensively.

"Well . . . okay." She was perplexed and agreed only reluctantly.

We walked out to the shore, where we thought we would be safe from discovery, and sat on the bulkhead, dangling our feet in the water. Abby showed me the contents of her kit—a pack of cigarettes, a plastic bottle filled with bourbon, and a package of peppermints. I had smoked a few cigarettes but had never learned to inhale. She tried to show me how, but I was soon overcome by fits of coughing. Mr. Steele, who was cleaning his boat across the water, raised his head from his work. We moved self-consciously and tried to be quiet, but my cough continued. "Quick, take this," said Abby, handing me the bourbon bottle. I took a big swallow, but it only made me cough harder. My throat burned and my eyes filled with tears. I crawled over to the trees and lay down. When I felt better, I was determined to try again. I had another cigarette and another swig of bourbon. I repeated this until I was talking and laughing nonstop. Abby and I were having a fine time. When it was time to go we split the pack of peppermint Life Savers and staggered back to the house. I saw Mom and Dad only long enough to state with studied precision that I had an upset stomach and was going to bed without supper. It took me all night to recover. But in spite of my physical discomfort, I felt exhilarated. Freed from inhibitions, I had had fun—real fun.

Two other summers came and went, bringing a few further lapses into Abby's vice kit. The lapses were only occasional; the Billinger Ethic pervaded most of what I did. But the older I grew, the more I became aware that this freer, lighter-hearted side of me was just as valid as the Billinger side. I realized, too, that this part of me was woefully underdeveloped, and I couldn't think of ways to develop it. I read the poetry that Abby wrote and knew that, far from being able to write anything like it, I couldn't even share its depth of feeling. I watched her burst out with spontaneous gaiety, bringing smiles of appreciation from everyone around her. I knew that I could not do the same. Whether I liked it or not, the Billinger Ethic had blanketed me. Grandfather's ghost was hard to shake off.

THE BILLINGER GHOSTS

I graduated from boarding school and went on to college. There I made friends with people who seemed to show the spontaneity that I so lacked. I was attracted to that spontaneity and was hoping it would rub off on me.

On my nineteenth birthday, I invited two of my new friends—Andy and Kate—to Southport to celebrate with me. All three of us were working in the city that summer and we were eager to let go and relax for a weekend in the country.

Just how they were planning to "let go" I didn't know at the time. But I found out after dinner on the first night when Andy came up to me and said he had this drug. Would I like to try it? I was surprised and frightened. I hung my head in doubt, trying to imagine what it would be like and feeling the Billinger ghosts hovering close about. But the prospect also excited me. Emotion and intellect were again at war within me. The resolution came as it had to. Andy and Kate thought it would be good for me, and they tried to persuade me. In a moment of uncertainty, I took the pill. I could never have done it on my own.

Immediately afterwards, we went to a James Bond movie in Westport. Two hours later, when we came out of the theater, the world looked and felt exactly the same to me—but not to Andy and Kate. They talked about how they had seen the end of the movie at the beginning and the beginning at the end; to them, the movie had been one big circle converging on itself. I was puzzled. I thought that perhaps I wasn't allowing myself to let go and so forced myself to lose as much restraint as I could. All the way home, I chatted volubly, and everything I said brought fits of laughter from my friends. This led me to think I might have a sense of humor after all.

A little later, the three of us went outside and sat in the hammock. Every now and then Kate would get up and dance a small ballet in the dark. I sat very still, staring at the house, until gradually, without my noticing it, the house began to change. Against the star-speckled sky it began to take on a life of its own, as if it were a needlepoint picture and all the stitches were twirling around. I realized what was happening and told Andy and Kate. "Just like you, Helen," Andy said, "getting off hours after everyone else."

I felt like a child exploring new territory and was thrilled with my discoveries. Nature was coming alive. I could see the grass and trees grow. My own body, which before had always been used to demonstrate physical skill, was infused with a new interior freedom. Every bone and muscle felt its own pleasure at being. I wanted to move so that my body could grow like the trees and absorb the gentle salt breezes. I wanted to feel like this forever.

"Helen!" a sharp call came from the kitchen door. It was my mother. I fell off the hammock in panic. "Andy," I whispered urgently, "I can't handle this, please help me." He got up, walked across the lawn and told my mother that the three of us were outside talking. She had wakened, noticed that all the kitchen lights were still on, and worried that we hadn't returned safely from the movie. After Andy reassured her, she went back to bed. But my own fear remained to haunt me. I knew I couldn't possibly confront my mother and her common sense. I couldn't fit into any traditional structures. Once my mother had entered the scene, there was no longer any freedom for me, only the fear that she would return and I would have to talk to her. I told Andy that I had to go to my room where I could be safe. We all went to bed.

That was a mistake. Once in my room, I was pulled mercilessly through swirling visions that were unfamiliar and frightening. I felt as if I were riding a satellite, attached to the earth only by a most tenuous thread of gravity which could snap at any time. Using all my energy, I struggled to keep the thread from breaking by focusing and refocusing on familiar objects like the light beside my bed. I would strain my focus until it looked like the lamp I knew and then, from pure exhaustion, I would relax, watching the lamp disintegrate again into a mass of twirling stitches. I repeated this immense effort over and over again for hours. I couldn't relax for long because I thought if I did I would be lost in space forever. I began to cry with frustration. I thought the whole thing would never end. I longed for the hours to pass, but I also dreaded the morning, when I would have to face my parents. All hell would break loose if they saw the state I was in. I realized that I had made a big mistake to do this at home; I would have been better off somewhere where the ghosts were not so strong. Fortunately, I had to use so much energy just keeping my hold on reality that I had no room to worry about Grandfather's disapproval. It only lay in wait.

When morning came, I had gained more control, but I was horrified to see a very puffy face scarred with tears and smudges in the mirror. More than anything else, I wanted to reach Andy, but I couldn't get to his room without first going through the kitchen and passing my mother at breakfast. Repeatedly, I would start down the back stairs and then, like a frightened puppy, dash back to my room again. On the fifth try, I managed to get into the kitchen. Keeping my back to my mother, I made my way to the stove, where a frying pan of sausages was cooking. I turned the sausages over and over while my mother chatted about the morning news at the kitchen table. Then, as casually as I could, I said I would go see if Andy was up. I found him awake and started to tell him about my night. My words became sobs, and my face, which I had tried so hard to get into shape for my mother, disintegrated again. Finally, I told Andy he should go and have some breakfast and I would meet him and Kate at the tennis court afterward. I climbed out his window and ran to the court.

By this time I was feeling better. Andy's understanding and my own hard-won ability to keep a grip on reality made me feel good. The danger of parental confrontation had passed and I felt only high and loose.

It was a good feeling. My youngest sister Louise rode up on her bike and stopped to chat. She began to talk about her dreams of the night before and I found myself full of thoughts and imagination, of energy and creativity, and of a desire to share my newfound inner resources. Louise looked at me quizzically as I talked on and on. She wasn't used to this aspect of her older sister. "Well," I said, "dreams aren't real although they seem to be when you're having them. They're only thoughts. But thoughts are real. Gosh, I don't know what is real anymore."

"Coke is!" sang Louise, imitating the TV commercial. "It's the thing of your life. It's a sparkling delight. It's the real thing." With a fling of her head, she rode off on her bike, singing the jingle again. I sat on the green grass beside the court and laughed and laughed. Children, I thought, are high naturally.

When Andy and Kate had finished breakfast, they came down to the court and we spent the rest of the day walking, lazing in the sun and sharing our thoughts. I had so many—all about the mind and body, my surroundings, and the world beyond. So many thoughts tumbled one upon the other that my speech couldn't possibly articulate them. (It had always been the other way around before.) I would have a startling mental vision as if I had discovered an unusually important truth; yet, when I tried to describe it, my words would come out sounding somehow incomplete or trite. No doubt my thoughts *were* trite, but at least my mind was exploring and creating, excited and active, not just diligent and plodding as it always had been before. More important than this, my heart opened up. I felt I was able to express my feelings more than I had been able to do before. We held hands—Andy, Kate, and I—as we walked about, and it felt natural to do so no matter who was around. They told me I sounded and acted like a new person.

That afternoon, when my cousins came down to the tennis court, I sat among them chatting and joking with an entirely new sense of ease. I didn't worry, as I had before, that I was sounding pompous or too intellectual. I didn't struggle to fill the time with stilted habitual exchanges, "Nice day," "Good to see you," "School's hard work." I felt free and relaxed.

And so the day ended. The next day I was my former self again, as if Grandfather's ghost had taken hold of me in my sleep and given me a fresh dose of the ethic. But I was not without memory. For a day, I had experienced new sensations that I would never forget. It had been as if the underdeveloped side of myself had blossomed for a moment and then closed up again. The brief glimpse of what life could be strengthened within me the will to change, which would eventually make change possible. I had seen another kind of future, I had liked it, and I was determined to recapture it for keeps.

For me, it took something as powerful as a drug to loosen my rigid control over my emotions for a day. But I knew that I could not rely on an external stimulus to create the change I wanted within myself. There had to be other ways, and there were.

After my nineteenth birthday, I came to realize that more than anyone else it was my father who could help me change, for in a way, he was fighting a similar battle against the Billinger ghosts. Gradually he began to talk more freely about his own disenchantment. Now and then he spoke of his loneliness in his senior year at school when he was the student-body president. He would say offhand that he never cared much about awards. They could never fill the gap created by the fact that no one really knew him.

When I heard him say these things, I knew that my experience had been much the same. I had won awards at school, but I knew, as Dad knew, that I would have given them all back in exchange for the warmth of cameraderie. The Billinger Ethic had implanted in us both a core of moral rectitude and ironclad self-discipline. But it had neglected to give us any clue as to how to deal with situations which did not call for rectitude and discipline. Despite all the good it had given us, in this respect, the ethic had failed us.

As time went on, it became easier for me to change, partly because Southport itself began to change. Last year, the town put in a new shopping center at the end of Beech Lane. Housing developments have crept up to our property's boundaries. The water in The Sound is so polluted that you can't swim without running into a dead fish or someone's garbage. Now the barn-gym is covered with a layer of dust, and there is a lock on the door and a sign on the loft ladder saying trespassers will be prosecuted. No one lives on that side of Valhaven anymore. My aunt has sold her house and Mom and Dad talk about selling our place. I know they won't as long as Grandmother lives. Grandmother herself can't understand the change, and it has brought great sadness into her life, as it has into mine. Valhaven was once heaven to me. As a child, I was happy and safe and thought this the most perfect of all worlds. But the change has also brought me joy. I know I am free to move on now, to look for a new kind of Manderley, built on some old foundations, but with new views of its own.

Edward Augustus Billinger will have a special place in my new Manderley. I will never want him to leave my side completely, as he has given me much that is good. But I want to be able to face him as an individual and say, "Here I am, Helen, your great-granddaughter Billinger. But first let me be Helen. Then let's be friends."

HELEN – LAWYER

*H*ELEN's declaration of independence from the ghost of Edward Augustus Billinger catalyzed her mood of that spring and pushed her into action. In the middle of writing it—"on a crazy impulse" at semester break—she flew off to Switzerland for "just a week" (unheard of in the Billinger Ethic) to join her parents and sisters on their somewhat longer and "more sensible" spring skiing holiday. She schussed down the mountain slopes, danced in the discotheques, and had such a good time that, on returning to Yale, she was determined to go back for the summer. "That week was like my drug experience —I was dazzled by the mountains, dazzled by the life-style; I wrote poetry, did silly things, made people laugh. I absolutely amazed myself."

But returning to Europe meant canceling her well-laid plans to spend summer in Boston with her longtime friend Andy and to work in a bookstore there. She didn't like going back on her word, but just across the Atlantic was all of Europe . . . waiting. There she felt she could be a completely different person—spontaneous, creative; the ghosts were not so much in attendance. Andy was not overly pleased by this turn of events, and Helen felt guilty. As soon as school let out, however, "I just packed my bags, got a plane ticket, and flew off to Germany. That was very unlike me." She spent the rest of the summer carefree, wandering Europe with friends, running off to Wimbledon on impulse, flying to Greece for a musical arts festival in Lawrence Durrell's villa on Corfu. She ran across an old school friend, and together they "zipped over the island" on motorbikes, imagining themselves in Greek myths. "It all sounds overdone," she told me shyly, "but I've never been happier in my life." Although she wrote Andy faithfully all summer, her thoughts were not with him, nor her family, nor anything on the American side of the Atlantic. At the end of August she returned home reluctantly, fully determined to return to Europe when she graduated. At Yale she signed up for intensive German.

Living with Andy that year was awkward for both of them. Helen was interested in having a "best friend" but not "a husband"; Andy wanted a closer relationship and a longer-term commitment. "I was not very courageous," said Helen. "I should have put an end to it altogether. But a big dependency had grown up between us—over three years' worth—and it was as hard for me to break it as it was for him. We both were rather miserable." After graduation, when Helen left for a year's job in Heidelberg, Andy "quite understandably" wouldn't have anything to do with her. He married another woman not long after.

In Heidelberg, Helen was lonely and cold—the house she lived in was heated only three hours a day. To improve her German—which was now quite good—she lived with a middle-class German family who had lost most of their belongings and assets in World War II and were now trying to recoup some of their losses. They were humorless, hardworking (the father worked from 4:00 A.M. to 2:00 P.M. every day at the post office), thrifty to the point of penny-pinching, and obsessed with possessions, TV, and crime. There was a double lock on every door. This not very ebullient scene left Helen miserable from the cold and with not much to talk to the family about. Her job—helping to run a junior-year-abroad program for American students—was interesting enough and Germany's arts and music festivals delighted her, but after a year she was ready to get back to New York, her beloved and "innovative but problematic"

167

home town. "By then," she said, "I wanted to be really involved with New York; to be able to do something productive there." Helen's *wanderjahr* was over. The Billinger ethic was reemerging.

Before Helen had passed the Statue of Liberty, she decided to go to law school. If she were to be "productive," she reasoned, she would need more training and law would provide her with "the best tools" and give her credibility and professional status. She found a job with a population control organization, got herself an apartment not far from her family, and put her major energies into preparing for her qualifying exams and applying to law schools.

Then, just after she had been accepted at Georgetown—the place she most wanted to go—she fell madly in love with a classmate she hadn't seen since college. He lived in New York and he just happened to be a law student. She had a few momentary doubts about going as far away as Washington, but not many. "I was scared of going to law school, scared that whatever enthusiasm I had about becoming a lawyer would be snuffed out by the experience. When work becomes a burden to me, I simply don't enjoy or retain any of the material. I wanted a school like Georgetown that wasn't intensely competitive. I wasn't going to give that up for love. I was too liberated for that!"

Helen went to Georgetown, but she found it terrifying and demanding—"devastating to my self-confidence"—and commuted weekends to New York to be with Tim, which made the week's work just bearable. Early that summer they were married in a large and formal wedding at the Episcopalian church where her father was a vestryman, and then they went off to her beloved Europe for their honeymoon, "so I could show Tim all the places I loved best." In the fall Helen transferred to a New York law school.

In the early summer of 1979 I found Helen and Tim in their lovely small apartment in Brooklyn Heights—perfectly appointed with a yellow and orange chintz sofa and matching chairs, an old English coffee table, plants in the windows, and many family photographs in silver frames. Very cozy and completely belying the hard work both occupants were engaged in. I didn't see a brief or a paper anywhere—not even on the leather-topped desk in the small study. Helen had just graduated from law school and was preparing for her bar exams; Tim was clerking for a judge. In the fall, both planned

168

to join law firms on Wall Street. When we finished dinner, Helen wanted to talk about the halcyon days in Europe, but I was eager to hear about her further experiences in law school. Tim, after helping with the cooking and washing the dishes, disappeared into the study to work on a brief.

"I really hated law school—all the way through—and I haven't yet figured out exactly why. Probably because I was scared silly that I wouldn't be able to make it and felt constantly that I was hanging on by bare threads. The way they teach you to put up a good argument is to attack everything you say, and you're made to feel all your theories are worthless. It's like being thrown up against a brick wall time after time." From the very beginning, Helen had felt strongly about working in the public sector—hopefully in the art world that she loved so much. Whenever she had an elective at law school, she did research on the legal problems of museums. However, to be useful to a nonprofit organization, she felt she must first get training as a practicing lawyer. She was pleased that the firm she was joining on Wall Street represented many public institutions; but eventually she thought she wanted to work within a nonprofit organization itself. "For me, it has always been important to work for an organization whose mission I believe in, and it's hard to believe in the mission of a law firm."

Helen's voice always changes when she talks about her family or Valhaven. It loses some of its earnest quality and takes on a warm lilt. She was very happy for her mother, who had gone back to school, finished her own doctoral degree in psychology, and was now deep into a research project about women who had resumed careers after raising families. Her father was busier than ever in church affairs. One of her sisters was still at Yale, but the other, Abby, her "vice kit" sister, was deep into a profession—photography. She lived nearby and borrowed Helen's casseroles. Her grandmother had just had her ninetieth birthday and was now very crippled with arthritis. Her immediate memory was slipping; she had difficulty conversing. Helen went frequently to visit her, and together they pored over photographs and old mementos just as they had in her childhood days in Valhaven.

"Grandmother knows she can't carry on a conversation. So she has a sofa piled with boxes, and when I come in, she asks me to bring over a box—she doesn't care which—and then, with a tray in front of her, we go over all the things in the box—old letters and Christmas cards, pictures and junk mail. I keep finding things I'd never seen before, like the rough draft of a letter my grandfather wrote to the cellist Gregor Piatigorsky saying how happy he was that Piatigorsky had his old cello. I loved finding that. All these things enable Grandmother to talk; they trigger her memories. We always find something that makes us weep or laugh." On one of these afternoons Helen read her grandmother her story—"naturally eliminating certain parts"—and they cried together.

Some years earlier, Helen had shown the whole story to her parents, with great trepidation about the drug scene. As it turned out, they liked the story and were "as understanding and objective as could be hoped" in learning about the episode. "That was such a relief to me," she said. However, when it was considered for publication, both parents were greatly concerned that the story implied too strongly that it was only the drug and not other things going on at the time that had changed her. And Helen, herself, became worried lest it look as if she were advocating drug taking. "I feel that even though it was a positive experience for me and can be for some others, I would never recommend it to someone, because it is awfully dangerous if not done under the right conditions."

So Helen had revised some of the story's emphasis to make this clear but, with her usual tenacity for honesty, she had not considered eliminating the scene or denying the value of the experience to her. Nor would she change a remark she felt was true but which embarrassed her dreadfully—about how the gas station's owner's wife had been so grateful to be "included" at the family weddings. "It was true," she said, "but I think there's something horrible about the fact that I would recognize that." Her parents stood strongly against the elitist, condescending quality of *noblesse oblige*—"Christian acts of charity"—so much so that her mother had asked her to omit the word "charity" from her wedding ceremony because it had so many overtones for her.

To protect her family, Helen had always known that she must use a pseudonym. So, with great care for authentic detail, she had carefully chosen new names for herself ("It had to be a straightforward name, not embellished or lyrical") and all her family members —living and dead—that would conform as much as possible to historical accuracy for her "disguised memoir." She felt "Billinger sounded appropriately German," but I'm proudest of thinking up 'Valhaven.' It sounded like the name of a home; it connoted peace and quiet, and sounded like Valhalla, which the dictionary tells me was the gathering place of fallen heroes."

In the last few years, she told me, Valhaven had come back to life in a new way. Although one aunt had died and the rest of Helen's many remaining aunts and uncles were not using the place any longer, her immediate family was expanding and gathered there frequently. Her grandmother had become too old to summer there anymore, so Helen and Tim used her grandmother's house, which they found a wonderful weekend retreat from the pressures of the law. "Tim really loves Valhaven," she said, beaming. "I'm so happy he does. I mean, who likes to be with their in-laws a lot? But he doesn't seem to mind." Helen brought out a map of the compound she'd drawn when she was homesick in Germany—the Sound, the barn, the tennis court, the island, her house, her parents' house, the beech trees.

Then she showed me a bright-colored poster of Austria on her bedroom wall that read, "Explore the Mountains with a Guide." She turned wistful. "You know," she said, "I thought you might ask me if I feel I've lived up to my promise in the story or whether I feel that I've slipped back into old ways."

"What do you feel about that?"

"Well, the story was undoubtedly caused by a lot of the change I was feeling at the time and it helped enormously to move that change along. It helped to make me realize I needed to break out —that I had a lot to break out from—and then it helped me to plan what I should do and then do it—like going off to Europe that summer." She paused, looking reflective. "I don't know about maintaining that feeling. Certainly, I'm not tied to my family in the way I was. But I haven't really done much to develop my creative side."

I said that it must be hard to be "creative" while one was struggling with the demands of law school and then asked her if Tim helped bring out her more carefree nature.

171

"He's a wonderful person—so much like my father in so many ways: dependable, very caring, intelligent, and with many of the same values. Really a remarkable person. I guess people really do look for husbands like their fathers." She knitted her brow and was quiet for a moment. "I think it's up to me to find my own creative pursuits. . . . I keep thinking back to that wonderful summer in Europe."

PORTRAIT OF AL-NOOR

*W*HENEVER Al-Noor walked into class—usually late and gently apologetic—a spirit of friendliness and enthusiasm swept in the door with him. His slight and agile frame was topped by a head of wonderfully black curly hair, and his face radiated a smile that was either present or imminent. He was intuitively sensitive to the needs of other members of the class, myself included. For Al-Noor, people were good, life was good, and both offered intriguing and unending opportunities.

He also brought to class more palpable offerings: tickets to the latest bluegrass concert, a collection of brightly colored cloth khangas from a new shipment he'd just received from East Africa. Although he would blush red at my saying so, he was every inch an Indian trader; we never knew what goodies would pop from his pockets or tote bag next.

Part of his trading activity was the result of his being a scholarship student and needing to work his way through college. But part was pure and simple heritage from a long line of imaginative Indian traders who had made their way from India to Zanzibar and eventu-

173

ally had come to rest—for the moment at least—in Dar es Salaam. Unlike other scholarship students, Al-Noor never seemed to work at the usual bursary jobs—clerking or typing in Yale offices or waiting on tables in the dining halls. Instead, he could be found running a hot dog concession, organizing the weekly bluegrass concerts, peddling his African wares, or, dressed in an immaculate suit, managing the toy section of a department store. After our class ended in the late spring, Al-Noor invited me down to the Westport Playhouse and this time I found him, smiling and elegant, acting as maître d' for the Playhouse Tavern. Perfect.

In retrospect, I find Al-Noor's energy and optimism of those days astonishing. For, as I was to learn, his life had not been easy, but buffeted by political upheavals, geographic displacements, his father's early death, and severe family economic seesaws. And only very recently have I discovered that these experiences hadn't completely passed by him without leaving a mark. He now tells me that, behind his cheery demeanor, he suffered some black moments that he didn't expose except to his most intimate friends. For us in the class, however, his gaiety and gentleness were always present.

Two years before he took my course he'd passed through one of those adolescent periods when everything seems to go wrong. Of course, it was his sophomore year. In a bureaucratic mixup, his scholarship was withdrawn; he worked long hours and moved off campus to save money; he was worried about and lonely for his mother and brothers, now living uneasily in Switzerland. He was beset with insomnia, and if after a long struggle he finally fell asleep around 3:00 A.M., he'd miss his morning classes. He flunked three out of five courses, struggled mightily to make some up in summer school—the oldest son of Abbas does not flunk out! Finally he followed his dean's advice to take a year off. To make ends meet, he moved illegally into St. Anthony Hall, his society at Yale, where he slept on a bedroll on the fifth floor, hiding it in a drawer during the day. At the core of his worries was his mother, who couldn't obtain working papers in Switzerland and was living off the obligatory generosity of her sister and brother-in-law.

After saving money for airfare, Al-Noor flew to Europe, where he persuaded his mother to move to the United States. Together they decided on Westport, which was not too far from New Haven and had a good high school for his youngest brother, Aboo. While his mother settled the small house and applied for her resident visa, Al-Noor worked at his usual potpourri of jobs—sweeping the floors of Macy's and Malley's, peddling Indian silks and sheepskins, selling youth fares for a student travel organization. He also took two courses at the Norwalk Community College, a requisite for his return to Yale. In spite of money being short, Al-Noor was now a lot happier, his family worries were lessening, his mother was nearby, and he was functioning effectively in his role as eldest son—a role he took very seriously.

Al-Noor's family history is closely interwoven with East African political history. At the turn of the century, his grandfather, Dadabapa—then just a child of seven—was invited by his uncle to leave overcrowded India and go with him to Zanzibar to seek their fortune in the rich lands of Africa. Dadabapa's parents were pleased at this opportunity for their son, and the uncle, for his part, promised to raise the child as his own. They were all devout Muslims of the Ismaili sect (a sect originated in nineteenth-century British India by Hasan Ali Shah, the first Aga Khan). They set sail in a dhow from Bombay, and the journey, hindered by monsoon winds and interrupted by frequent stops, took many months.

On arrival they found an old friend from Kutch, and the uncle was soon in business as a cart peddler of fruits and vegetables. Dadabapa had his job cut out for him as assistant to his uncle, and in this way entered the entrepreneurial world at a very tender age. The business thrived and they became prosperous. Dadabapa grew up, married Khadija, and had children of his own. Then, in 1928, the Aga Khan advised Dadabapa to move his family across the straits to Dar es Salaam on the mainland and open a business there. World War I had given German East Africa into the possession of the British, who now called it Tanganyika. Dar es Salaam, the capital, was a beautiful colonial town with turn-of-the-century government buildings and wide streets, shaded by baobabs and flowering acacia and almond trees. There, Dadabapa developed an increasingly prosperous textile business that manufactured khangas—the gaily colored cloth wraparounds worn by most coastal Africans. A local artist designed the prints, which usually included a popular Swahili saying, and the cloth was printed in Holland.

But the core of Dadapapa's life was the rapidly developing Ismaili community in which he played a significant role as an organizer and philanthropist. Apart from establishing businesses—insurance companies, banks, textile mills—the Ismailis built hospitals, foundling homes, and many schools, which were very important to them. They organized councils to oversee religious and social well-being, tribunals to solve conflicts within the community, and marriage committees to facilitate introductions between young Ismailis—especially whose who lived in Tanganyika's outback. It was in the midst of this bustling Ismaili growth in a British colony that Al-Noor's father, Abbas, grew up—and, in turn, Al-Noor himself.

Dadabapa died young, in a rather astonishing incident that Al-Noor will tell you about, leaving Abbas at seventeen a sad and intensely lonely young man. The family and Ismaili community rallied round, encouraging Abbas to marry early, and at twenty-four he found Zaytoon, who shared not only his religion and community but also his adventurous spirit. He was happy again. But as you will also read in Al-Noor's tales, things were to change significantly for this close community when Tanganyika became independent in 1961 and then joined with Zanzibar to become Tanzania in 1964. The new black socialist government was not very much fonder of the Indian merchants who had prospered under British colonial rule than they were of the British themselves. Major sections of the economy formerly dominated by Indians and Europeans—banking, importing and exporting, agriculture, wholesale and retail distribution—were nationalized. Although in Nyerere's Tanzania the changes were not racially motivated, it was the Asian capitalists who were most affected by the change. Things were not so benign in neighboring Uganda, where Idi Amin was to expel in the years to come thousands of Asians, many of whom had been born in Uganda. And in Kenya the rumors were out that, when the aging and ailing Jomo Kenyatta died, revolution would erupt, leaving the Asians as victims.

It was in this period of frightening upheaval, when Al-Noor was in high school, that he began to struggle with the dispossessed

176

feelings that came from always being considered foreign. This somewhat stark theme gives his tales their title and underlies their otherwise delicate and gentle nature. With Al-Noor, one rarely saw his
particular pain directly on the surface. But one day, about midsemes-
ter, he made a very clear statement in the notebooks, in an uncharac-
teristically abrupt style:

> I am a foreigner. I have always been and always will be. At different
> times in my life I have lived in Britain, the Netherlands, Zaire, and
> Tanzania, and I now live in the United States. In Tanzania, where
> I was born and grew up, I was called *muhindi*—Indian and foreigner
> —for I am brown-skinned, eat spiced food, and speak Gujerati and
> Kachhi as my Indian immigrant parents did decades ago. Neither my
> parents nor myself have visited India, where, with our western and
> East African habits and life-styles, we would now be considered for-
> eigners.

If I hadn't known Al-Noor, I would have sensed bitterness. But
bitter is exactly what Al-Noor is not. It is my guess that his deep
sense of optimism and security came from his close family ties and
those with the Ismaili community that surrounded him.

Whenever I heard Al-Noor talk about the Ismailis—which he
rarely did when he was at Yale—I was struck by the tremendous
personal support they seemed to give each other in their many
international communities, which now number some 20 million
followers over all. I was also struck by how closely they seemed to
listen to and follow the advice—both spiritual and worldly—of their
leader, the Aga Khan. As a midwestern Protestant of vague denomi-
nation and an even vaguer church attendance, I can't imagine what
it would be like to go off to London, Paris, or Vancouver and find
a whole community and its support system ready to receive me—
doctors, lawyers, the whole bit. I'm sure there must be a drawback,
but part of me deeply longs for this comforting, extended-family
support.

The Ismaili Muslims (who bear as little relationship to Khomeini's
Muslims or the Black Muslims as the Unitarians do to the Seventh-
day Adventists or the Mormons) are a highly educated, progressive,
nonproselytizing sect that is now led by the young and handsome,

Harvard-educated Karim El Husseini Shah, the fourth Aga Khan. A descendant of the prophet Mohammed, he traces his roots down the years to the Fatimid caliphs of Egypt (who held sway in North Africa and Spain in the tenth century) into the Persian court—where the poet Omar Khayyám plied his trade (a good Sufi Ismaili was Omar) —and then into India. At the turn of the twentieth century, the Aga Khans moved to Europe, where they became an established (if, to westerners, a somewhat flamboyant) business and political family. My own childhood memory—completely midwestern USA—brings up visions of the old Aga Khan: looking like a bulbous mountain with a silk turban perched on top, he is seated on an immense scale being weighed so that his loyal followers can give him his enormous weight in diamonds. Or of Ali: dapper and urbane, he is strolling beside the race course at Ascot or Deauville. Or he is leaning languidly on the aft rail of his Mediterranean yacht, while his wife, film star Rita Hayworth, stands statuesquely beside him, smiling radiantly in her latest bathing suit. Oriental opulence and Ali Baba romance.

But Al-Noor tells me it isn't at all like that. The Aga Khans, he says, have been devoted spiritual leaders since 1800 and have looked after their flock with both practical and spiritual wisdom. The diamonds, for instance, were sold and the resulting $3,600,000 given back to the people to fund schools and other community projects. That's a lot better take than that from our midwestern church bingo games! In any case, there seems to be no question that devout Ismailis take the Aga Khan's advice—both spiritual and worldly— very seriously and have profited by it. Wherever they are on the globe, they keep in touch with their imam through the well-equipped councils that oversee the social, economic, and religious well-being of their communities. Al-Noor's father, Abbas, moved his family twice at the advice of the Aga Khan—once when he went to London (Al-Noor was an infant) to expand the family textile business and again three years later, when he somewhat reluctantly returned to Dar es Salaam to help out his brother, who had sought the Aga Khan's counsel. With guidance from the Aga Khan, Abbas originated the first Ismaili *jamatkhana* (prayer house) in London. As eldest son, Al-Noor—except for a brief period when he first came to Yale—has held firmly to this tradition and community.

178

As a writer, Al-Noor was no master of English prose; his sentences frequently wandered all over the place, and bits and pieces of information that belonged in one paragraph would appear suddenly in another three pages later. But Al-Noor had another and rarer gift—he was a born storyteller in the oral tradition. He could spin a tale around a small incident in a way no one else could, leaving the reader not only with a fine story but with all the sights, smells, and sounds of the seacoast on a Dar es Salaam morning or of the Congo jungle at dusk.

He was also the only student I had who wrote successfully about a sexual encounter. I had always warned my students against trying to write about sex; the most veteran writers, I said, ran aground when they tried. Al-Noor proved me wrong, as you will see in "The Overnight Guest."

From the beginning he wrote of himself in the third person—first as Gulam and then as Mustafa—because he felt it gave him the distance he needed to tell a story. He also used fictional first names for his family, which I've also used in this introduction. Hirjl or Jiwan-Hirji is the accurate surname for all.

Because his stories fell naturally into short pieces, we decided that he should keep to his distinctive style and do a series of short tales rather than a single longer one. His biggest writing problem was to make some connections that would help his tales hang together. On these he worked with me for many weeks long after the course was over, finally delivering the last two "connecting" stories on a computer printout a few weeks before this book went to press. So, true to his own tradition, he was late and as gently apologetic as ever. But I could never not forgive Al-Noor, especially since I love his tales and, even more, the gentle and humane spirit that moves them.

179

TALES OF A FOREIGNER
by Al-Noor Tajdin Jiwan-Hirji,
Dar es Salaam, Tanzania

FIRST TALE: THE BIG ESCAPE

Ahmed and Mustafa, the two brothers, were five and six-and-a-half when their parents took them on a trip to the Belgian Congo. They left their home in Dar es Salaam early one morning in the new green Ford "box-body" with the diamond-shaped emblem of the family business painted on the sides. They drove across Tanganyika northwest to Uganda, past Lake Victoria and on into Ruanda-Urundi. Each night, they stayed with business friends of their father. On the tenth day they arrived at Bukavu, a lovely town high in the hills of the eastern Congo. There the parents left the two brothers with a Belgian expatriate family so that they could travel further. The trip would take the parents through pygmy country in the rain forest to Léopoldville, then west to Matadi on the Atlantic coast of Africa. They planned to be gone a week. This seemed a long time to Mustafa and Ahmed.

The brothers didn't know any French and the Belgian family

180

didn't know any English or Kachhi, the Indian language of their grandparents. But since Mustafa and Ahmed were old enough to eat, take baths, and go to bed without help, they could manage. The two brothers could talk to each other and play without words with the Belgian children. Even so, Mustafa and Ahmed were lonely. They talked about why their parents had left them so long with strangers in such a strange place.

Mustafa, the older, was more concerned about being left behind than Ahmed. Since his parents always gave him the respect due to the oldest child, he could never understand why they would not treat him as a grown-up and take him along on their trips. In Dar es Salaam he always felt badly when they went to parties at night and left him at home. He was suspicious that they shared secrets he knew nothing about.

On the second day with the Belgian family, Mustafa decided he and his brother should run away. He told Ahmed, who always listened to him, that they would leave immediately after lunch when everyone in the house was expected to retire to his bedroom for a nap.

The next morning, Mustafa removed himself from the activities of the household. The little boy sat on a rock, legs hunched beneath him, and contemplated the prospect of the getaway. Ahmed, on the other hand, was enjoying himself as usual; he was helping the Belgian father, Monsieur Rolland, feed the hens and ducks and clean out the cages. Mustafa was disconcerted by this. He felt his younger brother should be more concerned with the impending escape.

Lunch was subdued. Nobody talked much and the food tasted bland, so unlike the spiced curries the brothers were used to. Immediately after lunch the two little boys went to their bedroom. A few minutes later, Mustafa, pretending he was going to the bathroom, left his room to make sure that everyone was out of sight. Then he returned for his brother, and very slowly and ever so quietly they dragged their large suitcase through the hallway into the backyard and out to the road. It was hot outside and they were sweating hard, for the suitcase was heavy. Once they had passed the hedge and were on the dusty, rocky road, they could breathe more easily. They talked now and took longer and more frequent stops. They planned to go into Bukavu to the shop of a good friend of their

181

father's, but they didn't know which direction led to town. It never occurred to them to stop a car and ask the way or to try to catch a ride. Hours passed. They grew more and more tired, sweaty, and discouraged.

Someone drove up and stopped beside them. It was Monsieur Rolland. He said nothing but helped them put the burdensome suitcase into the car. The brothers sat next to him and they drove back home in silence. When they arrived, Madame Rolland spanked them for going outside instead of taking a nap. Nothing was said about their attempt to run away.

Later that afternoon they were invited to play blocks with the Belgian children on the sitting room floor. Ahmed joined in. Mustafa sat on a rocking chair, brooding as he watched the others play; he was ashamed of running away and being caught. He stared out of the open windows. A slope stretched down from the house into a valley with a little stream at the bottom. There were clumps of trees on the near side of the stream, and on the other side the land sloped upward again, turning to forest. Evening was coming, and a gentle breeze blew into the room. Inside it was cool, and Mustafa felt a little better.

A smell of hot soup filled the air. The day's excitement had made them hungry. Soon they sat down to eat. Ahmed asked for the pepper and salt in French. Then Mustafa tried, looking at Monsieur Rolland to see if he had said it right. Monsieur Rolland was smiling, and Mustafa smiled for the first time that day. Then the Rolland children began pointing at the different foods and crockery on the table and naming them in French. The two brothers repeated the words. Soon they were all laughing and enjoying each other. The two brothers felt warm and safe.

The next few days went well. Monsieur and Madame Rolland were more parentlike and they all felt better for it. When their own parents returned at the end of the week, nothing was said about the "big escape." Nothing was ever said about it.

SECOND TALE: THE WITCH DOCTOR

As a little boy, Mustafa was very thin. This was a constant source of despair to his parents. At his birth he had weighed seven and a half pounds, and in his first few months he had gained enough weight to win a healthy babies' contest. But somewhere things had gone wrong, and Mustafa grew up skinny. Over the years he was taken to many doctors, who prescribed a variety of exotic diets. One included a half-pound bar of Cadbury's milk-and-nut chocolate to be taken daily; another included a tablespoon of white stout a half hour before meals. The remedies continued.

Mustafa's skinniness was of particular concern to his aunt Dolat-bai, who felt that Mustafa was a reincarnation of her dead father. She was convinced that the devil was keeping Mustafa scrawny to avenge sins committed by his parents. She decided she would have to trick the devil into thinking the boy was not theirs. So Aunt Dolat-bai symbolically bought Mustafa on the installment plan. She deposited one hundred shillings into a special savings account against an eventual 100,000 shilling purchase price. Thus, by her ostensibly owning the boy, the devil would be fooled and would let the boy grow as strong and fat as her dead father. But this remedy didn't work either. Mustafa stayed skinny.

Aunt Dolat-bai, however, was not to be easily discouraged. Over the next few years she took him to several homeopaths, who regularly visited Dar es Salaam from India. Then, one hot afternoon, unbeknownst to his mother, she tried a lady witch doctor, an old African who had been recommended by an Ithnasheri lady. The Ithnasheri had suffered from a chronic ailment. She was treated by many doctors and specialists, who prescribed hundreds of shillings' worth of medicines and injections, and yet she failed to improve. Then she visited Bibi Zainibu, the witch doctor, and was cured in a few days. Bibi Zainibu had established her reputation through her own rebirth. According to the story, she died, and just as her body was being carried off for burial, she sat up in her coffin alive and well again. Because she had been on the other side, she knew the spirits and could talk to them.

Mustafa didn't want to visit the witch doctor, but he was ten, grown-up, and known to be a sensible and obedient boy. He therefore could not refuse his aunt. The office car picked them up, ostensibly for an afternoon ride along the seashore. But instead they headed for a remote place on the outskirts of town. After driving on the main highway to Ubungo for half an hour, they turned off onto a narrow dirt road, which they followed until they reached a clearing shaded by wide mango trees. In the back of the clearing stood a small round hut. Its walls were made of dongo, a native red clay, and its roof was thatched with dry coconut leaves. A cool breeze rustled the leaves but no other sounds could be heard.

The driver was afraid to get out of the car. Along the way, Aunt Dolat-bai had been chatting with him in Swahili and had just finished telling him that the witch doctor had awakened from the dead. He sat determinedly at the wheel, looking with terror at the dongo hut. Beads of sweat dripped from his dark shiny forehead and nose. Aunt Dolat-bai and Mustafa stepped out of the car and walked to the door of the hut.

"*Hodi! Hodi!*" Aunt Dolat-bai called into the darkness.

"*Karibu.*" A sharp cackling voice invited them to enter.

Inside, it took Mustafa a few moments to grow accustomed to the dark. Slowly he made out an old lady with wrinkled black skin, sitting on a stool in the corner. Talking to her in Kiswahili, Aunt Dolat-bai introduced herself, saying she had been sent by Mama Khadija, the Ithnasheri woman. Then she carefully explained how Mustafa could not put on any weight.

"*Kaa mwanangu*" (Sit down, my son), she said, looking at Mustafa and motioning him to the stool next to her. Mustafa did as he was told and Aunt Dolat-bai laid her ungainly body on a bed pushed against the wall. Mustafa watched as Bibi Zainibu mumbled and chanted strange sounds. After a few minutes she stood up and went outside. When she returned, she was clutching an assortment of dry roots and twigs. She sat down on a stool in front of Mustafa, cackled an incantation and waved the twigs rapidly around his head. Then, very suddenly, she was quiet. Mustafa knew she was listening for the devil. When she saw him, she shrieked. The skin on her face tightened and shone and her eyes opened wide. She shook her fist at the devil and screamed her incantations. Then she became calm. The wrinkles returned and her eyes dulled. She put the twigs, which had become wet with the sweat of her hand, in a small piece of newsprint and gave them to Aunt Dolat-bai. She patted Mustafa on the head and whispered instructions to his aunt. "*Atapona, lazima atapona*" (He is sure to be cured), she murmured.

Aunt Dolat-bai dipped into her purse and pulled out a wrinkled-up ten-shilling bill, which she handed to her. *"Zawadi kwa watoto"* (A present for the children), Aunt Dolat-bai said. Mustafa was surprised at this remark, for he had not seen any children around. Later, his aunt explained that the old lady would never have accepted the money for herself, as she was supposed to be a holy person who did not need money.

Back at home, Aunt Dolat-bai brewed a tea out of Bibi Zainibu's twigs and gave it to Mustafa to drink. It tasted sweet. He was then instructed to follow Khalfani, Aunt Dolat-bai's servant, upstairs to the terrace, where Khalfani would sacrifice a chicken. Mustafa watched as Khalfani poised the blade of a knife under the chicken's neck and, with his other hand, pointed toward Mecca chanting *"Bismallah."* Khalfani cut off the chicken's head, and blood spurted as its body struggled in Khalfani's hands and the severed head opened and closed its beak on the floor. When the sacrifice to the devil lay still in Khalfani's hands, he washed the blood off his hands and went away to give the chicken to a poor family. Mustafa was impressed but not frightened. He had seen similar sacrifices in the village.

For a while after this, Aunt Dolat-bai was sure that Mustafa was gaining weight. But the facts were different. Then, one day a few years later, it occurred to Mustafa's mother and all his aunts that, in spite of being skinny, Mustafa had never been sick a single day in his life. Gradually, they gave up trying to make him fat. Today Mustafa is still healthy—and skinny.

THIRD TALE: THE FATHER'S DEATH

Mustafa's father, Abbas, had always wanted to live abroad. At seventeen he had been sent to school in England, but his time there was cut short when his own father died and his brothers asked him to return to Tanganyika to work in the family textile business. Four years later he tried again. With his wife, Zaytoon, and infant son, Mustafa, he returned to England to set up his own import-export business. But in another three years he was again recalled to Dar es Salaam—this time through the advice and recommendation of the Aga Khan, who felt his brothers needed Abbas's help.

Abbas liked the textile business well enough, but he found Dar es Salaam's slow pace stagnant and restricting. So when the textile crisis had passed and the business was doing well, Abbas again entertained the idea of moving to some such place as London, Beirut, Bahrein, Caracas, or Abidjan. But each time he began to make plans, he was discouraged from pursuing them by his older brother and sisters and his widowed mother, who wanted him close by.

After two more children were born, Abbas became even more eager to start a new life elsewhere. He wanted his children to have a better education than they were getting in Tanganyika, and he wanted a new enterprise for himself and his wife. But in choosing a place, he had to be careful that he didn't jeopardize his children's Ismaili training. Abbas himself was a devout Ismaili, a member of a Shi'a sect of Islam. If he settled in a place where there were few Ismailis, he worried that his children would not be adequately exposed to the Ismaili experience and would adopt another religion or, worse still, grow up without any faith at all.

In 1957 some of Abbas's Ismaili friends urged him to move to the Belgian Congo. They told him exciting stories about the beauty and prosperity of the country, and Abbas was eager to find out if it was as good as they said it was. He persuaded his older brother, his sisters, and his mother to let him investigate the Congo by taking a vacation there with his family. After three weeks of traveling to many towns and cities, Abbas and his family fell in love with a mountain town called Bukavu and decided that they wanted to spend the rest of their lives there.

Bukavu was a beautiful town perched on steep hills overlooking Lake Kivu. It had mild temperatures throughout the year and fertile land, densely vegetated and green. A small community of Belgian colonials lived there and they had a good school, taught in French, that was open to the European and Indian children. There was also a mission hospital, an airport close by, and a club with sports facilities. Business was excellent. The few Ismaili families who had settled there had built a *jamatkhana,* where they met daily for their prayers. Their children were instructed in Ismaili history, philosophy, and religious ritual and met at the *jamatkhana* to sing hymns in the evening. This was the ideal spot Abbas had been looking for.

On returning to Dar es Salaam, Abbas tried hard to convince his relatives that moving to Bukavu was a wise decision. They objected strongly, but within a year, when they realized that he was determined, they reluctantly allowed him to proceed. They were very sad, for they felt that they were losing him forever.

Abbas went to Bukavu ahead of his family to make proper living arrangements. Mustafa and his brothers, Ahmed and Shiraz, and their mother followed a few weeks later. They took a plane that stopped at Zanzibar, Tanga, Mombasa, and Nairobi. There they changed planes and went on to Entebbe and Usumbura, finally arriving in Bukavu in the late afternoon. It was hot and sunny when they landed. Mustafa's father waited impatiently for them to pass through customs and then everyone fell into each other's arms. He loved them dearly and had missed them. He told them he had found a beautiful place for them to live in the hills outside Bukavu, but he wouldn't tell them any more about it. He wanted it to be a surprise.

They climbed into an old car and drove for what seemed to Mustafa a very long time. They traversed seven hills. At dusk they arrived at a large farm with a stone farmhouse. The outside walls were covered with red and green creepers, and two immense clumps of bamboo stood on either side of the house. Mustafa and his brothers dashed into the house. There was a fireplace in every room and a huge one in the living room. Abbas led them outside to the garden. In the approaching darkness he showed them rosebushes with large roses of many colors, a hedge of ripe red strawberries, and rows and rows of colorful Roma flowers. The farm had been rented from a retiring Belgian colonel returning to Brussels, and Abbas had the option to buy it. It was a tea plantation and had outbuildings in the back for curing tea.

Since there was no electricity in the house, Mustafa's father went about lighting the kerosene lamps while his mother made hot soup on the wood stove in the kitchen. They ate bread and butter with the soup. Abbas and Zaytoon made beds for their children, and the family slept.

Mustafa loved his first days at Kadaka farm. It was wild and isolated, with hills on one side and forest on the other. He loved watching his father supervise the workers, hoeing the ground and preparing the land for planting. They broke the ground, cleaned out the weeds and grass, and then molded the rich soft soil into rows and

187

beds. Abbas traded salt to the local cowherds for sackfuls of cow dung and planted lettuce, tomatoes, carrots, potatoes, groundnuts, and radishes.

Abbas was enthusiastic about his new life; he knew he was going to make his fortune here. He had already negotiated a number of trade enterprises both in the Congo and abroad. He planned to truck the fresh fruits and vegetables from the farm to Léopoldville, the capital, which was still importing most of its fresh produce from Brussels because transportation was so poor in the area. Abbas planned to purchase his own trucks for this purpose and would be able to sell his produce at much lower costs than that imported from Belgium. In addition, Abbas had acquired the export franchise for strawberries for the entire country and planned to sell Congo strawberries all over the world. He had also agreed to supply Bukavu's restaurants and hotels with fresh lobster from Dar es Salaam. He was full of energy and ideas, and during the next few months his enterprises prospered and his dreams were being realized.

Then, one day, Mustafa's father was summoned to Léopoldville by the Belgian authorities to clarify his immigration status so that he could become a citizen. The day he left, Mustafa and his brothers cried. To make them happy, Abbas took photographs of them and promised to bring them lots of toys from Léopoldville. He kissed them and their mother and went away.

A few days later, at the saddest time of the evening, someone knocked on the door. Mustafa and his mother were in the kitchen and Ahmed and Shiraz were visiting a friend in town. Mustafa went to the door and opened it. It was the Mukhi Sahib, the head of the Ismailis in Bukavu, and four other men prominent in the community. Mustafa was puzzled by the visitors. Mukhi Sahib was a nice man and a good friend of his mother and father. Mustafa usually smiled at him when they met. But something in the man's tone discouraged him. "Is your mother here?" he asked gravely. Mustafa stepped aside and the men walked in and went to the living room, where they sat on the carpet with their legs crossed in front of them.

Mustafa ran to the kitchen and whispered urgently to his mother, "Mukhi Sahib is here." His mother hurried toward the living room but Mustafa ran to his father's room instead. The room was untidy, for his mother had pulled off all the sheets to wash them; the blankets, pillows, and bedspread were rumpled on the bed. He looked out the window. It was rainy outside. A terrible feeling of sadness crept over him. He knew that a horrible thing had happened. He sat on the bed, crossed his legs, and quickly said his DU'a twice. He left the bed and went into the living room, his head down. He looked up at his mother, she looked at him, and he knew in that moment that his daddy had died.

While the men waited in the living room, Mustafa's mother went to the bedroom to pack two suitcases, one with her things and one with her children's. Mustafa watched silently. Her face was taut and her eyes unseeing. She said nothing, and Mustafa felt a heavy silence within him. He heard the men in the living room talking softly in sad voices. When his mother was ready, she went into the living room and asked the men if they would like some tea. They thanked her and said no.

The sky was rapidly growing dark. The night insects had started their loud chorus that would subside as the dark grew deeper and would fade into silence just before the break of day. They climbed into the car. Mustafa looked back at the house; he could barely see it in the dark. As they drove away, the hedges of roses and strawberries looked like strange solemn shadows. He would never see Kadaka farm again.

Mukhi Sahib and Zaytoon left Mustafa in Bukavu at the house where his two brothers had been playing, and then drove on to Léopoldville to recover the body of his father. Ahmed and Shiraz did not seem to realize that sad things had happened, and they were happy to be spending a few more nights with their friend, where they could play exciting games and stay up late. For three days the brothers played, but Mustafa only pretended to. He spent a lot of time by himself, thinking.

Mustafa didn't know what it was to die but he knew that for some unknown reason a person who died never came back and that he would never see his daddy again. He had been told often that a person went up to heaven or down to hell, but he didn't really believe it. Nevertheless, he pretended to himself that he did because if there was a heaven, he knew that's where his father would go and he liked to think of him there. Everyone had liked his father. When they spoke about him, his friends used the word *jolly*, even when they talked in Kachhi. He was always in cheerful spirits and could make others laugh and feel happy and rejuvenated. Mustafa's father was also a strong person. Nanima and Nanabapa, the parents of Mustafa's mother, called him their *simba* (lion).

Mustafa was lonely with his thoughts and was glad when his mother returned. She was five months pregnant, but somehow Mustafa hadn't noticed it before. She had deep hollows under her eyes and looked dark and sad.

Shortly after his mother returned, Mohamedali, the older brother of Mustafa's father, came to Bukavu from Dar es Salaam. While their mother and Mohamedali discussed what the family was going to do next, the three brothers were taken for an ice cream cone at the best hotel in town by a friend of their father. When they returned from their treat, the brothers were told that they would all move back to Dar es Salaam. This had been a hard decision for their mother. She knew that her beloved Abbas would have wanted them to stay in Bukavu where she could send her sons to the Belgian school and where all his other dreams could come true. But her mind was numb with grief and she longed to see her own mother and father in Dar es Salaam, so she didn't argue with her brother-in-law, Mohamedali, who wanted her to return home. She prayed that Abbas would forgive her for being weak in her decision and asked his understanding in her time of weakness.

Their small chartered plane landed at Dar es Salaam at noon. The sun was directly overhead and brought intense heat. The children were hot and tired. A bigger plane, carrying the coffin with the body, landed a few minutes later. Relatives met them at the airport and drove them to Mohamedali's house, where Nanabapa, their mother's father, was waiting at the entryway on the street. Nanabapa was crying. His whole body shook as he held his daughter close to him.

They walked down the narrow corridor leading to the house, passing a concrete seat with *Abbas* engraved on it in handwriting. He had etched his name there many years before when the concrete was still wet. Inside the house they climbed a short flight of stairs to a dark landing with two large mirrors, one facing up and the other facing down. A line of mourners shuffled past, looking dull in the dark mirrors.

190

Two huge rooms had been emptied of all furniture. The male relatives and friends sat in one and the females in the other. Straw mats borrowed from the *jamatkhana* were rolled out on the floor to sit on. Mustafa went into the room where the men were sitting and sat close beside an uncle, who treated him as a grown person. Although no one spoke directly to Mustafa, the men talked quietly among themselves about his father's death and he was able to learn how it had happened. Abbas, they said, had been visiting the store of a friend and had told him that he was not feeling well. His friend had urged him to see a doctor, and just as he was leaving for the doctor's office, he had suffered a heart attack. His friend had rushed to help him but it was too late. The doctor who later examined the body said that although Abbas had been only thirty-three, his heart looked as if it belonged to a man of sixty-six. That was how hard Abbas had dreamed and worked and lived.

Mustafa felt very sad. He could hear his brothers in a nearby room playing and giggling with their cousins, whom they had not seen in a long time. Mustafa did not feel like playing. Just before the funeral began, he heard the other children leave for an aunt's house, but he stayed close to his uncle, and before long the men went into the room where the women were sitting.

Then Abbas's body was brought in and placed on the floor. It had been washed and wrapped in soft white cotton cloth. The Mukhi Sahib sat on one side of Abbas's body, near his face. There was a hush. First the widow, then the closest relatives and friends went forward and, one by one, knelt on the other side of Abbas's face and asked that God forgive Abbas any sins that he might have committed against them. As they came forward, the Mukhi Sahib sprinkled their faces with holy water. Mustafa stood just outside the door and watched. When everyone was finished, the body was put in its coffin and carried out of the room. As the coffin moved down the hall, Mustafa's great-aunt rushed toward it, crying, "Where are you taking my poor Abbas?" She was held back and she wept. Others wept. Then the funeral procession left the house, and Mustafa joined his uncle and the other men in a long line behind the coffin. The leader of the procession sang a strong mournful chant which the believers repeated in unison over and over again:

191

La illah Ha Illah la
La illah Ha Illah la
La illah Ha Illah la
Muhammed U Rasullulah

The procession wound its way slowly to the cemetery by the sea, where a grave had been dug. The body of Mustafa's father was carefully lifted out of the coffin, placed in the grave, and a wooden plank laid on top of it. Then, with a shovel, each man in turn replaced the earth and covered the body. Mustafa did not move close to the grave nor try to see his father's face again. A prayer was said in Arabic and the funeral was over.

That night Mustafa slept with his mother, his little arm around her waist. He knew she was sad and he wanted to comfort her as he knew his daddy would. In the middle of the night she woke up, and he woke up with her. She looked frightened, and he told her he would look after her like his daddy had. She looked deep into his eyes and stroked his face. Then they fell asleep.

FOURTH TALE: DADABAPA AND THE TEA LEAVES

After his father died, Mustafa had gone with his mother and brothers to live at her parent's house in Oysterbay on the outskirts of Dar es Salaam. Soon after they moved in with their grandparents, his brother Aboo was born. There were now four sons in the family—Mustafa, Ahmed, Shiraz, and Aboo.

Oysterbay was the part of Dar es Salaam near the sea, where most of the English and other Europeans lived. Many of the large houses had red stucco roofs, open verandas, and well-tended gardens with large hedges. The roads were lined with baobabs and Indian almond trees, whose wide leaves provided a cool shade that broke the heat of the sun. On the seashore nearby, the palms bore coconuts, the sand was pure white, and the Indian Ocean breeze blew gently. It was a lovely place to live.

Fatima, Mustafa's grandmother, ran a large household that included his mother's four unmarried sisters, an unmarried brother, and the wives and children of two other brothers who were out of the country on business. Frequently, there were additional aunts, uncles, and cousins visiting from Kenya, Uganda, or Tanganyika. Very early each morning the house emptied. Mustafa and the other children were taken to school; Mustafa's mother and the other adults were driven in the Mercedes to work, leaving Fatima, her servants, and the ayah to run the house and look after the baby, Aboo.

School lasted until one o'clock. At lunch the house overflowed with children and they all sat with their elders around a huge table that seated twenty—with Grandfather Ali at the head. After lunch Fatima would escape to her bedroom in a cooler part of the house to rest for a few hours. (But not before she had locked up the pantry!) The seven children would play marbles, make kites, play *iti-dandi* (a cross between juggling and cricket), *nagori* (a mixture of dodge ball and hide-and-seek), or scavenge the neighborhood for luscious fruit —guava, mango, tamarind, or *sita-far*. Sometimes the older children would go "out back" to play zanzibari—a card game—with the old family retainers, their wives, and visitors. There was always something wonderful to do.

In the garden, apart from the blossoms of jasmine, bougainvillaea, champelli, and thorny tamarind (tended by the loving green thumb of Fatima), there was a vegetable patch—peas, beans, groundnuts, maize, and cassava—which the children maintained in a fairly respectable fashion. The chicken coop was open so that the birds had free run of the yard. Robin, the Alsatian, who liked chasing the chickens, was kept tied on a long rope. The favorite pet, however, was Kasuko, the Congolese parrot, who conversed in the evenings with Grandfather Ali in four languages—Gujarati, Kachhi, Swahili, and English—while everybody else watched with delight.

During the long holidays the children spent most mornings at the beach—swimming, collecting shells, building sand castles, or exploring the wide reefs and pools exposed at low tide. On Sundays all the cousins were taken as a special treat to the town drive-in for spicy snacks—pani-puri, mishkaki, and seeq, washed down by sweet-tasting iced passion fruit juice. Then there was the leisurely drive along Ocean Road to Oysterbay and home.

Evenings were very special to Mustafa. On Fridays and special holy days the whole family went to town to the *jamatkhana* for prayers. But on other evenings, after sunset prayers, the grown-ups and children would often gather on the veranda, enjoying the cool night breeze, and telling each other stories. Mustafa loved to hear his mother, Zaytoon, tell stories of his father, Abbas. He remembered Abbas well, but Ahmed and Shiraz were too young when he died to have much memory of him. So Mustafa would often help Zaytoon tell the others stories of their life on the farm at Kadaka in the Congo and how his father had started a strawberry export business. But none of the boys—including Mustafa—knew much about Dadabapa, their father's father, for he had died long before any of them were born. So one night in the soft twilight, after they had talked for a while about their beloved father, Zaytoon told them about Dadabapa and the tea leaves—a story she'd heard from her husband many times, but which Mustafa heard for the first time that night.

Dadabapa, she said, had sent their father to study in England when he was seventeen. Abbas had boarded a large seaplane in Dar es Salaam harbor, not far from where they were now sitting on their veranda. (She pointed into the dusk toward the sea.) In England, Abbas attended a technical college run by Imperial Chemical Industries, where he learned various cottage industry skills—such as how to make strawberry jam, can fruits, tan leather, print textiles by hand —many of which he used later on the Congo farm. Abbas loved England and his studies, but he was lonely for his family so he was delighted when Dadabapa came to visit him in the early summer. Together they toured all of Europe, visiting Dadabapa's friends in the textile business and sight-seeing.

One day they were waiting for a flight to Brussels at Fiumicino airport near Rome. They were having tea in the airport restaurant when an Italian, dressed neatly in a gray suit, white shirt, and black bow tie, came over to their table and introduced himself. He said he was a fortune teller and could predict the future by studying the tea leaves left in the bottom of a teacup. Could he, he asked, read their future for them?

Dadabapa was a generous man. He knew the Italian needed money badly, and though he was deeply religious and did not believe in superstitions, he consented. In broken English, the Italian thanked Dadabapa effusively and then, sitting down, asked for

Dadabapa's now drained teacup. He peered into it carefully, handling the cup so as not to disturb the pattern of the leaves in the bottom. Suddenly, he looked startled and frowned. He turned to Dadabapa and said gravely that it would be dangerous for Dadabapa to travel north that day.

"Where you fly?" he asked in broken English.

"Brussels," replied Dadabapa.

"That north! Don't go today." He pleaded with Dadabapa: there was another flight to Brussels early in the morning on the very next day; Rome was the most beautiful city in the world; they could easily stay over for one night.

Dadabapa smiled. The Italian insisted. Dadabapa shook his head firmly. At that moment the loudspeaker announced the boarding of the Brussels flight and Dadabapa took out a five-lire note, paid the Italian, and said good-bye. As he and Abbas walked toward the gate, they turned back to wave. The Italian was very upset. He waved back and then, with his head down and muttering to himself, he walked away.

The sky was clear above Rome and the day lovely. After a while, Dadabapa left his seat and went forward to chat with an elderly Jewish couple he had met at the ticket counter. As the plane approached Brussels, the weather clouded in and heavy winds and rain began to buffet the airplane. All passengers were requested to return to their seats and fasten their seat belts. Dadabapa wasn't worried, nor was Abbas; the weather was not much worse than other rainstorms they had flown through safely. But then, rather suddenly, they were enveloped in very thick fog, and a few minutes later they heard that the pilot had lost all contact with ground control. The plane circled, trying to pick up radio contact and find its way to the airport. The passengers sat very still—tense and silent. In a short while the pilot announced on the loudspeaker that the plane was nearly out of fuel and that he was going to make an emergency landing in a small clearing. Dadabapa and Abbas looked out the window and saw they were flying very very low, just above the treetops. The engines started sputtering. The plane found the clearing and dropped lower; they could see the trees above the wingtips. They were just touching ground when the plane jerked suddenly to the left and a sound of ripping metal rent the air above the sound of the storm. The left wing had struck a tree and had torn off. The plane spun around on its undercarriage and stopped.

Most of the passengers were knocked unconscious by the landing. Thick smoke began to fill the plane. An air hostess grabbed Abbas, who was conscious, and Dadabapa directed them to a hole that had been torn open in the tail of the plane. Then Dadabapa went forward to see if he could help his Jewish friends. Abbas was outside the plane before he realized that neither his father nor the air hostess had followed him. He turned around just in time to see a flaming piece of wreckage fall over the hole he had escaped through. He ran back toward the plane, but two pilots—the only others outside the plane—ran after him and dragged him away. He screamed and struggled to free himself, but they held him tight, shouting that the plane was about to explode.

Then Abbas saw something he would never forget. Dadabapa was looking out from a window of the plane. He was knocking on it not so much to escape now as to wave good-bye to his beloved son. With one final heave, Abbas freed himself from the pilots. The plane blew up. Abbas screamed and then fell to his knees weeping.

For a long time the brothers and their mother sat still on the veranda, looking out at the lights in Dar es Salaam harbor. For many weeks thereafter they talked about Dadabapa and the tea leaves.

FIFTH TALE: IN THE NATIONAL SERVICE

Politics entered Mustafa's life for the first time when he was eleven. In that year Tanganyika became an independent state. The country was swept by a nationalistic fervor, and Mustafa, along with his classmates, was propelled into a deep loyalty to the new nation. He dreamed of the time when he would grow up and serve his country. He would become a farmer, a teacher, or better still, a fisheries expert to increase the supply of protein for the deficient diet of his people.

His aunt Roshan—his mother's youngest sister—had similar dreams. She was exactly his age and as caught up in the new national-ist spirit as he was. When, two years later, they both graduated from

196

primary school and took the territorial exam, they both passed with flying colors into high school at a time when there were so few schools that only one of every six students who qualified could obtain a secondary education. This privilege heightened their sense of duty to their new country.

Both were studying the same subjects at school—Mustafa at the Agakhan Boys' School and Roshan at the Agakhan Girls' School— and they frequently competed in debates or dramatic competitions between the two schools. Although their families were in business and, by tradition, capitalists, both Roshan and Mustafa were fervent socialists and carefully studied Nyerere's white papers on socialism and self-reliance. Wholeheartedly they espoused the new emphasis on the equality of all human beings and the idea that the nation should be run by its 99 percent black majority, who for so long had been the exploited group in the former British-run trust territory. Both were inspired by Nyerere and both were excited by the idea of helping their new country become strong and healthy. When, in 1964, Tanganyika joined Zanzibar to become Tanzania, both thought of themselves as Tanzanian citizens to their fingertips.

But in their idealism, neither reckoned with their Indian heritage, and that oversight was to bring both up short when they entered their army training.

After graduating from high school, Roshan was sent for her six-months national service training to Oljoro, a camp in the coffee country of northern Tanzania near Mount Kilimanjaro. Mustafa was sent west to Bulombola, a farm camp on the shores of Lake Tanganyika.

When Mustafa arrived at Bulombola, the sun was setting over Lake Tanganyika and into the mountains of the Congo beyond. As he got off the Land-Rover, he could smell the rich, lush earth—thick with vegetation—and he was happy. He would be working on the farm, growing food for his country; he would be helping his homeland. He would be living and working—twenty-four hours a day— with black Tanzanians from all parts of the country. In Dar es Salaam, he had been surrounded almost exclusively by Indians both at school and at his mosque. But unlike many other Indians, who tended to look down upon Africans, Mustafa had been brought up by his religious mother to be an egalitarian and found it natural to

197

be one. In every way, Mustafa was exhilarated with anticipation for his new experience.

"Muhindi njoo hapa," a friendly NCO called out to him from the administration tent. Mustafa was shocked. *Muhindi* was the Swahili word for Indian. Was he not a Tanzanian now? Why should he be singled out as an Indian? Anxiously, he walked over to the NCO and stood at attention. The sergeant put him at ease, gave him a bedroll and uniform, and directed him to his tent.

That night in the mess hall he was referred to again several times as *Muhindi.* Mustafa knew it was not intended derisively, but it bothered him. He didn't want to be singled out constantly as an Indian. Later that night, as he lay on the ground on his bedroll, he thought of the history of his country and began to realize that it was not going to be easy to be accepted as a native Tanzanian. Although he had been born in Tanganyika, as his parents had before him, he knew he looked different from the other Tanzanians, had a different religion, ate different food, and spoke English, Gujarati, and Kachhi as well as Swahili. He also began to realize that he was likely to be resented because his Indian origins implied that he came from a merchant family. Businessmen were not popular in socialist Tanzania. BUT, on the other hand (he rationalized before he finally fell asleep), there was tremendous diversity in Tanzania; it had over 124 different ethnic groups and languages; and "being Tanzanian" was still an idea in the process of being formulated. Hadn't Nyerere spoken of abolishing racism and discrimination and unifying EVERYONE? Surely this included the Indians, even though they made up only one percent of the population? It would take time, but it could be done. He would have to work hard for it. He wanted desperately to be accepted as a Tanzanian. To have a country.

As the days passed, although the *Muhindi* label never went away, Mustafa enjoyed himself more and more. He made good friends with his fellow Tanzanians, especially those who shared his tent: Paul from Moshi, Felix from Arusha, and Ponda from the Coast. He made a conscious effort to minimize his differences. Although, unlike most, he was a city boy and slight (Aunt Dolat-bai's incantations had never brought results!), he pretended that he was not exhausted by the five-mile cross-country run at 4:00 A.M., the long mornings of farm work, and the afternoons of military duty. He was getting physically tougher, and he was surprised and delighted at his greater capacities. In the evenings he volunteered to lead the singing of patriotic songs in Swahili that followed the political lectures in the mess hall. He was annoyed with and avoided the few other Tanzanians of Indian descent who were in the camp. Most of them had been reluctant to join the National Service and they would bribe the poorly paid officers with cigarettes for medical excuses from the military exercises.

But Mustafa's efforts to change his label were of little use. One night in the mess hall he found himself in an argument with his friend Paul. "Why," asked Mustafa, "do you keep calling me *Muhindi*? I am Tanzanian like you."

"Yes," said Paul, "you are—but I am Masai as well!"

Mustafa was not a member of any African tribe, nor could he ever become one. At that moment he realized fully that the new national identity would take a long time to become real—if it could be achieved at all. The tribal identity still took precedence, and no matter how many generations a "foreign family" had lived in the country, it would still be considered a family of outsiders if it had no tribal ties. It would take time to overcome barriers planted in minds for so many decades.

Roshan returned from Oljoro with similar experiences. Both now were less naïve and physically tougher. Their time with their fellow Tanzanians had made them more Tanzanian than ever; they now had friends from other parts of the country with whom their own lives connected. Roshan was admitted to University College in Dar es Salaam and eagerly looked forward to continuing her Tanzanian experiences. Mustafa, who had in his late high school years become interested in economics, had applied to Yale, a university known for its good economics department. In his last few weeks at Bulombola, he received word that he had been accepted.

He was torn. He felt disloyal and guilty at the thought of leaving Tanzania to pursue an American education at a time when most of his friends stayed and attended the University of East Africa. But he knew his was a tremendous opportunity that few received and, in the end, decided to go. He vowed that he would get the best education possible, study very hard, and then return to serve his country. In the meantime, Roshan would keep him closely informed about Tanzania.

SIXTH TALE: MUSTAFA AND THE BLACK PANTHERS

When Mustafa was accepted at Yale, Zaytoon decided to move to England for a few years to be near her two middle sons, Ahmed and Shiraz, who had been sent there to boarding school a few years earlier. Mustafa and Aboo helped her close their apartment in Dar es Salaam, and then the three of them traveled to Kenya, Uganda, and Israel to say good-bye to friends and relatives in that part of the world. After they arrived in London, Mustafa had only one short month's reunion with Ahmed and Shiraz before he had to say good-bye to them all—aunts and uncles living in London, his newly found brothers, and finally Zaytoon and Aboo.

It was midnight when Mustafa's plane left London for New York. He was frightened, for he knew that he would now be separated from his mother and brothers for at least four years. Except for his army service, he had never been away from home for more than a few weeks. He looked down at the receding lights of London. He missed his beloved family already and felt a bit like crying. But he didn't.

On the other hand, Mustafa was ready for new adventures and eager to experience life outside the close Ismaili communities he had always lived in. So by the time his plane had landed at Kennedy Airport (it was still midnight on this side of the Atlantic), he had put aside his loneliness and looked forward to seeing what would come next. In the limousine on the way to New Haven, he could hardly believe that American roads were so wide and that Americans talked so much slang and so fast. By the time he arrived with all his luggage at the huge Gothic gate to Calhoun College it was three o'clock in the morning. But he was delighted. He felt he was entering a medieval fortress and an entirely new world. The gate was locked, but a sign scratched in pencil on a cardboard carton dangled down, saying, "Welcome to the Calhoun Hilton—pull string." Mustafa couldn't find the string, so he shouted up to an open window. A baby-faced boy in shorts came down, led him to a room, and gave him clean linen, a blanket, and a pillow. Since it was forty-eight hours since Mustafa had slept, he lay down without making the bed and pulled the blanket over him. He was happy to be in America, happy to be at Yale.

The next day he made his way to the Old Campus, where all freshmen at Yale lived, and was shown to his permanent rooms at 394 Farnam Hall. His roommates had arrived before him. Thurgood, a tall and lanky youth, was from northern California, and Stewart, short and stocky, was from Garden City, Long Island. As the weeks passed, Mustafa learned more about them. Thurgood was an Episcopalian, the son of a banker, and deeply interested in politics. After college he planned to enter the diplomatic corps and eventually become president—nothing was too good for Thurgood! He soon joined the Yale Political Union as a member of the Republican party. Thurgood thought he was thoroughly acquainted with East Africa, since he had once taken a trip there with his parents to visit a brother, a Peace Corpsman in Kenya. Thurgood was always well organized and never perturbed by anything around him.

Stewart was a Catholic and an excellent photographer. His ambition was to become a photojournalist for the *National Geographic* magazine. He also had a fine singing voice and soon joined a college singing group. In his senior year, he became a Whiffenpoof. Both Thurgood and Stewart were highly accomplished put-down artists. Their favorite tease for Mustafa was that they would invade Tanzania and install him as the president. Mustafa was not amused—principally because he could never think of a remark cutting enough to shut them up.

Give or take his roommates, Mustafa felt suddenly liberated at Yale. Nothing had the recognizable limits he was used to. The scale of everything was bigger; ideas ranged widely; the academic pace breathless; and the variety of things to do was almost infinite. He was fascinated with this new style of living. For the first time in his life he found himself questioning and experimenting with some of the basic tenets he had always lived by. He was now cut off from the religion he had practiced since early childhood, from his culture and its mores, and his mother—the nucleus around which he had stabilized himself for so long. With great trepidation, he stopped saying his morning and evening prayers. He wanted to see what would happen. He disliked tobacco smoke and so never tried breaking that taboo but he started taking sips of alcoholic drinks when they were offered to him. He tried eating pork, ham, and bacon, but after so many years of not doing so, he always had stomachaches whenever he did and soon stopped trying. He had a hard time making friends with his roommates and found it easier to make friends with upperclassmen and foreign students, whose very non-American-ness encouraged a certain solidarity.

And of course he had to contend with his nationality. At Yale, no matter how hard he tried, most people would not recognize him as a Tanzanian—nor for having anything to do with Tanzania. He was consistently introduced as Indian (or Persian or Arab), even after he had explained many times that he had never been to India and had been born and raised in Tanzania. He found it most difficult of all to explain this to his black American friends, for he felt they believed that all *real* Africans were black. Moreover, he was often ashamed to admit his Indian ancestry to well-informed black students, because they, he presumed, knew that Indians had been one of the groups who "exploited" Tanzania during colonial times. When he told them where he was from, he could detect distrust in their eyes and felt ill at ease.

Such was Mustafa's situation when the upcoming trial of Bobby Seale and the Black Panthers began to focus national attention on New Haven. During the pretrial hearings in the fall of 1969 and the early winter of 1970 there had been disjointed rumblings about whether or not the Panthers would be given a fair trial or would be "ripped off" again by "the pigs," Nixon, and "Whitey." (Mustafa was amazed at the colorful slang; indeed he had a hard time translating it.) The Panther Defense Committee, established in town by white radicals, began sending out leaflets, declaring that an immense rally would be held on May 1 to end the trial.

By early spring the whole town had become tense. The newspapers reported that other radical groups from across the nation—the Weathermen, the November Action Coalition, Youth Against War and Fascism—had singled out New Haven for a massive May Day demonstration. Signs scrawled on walls in Philadelphia, Chicago, and Cambridge proclaimed: "Blow up Yale—May Day 1970," "Come to New Haven for a Burning on May Day." In mid-April the newspapers predicted that some 50,000 demonstraters would march on New Haven—among them the Hell's Angels from California. Rumors were rife about Molotov cocktails, tear gas, bombs, the National Guard. Then one day two Panthers who were observing the pretrial hearings were sentenced to six months in jail for talking in the courtroom. This harsh treatment by the judge mobilized the students into action. The following day a huge student rally was held in Harkness Hall, calling for a moratorium on classes. On the day following, the "strike" was ratified by a majority of students who voted in meetings held in their residential colleges. But nobody knew what the faculty would do or whether classes would really continue or not. Mustafa attended the strike meeting in Calhoun College and then returned to his room to inform his roommates.

Stewart was there with two friends from his high school days. Thurgood was stretched out on the expensive sofa he had bought. When Mustafa breathlessly broke the news of the strike, they all remained blasé—if not snide—and started teasing him again about becoming president of Tanzania.

"Are you going to classes tomorrow?" Mustafa asked.

"Of course we are!" Stewart replied smartly. He laughed loudly and they began to tease Mustafa about being a revolutionary with nefarious intentions. Mustafa was hurt and angry. He had only been trying to give them the news. He couldn't understand why, no matter how hard he tried, he couldn't be friendly with his American roommates without being made a butt of their jokes. Nor could he understand how they could be so little concerned with the momentous events unfolding around them.

He retired to his room and stared out the window. He could see the New Haven green, where the demonstrators would mass for the rallies; he could also see the courthouse, where the Panther hearings were being held. In his mind he pictured bombs, bullets, tear gas, and explosions. He didn't know where he fit into all this. He knew he sympathized with the blacks in his country; he felt closely aligned with his good friends Felix and Ponda. Were the blacks here equally deprived of their rights and opportunities? He thought so, but he had not studied the history of blacks in America and he didn't know exactly how the Panthers fit into the overall black movement. He did feel that the judge's six-month sentence, just for mumbling in court, was outrageously severe and highly prejudiced. Could he count himself as one of the blacks here? But the black student groups would not accept him. He could certainly understand that; he knew so little about politics and he had never had their experiences. But he had even less in common with the white student organizers, who were mostly suburban, middle-class, and—after all—white, which he was not. He felt he belonged nowhere.

He determined that he would learn as much as he could. During the next week, while 75 percent of the student body remained absent from classes, there were workshops and rap sessions everywhere. Mustafa attended every meeting he could and assiduously collected and read as much of the literature as possible. It was so confusing! Everybody's position seemed to be changing all the time. Moreover, he didn't dare speak out at meetings or sign any petitions. His foreign student friends had told him that CIA informers were attending all meetings and that petitions were copied and filed in the national internal security data banks. As a foreign student, he was warned, he could be deported with no questions asked.

Mustafa was in a most distressing position; he could neither truly join in the strike nor remain apart from it. He felt rejected and alone and lived in private anguish. He began to spend more time in bed. The old questions came nagging back at him. Who was he? Tanzanian? Indian? English?—English was his first language. He didn't feel American although he felt more sympathetic to the Americans day by day. Who was he?

As May Day approached, the trickle of outside visitors became a flood. The speeches grew louder and more violent. Hundreds of guns were stolen from a truck outside New Haven; someone started a fire in the underground Law School Library; an explosive chemical was taken from one of the chemistry labs. The shops on Broadway and York Street began to board up their windows. Everyone was certain that violence was about to erupt. Many students left town. Parents were calling those that remained, urging them to leave. Stewart and Thurgood removed their stereo equipment from their first-floor rooms, put strips of tape across the window panes to prevent them from shattering, and then left for Garden City. They wanted Mustafa to go with them.

Mustafa was determined to stay. He wanted to because he believed in the strike and the nonviolent way the students planned to handle the march on New Haven.

May Day came. Huge parachutes hung from the trees, festively decorating the Old Campus; posters were tacked everywhere; students were manning food tables for out-of-town demonstrators in the courtyards of every college. The crowds—students and outsiders —milled around in the sun, talking and eating. It was like a big picnic. But the atmosphere was still tense in anticipation of the demonstrations to come. Throughout the day and evening, Mustafa wandered from one speech to the next. He listened to rock bands on the Old Campus; heard playwright Jean Genet speak in French on the green; saw Jean-Luc Godard's latest film in Saybrook College; listened to Jerry Rubin scream "Fuck Richard Nixon" in Woolsey Hall and Abbie Hoffman hurl invectives and obscenities in Stiles College. In the late afternoon, he watched the National Guard mass their army along York Street in front of Davenport College. A few students yelled insults at the guardsmen, who didn't move a muscle. The worst was expected when darkness fell.

When the tear gas began later that night, Mustafa was in the Branford courtyard. Earlier he had seen people running toward Elm Street and had heard that some outside group had started a march on the green—forbidden territory after sunset—and that the police were mobilized and confronting the demonstrators. People with gas masks rushed by him. He decided to return to the Old Campus. It, too, was crowded with people and filled with tear gas. A Panther was speaking from the platform and Allen Ginsburg sat cross-legged behind him, intoning in a deep bass voice, "Oomm, Oomm," while someone washed out his eyes with a wet rag. From the street he could hear more shouts and scufflings as the police and demonstrators met head on. The whole scene was bizarre. Mustafa felt he was wandering in a dream or had been caught in a Jean Cocteau film.

Moreover, he could barely see. He made his way to a first-aid station, where a doctor from the Yale–New Haven Hospital washed out his eyes. After resting awhile, he returned to his room. Gas was still strong in the Old Campus, but everything was quiet—only a few people wandered about. Shortly after midnight he fell asleep.

The next morning, everybody seemed cheered up. Not as many

out-of-town demonstrators as expected had shown up, and—in spite of a bomb explosion in Ingalls Rink—nobody was hurt in the melee of the night before. There was still another rally on the green to come, but nobody expected much to happen. The Panthers themselves were asking everyone to "cool it," and the visiting Yippees and white radicals couldn't go against them. The Panthers and the Yale students had won the day.

Mustafa wandered around among the groups hanging out in the sunny college courtyards discussing the "revolution," but his mind was having its own dialogue. Tomorrow his roommates would be returning and everything would return to normal, but he was still fighting the battle of his nationality. Mustafa was depressed. A revolt was going on inside his head. Who was he? He told himself that he would have to accept that he was not a "normal" Tanzanian, nor would he ever be accepted as one. Nor, for that matter, was he a "normal" Indian. He could call himself, he supposed, an East African Indian with a Middle Eastern religion. But that didn't quite fit. Besides, he was growing tired of labels—especially national labels. He reminded himself that he had once wanted to be accepted as an Ismaili among Ismailis; then as a Tanzanian among Tanzanians and now as a student, like any American, among his college mates. He realized that none of that was going to work. He was a blend of almost as many cultures as he spoke languages—Gujarati, Kachhi, Swahili, English, French. He was himself—part Ismaili, part Indian, part Tanzanian, part European, and soon, inevitably, part American. Such, he reassured himself, was a rich heritage and would give him a special view of the world and its peoples. Nations were fickle; they formed and unformed. He had been born in this world; the world would endure and the world would be his home. Why label himself with any nationality? He would be a citizen of the world.

In the meantime, he decided, he would return to his religious practices and his responsibilities as the eldest son in his close-knit family. This would give him a deeper sense of his own personal history.

That night he said his prayers. Mustafa was feeling better.

The Monday after May Day a friend introduced him to another student.

"What are you?" the student asked.

"I am from Tanzania," Mustafa replied.

"Is that in India?" the student asked.

"No," replied Mustafa, "that's in East Africa, but my grandparents were Indian immigrants to East Africa at the turn of the century, so I look Indian."

He was smiling broadly as he spoke. That was enough of an explanation for the student. But Mustafa knew exactly who he was. At last, it was all all right. He hoped the Panthers would be all right, too, and that their trial would proceed with justice.

SEVENTH TALE: THE OVERNIGHT GUEST

It was eleven o'clock Saturday night. Mustafa had been struggling with an art assignment for three hours and was getting nowhere. He was supposed to divide a small photograph into squares and transfer the image onto a larger sheet of paper with larger squares. He couldn't make it work and was becoming more and more frustrated. A light spring breeze was blowing, and Mustafa was tempted by the sounds of a rock band playing in Davenport College across the street. Disgusted with himself, he threw down his pencil and left his lodgings.

As he entered the Davenport courtyard, Mustafa took a deep breath of the wisteria air. He sighed. He loved Davenport College with its Georgian red brick walls and white doors and windows, and in particular, he loved the courtyard—especially at night, when floodlights illuminated the clock and gold dome of Pierson Tower. It was a lovely place.

The rock band was playing in the common room and students, either drunk or wrecked on drugs, were lying on the thick carpet all around. Mustafa spotted a few seniors whom he'd met on a plane from Europe a few days before and went to join them. They were grouped around a huge box of potato chips. When the band was taking a break, a girl came over to get some potato chips and Mustafa started talking to her. She chatted easily—about the potato chips, about the rock band, about herself. Her name was Dana, she was from Mount Holyoke, and she and a girlfriend had come down to Yale for the weekend.

He asked her if she had a place to stay that night and offered her a spare room if she needed one. As he said this, he wondered about his motives. Was he propositioning her? he asked himself. No, he was just being helpful. He wouldn't do anything bad to her; he could rely on his sense of good intention. After all, she was from out of town and might need a place to stay.

Dana looked at him. "Is your place far from here?" she asked.

"No," he said. "Right across the street. It's not a Yale building, but it's on campus."

"Are you sure you have room?"

"Of course I do. One of my housemates has gone away for the weekend, so I can borrow his room and you can have mine." The band started playing again. They had to shout to hear each other.

"Would you like to go someplace where we can dance?" Mustafa asked her. She said she would. It was quiet outside and cool. As they walked toward Branford College, he looked at her a little more. She was pretty, with brown eyes, rounded features, and short brown hair that hung loose. She was of medium height, slim but with soft edges. She walked without much grace, and her worn-out blue jeans and sweatshirt were covered by an expensive-looking blue coat with shiny metal fastenings. She wore dirty tennis shoes. At Branford they danced for a while, but it was hot inside and so they soon decided to leave. It was a clear night with a mild breeze. In a few minutes they had walked down Park Street to Mustafa's place.

The big clapboard house was owned by St. Thomas More Church next door. Originally white, it was now quite gray and run-down; half the shutters were missing. But for Mustafa it had a friendly feeling, and he loved his place. Over the years it had been occupied by many different kinds of people. At one time Carmelite nuns had lived there; at another, it had been a two-family house. Except for Mustafa, who was a sophomore, the present occupants were all graduate students from a variety of countries and a variety of academic disciplines. There were pot smokers and alcoholics, guilt-ridden compulsive workers, and perennial goof-offs like Mustafa. There was Dolph, who was the coordinator of the Gay Alliance and a savior to the many homosexuals who confided in him. There was Matt and his girlfriend Alice, who were always looking for handouts—especially of dope from the guy upstairs who worked at the post office. There was the Italian who had been brought up in Belgium and spoke English with the "blokes" and "mates" idiom of a rugby player. Mustafa found the variety of friends who lived in the house endlessly interesting.

When Mustafa and Dana arrived at the house, nobody else was around. Everyone was either asleep or away. They went to his room, which was right next to the front door. It was small but adequate. It had a bed, which he always kept neat, an old cupboard, and a closet in a sloping section of the ceiling. He had made a table out of a board propped up by the radiator on one end and two spindly metal legs on the other. He had a chest of drawers, a rickety little folding chair, and a big black chair with a stuffed red seat, which he'd taken from the laundry room in Pierson College. Hangings from Tanzania and posters from Poland decorated the walls. An old big table lamp with a massive shade gave the room a warm feeling.

Conversation flowed freely between them. Dana admired his Polish posters and so Mustafa told her about his latest trip to Poland to see Natasha, his longtime Polish pen pal. Because he had just returned, he talked a lot about Natasha and how they'd first written to each other when they were twelve, he in Dar es Salaam and she in Warsaw. He showed her pictures of Africa and Europe and his vacation trip to the Mexican pyramids. Dana seemed interested in all he talked about. A friendly but innocent atmosphere pervaded the little room.

As it was growing late, he offered her a towel and an old pair of pajamas and showed her the bathroom. She was grateful. While she was showering, he straightened up the room. She came out feeling refreshed and thanked him again. She had used his bottle of cologne. He kissed her good-night on the cheek and pointed to the door across the hall where he would be sleeping if she needed anything. He closed the door behind him and went off to wash.

Mustafa wondered if she wanted him to make love to her. Was that the reason she had come to Yale in the first place? Was that why she had accepted his offer to put her up for the night? He didn't really know. For himself, it would be fine. It wasn't that he felt any active physical desire just then. It was just that he knew that he could make love to her if she wanted him to. He liked sex and knew it was good for him. But he decided not to impose himself. He felt he had made an innocent offer of a place to stay; that had been his original intention and that was what it should remain.

But what if he didn't try? Maybe she really wanted him to. Wouldn't he look foolish if he didn't even approach her? But if he did, he might lose her friendship and trust. What would an American have done in his place? He didn't know just what the cultural requirement was in this case.

He was at a loss. He was barefoot and dressed for bed. Silently he paced up and down the little hallway in front of her door. If she really desired him, perhaps she would come look for him. But on the other hand, she might not dare approach him even if she wanted to; she might feel that was being too forward.

Mustafa saw himself as host. It was dishonorable to take advantage of his position. He knew what his hero Zorba would have done. But then, this girl was not a widow and they were far away from Crete. She might be a member of the woman's liberation movement, and if he did not bring up sex, she might have less cause to hate men's attitudes. But Zorba would say that she was still a woman and wanted to be desired and made love to.

Mustafa decided to talk to her and find out. He might look awkward, but at least he would be able to sleep, knowing that all was as it was supposed to be. He knocked on her door. She said to come in. She was in bed. Could he see any hint of encouragement on her face? He wasn't sure.

"There is something I want to tell you. . . . Ummm . . . I . . . well . . . Were you asleep?"

"No," she said, "I wasn't. I was wide awake."

He asked himself if she could have been waiting for him. He sat down on the edge of her bed.

"I just don't know what is expected of me," he said. "This may sound silly but do you want me to make love to you? I mean, I could if you wanted me to. I mean, not as a favor. I like sex and you are very attractive. But I didn't want to . . ." Words were coming slower to him now. She didn't look scared but seemed puzzled by his approach.

"Do you feel ready?" She saw he had no erection. He told her that he was restraining himself. He still wasn't sure if she wanted him.

210

"Would you like me to kiss you?" he asked. She nodded. He kissed her lips softly, touching her teeth with his tongue. His hands caressed her face and her shoulders and then lightly touched her breasts under her shirt. He kissed her cheeks and moved one hand between her legs. She was wet.

"Do you want to?" he murmured. Her hands were moving too. She said she did. He asked if he should use a prophylactic.

"Yes, please," she said. He gently eased off her and went to fetch it.

When he came back with the package in his hand, she said, "I guess I don't want to."

"All right," he said slowly. "But I'm curious. Why did you change your mind?"

She said that she felt she was not being fair to the Polish girl. He told her that their making love wouldn't affect that relationship, but he didn't press the point. If she didn't want to make love, it was all right with him. He asked if he could kiss her good-night, for he had liked kissing her very much. She said yes.

He kissed her. All night they kissed, caressed, and moved with each other, and made love.

"Do you like it?" he asked her.

"Yes," she answered. But she wanted him to come too. He told her not to worry about his coming; he was expecting to, but it was nicer when it was not hurried.

Soon the early morning light began to filter through the blinds into the room. At nine o'clock he got up and made pancakes for them. They ate in the kitchen. She told him she had promised to meet her Holyoke friend at ten thirty in one of the churches on the New Haven green and possibly hitchhike back to college with her. But she wasn't sure which church it was.

They left the house and walked toward the green. All Yale was fast asleep. It was a lovely morning, cool and sunny. He wanted to put his arm around her, but she felt shy in public. As they walked, she talked about her family. She said her father was a nice guy, a scientist in a top-secret government lab. Her mother had given all her brothers and sisters names from the Bible.

There were three churches on the green. The congregations were gathering, and Mustafa and Dana looked like street urchins in their

211

faded blue jeans. Feeling self-conscious, they searched for her friend in each of the churches. There was no sign of her, but it didn't seem to matter. They both felt relaxed and unpressured. They walked arm in arm around the lovely green. He felt hungry again, and they bought coffee and doughnuts in a shop nearby and ate them in the shade of a maple tree.

Mustafa asked Dana if she would like to stay another night to see a review with songs by Jacques Brel. She said she'd love to but she had a chemistry exam early the next morning and, even though her friend had not turned up, she felt she ought to leave in order to study for it.

Hand in hand, they walked toward the New England Turnpike. She spoke more openly now. She told him that she never before had enjoyed sex so much. Her remark was more a passing thought than an intended compliment. He was happy she had said it. Although there wasn't anyone around, she was too shy to be kissed on the street. He kissed her in the privacy of an office building doorway.

When they reached the highway, she caught a ride almost as soon as she started thumbing. He waved. She smiled and waved back.

AL-NOOR—
INTERNATIONAL TRADER

*W*HEN I drove into the Hirjis' yard in Westport on a hot Sunday afternoon in 1979, I was welcomed by Al-Noor's mother, Zaytoon, and his three brothers, Ahmed, Shiraz, and Aboo. Al-Noor was out running an urgent errand and was late. I would have been disappointed if it had been otherwise. When he arrived a half-hour later, he was—just as he'd always been—gently apologetic. His smile was bigger than ever.

The *big news* in the family was that, after nearly twelve years of separation, they were all together at last and they planned never to live apart again. "I guess you could say we've thrown our destinies together," said Al-Noor. They had started their own New York travel agency, Traveling Taj, which was beginning to thrive under Shiraz's able management and gradually would expand to include, they said, many other enterprises—such as their own airline and hotels. They had decided on a corporate structure, which they hoped was big enough to encompass all this. I was stunned at the enormity of it all—but only briefly. When I looked around the room at each

213

of the new entrepreneurs from this old trading family, I had no doubt whatever that it would all materialize.

Shiraz, tall and very handsome with a large black moustache, radiated energy and enthusiasm. "We elected Zaytoon chairman of the board because she's the most patient and sensible person around. And Al-Noor, of course, is president, even though he's not working full time in the business yet." Shiraz went on to describe how they had started Traveling Taj and how it would develop. Eventually, he explained, the whole family would work in the business but, as yet, Traveling Taj was too newly born to support them all—especially since they wanted to plough back the major portion of the revenue. But everyone, including Zaytoon, filled in on off-hours when it was necessary. Shiraz had graduated from the International Hotel and Tourism School in Switzerland and then, after working in a number of London hotels, had come to New York's Waldorf Astoria, where, with his hotel background and his many languages, he was rather quickly promoted to manager of the international department. "Then," said Shiraz, "one day I woke up and I said, 'Why am I working for Hilton? That's no way to make money.' " So when Ahmed returned to New York after completing his degree in travel industry management at the University of Hawaii, they opened Traveling Taj. They found an office in the Graybar Building in midtown Manhattan and "set to work like crazy."

Meanwhile, Al-Noor had graduated from Yale and was working by day as a statistician at the United Nations while he pursued his master's degree in business administration at New York University at night. Zaytoon, when she first came to the United States, had found a job in sales promotion with a New York advertising agency and was now working as a part-time typesetter with the *Westport News* so that she could be nearer home. (In Dar es Salaam, Zaytoon had worked for many years as the assistant to four consecutive Israeli ambassadors. It says something about the Hirjis in general, and Zaytoon in particular, that the new Jewish state trusted a Muslim so completely.) Aboo had completed high school, gone on to Vassar, and had just this month graduated with a degree in economics.

Kodacolor snapshots of all the graduations spilled out of a large cardboard box on the coffee table: caps, gowns, and big smiles

214

everywhere, with Zaytoon always looking lovely in a sari, and standing beside each one of her graduating sons in turn.

"That's a lot of graduations," she said, "and each of the boys has done so well. Each one brings a very different talent to the business."

"Eventually," said Shiraz, not to be deterred for a moment from laying out the Hirji master plan, "we all want to live in the same family compound—each brother with his own house and family and Zaytoon can live with one or all of us or have a house of her own."

"Like the Rockefellers?" I asked.

Shiraz laughed.

"And what if your wives don't want to live with so much family around?" asked the practical Zaytoon.

"Then we won't marry them," said Shiraz definitively. "If my wife loves me, she'll have to accept the whole family." Zaytoon smiled and looked askance.

"When *are* you going to be married?" she asked. "Don't you think it's about time you found a nice wife?"

"Not until I can support her in a good way," said Shiraz.

"Well, she can work too," said Zaytoon. "She may want to work."

"Yes, but I want to be able to give her the choice. If she wants to, she can. But I don't want it to be necessary."

Therein followed a family discussion on whether wives should be expected to work or not, with Zaytoon taking the more radical position. In a more serious tone, they talked about whether or not it was important to marry an Ismaili girl. Al-Noor felt he would not be happy if he did not; the younger brothers were not so sure. Zaytoon stayed out of this part of the discussion altogether. I sensed she was torn between her belief in freedom of choice and her loyalty to tradition.

Later she took me on a tour of the small house and showed me what normally would have been a playroom, with glass sliding doors opening to the yard. Floor cushions in Indian prints were neatly piled on the carpeted floor and a huge color portrait of the Aga Khan hung on the wall. Otherwise the room was bare. It had been set up as a *jamatkhana,* and Zaytoon held weekly prayer meetings here for some forty Ismailis who lived between Westport and Hartford. I told her how much I admired her spirit and wondered at the many changes she'd gone through since her childhood days in Dar es Salaam—London, the Netherlands, the Congo, her husband's early death, the loss of much of the family business after Tanzanian independence, the uncertain years in Switzerland, and now a ranch home in America! She admitted that it hadn't always been easy, but she said, "I have my family and my God, and I trust in Him." She smiled and continued in her more practical vein, "Al-Noor has done a lot of dirty jobs for all of us. We now have a happy future—all due to Al-Noor."

Al-Noor, of course, had said the same of her. As had the other brothers of both of them.

We all had curry—a splendid twelve-man very hot curry—around a big and perfectly appointed table, and then Al-Noor and I talked privately under a big tree in the backyard. He said his mother worried about his not getting married and sometimes he worried too. "I am keen on writing a short short love story—very intense—but essential. It would probably be super soppy and perhaps I ought to be in love—a torrid love affair—before I do it. But I avoid, it seems, any such direction. I don't have the time—or so I say! Or maybe I don't have the emotional togetherness. Either way, I see myself shying away from emotional contact with women." For the moment, however, Al-Noor was concentrated on a more imminent problem—his first-year business school exams. "What a pain!" he said. "When that's all over and I finally get my MBA, I guess I'll just have to go old-fashioned wife hunting. Not to worry now."

Al-Noor told me he had not yet shown his stories to his mother or brothers and I asked him why. "I don't know," he said. "Perhaps I'm shy . . . perhaps I'm uptight about it. Maybe my mother's interpretations of those times are different . . . it's all so personal. Besides," he continued, "we are merchants. Practical. We don't *write*. I can't be talking about such things."

We talked for a long time, and when I left, Zaytoon and the brothers came out to say good-bye. "Be sure to put down someplace," Ahmed called after me, "that none of this would have happened if it hadn't been for Al-Noor." I promised I would.

Since that Sunday evening, Al-Noor continues to struggle with business school and, although still working at the U.N., is beginning to search out a bigger position for the time when his MBA is in hand.

Aboo is working in New York for an international firm that sends him on frequent business trips to East Africa and the Middle East. Traveling Taj, although not yet big enough to incorporate all family members, has expanded, sending Ahmed to Vancouver to open a branch office there. But he commutes frequently to New York to be with his mother and brothers in their current home, a large family apartment on Roosevelt Island in the middle of New York's East River. "New York, I guess, will always be headquarters," says Al-Noor. "We all think of ourselves as essentially American now."

I, however, have my doubts about their wanderings being over. Zaytoon visits Vancouver frequently both for its beauty and its large and expanding community of some ten thousand Ismailis. More than ever, she is involving herself in international Ismaili councils, both religious and secular. Al-Noor, too, has become more involved in Vancouver and Ismaili affairs. As I write this, he has just returned from a business trip to Vancouver, where he saw some architectural drawings for "the most beautiful mosque you ever saw—contemporary and done by a Canadian architect but combining a lot of traditional Islamic culture. Space and light. Really wonderful stuff. The Aga Khan is encouraging this all over the world." Al-Noor exuded enthusiasm. And of course, Ahmed is in Vancouver more than half the time.

So I would make a guess that the family compound—"with houses for all"—for this East African trading family will eventually be built in rainy, green Vancouver, almost exactly halfway around the world from the hot, dry winds of Dar es Salaam. And that on the grounds of their new home, pines and laurel will replace the baobabs and jasmine that surrounded them when they were born.

PORTRAIT OF MICHELE

MICHELE Lewis (pseudonym) was one of those students I knew was troubled about something, but I wasn't quite sure what. Nor did I feel she could put her finger directly on it either. Sometimes she would involve herself energetically in class discussions—talking intensely in her soft persuasive voice—and at other times her mind seemed to be off in some distant place and she barely spoke a word. During some weeks her writing assignments were clear and concise; during other weeks they rambled for pages through Christian doctrine before making their point—if then. She had a hard time delivering papers on time. But one thing was clear: she was deeply concerned about how to live a Christian life—not just in abstract terms nor at some future date but right then in her daily life at Yale. Her relationship to Christianity—so clear to her in her younger years —was undergoing some rough adolescent and cultural upheavals.

In her application to the seminar she had written that she wanted to take the course "to sort out in writing some confusing experiences from my personal life"; that she found most of her Yale courses "heady"—by which she meant dryly intellectual—and wanted to write in a personal vein to balance them out. She was more interested in what she might learn about herself and her life from writing than she was in producing a tale for someone else to read.

When we met in private conference, the first thing that struck me was her earnest concern to "understand" and "love" other people. Although she was sometimes perplexed by the behavior of others, she struggled so mightily to understand them that she would occasionally tie herself up in knots. *Love* and *forgiveness* were key words in her vocabulary, and at that period in her life she allowed herself almost no direct anger; the word *hate* never escaped her lips. I sometimes wished she'd spew out a healthy, nasty remark about someone who'd taken advantage of her so that she wouldn't have to struggle so hard "to understand." "To hell with him!" would have cleared the air.

For Michele was passionate as well as puritan. Beneath her earnest exterior were very strong feelings—as well as high standards. Her body suggested this. Although she was not beautiful in a Madison Avenue sense, there was an aura of the earth mother about her, and if she'd been an Italian farm girl instead of a Presbyterian pastor's child from the steel towns of Pennsylvania, I would use the word *voluptuous.* I could imagine her in a De Sica film like *Field of Rice,* running across the sheep pastures, laughing uproariously while being pursued by a handsome young swain. Her long, brown, curly hair frequently fell with abandon over her round face, and her way of proudly tossing her head to clear the hair from her eyes was very attractive. She had full lips and large brown eyes, which usually were filled with earnest concern but every so often sparkled with defiant delight—giving her a hint of wildness. When she was preoccupied, she was apt to slouch, but at other times one was aware of her tall, proud, buxom figure beneath her worn but immaculate jeans and baggy shirt.

Michele was the second of five children who made up the close-knit "Christian family" her parents worked hard to create. Her early years were spent in Manchester, Pennsylvania, where her father was pastor of a Presbyterian church and her mother a devoted and energetic pastor's wife. Her parents had married young—in their late teens—and had devoted themselves completely to each other, their children, and their ministry. Work and family life were closely tied together, with the children helping out in the many aspects of church life—church suppers, prayer retreats, missions to the needy. From an early age Michele had accompanied her parents on civil rights picketing lines and Vietnam peace marches. Helping others —"joyfully"—was the whole family's mission. When Michele was in her late teens, her father became a professor in a theological school near Philadelphia.

Although Dorothy was the eldest child—and the one about whom Michele writes her story—Michele was most like her father. She admired him deeply and was somewhat frightened of him. "Although I can't think of a time he criticized me, I was fearful of his judgment; he seemed so perfect—he was my model—he was *it*. And I was a sensitive child. All he had to do was look at me in church and I would run home and burst into tears." To live up to her father's example, Michele tried hard to be "a good girl." She related to her father by becoming involved in his intellectual interests and "doing things in his realm," though she worried that she wasn't doing them quite right.

At Yale, Michele didn't feel comfortable with "the Old Blue image—at least, the stuff coming out of [Yale president] Kingman Brewster's mouth." Her early life in a steel town made her feel out of place at elitist Yale; it also made her somewhat disapproving of it. Although her parents were educated, her friends hadn't been, "though they were cooler kids than I was." It was hard for her to feel at home among "the heavy intellectual types—the facile talkers —because of their lack of feeling for other people." So Michele found her "home" and spent most of her time with the Yale chaplaincy and the Downtown Cooperative Ministry—an ecumenical welfare and social action group that included both the Yale chaplains and the ministers from New Haven's churches—many of which were black. "It was exciting," she said, "to work with people who really cared about making changes within the city. I could relate to New Haven in a way I couldn't relate to Yale." Appropriately, Michele's financial-aid job was assisting in the chaplain's office and acting as sexton for Battell Chapel, Yale University's principal church.

Her mentor at Yale was Rabbi Arnold Wolf, the Jewish chaplain. She took courses from him, found him a "brilliant man," and used him as her personal counselor. "Some of the counselors," she told me, "are nondirective—the nodding, 'I know what you're saying' types . . . and never tell you anything. When you're a confused college student and have a definite problem, you want some advice. Rabbi Wolf's method is just to tell me exactly what he thinks I should do. Then I go out and do it and find that he's always right."

As might be expected, Michele lived off campus in a cooperative house for most of her college years. In her junior year she was tapped for a secret society that she had been told was "not like the others —they have blacks and women and are interested in helping the New Haven community." She went to initiation but never returned, because she found "the members too hedonistic. It really isn't too different from any other Yale club, and I don't want to play pool and talk to preppies, even black preppies."

So far as all that went, Michele felt good about herself. What was at the core of her confusion and troubled conscience—although I didn't know it at the time—was a break with parental mores about marriage and sex. With a family background that linked Christianity closely with "no sex before marriage," living with a fellow student was a tougher problem for Michele than for most others at Yale. It was even more worrisome because Michele found she enjoyed her sexuality and felt completely "swept up" by her first relationship. "I lost myself completely," she told me much later. "I just thought it was so wonderful to be in love and be around somebody you enjoy. I was intoxicated with that—it was almost like a drug. I wasn't going to all my classes, though I didn't miss a church meeting—I never compromised that. But I compromised everything else, including my own values."

Michele also had a tendency to become involved with immature, conflicted men. During her first two years she found herself in love with another "preacher's kid," who eventually turned out to be a "bleak soul—writing endless papers on Kierkegaard" and who would disappear and reappear, commit himself, and then go off with someone else in unpredictable bursts of behavior. In her last two years she found herself caught up with Paul, an evangelical Christian who was striving to live "a perfect life," which meant, among other things, "a pure life." He took her to charismatic services where people spoke in tongues and where he sought "a personal relationship with Jesus."

Michele tried mightily to understand the evangelicals but was disturbed by their concentration on a direct relationship with God and by their separating evangelism from social action. When, with Michele, Paul fell short of his ideal of sexual purity, he made Michele feel "like an immoral woman." Michele struggled to live up to his standards—"to be more like his fantasy girl, the sweet midwestern farm girl from the musical *Oklahoma!*, but I didn't fit the role. I even asked my grandmother to make me a long *Oklahoma!* dress for a costume party we were invited to." Their relationship ended when Paul's brother committed suicide and he "shut himself off completely—I couldn't reach him at all."

It still boggles my mind that students are able to weather such stormy, intense relationships and complete their studies at the same time. And a scholarship student like Michele also has the time-consuming duties of a financial-aid job. Of course not all students do make it through—but a greater majority than one would expect from looking at the disjointed fabric of their daily lives. Youth, as Erik Erikson points out, can look extraordinarily wacky and self-destructive, only to emerge a few years later with good ballast in place. It also never hurts to be endowed with high intelligence and physical energy—and Michele had a high quotient of both. She also had the ability to analyze herself—if sometimes a bit too judgmentally—and eventually choose paths appropriate to her.

"In college, I didn't have any perspective on my sexuality at all," said Michele much later. "It was all so new and overwhelming, and my parents really never sat down and said, 'This is what you're going to encounter—how are you going to deal with it? This is what we feel about it.' I got their message by osmosis; my parents were so pure. They married young—neither had been in love before—and they were totally faithful with a strong belief in sex, but sex only in marriage. My mother committed herself to my father totally and built her life around his. So, in college, I think I was looking for someone I could completely commit myself to. I have a tendency —I think all the girls in our family have the tendency—to give myself completely; and there just aren't very many men in their twenties who can deal with that. Of course, my mother chose the right man, while I made the mistake of twice getting into a masochistic relationship and not being myself in my thinking or my

223

values. Whoever it was, I thought that I had to dedicate myself completely to him. I was very unliberated. But you're not liberated until you're liberated no matter how much ideology you have."

While Michele remained close to the church in spite of "compromising my Christian values," her older sister Dorothy, in her adolescent break from the family, did not. Dorothy's rebellion, like that of many ministers' children, was more severe and more dramatic. Although (or perhaps because) she had always been the most devoutly religious child in the family, in the summer following her freshman year in college Dorothy was swept into the drug culture. Just how deeply she was involved with drugs the family never knew. And then, a year or so later, she joined a Hare Krishna group in Hawaii. This was, of course, an enormous shock to the whole family, and although the incident had occurred two summers before Michele entered Yale, it was still "one of the confusing experiences of my personal life" that she was trying to "sort out." She decided to write her long paper about it; it would be an easier event to get some perspective on than her current experiences at Yale.

In first draft Michele's story was a patchwork of descriptions and excerpts from letters exchanged between Michele and her younger sister Debbie in their efforts to understand what was going on with Dorothy. As might be expected, the paper was more a document for her own understanding than a story for the eye of a reader not acquainted with the situation. But the draft also showed that Michele had a strong talent both for drama and for storytelling.

After much cutting and filling-in of needed information, her story, by the third draft, was all of a piece. In reading that draft, I was astonished that her feelings and opinions seemed to come across much more strongly on paper than they did in person. This is not unusual for shy people, but Michele had given the effect not of shyness but of confusion. In the writing there was no confusion.

"Dorothy and Hare Krishna" is also, alas, an all too classic tale of our times.

*D*OROTHY AND HARE KRISHNA
by Michele Lewis,
Germantown, Pennsylvania

*M*Y parents had a vision of building a Christian family—and there were five of us preachers' kids (known in the trade as P.K.'s) to carry the standards aloft. From the moment each of us first realized that we were P.K.'s, whatever we did was affected by that vision. It affected us and our lives both privately and publicly.

If you had been in Washington Park in Manchester, Pennsylvania, on a late June day in 1969, you would have seen us bearing the banners—quite literally. *The United Church Herald* had heard of our family—and the rather spectacular banners my mother made —and so a reporter had been sent to photograph us. It was a windy day, and we were struggling to keep the banners from blowing off their poles. But the reporter was dogged. "Just once more around the hill," he said. "I have one roll left."

I was beginning to feel silly when a hippie came up to me and asked, "Is this a happening?"

"No," I answered. "It's my family."

Grandma led the procession with a banner marked JOY. Next came Dad, carrying SHALOM. Religion had infused every bit of his being. After ten years as a parish minister in Pennsylvania mill towns, he was now a professor in a theological school.

Mom followed Dad, holding HOPE—her favorite banner. Then the P.K.'s followed in chronological order. First came my older sister, Dorothy, bearing VULNERABILITY IS THE PATH TO FREEDOM. She had chosen this one not only for its Christian theme but also because the slogan was the credo of an encounter group she had gone to. I followed with FLESH and a gold star. This symbolized holy flesh—the fact that Jesus had taken on a human body and come to us. My mother also intended it to symbolize people who, like Jesus, pitched in and dirtied their hands in the struggle to solve the problems of the earth-bound world. That kind of "flesh" was a family precept. We had, for instance, always marched in demonstrations. I went to my first when I was ten— picketing a store that wouldn't hire blacks. My father had led the march in his clerical collar, and we P.K.'s followed, with mother bringing up the rear, pushing my little brother in a baby carriage.

The next banner was carried by my younger sister, Debbie, who was being perverse that day, quite as usual (Debbie and I were always scrapping). The banner she carried was an experiment of my mother's—a circle of cloth sewn over a Hula-Hoop, with a watch face sewn on it. In the middle of the face were the words LIVE AWAKE. I thought that was ironic—as if that was what Debbie was doing! Dorothy and I never saw much of Debbie in those days. She stuck close to her room, her private journal, and a group of friends she didn't want me to talk to.

Becky, my youngest sister, was next in line with a banner shouting YIPPEE over a bright silhouette of the risen Christ. She kept turning to nag Scott, last in line, who kept letting his ALIVE WITH POWER banner fall on top of her head.

But this story is not about banners. It is about my older sister, Dorothy, and her passion for religion. Dorothy had always taken her oldest-sister role very seriously, in spite of the fact that I tried my best never to let her lord it over me. But somehow she usually managed to do so.

One day, for instance, when we were all going to New York to hear my father give a speech to a group of clergy, she took command of our rooming arrangements and ended up giving us a sermon besides. She was then fifteen; I was twelve and Debbie, ten. En route in the car, Debbie and I had been scrapping in spite of warnings from Mom. When we arrived at the George Washington Hotel, Mom suggested the three oldest sisters draw lots to see who would get the single bed in the room the three of us were to share. Dorothy won and I had to share the double bed with Debbie. I knew Debbie would try to steal the cover, so when we got into bed that night, I told her she better not try.

"Shut up," said Dorothy officiously. "I'm trying to get some sleep." Debbie and I fought over the blankets anyway, until Dorothy took over and told me to sleep in the single bed. She would sleep with Debbie.

I was about to hold my own when we were stopped short by loud argumentative voices coming from the next room. A woman was demanding money and the man kept shouting, "You bitch! You bitch!" Dorothy became very dignified and explained to us in schoolmarmish terms what was happening. I pretended to be bored, especially when she turned the whole thing into a sermon on Jesus and following the Christian path. That was Dorothy's favorite subject. She was going to be a minister like my father when she grew up.

Debbie, on the other hand, played little sister to the hilt. She sat at Dorothy's feet, listening intently as her older sister talked about heaven.

"Do you think I'm saved?" Debbie asked, a bit troubled about the thought that she might not be.

"God always tells you if you are," Dorothy answered gravely.

"Are *you*?" I interrupted accusingly from my exile in the single bed.

"Yes, I am." She answered with conviction.

"Huh! You sure don't look it to me." I had to regain my own status somehow.

As we grew older, we—like other children—fought and competed less. During a year in England, when our family lived there for my father's sabbatical, Dorothy blossomed into a first-rate folk singer. Grandmother had given her a twenty-seven-dollar guitar, and she made the most of it. She was eighteen by then. She had written a song for our arrival in England and played it for us at the first family meeting:

How shall we sing the Lord's song in a strange land?
We shall work and we shall heal and we shall spread our Lord's
    Shalom!
We shall laugh and we shall cry and we shall stamp our feet in
    joy!
We shall clap and we shall dance and we shall sing the song of
    God!

From that time on our family had two new themes: hope and celebration of the future time when love would triumph and the world would be reconciled to itself. Dad had explained this "theology of hope" in a book called *The Rainbow Sign.*

Encouraged by Mom and by Dorothy's eagerness to play her guitar, we all began to sing together spontaneously when we found ourselves gathered in the living room. By this time Debbie had a guitar, too, and the rest of us shook and banged various simple instruments—tambourines, drums, and maracas—that Dorothy had collected. I especially liked to sing. Often, I would go looking for Dorothy to ask her to get her guitar out and play. One night she invited me to sing with her at a girls' school where they had a hootenanny every Saturday. After that, we became partners. We had come a long way since our earlier rivalry.

When we returned to the United States the following spring, Dorothy began to perform at the various church conferences around the country where my father lectured each summer. She loved to perform and had a special talent for getting people to sing along. I admired her patience in sticking to the songs that everyone knew—inevitably "Blowin' in the Wind" and "Michael Row Your Boat Ashore." When our family led the worship at a conference, we always planned a swinging service with Dorothy in charge of the music. Dad even began to take her to his individual talks, where she would lead a song at the beginning or end. For these she would write special songs or hymns that would fit the subject of Dad's talks.

That fall, Dorothy—the first to leave the nest—went off to college in a small Pennsylvania town. I don't think she liked it. The school had a middle-class collegiate atmosphere and doted on such things as debutante proms and elite social cliques. The "greening of America" had just begun on the larger campuses and hadn't yet come to the Pennsylvania hills.

The next summer brought a radical change for Dorothy. She took a job with the Yellowstone National Park United Parks Ministry and joined a group of other college students who worked at the concession stands and helped run the chapel programs. But her letters home were worrisome to my mother. She called me into her bedroom one day and asked if I would look at one and tell her what I thought. "What's the fuss?" I asked. "It's just a bunch of rapturous poetry about nature." Dad read it, too, and couldn't see what was upsetting Mom.

"She's taking drugs," she protested. "I know she's smoking pot and taking drugs." Dad and I pooh-poohed that. Later I was astonished by my mother's perception. She had been right.

The next year, Dorothy dropped out of school and worked for a few months in our town doing odd jobs, like stuffing envelopes for various organizations. My parents agonized; they couldn't understand what had caused her to leave school and start taking drugs, and they didn't know what to do about it. I didn't know how to take it either; the fact that she had some mescaline right in her room seemed strange but didn't bother me nearly as much as the rupture her conduct seemed to be causing in the family. I disapproved.

Later in the year, at Mom and Dad's suggestion, she took a job at a mission in a poor section of Biloxi, Mississippi, to help clean up hurricane damage. My parents were hoping that a dose of the reality of poverty would shock her into being more responsible. We all took her to the bus when she left. When she returned three months later, she had little to say about her experience, and she seemed as out of reach as before.

That year Dorothy also attended a two-week encounter group. She and I had planned to go together, but at the last minute I had to stay behind to take my SATs for college entrance. I was relieved not to be going; I had never been through a marathon and was frightened by the stories I had heard about "taking the hot seat" and having to expose one's intimate secrets to fifteen strangers. Dorothy, on the other hand, looked forward to the close community feeling created by an intense marathon where, in her words, "everybody usually comes out hugging everyone else." She told me she wished our family was more like that. Unlike Biloxi, the encounter group made a deep impression on her. We held our breaths about what she would do next.

She decided to go back to school, but this time as far away from Pennsylvania as possible. Spurred by Mom's and Dad's stories about Hawaii (they had been to a fiftieth-state celebration the year before), she applied to and was accepted at the University of Hawaii. She planned to leave early in the summer.

I, too, wanted independence. In the previous summer, the usual family vacation had been a disaster—stifling days on the road and hot nights with hay fever in motels—as we drove to Colorado and back for yet another church conference. Moreover, Debbie and I had continued our cold war, which had become even more intense in the three years we had attended the same junior high school. She picked at me constantly, while I treated her with civility and condescension. So, just after my sixteenth birthday, I got myself a summer job as an apprentice housekeeper and cook in a conference center in Düsseldorf. I would go to Germany by myself!

Suddenly, in the spring before either Dorothy or I had left, my father received a surprise invitation to become a visiting professor of religion at the University of Hawaii for six months and theologian in residence at a church there. This was a blow to Dorothy, but she reluctantly agreed to fly over and live with the family for the summer and her first term.

In Düsseldorf, I received a letter from Dorothy. She loved Hawaii and had written some new hymns—joyful ones—for the singing services she often led at Dad's church. She sounded happy and alive again. But what "really turned her on," she said, was the Hare Krishna group who held open meetings every Sunday night in the Fellowship Hall of the church. The Krishnas, she wrote with some awe, worshiped God not just on Sundays but twenty-four hours a day. She attended—as a guest—the Sunday celebrations, where she listened to the guru, Sai Young, and joined in the singing and dancing and something called psychic sleep.

Her letter should have been a tip-off that further family trouble was brewing, but I felt pleased that she was happy again. Then I began to receive letters from Debbie. That fact in itself was a shock, but it was an even greater shock that the letters were gentle—no sarcastic barbs—and her salutation read "Love, Debbie." That made my hands tremble when I read it. But it was Dorothy and the Hare Krishnas who were the subject of most of Debbie's letters:

> . . . Dorothy's sound asleep. She had a hard day at the pineapple factory. She wakes up at 5:00 A.M. to be there by 6:30 and guess who's her lucky roommate? The Hare Krishna people were going strong last night and Dorothy stayed till about eleven. I was gonna go in for a while, but one look at a roomful of kids laying on the floor practicing psychological massaging was enough to spook me back to my room.

Within a few weeks, Dorothy quit work at the pineapple cannery. The Hawaiian women gave her a hard time for being a Haole (a white mainlander). Debbie struggled to understand what it was that attracted her to the Krishnas. She wrote me about sudden family meetings called when Dorothy didn't come home at night and about Dorothy's increasing secretiveness.

I finished my job in late August and flew to Honolulu. Jet lag, no sleep for thirty hours, and the sudden switch from a Germanic city to a Polynesian island left me completely dazed. When I first saw the islands from the plane, I couldn't believe they were real— accidental bumps in a huge aqua sea. The family met me, piling leis over my head and talking excitedly about rainbows, blue skies, volcanoes, and surf. My little sister Becky had turned a beautiful chocolate-brown. Dressed in a bright-colored muumuu, she looked like she belonged to this exotic place. Scott, full of a seven-year-old's shy dignity, ceremoniously presented me with a cup of pineapple juice from the free dispenser Dole had set up at the airport. The others hoisted my bags and guided me to our VW bus for the ride home. I spent the next three days alternately sleeping, trying to soak in Hawaii, and exploring our Japanese-style house.

Our house was just two doors away from the church and a hedge of oleander lined the sidewalk between the two buildings. In our backyard, the most extraordinary trees grew everywhere. A huge mango at the far edge of the yard screened out a freeway and an exit ramp that curved over the church property. In front of the mango were two plumeria that blossomed continuously, and all around a small patch of sun-drenched grass were banana and papaya trees intermingled with strange and beautiful flowering shrubs. Our *lanai* overlooked it all, and in the cool of the evening I would lie there, letting the magic of the air, the sound of Dorothy's guitar, and background swoosh of cars lull me asleep.

When I had recovered enough to rejoin the daily life of the family, I realized that Hare Krishna had become a highly sensitive topic. After her first visit, Debbie had never gone to a gathering again. ("Mikey, they worship that guru!" she told me in horror.) Mom kept pointing out how such a practice was idolatry; Dad attended several meetings, trying to fathom what it was that enthralled the group of young people. He was saddened, he said, by the cultural decadence that allowed their religious hunger to seek such outlets and the failure of the church to meet their needs. On one occasion, Dad invited Sai Young to speak to the adult forum he led before church each Sunday. Sai didn't come but sent in his place his second-in-command, Kirby, who touted Sai's group as a successful center for drug rehabilitation. His pitch was carefully designed to appeal to the middle-class Orientals and whites who made up the congregation.

I didn't meet any of the Hare Krishna people until my parents took me to Waikiki one night. We had walked along the beach to see Polynesian drummers and hula dancers in the floor shows put on by the fancy hotels on their torchlit outside dance floors. Afterward, we walked over to the International Market Place opposite the hotels' street side. Here we heard a different beat and a new chant. A short white man—his head shaved except for a ponytail on top —came up to me. "Hare Krishna," he said.

I was excited to meet my first Krishna and eager to hear about the sect firsthand.

"What do you mean?" I asked.

"Krishna is God. We chant his name and take away the bad karma of all whom the vibrations reach—"

"How did you find this out?" I interrupted.

"I was living on the street, spaced out on drugs. I was nowhere, man. Then I met Sai. He told me to forget the drugs and sing the names of all-powerful Krishna. None of the suffering in this world is real. You are not a body, you are pure spirit soul. Believe me, Krishna is the answer. Hare Krishna." He turned to talk to someone else. Some of the devotees swayed and chanted while others button-holed passing tourists. They were earnest, if difficult to talk to. They all said the same thing.

Further down the street was another group chanting Hare Krishna. The people in this group were dressed in identical saffron robes, and the men all had shaved heads. One tried to sell me some incense and I asked what the difference was between the two groups. His face hardened and he said that his was the only official group of the International Society for Krishna Consciousness (ISKON) in Hawaii. They kept all the disciplines—wearing robes, bathing three times a day, abstaining from meat, alcohol, drugs, and nonmarital sex.

I was curious enough that when Dorothy urged me to go with her on Sunday, I agreed. Dorothy told me that the guru, Sai (Chris Butler in his former life), had been a notorious junkie and pusher, but had given up that career to lead people to Krishna. Sai—who was now twenty-two—and forty devotees had lived in various places throughout the city. From time to time they were systematically evicted from their dwellings by the board of health. The group also had a banana farm commune on the island of Maui.

I learned the details of the strained relations between Sai's group and ISKON at a later date. Evidently, Sai, in the hearts of his followers, had replaced the official but far-off swami in India, and ISKON considered him a renegade, both for his disregard of author-ity and for allowing his followers to have long hair. Sai's devotees claimed, in return, that they were able to reach more people on the street than ISKON and that they had never sunk to panhandling from Waikiki tourists like ISKON. From the outside, I thought their street competition was amusing—especially when the Jesus Freaks marked out a terrain across the street and sang "Rock of Ages" loud enough to blot out the Krishna chanting of both groups.

The next Sunday, Dorothy took me to my first gathering. Even before we reached the churchyard, the hot night air was filled with the sound of drums and nasal chanting, and a piny incense my brother called "the Hare Krishna smell." In the church courtyard,

233

a group of sandaled women were preparing a feast. A huge pile of zoris and sandals were stacked by the open doorway to the hall. When I stepped inside, I couldn't believe the transformation—the Fellowship Hall had become a Hare Krishna temple. Ten potted palms lined the walls, prayer rugs covered the floor, and flowers were strewn everywhere. On the stage, the devotees had set up several little altars, each decorated with a candle and a blue picture of Hare Krishna. At center stage they had raised a large plush lace-covered dais with an elaborate microphone and speaker system placed next to it. The room was dark except for the light from the candles; incense and chanting saturated everything.

During the first hour people drifted in and out of the hall, while various devotees took turns chanting the names of Hare Krishna into the microphone. The hypnotic rhythm was controlled by the drumming of an ecstatic devotee who was backed up by a group with finger cymbals. Over and over again, we all chanted:

> Hare Krishna Hare Krishna
> Krishna Krishna Hare Hare
> Hare Rama Hare Rama
> Rama Rama Hare Hare

More people arrived, and our numbers swelled to well over a hundred. Then the music stopped suddenly and everyone turned expectantly toward the back door. Enter a long-haired young man dressed in an immaculate white sari. Ecstatic cries of "Sai, Sai" filled the room. More drums and clanging cymbals. Slowly he made his way along the flower-lined path to the stage, assumed a semilotus position, and adjusted the mike. The chanting died down; he looked around the room and said, giggling, "Hare Krishna."

Then he launched into a rambling talk on pure spirit soul and something called shining effluence. Like a hypnotic refrain, he chanted repeatedly, "You are not the body, you are pure simple soul." Such a thought is surely one of the greater Christian blasphemies, and yet I found myself almost believing it. At the very least, when a devotee greeted me with "Hare Krishna," I found it impossible not to reply, "Hare Krishna."

I looked around to find Dorothy. She had moved to a group near the front and was listening to Sai with rapt devotion. I, too, found myself strangely drawn to Sai and longed to attract his attention. I suddenly felt jealous of everyone in the room.

When his talk was over, I rose and asked a question, "How can psychic sleep stop the war in Vietnam?" It was a sincere question —not a provocative one—and at that moment I genuinely thought he might have an answer. He treated it, however, like an aggressive put-down from an unbeliever and pointedly ignored me. Fifty people turned to stare me down. I felt shamefully embarrassed and unjustly accused.

That slap broke his spell over me and I retreated to the back of the room, where I tried to join the dancing and chanting which had begun again. But my heart wasn't in it. I left in the middle of the psychic sleep exercise.

After that, Dorothy tried to avoid me. Going up to my room, I would pass her on the stairs and try to catch her eye, but she always stared beyond me as if she were stoned. When she came to dinner, she was either irritable or haughtily remote and wore a glazed half smile that never changed. After a few days I couldn't stand it any longer and confronted her. "Why are you ignoring me?" I asked. She burst into anger, blaming me for asking a "Pharisee" question that Sai wouldn't like.

"What are you saying, Dorothy?" I looked at her. She snapped out some words I could not catch and stalked off.

She began to avoid all other members of the family as well—even Becky and Scott. Each time anyone said anything to her, she would put on that same strange smile and turn away. We grew more critical of her and held family meetings to analyze what was happening. One day Mom called me to her bedroom and confided that if she had known about Hare Krishna she never would have encouraged Dorothy to come to Hawaii.

Dorothy herself wasn't around much. When she wasn't chanting in the streets, she hung out under the freeway ramp behind the church with the drifters who found it a sheltered place to spend the night. I walked by the ramp every day on my way to school but was too afraid of the strange people there to go over.

One morning I awoke not only to the familiar sound of rushing cars but also to the sounds of chanting close by. I looked out my window and saw one of the devotees picking flowers off the plumeria tree. Sai's group had been evicted again, and he had decided to put up a tent under the freeway ramp on the church's property. That day the executive council of the church met in emergency session and voted to give sanctuary to this rejected group just as they had sheltered over forty AWOL G.I.'s the year before. Dorothy was overjoyed and spent many hours chanting with them there.

The Hare Krishnas soon became as unpopular in our neighborhood as the G.I.'s had been controversial. Just as the body wasn't real for them, neither were private-property laws. They helped themselves to the fruits and flowers in neighboring gardens on the block. Our friendly Japanese neighbors put up large NO TRESPASSING signs on their lawns.

At home the climate became even more intense. It didn't help that we were having a spell of *kona* weather; the trade winds weren't blowing and it grew unbearably muggy. Everyone was touchy. Mom jumped on Dorothy for offering our washing machine—already on its last legs—to the camping Krishnas.

The following day Dorothy walked in the house proudly wearing a new cherry pit necklace that Sai had given her. She was thrilled that he had noticed her and was in an ethereal mood, paying even less attention than usual to the rest of us. When mother saw the necklace at dinner, Dorothy clutched it, then took it off and slammed it on the table. Her fixed smile disappeared and she was just angry Dorothy again.

That Saturday night, as I was coming home, I heard the noise of chanting from a block away. The beat seemed intensified . . . almost triumphant. When I walked in, I found Dorothy and my parents sitting in the living room. She was clutching her guitar case and the bag she carried her hand instruments in. I started to retreat, but mother, in an intense voice, asked me to find Debbie and return to the living room, because Dorothy was leaving to join the Hare Krishnas that night.

I was shocked. As much as I realized the power of her attachment to the group, I never thought she would actually leave home to live with them—giving up her family, her school, and most of all her faith. I think that was the hardest blow to my parents—Dorothy surrendering her soul. To worship Sai like Jesus! Mom said later that the reason the Krishna chanting was so loud that night was that they felt they had hooked a prize—a folk singer and the daughter of a Christian theologian. Such a conversion would make them seem more legitimate.

I found Debbie upstairs and asked her to come with me. Scott and Becky were asleep. In the living room no one was saying much of anything. Mom or Dad would start a sentence and then drop it in the middle, fearful that a wrong word would drive Dorothy out of the house. Evidently the three of them had just returned from Waikiki Beach, where Mom and Dad had taken Dorothy on a last try to get through to her. For a half hour they had walked in the dark along the edge of the surf, but nothing Mom and Dad said drew a response from Dorothy. In a final desperate effort, they had tried to rebaptize her. Mom had attempted to dunk her under the waves to wash away the Hare Krishna spell—like washing away sins. But at the last moment, Dorothy had pulled away, leaving Mom on her knees in the wet sand. Then they had all driven back to the house.

It was now Debbie who stepped into the breach. Very rationally, she tried to put forth all the right arguments to explain to Dorothy what she was doing and to convince her to stay. Dorothy pretended she didn't hear and then, dramatically, stood up and asked each of us to say good-bye. Much to my shame, I did just that. I was too fed up with Dorothy to realize that this scene was more serious than all the others. Debbie turned away, and neither Mom nor Dad said a word. Dorothy shrugged, picked up her guitar, and turned to go. Mom called her back. "You're not just going to walk out of here, you're going to have to break out," she said, and quickly stretched out her hands to the rest of us, urging us to form a circle around Dorothy. We locked arms, leaving Dorothy in the middle. Debbie and I were sobbing. The desperation of weeks of trying to reach Dorothy suddenly came home to us as we acted out our refusal to let her go. And yet we knew we couldn't touch her anymore. At first Dorothy laughed and treated it like a game. But when she tried to break out of the circle between Mom and Dad and couldn't make it, she became furious and flailed helplessly against them. Then, for the first time in many weeks, she suddenly broke into tears. We all fell away and Dorothy just stood there, racked by sobs. She cried with her whole lungs as a baby does.

237

Again we made a circle around her, but this time to hug her into a tight ball. After a while we sat on the floor around her. Debbie and I held her hands, and I tried to look into her eyes. For the most part, Dorothy just stared. She glanced at me momentarily when I took her hand and then went blank again. I didn't know what to say. Rather strangely, I blurted out, "It's like you're dead and we can't have a funeral." I was moved by Mom's and Dad's anguish and really wanted to yell at her, but I couldn't make contact with her. Debbie and I began to weep again as we held her lifeless hands.

My father, who had been sitting in a corner with his head in his hands, cried out, "You're breaking our hearts, Dorothy," and then let out two anguished sobs. Dorothy didn't flicker an eyelash. I kept wondering what more I might say and somehow felt an urge to call her "sister." I knew how she liked to play the role of big sister, but I never thought of her in that way and the words stuck in my throat. Everyone was silent for a while. Dorothy was hunched over, absently twirling her hair. My leg began to cramp but I didn't dare move, and the word that I knew I should say was pounding in my brain. Suddenly, I blurted out, "Come on, sister."

She lifted her eyes and looked at me questioningly—as if to say, "You've never used that word before, what are you up to now?" I said it again, this time realizing I meant it. Debbie said, "Dorothy, I don't want you to go, please don't go."

Then Mom asked quietly if we could have a communion service. Dorothy nodded vacantly and I ran upstairs, fighting tears, to bring down the bottle of Rhine wine I had brought from Germany and was saving for Thanksgiving. Dad opened it, trembling as he pulled out the cork. We poured the wine into paper cups and sat around on the floor. Dad closed his eyes and repeated the words of the service. "And He took up the cup saying, is this not the New Covenant in my blood, which was poured out for you? Take, as oft as you drink it, in remembrance of me."

We drank, and together said the Lord's Prayer. A long silence followed, and then Dorothy looked at us, almost cheerfully, and said, "Okay, I guess I won't go tonight."

Dad staggered to bed, gray and drained. Mom took a gold ring off her finger that her mother had given her and gave it to Dorothy, making a final statement for all of us: "We love you." We all went to bed.

When I came home for supper the next day, Dorothy wasn't there. Mom said she had gone to the University to a meeting. It was Sunday and I knew she would have to walk past the seductive door to the Fellowship Hall on her way home. I went outside and waited for her on the front steps.

The meeting was supposed to be over at eight thirty. At nine she still hadn't returned. I kept waiting. About nine thirty she appeared from behind the oleanders and stood on the front walk, startling me out of a worried reverie. She was crying. I ran out and hugged her. I started to cry, too, and asked her what had happened.

"I heard them chanting," she said, "and stood in the doorway looking in. Sai was there. He gave me a nasty look and then kept on chanting. I watched for a while, but didn't go inside." She seemed exhausted but clear and strong.

We went into the house. Debbie was there waiting for her. Dorothy laughed and embraced us both and said, "Don't worry, you have your sister back."

MICHELE–MINISTER

*T*HAT Michele became a minister did not surprise any of her friends, but for some reason it surprised me. And it surprised Michele herself. She had planned, vaguely, that after graduation she would work for human aid projects—CARE, Asian relief missions, agricultural assistance, or the like, but to preach the word from the pulpit—"No! It was the last thing I wanted to do."

It was Michele's mother who had stepped in at a propitious moment. In the fall after her graduation, Michele was back in New Haven, planning with friends to open a low-cost cooperative restaurant in an abandoned town house, when her mother telephoned and told her in no uncertain terms that she was frittering away her time, running away from her future instead of embracing it. "I was shocked," said Michele. "My mother had never spoken that way before—but it worked. And I had sworn I would not go back to school—ever!" Michele agreed to go home to Philadelphia and try out the seminary for one semester.

Still undecided at the end of the term, she went to the Philippines for the summer to work in a church mission, helping Filipinos who had been displaced by Marcos from the Manila slums move to small camps in the countryside, where they had no idea of how to grow their own food. She was surrounded by agricultural and nutritional missionaries who knew their stuff and were working on small farms with people who desperately needed help. At first Michele felt she had found her ideal vocation, but as the weeks went on, she became bored. "Then it hit me one day: what was really important for me was not breeding a new strain of rice or teaching people how to plant it, but rather addressing the basic spiritual questions *beyond* bread. I returned to seminary really excited! A pastor, after all, has got to have a lot of interests and be many things to many people. I wasn't sure how I'd like all the school work, but I came home from that summer determined to get through seminary whether I liked it or not."

The determination was still in her voice when I reached Michele by telephone in the early spring of 1980. She was co-pastor—together with her husband—of a Presbyterian church in a small town, Crescent Falls, in upper New York State and was about to perform her first Easter service. I decided to drive up from New York City for the occasion. As I made my way through the Pennsylvania hills, still wintry and barren, I wondered how one managed to share a pulpit on a completely equal basis with one's husband or wife—especially in a small church. Earlier in my life, I'd known a number of ministers, and I couldn't imagine any one of them happily stepping aside from the pulpit for that precious twenty-minute Sunday show. A visiting preacher is one thing, but a co-preacher living in the same house? And suppose they disagreed on the Scripture? I was eager to see it. I was eager to meet her husband.

It was well after dark on Holy Saturday when I pulled up in front of the white clapboard church with its tall spire. The small parsonage was next door—just a few feet away—and I found Michele and Glenn inside, busily preparing for the next day's activities. Glenn was a short, slim, handsome man with Nordic features and fair hair, in striking contrast to Michele's almost Mediterranean aspect. He had a limp on his right side and lacked full use of his right arm but seemed completely at ease with these disabilities, as if he'd been acquainted with them for a long time. Although witty and welcoming, he was necessarily preoccupied with the upcoming Easter cele-

241

brations—as was Michele—and I knew enough not to hang around and be sociable on the night before a sermon. But as I started upstairs to bed, Michele could not hold back the *big news*. "I'm pregnant," she beamed. "We waited until we were established, then we decided it was time to have a baby! This is an ideal job for raising a family—with neither one of us working full time." The earth mother radiated joy.

In the frosty dawn the next morning I walked a block away to a neighboring Methodist church where Michele and Glenn were to give a sunrise ceremony before performing the eleven o'clock service in their own church. Gladioli, Easter lilies, and tulips decked the steps to the altar, and a large red banner on the left of the chancel proclaimed "Hope, Love, Joy, For Thy Peace." A green one on the right read "Take One, Plant One," with a collection of potted seedlings placed below it. As the organ began, the twenty-four-member choir in gold robes with white collars marched down the aisle, followed by Michele and Glenn in almost identical natural flax robes. Glenn wore an orange and gold stole but Michele's robe was, by preference, unadorned. "We wanted," she told me later, "to have the same color robes so we wouldn't clash too much up on the chancel. I didn't like the usual academic robes; I don't like black, and I don't want to emphasize the academic side of the ministry. My robe's a choir robe and Glenn's is a monk's robe; they cost very little and both can be thrown in the washing machine." Michele, I could see, was a practical minister.

As Michele and Glenn mounted the steps to the chancel and sat down on two identical chairs covered in red velvet, I was struck by a new sense of dignity and self-assurance in Michele. She read the Resurrection Scripture in a mellifluous but firm voice, and then, when she invited all the children forward to listen to a short Easter homily about how butterflies were a symbol of Easter—"when faith takes wings"—she spoke with lighthearted certainty. Toward the end of the service a young couple brought their baby to the altar to be baptized, and as Michele took the infant in her arms, she quipped to the congregation, "I need the practice." She was completely in her element. And so was Glenn, but with a style that was more dramatic ("Thunder rolled, lightning cracked"), and one that, at moments, flashed with quick wit. Both seemed to know everyone in the small town and were warmly welcomed on all sides. After the sunrise service, Glenn helped cook the scrambled eggs at the big United Youth breakfast in the church basement before going on to the Congregational church for his next celebration.

When all the services were over for the day, Michele and I sat on the front steps of the parish house, talking and warming ourselves in the midday sun. We were interrupted now and then by a well-wisher passing by on the sidewalk and stopping to chat. "I was really lucky to have found Glenn," she said, fondly watching him enter the church next door. "You know, after those two rather disastrous relationships I had at Yale, I gave men up. In seminary, I said to myself, 'I have a calling—a vocation that I'm interested in—and I'm not altogether happy doing it by myself but I *can.*' Then just three weeks after I said that, I met Glenn and before you knew it, we were engaged. For me, giving it up was a precondition for having a healthy relationship. It's a Christian idea: you have to let go before you can receive grace; you don't go out and grab it. So, for me, finding Glenn was almost a religious experience. He's got his problems, sure, but our relationship is not based on mutual pathology. The other ones were."

"How do you find working so closely together?" I asked.

"Well," she said, "Glenn at first didn't think we could share a ministry—he would be trying it out for the first time, feeling his way, and I didn't have the same style as he did. I'd had a lot of practice by then; I knew a lot. I was frightened of besting him in a competitive situation and having to cover up what I was doing. Nor did I want to hold myself back. If he was going to compare himself to me, we were going to have problems. We have different gifts and he can do things I could never dream of doing. So at first we looked for separate churches—each full-time—but then this church came along, actually *looking* for a husband and wife co-pastor team, each half-time. I never thought that would happen. When we came for an interview they responded to each of us individually—and differently. They gave us two copies of everything. That's a small thing, but I felt it showed they understood the situation. And they have. That's one reason we ourselves haven't had to worry much about sharing and competition. Some people naturally turn to me for counseling, others to Glenn. We think that's great. So far, I've taught the adult classes because I like to, and Glenn has taken on the youth groups and the basketball teams because he likes that. Together we're offering people two different styles of ministry."

I mumbled something about how extraordinary I thought it was that they were able to divide the many facets of the job so compatibly.

"Well," laughed Michele, "it's not all peaches and cream. There are some chores—like taking out the church trash—that neither of us wants to do and then we nag at each other or feel guilty because neither of us has done it. But the really difficult part is that we constantly talk to each other about business. Being a pastor is an around-the-clock job. On our day off—Monday—we try hard not to mention the church at all. It's a matter of survival. But when you're both on the same job, it's hard for either person to pull the other away from it."

At that moment a little old lady—complete with knitting bag—came up to the steps to chat about the Easter service; she found it "lovely" but hoped no one had scrimped on their donations to the collection plate. She stayed for some time; Michele was concerned and patient. When she had left, I asked Michele whether she had found any resistance to a woman minister in such a small town.

"The women here are my staunchest supporters. A lot of them have liberated their heads and they won't take any nonsense about me being less than full pastor. I haven't had to make an issue out of it, which is lucky, because if I had to spend my ministry defending my rights, I wouldn't be free to do my job. No, the biggest drain is always being available to people—like the woman you saw just now. Our job is to listen, to really pay attention, to really care. And there are so many who need it. But we can never seem to get away from it—unless we go out of town. As long as we're here, I feel we must be available."

I asked Michele how she counseled young couples on premarital sex.

"Well," said Michele, "I tell them what I believe—that sex isn't very valuable without a real commitment like marriage—and I tell them I had to learn the hard way. As you know, I did. The hardest thing for me in college was believing in my parents' values and yet not living up to them. All the couples we've married so far were living together before they married. That doesn't bother me. It's an ideal I have rather than something I expect from people; it's a belief that that's what God wants. But there are a lot of things we people don't live up to and I don't think premarital sex is the worst sin by a long shot. The worst thing about it is that it creates children who end up in a bad situation. I don't like abortion—who does?—but I'm certainly pro-choice in the abortion movement. We don't need any more human suffering than we already have."

Her remark reminded me of Dorothy, and I asked Michele what her sister was doing now. For the first time on that Easter morning, her face clouded over and she looked troubled. "It's really worrisome," she said, shaking her head and looking at her hands. "She seemed all right for a while, but she's never really pulled out of her rebellion—or whatever it is. She never got mixed up with Sai again. He dissolved his special group, shaved his head, gave all his property to ISKON and joined the straight Hare Krishnas, if you can call them that. Some of his devotees followed him; one joined the Jesus people and another two were drafted and almost immediately were given dishonorable discharges because they drove their sergeant crazy with their chanting.

"Dorothy finally finished college—but it took her a long time, and then she went to divinity school, but there she refused to complete her last credit, saying she didn't believe in credentials and that sort of thing. But all along the way her thinking has been skewed. When she was in divinity school, she became involved in prison reform— first as part of the church and as a church representative. But then she got personally involved with the prisoners themselves—especially the blacks. She's always had black boyfriends. Now she spends most of her time at the prison visiting a lifer—a two-time murderer —who's as old as our father. She wants to marry him and has told the family, 'If you don't accept my marriage to this guy, you don't accept me.' They said, 'We accept you but not everything you do.' It's the same sort of thing as the Krishna episode. But this time, the family decided they wouldn't intervene—wouldn't go after her like at Waikiki. We were all helped by the story of the prodigal son, whose father let him go and he came back when he wanted to. In the Hare Krishna stuff, we didn't let her go. It was bad for her and it was bad for us."

245

I asked Michele what she felt was at the root of Dorothy's problem. "I don't know," she said. "Drugs?—we never knew how deeply she was or wasn't involved with drugs. Psychological distress?—she would never enter any therapy, even family therapy. My mother thinks it may be an inherited predisposition of some kind. We simply don't know. She always had trouble relating to our parents. She seems tied to them in a negative way. She always dramatically involves them in her actions—appearing suddenly and then disappearing again. She is very suspicious of me. She identifies me with Mom. That hurts me. She's hurt everybody so much, I guess we're all pretty exhausted and angry."

Michele obviously wanted to close a painful subject, and I was glad she was now able to do so without feeling she needed to explain or to struggle to understand all points of view. I told her that, to me, she seemed much more self-assured and had a new sense of authority. I asked her if she felt that way too.

"I do," she replied without hesitation. "I feel I've grown a lot and learned some things. Partly through writing about them and making my values clear to myself. Resolving what I would do when I grew up was a big watershed for me."

At that moment Glenn came around the corner of the house and obviously needed to consult with his co-pastor. I made them promise to let me know when the baby was born and then drove off down Main Street. As I passed the Methodist church, a woman parishioner, who was coming out of the front door with a pot of Easter lilies, recognized me from the United Youth breakfast and waved.

David Michael Lewis was born that August with ease, bringing delight to parents, grandparents, and parishioners. Michele's mother helped her out in the early weeks, and then Michele got back to work in the church. It was lucky the parish house was right next door. All went well until David began to be mobile, at around six months. Then both co-pastors realized that neither had been doing a part-time job: both had built their various enterprises into full-time employment. They now faced full force the modern dilemma: Which spouse would give up which activities to be with the baby, and when? How could they reduce the job so they could—on an equal basis—continue to enjoy their profession and still have unrushed time with

David? Neither wanted to put David in a day-care center, nor could they afford a housekeeper or nursemaid on their small joint salary. As much as they loved their present parish, they decided they had no choice; one or the other would have to take a full-time position with the other looking after the baby most of the time. After a few months of considering the options, Michele decided she didn't want to miss the child-rearing years with David, and she knew that Glenn, as much as he loved David, was not too keen on becoming the primary parent—even temporarily. "Neither of us was as liberated as we thought we were. When we became honest with ourselves, we faced the fact that I really didn't want to miss being a day-to-day mother and Glenn was not thrilled about stepping aside for a few years from his profession—even if he returned to divinity school for further study at the same time."

Glenn found a full-time position as an associate pastor in a large suburban church near Philadelphia not far from Michele's parents, which pleased both of them. After they were settled, Michele planned to look for very part-time work in another area—such as religious television programs, in which she'd had considerable experience both in seminary and with a small TV station near Crescent Falls. "As sad as it makes us to leave the people here," said Michele, "we had to put our family and our marriage before this particular job. It's really time, anyway, that we began to develop our careers separately. I'll get back to mine in time."

PORTRAIT OF PETER

PETER Werner (pseudonym)—a freshman—was at once a skeptic, a satirist, and a compassionate believer, and you never knew which side of his personality would surface next. Much of the time he sat quietly in class—his head of wavy blond hair tipped slightly forward —and carefully observed the proceedings over the tops of his clear-rimmed glasses. Then, quite suddenly, when he heard something that engaged him, a big smile would spread over his face, followed by a short, embarrassed chuckle. At that moment you were unsure whether he was about to speak out in enthusiastic support of some-one else or to burst forth with one of his deft and acerbic Bill Buckley put-downs. His opinions were seldom neutral, and he usually had a slant on a subject which no one else had thought of. He not only saw from both sides but from above and below as well. His dissenting opinion kept us all on our toes.

Peter could also write—and this showed up clearly in an early and rather simplistic assignment I usually give on likes and dislikes. I don't know what it was about this apparently fourth-grade exercise, but it had a way of spotlighting the students' style and craft as well as forcing them away from generalizations into specifics. On Peter's list of likes and dislikes, his direct style, his skillful use of words, his distinct tastes, and considerable imagination all became immediately apparent. You will notice he never substitutes "dislike" or "don't like" for "hate." No gray areas for Peter.

> I like hot apples and blue cheese stuffed inside a crepe.
> I like crowded, sweaty, dingy amusement parks on a hot summer night.
> I like the tired dull ache in my muscles after swimming a mile.
> I like to win.
> I hate to lose.
> I like the feel of stiff cotton pants when they're new and the soft secure feeling that they have when they're old.
> I like to sit with my roommate at a table near the entrance of the dining hall and make fun of all the people as they come in.
> I like getting ashes on Ash Wednesday.
> I like to complain.
> I don't like listening to people complain.
> I like horror stories, movies, and novels of the occult where the protagonist is menaced by unseen forces.
> I hate monster movies.
> I hate the Marx Brothers.

That last remark brought a flurry of reaction and the class divided itself between those who were horrified and those who were terribly grateful that someone had finally voiced their own unspoken thoughts. That was Peter. He could always stick a pin directly into a point of controversy—even if it was as unthreatening as the Marx Brothers. He was to do it again on even touchier issues.

Peter's main passion was defending anyone he suspected had been misused or slighted—especially by what he thought of as the "privileged establishment." A full scholarship student who was working at many odd jobs within the university, he was highly sensitive—as is clear in his stories—to the different salary levels, privileges, and life-styles of the many people who are needed to make Yale function. He felt his own life somewhat whiplashed between washing dishes with Mary in the kitchen of his college and sipping sherry in the master's living room with Norman Mailer and the like (if there is a like). In fact, he enjoyed both experiences, but the sherry had a way of turning sour if it meant that someone like Mary had to wait on him. And if when he was working the dining hall anyone spoke rudely to Mary, then . . . He was the conscience of the class and frequently brought to the surface discomfiting feelings that others had pushed aside.

But there was another conscience in the class—a black one in the person of Elías Aguilar. Although Peter and Elías appreciated each other's concern for the poor, their styles were very different—Elías's action-oriented, hyperbolic, and laced with the black rhetoric of the time; Peter's caustic, ironic, and expressed more openly in his writing than in personal confrontation. Elías had a platform; Peter saw much of life as a paradox (he even saw himself as something of a paradox). Both were compassionate and both tried hard to follow the mandate I laid down for all my classes: seminar members were not to critique each other's writing while it was in process; they were to help each other say exactly what it was each wanted to say, no matter what that happened to be. This stricture proved tough for Elías when Peter threw the first curve by writing in an early story:

"How much easier it would be if I were black or Puerto Rican. Then I would be expected to be poor. They could look at me and marvel at how I was advancing. 'Look, he goes to Yale.' But to be white and poor. The white rich really don't want to know about it. It upsets them."

Restraining his fire as much as he could, Elías countered in the notebooks: "I pounded my fist in anger on the last page of your piece on poverty ['A Phone Call Home']. . . . I admire your courage in writing this piece and my anger is a reaction to the content, not to its author." Whereupon Elías went on to enumerate—dollar by dollar and possession by possession—how much poorer his family was than Peter's and then pulled himself up short again with "I, too, question and torture myself for being here.

But the "black" remark was too much. Elías begins tentatively: "Does being black or Puerto Rican make being poor easier? That's the only part I must attack the author on, I'm sorry. You make it seem, So if it's more natural to be poor if you're black or Puerto Rican and therefore easier to bear . . . that some of the sympathy

251

offered us should be given to 'poor whites,' who are so much worse off because no one expects them to be poor."

And again Elías laid out all the data to prove his parents poorer than Peter's. It was difficult for Elías to see that what Peter was referring to was his social interactions with his wealthier friends, from whom he felt pressures to live up to their more extravagant life-styles—flying off to Bermuda for spring vacation or the like. Elías's friends not only expected him to be poor but required it of him. He was among equals. From that point forward, the contest continued to surface at odd moments throughout the semester without resolution.

Peter was one of those writers—and there are many of them—who feel more comfortable writing than talking. On paper he could express himself and his fantasies fully without fear of embarrassment or face-to-face controversy. His great strength was an unbounded imagination, which he could bring to the simplest situations in his life, creating small tales:

Communion

I moved toward the altar, letting myself be carried along by the line of people that pressed forward to receive Communion. My attention was focused on the faces of the people, imagining who they were, what they did, how often they had sex, what political party they belonged to, and how they would react in situations that were somewhat out of the ordinary. A "no-longer-a-believer-but-I-haven't-the-heart-to-tell-my-parents-or-maybe-I'm-just-scared," I was helped by this game through the tedium of Sunday mass, and sometimes I actually looked forward to it.

The steady flow of people that passed as they returned from Communion stopped, and I strained to see what was holding up the show. It was one of those eighty-year-old ladies in a fur coat from 1910 who can't walk but still goes to mass four times a day because she knows she's going to die soon and wants to go to heaven. Her daughter, a woman of about forty with the potential for being beautiful, stood behind her mother, holding her cane and trying to guide her down the steps.

My face burned with anger at the old woman. She had robbed her daughter of her youth (sob). In a few years she would die, leaving her daughter alone, unable to make friends, meet the husband, and raise the family that she might have had if she had not been caring for her invalid mother. She would live an empty life in a three-room apartment; perhaps work in a library. She had no spirit of her own anymore. Just look at her blank, expressionless eyes. Her energy, passions, and desires had been sublimated and rechanneled through a pair of purple knitting needles that click incessantly during the day, leaving a tired, empty shell.

However, my pity for the woman was threatened by my impatience for her stupidity. She should be standing in front of her mother, not behind her; and why was she carrying her cane? Her mother could use it on the stairs. If she just used some common sense, the line could move again.

Finally they finished their descent and came back toward me. I decided to give the daughter an understanding and compassionate look of "Have you tried arsenic in her tea?" After all, wouldn't that just make her day? She passed by and I looked into her eyes, but she didn't see me. A chill passed through me as I realized that she couldn't. She was blind.

She wasn't helping her mother on the stairs; her mother was helping her. The cane wasn't her mother's; it was hers. A cane that blind people use to poke around in the darkness.

Her poor mother. Forbidden to enjoy the rest and leisure of old age. Cursed to care for her blind daughter until death. Could she ever forgive me?

Me. Stinging with embarrassment. Once again the victim of my own hasty judgments. Once again forming convictions in the false light of appearances. Once again, reality had given me a good kick in the ass.

Peter and his twin brother were the eldest of eight children—six boys and two girls—from a devout Roman Catholic family in East

Meadow, Long Island. His youngest brother, Matthew, was born just before Peter entered Yale. His father, a third-generation Lithuanian, grew up in the hills of Pennsylvania; his mother, of German descent, spent her childhood years in Brooklyn, where her father was a fisherman. The big family had a comfortable suburban life until Peter's father, an aerospace engineer, was laid off in the Long Island space industry cutbacks of 1969. The family funds suddenly became sparse. His father had a difficult time finding work at a comparable salary and turned temporarily to real estate—which provided only a sporadic income. His mother, a resourceful and energetic woman, went to work as a practical nurse and began studying for her degree as a registered nurse. All this, as you will see, made as deep an impression on Peter (who was thirteen years old at the time) as the Great Depression made on many of those who grew up in the thirties. It must have been a difficult blow to his father's self-esteem, and Peter—as an eldest child—reflected some of the pain of that.

From their earliest years, Peter and his brother Joseph—who were fraternal twins—had very different talents. While his brother turned to athletics and music, Peter was the academic and a devoted reader of literature—the more wildly imaginative the better. With his delight in paradox and fantasy, Peter must have been somewhat of an anomaly in a family that was down to earth and practical. His mother wanted him to be a lawyer. Many of his brothers and sisters later turned—like his father—to careers in the applied sciences. When Peter came to Yale, Joseph went to the State University of New York at Buffalo and is now working for his graduate degree in urban design at the University of Pennsylvania. Differing in their approaches to life, they never developed the close bonds that many twins often experience.

Peter was torn about whether or not to use a pseudonym for the publication of "Both Sides Now." But this conflict was not unusual for Peter. He rarely showed his writing to anyone except the other class members and a few close friends whose opinions he trusted. When he did publish—usually in Yale's student literary paper, *The New Journal*—he was conflicted because he was never quite sure how his reading audience would respond to his special view of things. In one article for *The New Journal* he listed himself under the title

254

as "anonymous" and then, with typical ironic wit, ran a line at the end of the piece stating, "Peter Werner prefers to remain anonymous."

I asked Peter if he'd shown any of "Both Sides Now" to his parents. "No," he replied. "I don't know why exactly—they're kind of sensitive about the financial problems they went through. I think they'd prefer not to think I was affected by them much. And my mom would probably feel I was complaining about my childhood. I don't want to make them any more uncomfortable than I have to."

BOTH SIDES NOW
by Peter Werner,
East Meadow, New York

WHEN I was in high school, I don't know how many afternoons I spent upstairs in my bedroom, listening to the neighborhood kids playing roller hockey in the street while I struggled to play the guitar. I was trying to teach myself, and from a huge book of music titled something like *Greatest Hits of the Sixties with Simplified Chords*, I had chosen Joni Mitchell's "Both Sides Now."

The chords were simple, and the song seemed to demand a voice that wasn't too good. As with so many of the folk songs of that era, the lyrics seemed so much more earnest when sung poorly, as if the words demanded to be heard no matter what the quality of the singer's voice. I finally managed to learn the song, and a few more after that, before deciding that as bad as my voice was, it would never sound as earnest as Bob Dylan's, so there was not much point in going on.

And yet to this day I still remember the chords and lyrics to "Both Sides Now," for over the years the song took on an ironic significance as circumstances in my own life changed. What I should have learned from the song was how multifaceted and deeply layered these two sides can be.

When I was living at home, I thought I already had seen both sides. I grew up rather comfortably on suburban Long Island in a family that gradually grew to include eight children. My father supported us all with his job as a space engineer under government contract to NASA.

Then the United States landed a man on the moon, and my father was laid off along with thousands of other space engineers on Long Island. Suddenly we had no money and I saw the "other side." According to government statistics, we were living in poverty, but things weren't much different than before. They were just a bit more strained. For me, the two sides then were simply "richer" and "poorer."

Since coming to Yale I have had a chance to see more of these two sides. Here I learned that in many cases "richer" and "poorer" also define the distinction between "superior" and "inferior." Money, education, and family background all play their part in determining human value. Some people are meant to serve others; others to be served.

As a bursary student, I find myself in a strange position. One minute I'll be on one side, sipping sherry at a reception, while men and women in starched white uniforms offer me hors d'oeuvres from silver platters. The next minute I'll be on the other side, washing dishes in a hot kitchen of one of Yale's dining halls, or wearing a red jacket and serving my fellow classmates a French dinner. I meet students whose fathers are millionaires, then talk to dining hall workers who try to support a family on seven thousand dollars a year. When I joined the Duke's Men, an informal singing group at Yale, our spring concert tour took us through a series of posh resorts and hotels, a world of servants and masters, another world with two sides.

Here are some glimpses of the two sides:

A PHONE CALL HOME

Tom is one of my three roommates, a blond surfer from a Los Angeles suburb. Although our relationship was rather cool early in

257

the year, as the months have progressed we've become close friends. When we're drunk, we call each other by the names of characters taken from a Lawrence novel on our freshman reading list.

I can tell that Tom's family is well off, not by any of Tom's possessions but by his general demeanor and the fact that he's well traveled. I know that Tom thinks my family is comfortable enough, if not abundantly wealthy, and God knows I haven't done anything to make him think otherwise. We're among the last to be able to take advantage of an already slipping fashion dictate that demands that rich and poor alike wear nothing but jeans and cotton T-shirts, and so it's been difficult for me to guess just how much money Tom is used to, and impossible for Tom to realize how poor my own family has become.

We weren't always poor, but we were never wealthy. When my father still had his job as a space engineer, our family of ten lived in a barn-red colonial home in a suburban neighborhood and had a beige Chrysler Town and Country station wagon parked in the driveway. After my father lost his job, he couldn't find other work as an engineer. He tried his hand at real estate and lost money. There were no savings to draw from, and the family had a desperate struggle hanging on to the house and the car. When relatives had no more money to lend us, government assistance became a necessity, and my mother started training as a nurse in order to bring money into the household.

Tonight I find myself chiding Tom for his upper-class prejudices and social naïveté. This always confuses Tom, because he has no way of knowing where I'm coming from and no reason to suspect the personal vindictiveness that creeps into these "consciousness raising" sessions. Tom is trying to convince me that the reason he didn't have any friends among the Chicanos who attended his high school is not because they were poor but because they lived so far away. In fact he does, he insists, have white friends who are really quite poor.

"Listen to this," he says. "I have this friend. There are four kids in his family, and his father makes twenty thousand dollars a year."

I can't quite figure out the moral to this story, although I'm afraid of what's coming. In the best days, my father supported ten people on twenty-three thousand a year.

"Well . . . ?" I say, waiting for a conclusion.

Tom says nothing.

"Is that poor? Is twenty thousand dollars a year poor?" I ask, and my voice is angry and condescending.

Tom is annoyed that his humanitarianism is unappreciated. His head cocks back and his eyes go cold.

"Well . . . my old man makes a hundred grand a year."

Those words, that number, affect me as if I had just been drenched with a bucket of ice water. I want to shout back, "Well, my 'old man' is unemployed and we get six thousand dollars a year from welfare. So how do you like that?" Instead I say nothing.

Tom tries to press his point. He thinks I don't understand.

"Well, how much does your father make?"

"Fuck you," I reply.

Tom shakes his head in disgust and goes into his room to study. He's learned that there's no point in talking to me when I get into one of my moods. And like I've said, he's seen no sign of my family's financial state. When my parents visited on parents' day, the Chrysler was in good condition. My father still had his fine cashmere coat, and my mother's "simple black dress" did not betray its age. So he can't understand my anger.

I think about that number and I realize that there are some who would consider it pocket money, but still it's more than four times what my father ever made, and I resent it. I resent the way Tom takes the money for granted and I resent the way he takes it for granted that my own family is well off. I wish I had the courage to tell him the truth.

How much easier it would be if I were black or Puerto Rican. Then I would be expected to be poor. They could look at me and marvel at how I was advancing. "Look! He goes to Yale!" But to be white and poor. The white rich really don't want to know about it. It upsets them; they think it's disgusting. You're upsetting the order of things. Blacks are poor. Puerto Ricans are poor. They can't help it. They're not smart enough to handle money. But whites aren't handicapped. If they're not rich, it's their own fault. They're not living up to their race. They're a disgrace.

The noise from the stereo is beginning to annoy me. That weirdo David Bowie. It is Tom's record, not mine (which makes it all the more annoying). But the stereo is mine. None of us brought a stereo

259

in September, so the kid who's on welfare had to go home to bring one back. The same thing with the typewriter. The kid who's dad earns a hundred grand a year shows up at Yale without a typewriter. I spent half my summer earnings to buy a decent machine, half that summer slaving in a department store. And Tom just uses it whenever he wants.

Typical, I think. That's why his people are rich and my people aren't.

Bowie keeps whining. It is the same record that was playing when my brother Michael visited in December. Hearing the record, the first thing he said when he came in the door was, "What's going on here? Have you gone gay?"

Michael sat down without taking off his coat, and we tried to catch up with each other on the past few months. After about ten minutes he stood up to remove his coat.

"Boy, it's hot in here."

"Well, you should have taken your coat off."

"I just got sort of used to wearing it around the house. We haven't had any heat this past week."

"What?" I shouted, and broke into laughter. I pictured my family seated around the big oak table in the dining room, eating dinner in their winter coats, my sister Ann trying to avoid dipping her fur cuffs into her food.

"Dad wasn't able to pay the oil bill, so they stopped delivering." Michael was laughing too. He fell back onto the couch and the two of us sat there laughing until tears came to our eyes.

Remembering the laughter, I realize that it would take a great effort to make myself upset about the incident. My family isn't miserable in their predicament; they are able to laugh about it. They're as happy as ever. Then my anger returns when I realize that Tom is happy too.

It's easy not to mind being poor if you think the wealthy are miserable. It's easy to go to see a play or a movie or read a book where the rich are at each other's throats and they're lonely and unhappy and their lives are empty and half of them end up committing suicide. The rich are different and they get their just desserts in the end.

But Tom is really not so different from me. That is one of the reasons we're so close. I can easily see myself in Tom's position

260

through a simple quirk of fate called parentage. I might not have been happier but things would have been much more . . . convenient. Tom is no different, and yet he has so much more. Not only has he money, but he has the ability to enjoy it.

But now it's easy to let the heating incident upset me, and tears of anger burn in my eyes. I remember going home two weeks later for Christmas vacation to discover that, for financial reasons, my family had learned to make do without lunch. My stomach, conditioned to Yale's twenty-one-meal plan, was not pleased with this. In the afternoon I would rummage around the kitchen, looking for a quick snack to tide me over until dinner. But there was nothing that could be called "quick." There were no convenience foods that could be taken from a package. They were too expensive. Everything had to be washed or peeled and cooked, and a simple snack would entail a major production. There wasn't even a loaf of bread. My father made fresh rolls before each meal. It was cheaper.

On New Year's Eve, I was particularly hungry. My stomach nagged me all day and I looked forward to supper. But when supper came there was nothing but soup. Soup and the fresh hot rolls I had grown sick of—three to a person. I wanted to cry, but I held back the tears.

I don't now. I pick up my books and go into my room so that no one will see me. I'd like to hate Tom. I'd like so much to hate him but I cannot, and that makes me feel guilty. I am consorting with the enemy.

I try to hate, but the closest I can come to hate is jealousy. I want to have money also. Realizing this, the guilt presses against my lungs like stones. I want to travel. I want to have a swimming pool. I might enjoy a boat. Someday I might be able to have these things, but how could I enjoy them while others were miserable? How do the wealthy do it?

I try to escape to my books. I pick up my Religious Studies assignment. *The Documents of Vatican II.* The words become blurred as I read, the tears swelling in my eyes.

In His goodness and wisdom, God chose to reveal Himself and to make known to us the hidden purpose of His will by which through Christ, the Word made Flesh, man has access to the Father in the

Holy Spirit and comes to share in His divine nature. Through His revelation, therefore, the invisible God, out of the abundance of His love, speaks to men as friends and lives among them so that He may invite them and take them into fellowship with Himself.

The book lands in a pile of dust underneath the bed, for in my present state it seems more than likely that Christ was sent forth by Herod. Something had to be done to keep the starving masses from revolting.

My thoughts return to my family at home. My father has taken to going to our church each weekday morning and praying for guidance.

"Just trust in God," he always said. "Don't worry about tomorrow. Everything will work out according to God's will."

I had stopped worrying about tomorrow, but I'd never really trusted in God. And yet things had worked out. For me. But the rest of the family were still at home.

My mother had joined the charismatic movement of our church. She was going to be rebaptized in the Holy Spirit. Born again. But still she was able to say to my father, "Why don't you spend less time in church and more time looking for a job?"

My father laughed and called her a Holy Roller.

My sadness increases, and I want to talk to my parents. I want to call home and hear the voices of my family. They always sound happy. Mary will talk about her school play, *Oklahoma!* And in the background I might hear Paul practicing his French horn. That will cheer me up.

I wait until I've calmed down enough so that my voice will sound normal over the phone. I check my face in the mirror so that my roommates won't see I've been crying.

I go to the phone in the living room and dial my number. It takes a while for the connection to go through. The phone starts ringing, and then there is a click followed by a white fuzzy sound.

A nasal tape-recorded voice speaks.

"The number you have reached, five-five-five, four-eight-nine-five, has been disconnected. Please check the number you are calling to make sure that you have dialed correctly."

I let the receiver fall and the voice starts to repeat itself from the floor. I have dialed correctly. My parents haven't paid the phone bill again. Tears come, and then sobs, and there is nothing I can do to stop them.

In the next room, I can see Tom at his desk, concentrating on his chemistry.

KEVIN

Kevin is a full-time dishwasher at Timothy Dwight College. I work with him five days a week. He is twenty-five years old and mentally retarded.

"Peter, are you going home for Thanksgiving?"

"Yes."

"Where do you live?"

"Long Island."

"Are you taking a plane?"

"Kevin, I live on Long Island."

"I know. Are you taking a plane?"

I tell him where Long Island is. I tell him that it's two hours away by car.

The next day, Kevin starts again.

"Peter, are you going home for Thanksgiving?"

"Yes."

"Are you taking a plane . . .?"

This goes on every day for two weeks until Thanksgiving arrives.

His affliction is not severe. His speech is normal and he is physically healthy and coordinated, though he is barely five feet tall. He wears the same brown corduroy jeans and tan shoes to work every day, topped by a blue work shirt and a black rubber apron. I remember the pants and shoes when they were new.

"Peter, look what I got for my birthday."

Kevin has a thing about his birthday. He keeps track of it as if it might become lost if he didn't.

"In eight months and ten days I'll be twenty-six years old. Last year the students surprised me on my birthday. They came in and decorated the whole dish machine. The whole place. They didn't do it this year though. Maybe they'll do it again next year. I don't know. Maybe they will. . . ."

"In four years I'll be thirty . . . In five years I'll be thirty-one
. . . In six years I'll be . . . I'll be . . . How old will I be?"

He's obsessed with rules and instructions. They must not be
transgressed. Everything must follow a certain order. There is no
room for change.

"Peter, take some trays over there. They need trays. . . . No, not
those trays, those are for the coffee cups. Did you hear me? Hey!
Where are you going? Bring those back! Those are for the coffee
cups!"

Kevin might have the mind of a child, but physically he is a man,
and his mind doesn't quite know how to handle this:

"I know about sex. I read those magazines. *Playboy. Playgirl.* I go
to the movies. The filthiest movie I ever saw, *Superfly.* Oh, boy, you
should have seen it. . . .

"If I had a girl in bed you know what I'd do? You know what I'd
do? I'd suck her titties. That's what I'd do. . . .

"I got my back pay today. Almost a hundred dollars. Maybe I
won't give it to my mother. Maybe I'll get a girlfriend with it. Put
on my fancy clothes and get a girlfriend. Go dancing. Maybe she'll
let me play sex with her. . . .

"Is that your girlfriend, Peter? Ahhhh. I know you. I bet you're
a big lady's man. I bet you've even kissed her. You'll see. I'm gonna
kiss a girl some day. . . .

"I'm twenty-five years old and I've never even kissed a girl. Really.
Never. I ain't lyin'. Never."

He's proud of his job. He's proud of his salary. Thursday comes
and it's payday.

"Whad'ja get, Peter? Lemmee see. I made a hundred and sixty-
four dollars this week. Sunday I worked overtime. I'm a good worker.
Juan's a good worker too. I make more than he does."

His parents are separated.

"My father's down in Milford. He's married again. I make more
than he does."

Thinking about him, I realize now that I've never once seen Kevin
do anything to hurt anyone. He's never been selfish, never cruel. His
virtues are rather amazing considering the home life that he tells me
about.

"My mother takes all my money. She gives me ten dollars a week.

I can't do nothin'. If I don't give it to her she'll throw me out of the house. . . .

"My brother's in trouble with the police. He's been stealin' cars and pushin' dope. He got in an accident and the doctor found out they were carryin' drugs in their underwear. The car was stolen. He's sixteen years old. He has to go to a special school now. . . .

"I saw my mother playing sex with one of her boyfriends. I did. I went in her room to get something and there they were, playin' sex. Boy, she was mad. She said, 'Get the hell out of this room!' That was last year."

Due to the recent decision to lay off forty-three dining hall employees, Kevin faces the prospect of losing his job.

"Why does Yale want to do this to me? They have work. I'm a good worker. I never take a break. I'm workin' all day. Who's gonna load the machine if I'm gone? You? You, Peter? You don't know how. You're not fast. You'll be here all night. . . .

"I don't even know how to collect unemployment. I never did it before. I don't want to. They don't mail it to you. You have to go and pick it up. . . .

"They need me here. Who's gonna do all these things? . . . What's gonna happen when I'm gone?"

THE BANK COLLECTOR

During our spring break, the Duke's Men made a concert tour to Washington and some of the southern states. We spent one night late in our tour at the summer estate of one of the Dukes' girlfriends in Baltimore. Her father is a lung surgeon in Washington.

The estate was on a river leading into Chesapeake Bay. Bolstered by four white pillars, the house stood on a hill about two hundred yards from the private docks, where two sailboats and a motor boat were moored. Inside the house, the floors were covered with Persian rugs and the rooms were filled with antiques.

On one side of the house was a closed-in porch that had a lovely view of the river. It was pleasantly furnished with a green rug and white wicker furniture set against green walls. The large plants that hung from the ceiling thrived in the sun that poured in through the glass windows and doors.

Against one wall was a long shelf holding a collection of antique small mechanical banks. Little metal clowns, acrobats, hunters, and Uncle Sams stood poised, ready to spring into action upon being fed a coin. The amusing figures, painted in bright but now aging colors, created a carnival atmosphere that contrasted with the formality of the rest of the house.

What is it that is so alluring about a carnival? Is it that seductively evil force that always seems to be running through a noisy, crowded, rundown fairground on a hot summer night? Is it the false and deceptive smile of the Kewpie doll?

I looked down at the shelf of antique banks and that same force seemed to be present. The metal figures all wore unchanging smiles that seemed to say they had a secret. They were doing something wrong and getting away with it.

"I see you've found my banks," a voice behind me spoke.

I turned to face the doctor.

"Yes. They're very interesting."

"It's not a big collection," he said, sitting down, "but several of them are fine specimens. Quite rare."

I sat down in a chair across from him.

"It's a great hobby," he continued, "but it's expensive. That's why I've only got twenty-three."

I sympathized with him. I bet myself that some of his banks could have cost more than two hundred dollars.

"It used to be you could buy a whole collection for the same amount that just one bank costs today," he said nostalgically. "But now it seems like everybody's got their own collection. The banks are just about all bought up now. You won't find one just sitting around in an antique shop anymore.

"Every now and then someone will put an ad in the classified section of a magazine that he has one for sale, and he'll get offers from all over the country. I had a friend who answered one of them. He recognized that the bank in question was a very rare one, but the guy selling it didn't know it. It turned out there were only two of them left in the whole country. Well, he bought it from this guy for only two thousand dollars.

"The next thing he did was take it to a well-known collector, who was going to give him ten thousand dollars for it. But this guy got a better offer from the Shorelys—you know, the banking Shorelys. Oh, well. Anyway, he sold it to them for twenty-two thousand dollars.

"The collector thought he had it all wrapped up for ten thousand, and it was swept from right under his feet," the doctor chuckled. "Twenty-two thousand dollars. That's a twenty-thousand-dollar profit in just a few days. Not bad."

I was too dumbfounded to say anything. The doctor continued his monologue.

"Here, let me show you one of mine." He went over to the shelf, took down one of the banks, and set it on the table in front of us. The base of the bank was a blue circus pedestal, one of those round structures that trainers train elephants to stand on. In the top of the base was a slot for coins. At the back of the base stood a vertical bar that became a curved fork above the pedestal. A cast-iron acrobat balanced between the sides of the fork on a metal bar which he held on to.

The figure was dressed in a white clown's suit that had been painted on and had now turned creamy with age. He had red buttons and trim, a pair of red pointed slippers, and a red stocking cap. His black face was frozen in a leering grin.

"This one's a prize," the doctor said, giving it a pat. "Look at him. Not a scratch on him. That's all the original paint and there's not a scratch on him. He cost me seven thousand dollars just a few years back. I don't know how much he's worth now. At least twelve. Watch this," he said, reaching into his pocket. He pulled out a nickel and fitted it into the clown's cap. The metal figure bent slowly forward until his head was quite close to the base. The coin fell into the slot in the blue drum, and the figure swung back up again, grinning proudly.

The doctor's face fell. "He's supposed to do a flip, but he needs adjusting. Maybe with something heavier . . ."

He reached into his pocket for a quarter. This time he gave the clown a little push as he fitted the coin into the cap. The clown performed a full flip and he resurfaced with that same evil grin.

"There!" the doctor said proudly. "With something heavier, like a half-dollar, he'll do two flips."

The little metal acrobat swung back and forth on his stand,

basking in glory with his huge, gloating grin. I began to understand what evil secret that hunk of metal possessed. He held the power to keep a person fed and alive for several years. That was the power that ran through those atoms of iron. That was the force that give the metal man life.

The doctor was still speaking.

"You know, if you get your hands on some money these days and you want to invest it, you've got a problem. Look at the stock market. This country's economy is a mess." He smiled at his shelves of banks. "That's what's so great about these things. They're good investments. They're safe. People are taking an interest in these things again. Anything from the early days of America. That's where you should put your money these days, in anything American."

Anything American.

BREAKFAST AT TIMOTHY'S

In my job as a dishwasher at Timothy Dwight College I usually worked dinners, but one of the workers had asked me to fill in for him at breakfast one day when he would be away. I needed the money so I agreed, expecting to wash dishes. When I reported to work, though, it turned out that I was expected to work on the serving line.

At all of Yale's dining halls, a hot breakfast is served until nine o'clock. After nine, only continental breakfast is available; students serve themselves cold cereal, toast, or Danish. When nine o'clock rolled around, I still had some scrambled eggs, one piece of French toast, and one piece of regular toast. I decided to finish serving them, rather than bring them back to the kitchen, where they would just be thrown out.

At about ten after nine, a resident fellow of Timothy Dwight showed up for breakfast. He was a tall man, about forty-five years old, with stumpy gray hair and a pair of wire-rimmed glasses. He mumbled something and pointed in the direction of the French toast. I put the toast on a plate and served it to him.

"Okay," he growled, "would you like to give me some eggs? I asked for eggs."

I took another plate and gave him some eggs. He was angry.

"Now would you like to give me some toast to eat with the eggs?" I reached for the last piece of toast and put it on his plate.

"Now," he exploded, "would you like to give me two pieces of toast instead of one piece of toast?"

"That was the last piece," I told him as I put two more pieces of bread in the toaster. Then I remembered that it was after nine o'clock and that I didn't have to be making more toast.

"If you want breakfast," I said, "you should get down here before nine o'clock."

He looked at me, his eyes filled with contempt. He spoke through clenched teeth and the words fell from his lips like bird droppings.

"Tomorrow," he snarled, "you can come and serve me breakfast in my room before nine o'clock."

"Don't count on it," I said. I reached behind me to the toaster and pushed up the slices of bread, half toasted. If he wanted toast, he could make it himself. He stalked out of the kitchen.

When he left, I realized I was shaking. My eyes were burning and it was hard for me to swallow. If I had been alone in my room, I probably would have cried. It hurt to be treated as if I were inferior. I felt a hate for that man stronger than any hate I had ever felt before, and the strength of that hate scared me. I would have liked to see him dead.

IN OUR NATION'S CAPITAL

I sat at a table in the Crystal Room of the Sheraton Carlton Hotel in Washington, D.C. The Duke's Men had been hired to sing at a Saint Patrick's Day luncheon in honor of the Irish ambassador to the United States and of the hotel's manager, who was retiring.

People had gathered an hour earlier to sip cocktails in the Mount Vernon Room, and the Duke's Men hadn't passed up the opportunity either. We were among the first ones there, and we watched the room fill around us with Washington VIPs. The only one that most of us could recognize was J. W. Fulbright. Danny, one of the Duke's Men, whose father is a Washington lawyer, was able to point out important congressmen, aides, consultants, etc. They didn't look like much to me.

More interesting than these stale Washington politicians were the wives they brought with them. Their identities were concealed behind layers of face powder, and most of them were dressed all in green for the occasion. Each of them was responsible for maintaining and advancing the social status of her family, and they were all trying to engage in friendly conversation with women a step ahead of them on the social ladder, in hope that room might be made for them on that step. Their behavior reminded me of the tigers in "Little Black Sambo" who chased each other's tails around a tree in a continuous circle until they turned to butter. Lunch was called, and the women were saved from a similar fate.

I vowed not to sit with any Duke's Men, to force myself to eat and talk with some of these people. I saw it as an educational experience. I sat alone at a table and chased away any of the Duke's Men that tried to join me. Two unassuming men in clerical collars sat down and introduced themselves as monsignors with Irish-sounding names, and that was as far as our conversation went. I began to despair and was unconsoled by the chlorine smell of the hot tuna crepes on my plate. Then a woman who introduced herself as "Grosvenor" sat down and announced that the rest of the seats at the table were reserved for an important congressman, his wife, and an admiral. She greeted the two monsignors, whom she didn't seem very interested in, and started a conversation with me.

She asked me what I was studying, and I told her I was interested in writing. Her eyes lit up, and she told me that she, too, was a writer. She had been an editor for *Business Week,* and a Washington columnist. She was retired, and was now writing a book of amusing anecdotes about "all the famous people" in Washington. I listened intently as she rattled off a story about Prince Charles's visit to Washington.

". . . Well, he was standing on the reception line, and everybody had been carefully screened, you know, and there was a man there and nobody knew who he was or how he got in. . . ."

She was quite tickled by the tale she was telling, and her breath came in short little pants, like that of an overexcited toy poodle.

"Well, finally he reached up to the prince, and he shook his hand and the prince asked, 'And what is your connection?' And do you know what he said?" she gasped. "Do you know what he said? . . . 'Western Union'!"

She repeated "Western Union!" and I realized that I was supposed to laugh. So I laughed politely, trying to figure out the punchline.

The congressman, his wife, and the admiral arrived, and a waiter appeared and filled our wineglasses. Danny later informed me that the congressman was one of the five most powerful men in Washington, along with Ford and Kissinger. His wife was a huge woman with a beaked nose, an elaborate hairdo, and a double chin that danced when she turned her head. She was dressed in pink. The congressman was also fat, and both he and the admiral were bald, round-headed men whose faces were distorted by thick lenses set in jet-black frames. All of them appeared to be well into their seventies.

Mrs. Grosvenor introduced us, and I remembered to stand up as I shook their hands.

"This young man," Mrs. Grosvenor informed them, "has been most delightful to talk to. He's interested in becoming a writer."

"Awhh," the admiral guffawed, "you'd better tell him to find another field. There's no money in writing. He won't make a cent." He turned to me and looked at me as a father would. "Really, you'd better study something else. Why, you'd be better off in the army!"

"Listen to him," the congressman's wife advised me. "He knows what he's talking about. Why, since the admiral retired, he's simply been raking it in!" The table burst into laughter, and even the two monsignors, who had been totally uninvolved in the conversation, smiled sheepishly.

"He's been . . . He's been . . ." the woman tried to speak through her uncontrollable laughter. "He's been . . . working as a . . . 'consultant'!" And the table was overcome by renewed fits of laughter.

The admiral sat with a huge grin on his face, quite proud of himself.

"You've got to have money, son," he continued, suddenly turning quite somber, "because without money, you're nothing. You don't go anywhere without money."

"He's right, you know." Mrs. Grosvenor frowned. "Money talks."

I waited for more laughter. I waited for them to acknowledge their joke. But there was no laughter, no acknowledgment. These people were serious.

271

SPECIAL PEOPLE

Mary is a full-time worker at the dining hall where I work part-time as a dishwasher. She's one of those women who can be big and fat but somehow you never notice their size. Although she must be close to sixty, she has a spirited personality that might belong to a sixteen-year-old girl. There is something dry and clean about her; she is the definition of "baby powder fresh." Her hair is dyed dark black; her skin is white with a thin dusting of powder, and her lips bright red with lipstick. She always has a kind word for everyone, and all of the students love her.

One Saturday night, just as we were ready to close the serving line, a busload of Yale alumni appeared with their wives, ready to be served dinner. They were members of the Yale Club of Hartford and had been expected two hours earlier in the evening. But they hadn't arrived, and nobody was ready for them now. General havoc took place in the kitchen as the workers tried to whip up a last-minute meal for the Old Blues and their wives.

I became increasingly annoyed. It especially pained me to see Mary running around excitedly as the Yale Club sat there coolly, waiting to be served. She ran by me in a huff and shouted.

"Quick, Peter! Get some coffee cups! They need coffee cups!"

I walked up to the stack of clean cups with deliberate slowness and started counting them out onto a tray, one by one.

"Hurry up, for Christ's sake," Mary whined. "These people are waiting."

"All right! Don't worry about it. They'll get their goddamn coffee cups," I shouted at her, loud enough for the Yale Club to hear. They looked on in disapproval and Mary walked by them shaking her head.

"Boy, these student workers," she said. "They're so slow!"

I felt terrible.

I had taken my anger out on Mary when she was the one I was angry *for*. I hated to see her so subservient, and yet it was I who put her down further, and in front of them. So much so that she'd had to defend herself. I couldn't understand how everything had gotten so twisted.

She approached me afterward, when we were cleaning up.

"You know, Peter. You'd better watch it. You were wrong to wise off in front of those people."

"I know, Mary." I tried to apologize. "I'm sorry."

"Those were special people," she said, her face set in earnest, "and you had to go and get wise. They don't like that, you know."

"Oh, Mary," I said, exasperated, "those were not special people."

"Yes they were. The manager made a special trip down here to tell us to make sure that they were well taken care of. You'd better be careful, you know. They might report you. You might lose your job."

She turned to the counter and started shoving cottage cheese into a container.

I almost cried for her. I wanted to take her in my arms and try to convince her that there weren't any "special people," that she was as special as anyone else in the world.

I put my arm on her shoulder.

"Mary, there's no such thing as special people. People are people. That's all."

She stood there, shaking her head and shoveling the cottage cheese.

"Peter, you're wrong. Those were special people and you had to open your big mouth."

"Mary, look at them," I said, pointing toward the dining room. "What's so special about them?"

"Peter. Shush. They'll hear you."

"Mary," I pleaded, "can't you see that you're more special to me than any of those people? That's why I got so mad. I hated seeing you run around for them."

Her eyes suddenly glazed with tears and she hurried to the refrigerator with the cottage cheese.

"Peter, what am I going to do with you?" she called back. "You're gonna give me gray hairs. You're gonna get yourself in trouble too. You don't know your place. Those were special people."

PETER—
HIGH-SCHOOL TEACHER

*P*ETER graduated from Yale just a few weeks before we met in a Greenwich Village bar in the summer of 1979. He looked wonderful and had a new bounce. It didn't take long before he made his first shameful confession: he was thinking of joining the Yale Club of New York.

"Good God, Peter! What's happened?"

Peter grinned one of his big grins and chuckled. "Yes. Isn't it terrible? I never thought I'd do that. But when you're just out of college, it's very cheap to join—like $125 a year—and they have gym facilities. I can't join any gym in New York for that."

"So you're selling your soul for your body?" I needled him.

"That's not even the worst of it. Shall I tell you more?"

"Do you think I can take it?"

"Well," he said sheepishly, "I'm thinking of taking a job with a New York bank—a training position in marketing."

That was almost too much for me. I ordered another drink. "And are you also going to have motorboats tied up to a dock at the edge of your lawn and collect antique mechanical banks with clowns on them? You'll turn out to be a capitalist yet."

"No—I'll capitalize on my own talents, not other people's." Chuckle. "Actually, I hope to learn a lot about things I didn't learn at college—finance and how all that works."

However, as we talked further, it was obvious that Peter's heart and soul were still in the arts. He was full of new enterprises: 3-D photography; new ideas for plays; and covers from paperback books published in the forties and fifties, which he planned to make into an art-sociology book from that period. He started to fantasize about his future.

"You know what I'd really like to become? The male counterpart of Lena Wertmuller. *Seven Beauties* is a great film. So is *Swept Away*. She portrays the real stuff."

What Peter wanted for the moment was a "base job—not really base (chuckle) for four days a week," which would earn him his living and then allow him to "do real work—write, photograph, and work on my book for the remaining days." He was living in Fresh Meadows with his favorite grandmother—"a really hep person with a great sense of humor"—and enjoying all the action of New York's art world.

During his years as an upperclassman, Peter devoted much of his time to taking graduate courses in playwriting at the drama school. He also continued to write for *The New Journal*. In both, he ran true to form—producing fine but controversial material—mostly highly satirical. As usual, he drew fire. In one instance he was inspired by a news event that drew a lot of publicity in his junior year. A Yale freshman, who was admitted after presenting himself as a young self-made millionaire and international entrepreneur—complete with a fake name, a fake high school transcript, and fake SAT scores —was discovered and expelled. He turned out to be a house painter from San Francisco. For Peter, the story and the reaction of the student body had disturbing undercurrents. It seemed to reveal some unpleasant attitudes about who "belonged" at Yale and who didn't. He decided to write an anonymous piece for *The New Journal*—"a mirror-version of the house painter's fraud." Peter's story was about "a middle-class Jewish girl from Long Island who realizes she'll have a better chance getting into Yale if she pretends to be the daughter of a Puerto Rican domestic from Spanish Harlem. She figures that if she does this, the heavy recruitment of minority students for affirmative action will get her admitted. Although she usually scores high on exams, she decides purposefully to do only so-so on her Scholastic Aptitude Tests. Sure enough, she's admitted and then uses her book allowance to buy birth control pills."

Peter had hit target again. Yale's minority students were not amused and called the editor of *The New Journal* with heavy threats if he ever published anything like that again. The dean of minority students assembled a kangaroo court and asked *The New Journal*'s editor to have the anonymous author turn up to listen to a delegation of blacks and Puerto Ricans. Peter was distressed but he did not turn up. And he claims he was genuinely puzzled. "My piece was a satire," he protested to me. "It was supposed to be funny. I thought I was on their side." Whether Peter really didn't know that he was asking for it, I don't know. But he certainly had hit the bull's-eye in one of the most sensitive areas at Yale.

He also targeted another sensitive area: women. In his senior playwriting class, he wrote a one-act thriller called *Camera Work*, which was chosen as one of the two best plays of the class—and therefore slated to be produced. But the women actresses refused to act in it because it portrayed one of the women as sexually obsessive —"a role they felt was humiliating to women." Said Peter, "It was just another instance of people focusing on the wrong point. It had nothing to do with the real thrust of the play—which was a whodun-it—a *Twilight Zone* kind of mystery."

Peter was no red-neck, no John Bircher, neither was he a real leftist. He was really an existentialist of sorts and just seemed to have an uncanny ability to touch sore spots with biting humor. There was always enough of a grain of truth in his viewpoint to make it sting. Whether he was in fact unaware that his satires would kick up dust, or whether he liked to see the dust fly for its own sake, I can't guess. He did want to be very sure people saw things from all sides.

Almost all college students seem to have one year that is a "downer," when a lot of things conspire to stir up anxieties and confuse the picture. Peter's year was what he calls "my first senior year." He'd broken up with his girl of long standing and he was worried about that frightening time when one graduates—and then what? He found himself staying in bed more and more, "reading schlock magazines" and burying himself under his big down comforter.

"You were playing Oblomov?"

"Yeah—I had a great bed, a beautiful room, a big bay window, and I didn't see the point of getting up. And I didn't eat right. Also, the university was very depressing to me that year. The employees were on strike and picketing many of the buildings. It was sad seeing them shuffling around looking like they hadn't eaten in three weeks. I knew part of that was simply show to help them win the strike. But they looked awful. The whole university seemed to be an analogue of my state of mind."

Peter left Yale and took the rest of the year off. He lived at home, took on some free-lance writing jobs and a few courses at Nassau State College, and by the end of the year his spirits had returned. His family worried about him, but the year off was valuable—as it is for many students. "I felt better than I ever had," he said, "and I got along with people much better. I learned a few social amenities. I certainly wasn't helping the social situation any by lying in bed. I'm not doing people any favors just by feeling miserable about them or myself."

Peter enjoyed his "second senior year" with "good company and good times," but wasn't "intensely involved with anyone or anything. I kept myself at a distance." He was accepted in a graduate course in playwriting and worked with Howard Stein—"a great man." He worked hard, and when he had finished his last paper, "all of a sudden I let myself feel again. I knew I was going to graduate. I wasn't going to mess up again." He paused, quiet for a moment. "You know," he said, "someday I think I'll work out a happy medium between keeping my distance and getting too emotionally caught up in all the injustices I see."

When I called Peter again in the summer of 1981, he'd just returned from a vacation with friends in Maine, where he was hunting stereo photographs. Although he was still working for the bank, he had completed an intensive education course to qualify for teaching English in New York public schools, where he had taken a job beginning in the fall.

"I found working in the bank really very interesting," he said. "I had never dealt with finance before—nor did I know how banks work. But my real love is literature, and also I'm not comfortable being involved with business."

"Why not, Peter?"

"I don't know. I'm not very happy when people make a distinction between business decisions and moral decisions. If you ask how they can support apartheid by investing in South Africa, they say, 'That's a business decision, not a moral one.' And the staff—the people working here—they're treated as business units, not as people. I don't like places that depersonalize people in order to function."

"And teaching?"

"Well," he said, "I feel as if I'm almost entering a monastery and taking vows of poverty (chuckle) but I think I'll be a lot happier teaching literature. It's what I've always wanted to do. I used to have doubts about my motives—or my expectations. Sometimes I would imagine myself as a teacher on *Room 222* or *Welcome Back, Kotter,* and then I'd tell myself they were just TV shows—romanticized versions of the intense satisfaction of teaching. Teaching itself would be very different. But hell, the best classes I had in high school were right out of *Room 222.* It may not be expecting too much after all."

PORTRAIT OF MARY

MARY Sheldon was a member of the same seminar as Elías Aguilar and Peter Werner, and together the three provided a combination of characters that would stretch the imagination of the most enterprising of Yale admission officers. It certainly stretched mine. Helped along by occasional interjections from other class members, Peter and Elías would argue vehemently on almost every subject, from which one of them was poorer (a sign of some status in that period at Yale) to what was wrong with Edmund Wilson's essay "Detroit Motors." Meanwhile, Mary would quietly observe the battle scene from a chair that was usually pushed slightly into the background.

Although of average size, Mary gave off an air of porcelain fragility and the wide-eyed tentativeness of a little girl who had suddenly found herself surrounded by a group of adults in a hot political discussion. As Peter spouted caustic Ivy League humor and Elías pontificated with "motherfucking" gusto, in my mind's eye I would imagine Mary far away, curled up on the window seat of a thatched-

279

roof cottage somewhere in rural Sussex, quietly writing poetry while the English rains streamed down the leaded window panes.

But Mary did not live in a thatched-roof cottage nor was she so fragile. In her own shy way she had clout—which the class was soon to discover.

Although I think the other students knew that she came from "somewhere out there on the west coast," they weren't aware that her father, Sidney Sheldon, was one of Hollywood's best-known scriptwriters. This was before the days when he had published many novels, so the students had no occasion to spot *Bloodline* or *Rage of Angels* in bookstore or airport racks. Nor did Mary ever mention what her father did. This was smart of her as well as showing her innate modesty. Yale had its particular snobberies, and popular romantic novelists and filmwriters, by and large, were judged with academic scorn—especially if they made money. Erich Segal, a formerly popular professor of classics, had been mercilessly ridiculed for *Love Story,* and Charles Reich, a professor in the law school, was given similar treatment for *The Greening of America*— though he put his neck out a little further by writing about matters in the academic terrain.

What brought Mary respect from the class was her own writing. Drafted in immaculate but imaginative English, her material began to appear in the notebooks at a tremendous rate. And it was good —with a subtle self-spoofing wit that the class could appreciate. To the upperclassmen, her ability and output was made even more impressive by the fact that she was only a freshman. By the time we were three weeks into the semester, there was no doubt in anyone's mind that Mary knew how to write. And although she didn't speak up much more than she had in the beginning, class members were now glancing in her direction during a discussion to check out her reactions. Whenever she did speak—always in a breathless, almost gushy voice—her opinions were compassionate (except toward her own writing) and quietly definite.

The class had strong reactions to her writing. Once, when she had removed an early version of her long story from the notebooks because she thought it was no good, the class protested with vigor. With his usual passion, Elías wrote on the comment sheet in the notebooks: *"Miss Sheldon!!* If you don't put the first version back in the notebook and stop being Miss Self-conscious, I'll shoot you! I loved that piece. It had a punch and fluidity that's lacking in the revision. You made a great error in scrapping it. I'm pleading with you to return it." The rest confronted her in class. Mary demurred —smiling mysteriously—but the piece was returned the following week.

An only child, Mary grew up in close companionship with her actress mother—a southerner descended from the Sledges and Lees of Virginia—and writer father, the son of a traveling salesman. Her parents were her "trusted friends" and inspiration. "The worlds of theater and books," she said, "have always made my horizon as well as theirs. There was never a possibility that I would grow up to be a doctor or a lawyer—it has saved me a lot of time." Groucho Marx was her godfather.

Early in her life, when her mother and father were poor and struggling to establish themselves in their volatile professions, Mary was moved back and forth "many, many times" between the coasts; they lived in eighteen different houses and apartments, and Mary attended nine different schools. "There never seemed to be any continuity between one period in my life and the next," she said. "Sometimes I was happy in the new house, smart in school, loved. Other times I was miserable, hated by teachers and the kids alike, perpetually an outsider." By the time she was twelve, success was beginning to pay off and the family came to rest in Beverly Hills. Although there was now the occasional elegant dinner party at which Mary had to turn up appropriately starched and pressed, her family remained devoted, close-knit, and hardworking. "My father," Mary told me one day, "is the original believer in the puritan work ethic."

During her peripatetic childhood, Mary surrounded herself with her favorite animals, dolls, and books and the fantasy life that an only child is so often heir to. Mary's fantasy world must have been particularly engaging and, I suspect, not without a good deal of input from two extraordinarily imaginative parents. "Both of them thought I would eventually become an actress," she said. "Before I was born, my mother wanted to name me Flame—she could envision it blazing someday on a theater marquee. They believed I was so-o-o-o talented." Mary smiled shyly, basking in their blind faith and protesting that they were utterly foolish in their estimation of her.

For her early high school years, Mary attended Westlake School for Girls, a rather posh and pretentious private day school in Beverly Hills which prides itself on high academic standards. She found the girls at Westlake "dreadful (they kept saying 'Mary Sheldon, go to hell')" and dreamed of going to an old-fashioned English boarding school. After many insistent petitionings from Mary her parents finally relented, and she went off to St. Clare's Hall in Oxford for her last two years of high school.

Mary had gauged herself correctly. She found St. Clare's and all the fifty girls there "wonderful." She had a fine English teacher, who taught her to read "Jane Austen, Evelyn Waugh, and all those marvelous people." She felt completely at home in the rather cloistered and patterned daily routine of the English public school and loved its imaginative literary life.

Yale presented another striking change in her life. "After St. Clare's it was so huge, so heartless, it seemed to be run on wheels of steel." It was also her first coeducational experience and my class probably her first opportunity to exchange ideas with a ghetto black or a "poor white" (as Peter liked to call himself). It is no wonder that Peter and Elías should have left her wide-eyed.

Early in the course I had my own concerns about Mary's writing. Although she wrote well-constructed, light vignettes and an unending succession of fanciful poetry, I wasn't sure she could sustain the momentum to construct a long piece, or take herself seriously enough to write something that had real meaning for her. How much was she interested only in creating an effect, by shaping an amusing turn of phrase or by sketching a touching but passing scene depicting self-consciousness?

Daughter of the Household

The daughter of the household is a curious creature when she is shown off at her parents' dinner parties; especially if she does not like her parents' friends.

She sat, head of one of the three tables, and handed the butter around, a distorted miniature of her mother. At the table were three men and their wives, a pretty single woman, and a rumpled young boy.

"So you mean to say that criminals, no matter what they have done," the single lady smiled at her with predatory amusement, "should be allowed to remain absolutely unpunished."

The entire table seemed to titter.

Daughter of the household longed desperately for the way things were at the tables where her parents sat.

"No, no; that's not what I meant." She protested.

The single woman pursued her to the retreat: "But you just said—"

"I heard what she said!" cried the rumpled young man. "She said it because she is young and sensitive."

"Sensitive! What does that have to do with it? I am also sensitive!" burst out the single woman.

Daughter of the household let her fork drop limply. Young. He said, ". . . because she is young . . ."

Or how much was she interested in involving her deeper concerns in what she wrote and developing them thoroughly? I knew she would never expose her feelings directly—or at least, not obviously. (She was another of those students who had a terror of committing the cardinal sin of overexplaining. I think she would have dropped through the floor and disappeared forever if anyone had accused her of being "obvious.")

But I needn't have worried about all this. Her final decision (and it was made very early in the course) was to write her long piece about her relationship to someone who was indeed very close to her —the newly-met friend she'd run across in the library, a prelaw senior at Yale. I usually warned my students against writing about love relationships that were in progress, especially if they were fairly new. But Mary, I felt, could handle it. Besides, I had no choice; once Mary made up her mind, that was it. Her story revealed a playful side of Mary that we never saw in class.

Just when Mary gave her story to her friend to read, I have no idea. I rather imagine it was not until after she felt quite sure of his affection. But it was a question I didn't ask her; fiction, fact, and

283

privacy were all so closely bound for Mary that I would not have intruded even if she had allowed it. As to her father, I doubt whether she showed the story to him until much later. She would not have felt she needed to hide the subject matter, but exposing her craft to the master storyteller—ah, that was another issue altogether.

*L*EGAL MIND
by Mary Sheldon
Beverly Hills, California

*I*T was very hot. I had just come to Yale, was hating it, and couldn't figure out how to use the photocopy machine in the library.

A boy with red hair and a blue jacket was walking toward me. He struck me as being the sort whose nickels never jammed in the Xerox, and I asked him for help. After he obediently copied my pages, he nodded a good-bye, but I kept him talking. I make it a point not to be well behaved in libraries.

"So you're going into law. How splendid."

How splendid indeed. I never could resist the chance to make fun of a lawyer.

"As for me, well, I've always hoped to follow a career in bank robbery."

Perhaps it was because lawyers are usually mentioned along with doctors, and I have, since the day I received my first flu injection, always loathed doctors. Perhaps it was because my father had told me that I could marry anyone I chose, except for an actor or a lawyer. It seems that the first would eat me up in a year, and that I would eat the second up in a week. Or perhaps it was because I hate legal

285

minds; they are too much like legal pads—ruled, straight, and yellow.

"Do you like Yale?" the boy asked politely.

I said I didn't. "I've only been here a week, and I've already cut nine out of twelve classes. And I'm starting a campaign to get my physics teacher fired."

"You're a scientist?"

"Oh, yes," I said ardently. "Physics is my *raison d'être.*" Ha! The last science course I'd taken was when I was ten and failed in my paper model of a bee.

I felt no whisper of guilt about this lie. Lawyers deserve such treatment, after all. They do not send valentines.

"What's your name?" he asked me.

"It's Elizabeth." Elizabeth is the name I like best in the whole world. "But you can call me Pamela for short."

He laughed. "Where do you come from?"

"Arizona, and yes, the Grand Canyon is as beautiful as they say it is."

I looked up at the clock then, and saw that it was time for my history class. I said good-bye to the boy and rushed from the library.

Sleazy Sunday, early October. My roommate was away for the weekend, and I sat on the floor of our living room, reading. We had not had much time to decorate, so the room was bare, except for one aggressively athletic swivel lamp, a few tacky posters (my roommate's), my venerable azalea, and my cat, Isabella, who hated Yale even more than I did.

There came a soft knock at the door. I opened it and found a boy standing outside. He seemed very nervous.

"Hi," he said, smiling at me. "I just came by to see how you're getting on."

"Well, my, my," I rattled, effusively. "How perfectly splendid of you to come! I shouldn't admit this, I know, but I was hoping you would!" And it was quite a miracle of a smile I broke into then, considering that I had absolutely no idea who this person was.

"Aren't you going to offer me a bit of carpet?" he asked, coming in and sitting.

I chirped on like Billie Burke in *The Wizard of Oz.* Who on earth was he, and how could I find out without insulting him dreadfully?

My appetite for impossible deeds was whetted, for, as I had told Legal Mind a few weeks before, I have the sneaky soul of a bank robber.

Wait a minute. Hold on there. This person perched on my carpet was a redhead. Legal Mind—hadn't he had red hair also? Could this in fact *be* he? It? But another glance at the mysterious visitor reassured me. He was up on his haunches, barking at my cat.

I tried to remember everyone I had met in the last month. This person sitting on my carpet could be the boy who had lent me his *Canterbury Tales* because I'd dropped mine in the bathtub. Or perhaps he was the boy who reported me for having an illicit hot plate in my room. But surely he was the one who helped me to put out the fire when that same hot plate started to roast the curtains. No. This person was obviously someone I had taken quite a fancy to, for I seemed to have given him my name and address. Could it be senility setting in? A week before my seventeenth birthday?

The boy stopped barking at my cat, and began to purr instead. Isabella was enchanted. Then he looked up and grinned at me.

"It took quite some courage to come, you know. After all, you didn't even tell me your last name. Or your address. But I found you. I tried the easy way first, and looked through the freshman directory. But you didn't put your picture in. Then I tried the registrar's office. You told me your first name was Elizabeth, so I spent an afternoon looking up all the freshmen from Arizona with *E* as their first initial. There aren't any."

I blushed.

"But then I remembered that you said to call you Pamela for short, so I hunted out all the Ps. When that didn't work, I visited every freshman from Arizona in alphabetical order. Round about the Ws, I began to wonder if you came from Arizona at all. I spent a few more days in the registrar's office, and here you are at last. So tell me—how are things in California, Mary?"

"You are thorough," I said.

He smiled. "Yes. I think it's called 'having a legal mind.' "

I ended up spending quite a bit of time with this strange character that October. Shielding from the world his true identity, Legal Mind passed in daily life as "Robert Asher." Loyal and close-lipped to the core, I went along with the masquerade.

As I came to know him better, I gradually reached the conclusion that the creature was too miserable to be true. When I say I wish I were in ancient Greece, wearing chitons and eating olives, I want the person I am with to say "Of course!" I don't want him to say "Really? Isn't it awfully crowded over there this time of year?"

The time I barraged him with raptures about Elizabethan London, lutes, and ruffs, I was met with the plague, lice, and no drainage system. And yet, the time I said I simply must go to Maine that weekend and eat a lobster—well? If I didn't come into his room and find him scrutinizing road maps! Fool. I hate lobsters.

Why did he get so upset? Why can't I say I like something when I don't? I was just in a mood to be a lobster eater that day.

The reason I showed him my book was not because I thought he could offer any valuable criticism, but because I hoped to shame him into seeing what an uncreative wretch he was. And what did he say? "This reminds me of my first novel—except mine was better." Foul, unfeeling creature!

And when I failed my English essay, did I get comfort? Ha. True, he did offer to help me rewrite the paper, but did he have to find my sentence structure quite so amusing?

But maybe I didn't despise him as much as I thought. At the end of October he became, unexplainably, so very sad. I couldn't help worrying just a little. We went out to dinner, and I talked nonsense all through the meal, trying not to ask him what was wrong, because it was none of my business and because I didn't want to get involved. Finally I asked straight out.

Somehow, it had never entered my head that there had been a "last girlfriend."

"I've never been that close to anybody," he told me. "I've known her since I was seven years old. After I got her letter last Wednesday, I kept congratulating myself—I was taking it all so wonderfully. I wasn't hurt. I wasn't crushed. But I kept getting drunk, night after night, refusing to admit why." He laughed with bitterness. "The worst is that I knew her so well. I knew her thoughts before she did."

I shrugged. Robert had just touched on my secret and impossible dream—to be known well, and still be cherished—flaws and all.

I looked into my glass of wine, a wavering crystal ball, and saw myself. There was only one way to get rid of that unlucky image. Cannily and quickly, I drank the wine down. He was sitting across from me, also looking into his glass. I wondered what the crystal ball told him.

Now seems a good moment to tell the story of the most important thing that has ever happened to me.

When I was five years old, I had one ambition. Toy shops at that time were selling Disneykins—tiny plastic figures of storybook characters. I craved the whole set desperately, but perhaps more than any other, I wanted a little Alice in Wonderland to put in my pocket.

I was spending the weekend at my Aunt Lucia's house. She promised that she would take me to a shop and buy a set of Disneykins for me first thing Saturday morning.

My cousin Melody was also sleeping over, and I kept her up nearly all Friday night, sometimes by talking about the Disneykins, sometimes by being quiet and thinking about them.

When we got to the toy shop the next morning, we headed for the shelves where the Disneykins were, but saw there was only one set left. It had originally held twelve of the little characters, but some child must have sabotaged it, for every one of them had been broken off except the figure in the center. Alice in Wonderland.

"There's another toy shop a block away," my Aunt Lucia said, comfortingly. "We'll get a good set there."

But I wouldn't move. I was in an awful state. I yearned for every one of the Disneykins—for Dumbo and his silly ears, for Peter Pan and his green jerkin—but Alice was the one I wanted most.

"No, Aunt Lucia," I insisted. "I want this set."

She pointed out how foolish I was being, and I burst into tears. She could not change my mind. I had found Alice, and I would not leave without her—after all, how could I be sure that there would be another one in the toy shop a block away?

So Aunt Lucia bought me the little plastic figure, and we walked to the other store. In ten minutes, my cousin Melody came out with a big smile and a little paper bag. Inside was Alice—and the rest of the Disneykins too.

It has been that way for as long as I can remember. I have never trusted my luck. I have never trusted anything, certain that my heart's desire will be snatched away even as I touch it with my fingers. . . .

My October with Robert was no exception. I suppose I should have been happy when he told me he had broken up with his girl-friend. But I wasn't. It seemed too easy. If they had loved each other once, why couldn't they do so again? And then, suddenly, like a waking dream, a scene came into my mind.

He and she, the last girlfriend, were coming down some stone steps. From a party? It was night, and cool, for she had a wrap. I saw her push a lock of hair away from her eyes—she had that delicate green-gold hair, with a bend in it at the shoulder. He used to put his hand there, in that bend, quite absentmindedly, when he was thinking or trying to remember something. I could see what she was wearing. Not her dress, but the buttons on it. They were tiny and red, like earrings —and her earrings were little golden loops.

Those earrings, especially, made me want to weep and curse and curse and weep. I—coward that I am—had canceled three appointments with Doctor Marcus, sure that ear piercing would end up with ear amputation.

I told myself that these insane hallucinations were caused by nothing more than my damned unfinished English paper.

I used to think a lot about his name being Robert. It seemed so puny. I felt happy the day I discovered that he had a middle initial. I never asked him what the *J* stood for, but it made things a lot easier. On his black turtleneck sweater days, I was convinced it stood for *Jon*. On the days when he'd scowl that I'd interrupted his reading, I'd comfort myself, certain that his stodginess was due to his having *Jerk* as a middle name. The nights we went bowling it changed to *Jerry*, and once, during a church service, the glorious possibility occurred to me that it might be *Jehovah*.

I was looking forward to going to the Halloween party with Rob-ert, for going to parties is one of the things I do best. I am absolutely charming and it is horrible. Not because I am phony, asking people what their names are, what they do, and then forgetting—no; I remember. What is horrible is that it is such an effort.

What is also horrible is that the people never guess; for, as I say,

I am charming. I talk to everyone. I single out lonely boys in corners, I bring drinks to the ones in the loud shirts, I flirt with the ones who wear glasses.

The reason? Very well—why not tell you? When I went to my first real party at age thirteen, no one danced with me, even though I was wearing my green chiffon dress.

So when Robert and I came into the party on Halloween night, I left him almost immediately and went off to be charming. The next time I saw him was at two in the morning, when he said he'd better take me home. He looked at me very quietly and asked me very slowly, "Why did you do that?"

I just stared at him. Why? Why, it was all for his benefit! I wanted him to see that I was not a socially graceless wallflower but a desirable human being. I wanted him to be so stunned by my air of sophistication that scales would plunge from his eyes and he would suddenly forget all my past shyness and childishness and see me for the woman I truly was—even though I truly wasn't. I wanted him to think of me as a dangerously flirtatious girl who was never, never to be taken for granted; someone whom, as a child, nannies had shaken their heads over and who they prophesied would come to a bad end.

So I told him. "I did it for your benefit." And after he left, I sat up in bed, awake until morning, crying about the delicate and puzzled hurt of his good-night kiss.

I never know if I am in love with someone until the moment I tell him that I am in love with him, and only then, when he blurts out that he loves me too, do I realize that the whole thing is a mistake.

When the time came, on November fifth, Robert told me this: that I had said I loved being alone "above all things," so how could I love him? I had said I loved Venice, and my Aunt Lucia, and going swimming, and ice-cream sandwiches. I had said I loved the scores of boyfriends in my life. So why should he care if I said I loved him too?

And he did not say he loved me.

The afternoon I asked Robert to play the song "Day by Day" for me, he sighed. "That song. It brings back too many things."

I also had memories embedded in that song, but they were wiped out instantly, like dust on a windowsill, by what I imagined his to be.

He used to pick her up for the evening at her house. She would always be sitting on the plaid sofa, on the middle cushion.

The living room of her house was a thing of completeness. Blue curtains, once bought to match a chair long since re-covered in orange. The bowling trophies. The tank of tropical fish.

Robert was always eager to rescue her from the room. She didn't fit. She was a different texture, a different color. But she never noticed that she didn't belong in her house, with her parents, the coffee cake in the refrigerator, or her older sister's turquoise nylon net prom dress. Because she never noticed, he felt protective, and so led her out of the house quickly, his hand on her hair.

The two of them would return from their evening and park in front of her house. I could see his arm around her shoulders, but though I strained terribly, the only thing I could hear was that song "Day by Day" playing on the radio, and nothing else but the intimate intensity of thought.

Who has the power to fight a silence? I did try. I wrote myself notes each morning, saying that there was nothing to be afraid of, that the past is dead, that this time I must have a bit of faith in myself.

But it did little good. I was the character in the song "Loch Lomond." No matter how quickly and carefully I ran down the high road, there she was, the last girlfriend, down below my sight, slipping along the low road. How far ahead of me was she now?

Oh, but I am a sneaky fighter. The way that ants storing up grain against the winter are sneaky. There had to be some method of storing Robert up for loveless January days. I tried weaving a cloak of poetry, webbing him in the threads of meter and metaphor; for poetry, typed in black ink on paper, lasts through the winter.

But Robert struggled against my threads as impatiently as Gulliver against the threads of the Lilliputians.

November seventh, Keith died. He was eighteen years old. We had had many special times together, my cousin and I. I thought of them now. The day he fell in love with the seal at Marineland. Those musicals we put on, and the Beatles songs he sang incorrectly in his raucous voice, "Please please me like I please you!" I thought of his cowboy hat, and a haiku he wrote. "Ha! I'll prove them wrong!" was the last line.

I'd loved Keith all my life, but when they called and told me about the accident, the only thing I could feel was exhilaration. I went out and bought a doughnut. The air seemed finer than usual. The pavement seemed harder, the leaves were surely crisper. I ate the doughnut slowly, and saw Keith's pointed mischievous face before me.

I don't know exactly when this wonderful sense of life left me, but sometime that afternoon it was gone, and I was alone. Afraid to die, and Keith already dead.

Looking for a lifeline, I telephoned Robert and told him to come over as soon as possible.

He came.

"Keith is dead."

But Robert had never heard me speak of my cousin. He had never seen his picture, or his cowboy hat.

"I'm sorry," he said.

I couldn't believe it. "I'm sorry" is what my roommate had said. And the chaplain. My father on the telephone had also said "I'm sorry."

What I expected Robert to say, I don't know. He was the Legal Mind, and he could have somewhere found a clause in the contract saying that Keith could live on forever.

"I'm sorry."

He said it a little louder this time.

I spent the afternoon alone, reading biographies of dead film stars and growing angry. When Robert came that evening to take me out to dinner, I sat in my white lace blouse and skirt, a cold cameo, and began to accuse him. In a voice of remotest pearl, I accused Robert of committing every evil I could think of, because I could not, after all, condemn him for the one sin he *had* committed: he hadn't stopped my cousin from dying.

Finally Robert turned to me. "That will be enough, Mary." But I kept on.

All my life, I have never really minded having fights with people. I used to wear fights rather like badges, the way I wore the Band-Aid the nurse put on my arm after the shot. The fights never lasted long, and after they were over I was very good at being comforted back to smiles—regardless of whether or not I had started the argument in the first place.

But it was a strange thing, my sadness now. Robert and I had ended the last tearing, ripping hour promising each other a "fresh start." But there could be no fresh start. Not really.

I didn't trust Robert for a long time after that, and he didn't trust me for the same long time. The atmosphere was a peculiar shade of sad.

One day I decided that I had had enough—that it was time to go into action. I would Use Tactics; and I admit, Using Tactics is one of the things I do best.

I hated to do it; I hated to admit that Robert was just another someone to be manipulated; I hated to admit that the word *manipulated* was in my vocabulary.

But before Robert came, I knew the scene would be word-perfect.

Act two, scene one: Enter the wounded Faun! (And it would work. Robert, being a man like all the other squashy men I know, would absolutely fall at my hooves.)

(Robert enters. Mary is sitting on bed, hands tracing the coverlet pattern, with small and wan gestures.)

Robert

Hello.

Mary

(Suddenly looking up. For a moment we see a glance of naked emotion dart into the warm brown eyes, then they return to normal.)

Hello.

Robert

How are you today?

Mary

(very intensely)

I saw a child today walking with his elder sister. The girl held his hand as if it were as fragile as a sugar cookie—the *two of them smiled at me as I passed, but I wondered. What would happen when they turned the corner? Would she drop his hand? Would he drop his smile, as soon as I had passed? (Mary, with a pale smile, returns to tracing the pattern on the coverlet.)*

Robert

(shaken)
    Hey—are you all right?

Mary

(looking up abruptly; eyes are now luminous)
    And I passed an old woman doing her Christmas shopping. I saw her in the toy store, knowing exactly what she wanted, proud that she was buying just the things her grandchildren longed to have. I couldn't see everything—only enough to know that she was buying the wrong presents.
(She looks up suddenly gay.)
    My goodness! How morose! Enough of this. Tell me about your day.

Robert

Never mind about that. Mary, you're acting so strangely. Please tell me what's wrong!

Mary

(after a long silence)
    It's odd: I never would have noticed those things—before. Before—I would only have seen the sweetness in the children. Before—I would only have seen the pride in the toy shop woman's face. But suddenly I'm seeing all these other things. That's because it's no longer Before, is it? It can never be Before again.

I decided to end the script there and let him take it from that point forward, and improvise his own lines of comfort, his own phrases of consolation.

There came a knock at the door, and I scurried into position, stage right.

"Hello." Robert dashed into the room. "What are you looking so morbid about?"

295

"I'm not. I saw a child today, walking with his elder sister . . ."

When I had finished my first speech, and I did it rather well I must say, there was a deep silence.

"That's not bad," Robert said finally. "Of course," and his face fell, "you haven't a hope in the world of its working, but," he brightened, "it does show a lot of talent! Let's see—my guess is that you were being a homeless bird. Am I right?"

I was knocked flat.

"Well, am I right?"

I suddenly remembered something; the night at the restaurant, where I had stared so longingly in my wineglass, wishing to meet a man who would *see;* who would see what I had tried carefully to hide; who would understand all my ruses and my motives and care for me anyway. Ah, the impossible joy of knowing that he knew that I knew that he knew. . . .

"You're a fool, Robert." My voice was unsteady. "If I were a homeless bird, I'd be all hunched over, wouldn't I? Wouldn't I? Can't you even recognize a wounded faun when you see one?!"

Well, after that, things seemed to be all right.

I told nobody about the absurd little things Robert did to cheer me up that winter.

In January I was ill with the flu, and he came to visit. "I've stopped by on my way to dinner. Have you eaten yet?"

"No," I told him blearily. As if my tortured body could be coaxed into spending half an hour at a college dining room!

"Oh." And suddenly, unexplainably, he was gone.

As I lay there, deserted, I tried to be rational; men regarded illness in a different light than women did, after all; he didn't realize how sick I was—I ought to be glad that I didn't have to worry about him worrying about me; I ought to be grateful that he was strong enough to shut me out of his mind and spend a quiet dinner hour in the stimulating company of his friends. I ought to be pleased! But after forty-five minutes had passed, I was in tears.

Suddenly, Robert charged into my room, with something covered by a napkin. "I've brought you a surprise." I lifted the paper, and there lay a sandwich; the most drippy, mangled, tormented fragment I have ever laid eyes on.

He hovered over me, eyes like a little boy's. "Eat it! What's wrong? Aren't you going to eat it?"

As I choked down the sandwich, he revealed the secrets of his concoction.

"You have no idea how long it took to steal the bread, melt the cheese, freeze the apple, buy the dressing, heat the ham, shred the lettuce, spread the peanut butter, and cut it up into eighths," he told me chattily. "And when I looked at the clock and saw I'd spent forty-five minutes making that sandwich, I had the most terrible fear that you'd think I'd spent the time eating my own dinner and talking with my friends." He watched me anxiously. "You didn't think that, did you?"

"Certainly not." I laughed as deprecatingly as my laryngitis would allow.

In February, the evening before one particularly dire drama exam, I flung myself upon his floor and announced that I had ten pages of notes left to learn, no time to learn them, and that I intended to contract bubonic plague. Robert, in the midst of his own exams, tested me on the notes for over two hours. He asked me the questions about German drama in a thick Rhine accent, threatening me with the kaiser every time I forgot that Gottsched wrote in alexandrine verse; he tested me on French drama in a crumbly Gallic voice, kissing my hand and making indecent offers every time I got a date right. When, on the English drama section, I mentioned Queen Elizabeth, I was severely chastised, in the most Mayfair of tones, for not springing to my feet—and my informative offerings about American drama were greeted by a scratching of the chest à la Brando.

It was a most entertaining evening—and the only reason I failed the exam the next day was that Robert and I had studied the wrong set of notes.

It was Robert who got me to stop biting my fingernails. It was Robert who taught me how to find a square root. It was Robert who taught me that twilight does not have to be a death time.

He rescued me from overwork and large black dogs. He stole apples for me from the college dining hall, and showed me that having a piece of chocolate cake did not mean I was unhealthily undisciplined and would soon weigh two hundred pounds.

Finding out by subversive means what my twenty favorite songs were, he managed to dig up recordings of them all and make me a tape. Deciding that my education had been neglected, he bought me a copy of *Anna Karenina*. He also bought me violets, but only after I'd asked.

He remembered that I take my coffee with milk and sugar. He remembered all of my aunts' names. He taught me to spell *moreover*. He said nothing when I left purses in libraries, keys in rooms, tickets in "the other coat," and his best pen in the rain.

For weeks at a time I did not think of the last girlfriend.

Then it was March, evening, a week before the spring holidays. We were at a party. Robert, who had been talking to his history teacher over in a corner, walked up to me.

"Hello, miss," he said in a heavy English accent. "Would you mind being joined by a stranger?"

I didn't mind. He looked a nice sort of fellow.

"My name is Jeremiah," he informed me. "I drive a school bus. It's a boring job, but it seems good to me. I used to be a bullfrog." Then he winked and leaned toward me. "I bet the bus wouldn't be so boring if I could drive pretty girls like you to school every day."

Oh, dear. I do dislike obvious men.

"It so happens that I don't go to school," I told him with a smirk. "You see, I work nights."

He leered at me. "Have you got a specialty?"

"But of course."

"Hey, hey, hey. And what's your name, ducks?"

"It's Rachel."

There was a pause, and when Robert spoke again, the English accent was gone.

"Rachel?" he asked.

Rachel.

And that is how I found out what the girl on the low road to Scotland was called.

Knowing her name changed everything. She stepped out of the past for me. It was queer to think that at this very moment her name was somewhere in the telephone book. And that her mother might even now be shouting, "Rachel! Drat that girl! Where *has* she gone off to?"

And knowing her name changed something else. I had been wrong to imagine her with green-gold hair and waif eyes. That was Alexandra. Rachel had black hair like Anna Karenina, and gray eyes that looked slightly mad. She had windswept cheeks and always wore red tam-o'-shanters.

I tried. I tried not to be jealous, not to be morbid, but in the days that followed things happened that stopped my trying.

Robert was telling me about a phenomenon: people buying presents for others that they want themselves. "Last Christmas I bought—this girl—a radio, and she bought me a shirt."

A few days later I came to Robert's room early to wake him up for breakfast. Sleepily he told me to go to the closet and pick him out a shirt to wear.

The agony of standing there, certain I would choose the one she had bought him. The green. I mustn't pick that. Green was Robert's favorite color, and Rachel would have known. The white with red stripes? No. I thought of the tam-o'-shanter. She might have bought him something with scarlet in it so that whenever he wore the shirt he would think of her.

I finally chose the black and white one. Robert put it on without comment.

And I said, "Let's go bicycling sometime!" Robert smiled. "No. The last bicycle ride I took was too perfect a time for me to even try and repeat."

"Just wait here on the steps, Robert." Her mother patted them. "Rachel'll be along shortly. Her bicycle has a flat, so she's gone to borrow another."

He sat there in the spring sun, waiting.

"Rachel!"

He jumped up. "My God! Where in Heaven's name did you get that?"

He looked down at the tiny tricycle with the ribbons on the basket.

"You crazy woman—you're never going to be able to ride that thing down the driveway—much less to the beach!"

299

"Wait and see!" Rachel pedaled off, the absurdest of grasshoppers, her knees bobbing above her head. Robert was on the ground with laughter.

It is a strange thing, living with a rival who isn't there. You look in the mirror and see not only yourself but her also. You are ugly. She is beautiful. Her hair curls like Christmas sausages.

Or you pick a fight, are cruel, and then want to hang yourself from the highest tree when you think of the gentleness she would have shown. Rachel, strain of music!

After that one night in October Robert never mentioned her again, but the more I knew him, the more deeply I could sense what it was that Rachel had been.

Like a little Proteus, Rachel changed for me all the time. When Robert showed me his seriousness, I saw clearly that she, too, could have been nothing but serious. When Robert was frivolous, I saw —how could I have ever thought otherwise—that Rachel was also the most fun of persons. Someone fond of flinging her shoes into the air.

Understand me. Robert deserved the best, and the best was Rachel. Not me.

I went home to California for the spring holiday. Robert took me to the airport and kissed me at the door of the airplane. My parents were glad to see me, and asked if I'd made many friends at college. I did not tell them about Robert.

I didn't do much that vacation. I knit a hat for my father. I thought about Robert. I'd lie in bed but I would not be able to picture his face. Of if I could summon it at all, it wouldn't be the same Robert who had kissed me beside the airplane. It would be another one, a younger one. The one who had first known Rachel. And I would lie in bed, sometimes all night without sleeping.

Senior year of high school. The halls filled with students. Yes, he'd had a nice summer, but yet, it was good to be back. New York in early autumn is acid and brash. It was a relief to leave the building and walk outside in the noontime. He headed for the gym.

Inside the locker room he caught sight of himself in the mirror. He

*looked preoccupied, and he knew he was. With acceptable things—
college, career, girls. With unacceptable things—what it was like to
grow old.*

*Far away on the gym field, the cheerleaders were having their first
practice. Robert stood by and watched them. He knew calmly that he
would always remember this moment—standing by and watching the
cheerleaders go through their monotonous rites. Their voices were like
the flutter of hands.*

*And they would never know. Never know that when they were old
women and he was an old man, that just by remembering them at this
moment, he would make them seventeen years old once again.*

He left the field and went back into the school building.

*After school, Rachel Billings came up to talk to him. He had
known Rachel nearly all his life, but distrusted her as a rival who tried
to get higher grades than he did. Seeing her now, he frowned, vaguely
annoyed at her peppiness, at her Miami tan, at the fact that she was
beautiful.*

*"Well, Robert," she said. "I saw you watching us this afternoon.
You stayed an awfully long time."*

*Robert wanted to gush out his secret to her—that through his
memory, she would be granted eternal youth. But he didn't.*

*"A cheerleader is so horribly high school," she said suddenly. "But
I like high school. No matter how wrinkled and ugly I get, I can point
to my picture in the yearbook and know that once upon a time I
looked good in gym shorts. Or were you too far away to notice?"
Enter: the dimple.*

It was a rainy Sunday. My parents were playing gin rummy with
their friends the Davises, but I didn't want to go. I stayed home,
looking through books I had had as a child. It was incredible how
short those same books were that I had remembered as being such
tomes—and how simple the descriptions that I had recalled as being
so intimately detailed. God, how I must have put myself into reading
those books. It made me sad, thinking that I could never do that
anymore.

Then I caught sight of my all-time favorite. My mother had given
it to me when I was eleven. *How to Get a Teenage Boy, and What*

301

to Do With Him When You've Got Him. I glanced through it again, amused by its brashness. How to meet a boy. How to make him notice you. How to make him love you.

Then I frowned, remembering Rachel's cheeky exit line the day she met Robert in the school hall. From what I had heard, it sounded as if she were familiar with my favorite book, also.

Or was Rachel just naturally good at this? When she wanted to get to know Robert, did she need a book at all?

Their first date:

It was a glowing October afternoon, the restaurant was quiet, full of people tired from raking leaves.

Robert was wary, puzzled by the way Rachel was behaving. He was used to girls asking all about him, wanting to know about his family, his career ambitions. He was supposed to be flattered by their interest, he knew, but he was bored.

If he had expected Rachel to be different, he was disappointed. She asked him about the same subjects which had interested the other girls, but Robert found her questions a little odd. Would he cheat to pass a college exam? Would he stay close to his family when he graduated from high school? Would he go to church service every Sunday at law school? And when he became a lawyer, would he buy four-hundred-dollar suits at Brooks Brothers? Would he send his children to a private academy?

This last question made Robert nervous. It occurred to him that Rachel's entire routine might have been a joke.

He glanced up quickly, and knew it was no joke. Rachel looked ravenous. Her mouth open like a baby bird's, ready to be fed his next answer.

So he answered her question.

The hunger dropped from her face, her eyelids lowered, and he watched, fascinated, as she tasted and chewed what he had said.

It was an incredible feeling. Robert was somehow sucked out of himself and into Rachel. He wanted to know why she was doing it. He knew.

"And what about you, Rachel?" he asked casually. "What do you plan on doing with your life?"

She relaxed her grip on him. "I have no plans," she said bluntly.

302

"There's nothing I'm going to do. There's never been anything I ever really wanted to do."

Oh, grief. That was exactly the sort of thing that Robert, who is a protective, paternal pussycat, could not resist. Blast him to hell.

The fall term passed slowly—school notebooks gradually became heavier, posters for dances went up and went down, teachers changed from "Mr." to "Old."

Everyone grew used to seeing Rachel and Robert together in the halls, eating lunch together, sometimes with Robert's group, sometimes with Rachel's. When they ate with his, the conversation centered around sports and colleges. With hers, the talk thrived on parties and what everyone had worn.

And sometimes they ate alone.

And then there were the school dances. The night of the Autumn Dance was tender and cool. Robert came over to Rachel's house to pick her up, but she hadn't come downstairs yet. So he watched her father and brother play checkers for a while.

Robert hated complimenting girls on how they looked. The thought that they had spent so much time making the most of their faces embarrassed him.

When Rachel came down the stairs, dressed in an Empire gown of blue velvet, she resembled nothing so much as a faraway photograph of someone's grandmother when young. Robert had no trouble telling her that she was beautiful, but he had to add that he liked her better without make up.

When Robert and Rachel came into the gym, laboriously converted into a dance hall, the first thing they saw was a blond-haired girl in the corner, wearing the same blue velvet dress.

Whee! Did I ever enjoy that!

Robert danced with Rachel all evening. But in the middle of the last slow song, Rachel ran off. Robert called after her, then followed her through the crowd, finally catching up with her next door in the locker room.

As she turned, he saw her face. He put his hand on her cheeks, as if by reading her tears like Braille he could understand why they were there.

"Is it Maxine having the same dress as yours?" he asked her. "I'm glad she wore it, because it gave you a chance to outshine her."

She continued to weep.

"Did I say something to hurt you?"

She shook her head, and he turned her toward him.

"Then what is it?"

She spoke so low he could barely hear her reply.

"It's been a month now, and you haven't kissed me once."

He was still kissing her in March. Not the same kiss, of course. Well, perhaps it was the same kiss, but interrupted by car rides and picnics and telephone conversations and concerts and exams and restaurants and simply looking at each other.

I looked, too, that spring—looked into the cracked mirror I found in the purse I'd had since I was five. Then I closed my eyes and looked away.

But the kiss in March was sweeter.

Robert was relaxing on his back by the shore of the lake, trying to get a suntan. Rachel was thwarting his ambitions by lying on his stomach.

"You know when I had my first crush on a girl?"

She told him no, she didn't know, and didn't care anyway.

"When I was five. It was on Mrs. Craddock, my first-grade teacher. She always wore sweaters pushed up on her arms, and she let me empty the goldfish tank." He laughed and put his arms behind his head. "Her first name was Rachel, and I've always resented any other girl who was called that."

Rachel dumped her head down on Robert's chest, and her voice was muffled.

"Still?"

He thought a moment.

"No. Not still."

Rachel even did things wrong. She had fights with her family: once she flung a vase at her mother's pet sheep dog. She would also laugh "far too loudly for a lady," as her aunt complained.

304

A coward she was not; once she stood up in assembly and denounced the school principal for giving them what she considered an unfair detention. The punishment was not rescinded, and Rachel was given an extra one. Once, dancing at a lodge meeting, she told an old friend of her stepfather's that he was a lecherous beast.

Rachel's teachers found her outspoken and sometimes rude; they did not, after all, see her weeping in the girl's rest room the day she felt she'd made too caustic a joke about her history professor.

It was only to be expected that she was wildly popular with her classmates. Black widows usually are.

It was April. Robert's mother sat down stiffly on the chair. "When I was growing up, Robert, in the days before there were airplanes, when the railroads running through the towns divided them into two halves, there was a name for girls like Rachel. It was said that they were 'from the wrong side of the tracks.' "

I felt pain for Rachel when Robert lowered his eyes.

The day of college acceptances.

Although Rachel was in her bedroom, supposedly studying French, she was listening so carefully that she might have just as well been in the living room.

"Herman!" One of her stepfather's friends had just come into the room. "Janet tells me that Rachel got accepted to every college she applied to!"

"That's right." Her stepfather sounded so unenthusiastic that Rachel couldn't help wanting to laugh. "But you never know about these things—the schools probably had a sex quota to fill, and they took Rachel because she's a girl."

Rachel slammed her textbook down and went to the bathroom for an aspirin.

Later that morning, Robert telephoned.

"Hi, Rachel."

"How did you do?" she asked.

"I got in everywhere, and breakfast in bed. How about you?"

"The same, except no breakfast. Only advice." They laughed luxuriously.

Rachel had her first real daydream about the future that morning.

She saw herself, forty years old, entertaining guests in a penthouse apartment. "And this," she heard herself say, pushing aside the green and golden draperies, "is the river." Quite as if the view were as much a part of the apartment as the Georgian silver teaspoons. Behind her, trying to untie the ribbons on her hostess coat, were two children dressed in clothes from the sixth floor of Bergdorf's.

I could see that her children were beautiful, but I did not know if they were boys or girls. They were pale and misted over, like figures in a Renoir pastoral.

The last two months of high school were lived on Mount Olympus. The weather was what did it. It brought everyone outside, made teachers mellow, made picnics and rowing and waving at people you didn't know a necessity.

The night before graduation, Robert and Rachel were standing outside, very close together.

"Tomorrow's the end of high school," she said quietly.

He tried to make her laugh. "Guess what I noticed this afternoon?" he asked. "Raymond Miles's eyes. They're crossed as two swords, and I never saw it until today. What a waste. We could have teased him about it all these years."

Rachel didn't laugh.

"Hey," Robert said with concern. "You're not going to do anything stupid like cry during the graduation exercises tomorrow, are you?"

"No. Have you been practicing your address?"

"While I'm asleep."

"Are you still going to say all that about the seventh-grade lockers, and the bit about May Day in ninth grade, and that line: 'The cheerleader and her friend from chemistry must part'? Is that still in?"

"Yes."

"Well. I may cry a little after all."

One day while I was still at home, I got a letter from Robert. He said that his plans for the summer weren't certain yet, but that, as soon as the college semester was over, he wanted me to spend a few weeks at his house. That part of the letter was lovely. But then he wrote about all the things that we would do together, and they tumbled out in a great rush, as if he had done all the things before.

With their long brown legs and their short bright clothes, Robert and Rachel melted in with the summer they spent together. It was slow like a back rub, long like the best kind of Popsicle, hot like midnight singing.

It was the middle of July, and Rachel was depressed. Robert had by this time gotten a daytime job as a paralegal, so he could see her only at night. Her mornings weren't bad—she slept and ate—but the afternoons were tedious.

Browsing through a magazine one hot day, she saw an advertisement: Ornaments, hangings, bowls, even windows. Make your own! With our deluxe stained-glass kit, you too can . . .

Rachel put down the magazine. Stained glass! Her summer was solved.

For three weeks, after she'd borrowed the money for the kit and sent away for it, she searched the sunsets for new color combinations. She explored the fields for new flowers. When Robert mentioned an album cover he liked, she promised she would copy it for him in glass. And her mother's favorite Vogue poster, and a baseball for her brother's window shade, and spectacles with rose-colored frames for her stepfather. She went out and bought a potter's smock. She asked if she could have, instead of the regulation Fourth of July fireworks money, a wildly expensive book on Chagall's windows—as research material. She even made the supreme sacrifice. To keep her hands flexible, she cut her fingernails.

Then, one early afternoon, she came home from the lake, and to her suffocating delight, the parcel had arrived.

In Robert's office, the phone rang.

"Robert?"

"Rachel! Is something wrong?"

Came a wail. "Everything's wrong. It came this afternoon—and all it is is—nothing! NOTHING! It's not glass at all—it's plastic and horrible luminous watercolors. And when the lights are out, the luminous paint makes the plastic glow purple and green and orange in the dark."

The only reason Robert didn't laugh is because he didn't dare to. But after he hung up the telephone, he didn't feel like laughing anymore. So her new toy was a disaster—but there was certainly no need to carry on so!

After work that afternoon, he stopped by her house.

"She's in her bedroom," Rachel's stepfather told him. "Been in there all day."

Robert frowned and knocked on her door. She said to come in, but her voice sounded weak, as if she had been crying for hours. When he opened the door and found the room unlighted, he grew apprehensive.

"Rachel?"

No answer.

Then a noise behind him made him turn around. There, standing in a corner, glowing wickedly at him from the darkness, was a stained-glass Rachel. Dressed in a bathing suit, she had painted every available inch of herself like a Chagall window.

What Robert wanted to say was that he appreciated it. That he was relieved that she saw the humor; that he would buy her a real stained-glass kit tomorrow, silly, silly girl; that he loved her; and was she sure that the paint would come off?

What he actually said was, "Are you sure the paint will come off?"

That summer also held the story of the scarf.

Robert and Rachel were at the lake. It was very hot. She had no shirt on, only a halter-top scarf arrangement.

"Stop the sun, Robert."

"Silly. Take off your scarf."

She laughed. "But I have nothing on underneath."

He looked up slowly. . . .

How odd. I'm beginning to feel decidedly unhappy. I believe I'll leave off that scene right there.

Well. So that was their summer, Robert's and Rachel's. They finished up with suntans; Robert's hair had grown lighter, Rachel had taken to curling her eyelashes; Robert was offered a future job in the law firm he had worked for, Rachel's brother won his pitching championship, and Robert wrote music for his guitar.

Robert said good-bye that summer when he packed his suitcase for Yale. But it seemed to him impossible that he could be leaving his house. There were his old baseball cards, but the players no

longer were young like they appeared on the pasteboard squares.
Most of them had left baseball and gone on to become insurance
salesmen. There were the posters he'd bought when he was fourteen.
The bed lumpy from serving as a trampoline. His mother's eyes,
splashed red from saying good-bye, worse than when he'd had his
tonsils out.

"Good-bye," he said. And then Rachel picked him up and they left
for the station.

They were together for three years, Robert and Rachel, but I'm
ending their story here. I've told all I want to—all I can. I don't know
what happened later. Perhaps they grew apart. Perhaps it was because
they went to different colleges, though I'm sure Robert visited her
every holiday. I'm not sure. . . .

All I know is that when I met Robert in the library that September
afternoon, Rachel was not standing beside him.

The spring holidays were now over. I kissed my parents good-bye,
gave Papa the knitted hat, and went back to school.

That April was a dreary one, damp outside, damp inside.

Robert had too much work, and the college kitchen went on
strike, leaving me to fend off starvation with egg salad sandwiches.

I had a good many colds, but I used to pretend I was a lot sicker
than I was, to enlist Robert's sympathy. So don't believe me when
I say I was dying. Believe me when I say I was unhappy. You see,
although Robert was the most giving person I have ever known, he
never once gave me what I wanted most—the upper hand.

The last afternoon in April was nearly as bad for me as the one
which saw my cousin Keith dead.

Robert and I had a dinner date, so at six o'clock I walked upstairs
to his room. He was not there, but his door was open, and I walked
in. The last time I had visited him, I had left my one and only pen
in his desk, so I started to look for it.

It sounds too absurd to speak of an envelope with the same fear
that a bomb would be spoken of, but they were the same to me. The
envelope was unopened, and it was addressed to Robert. The return
address told me that I had been wrong when I imagined her last
name to be Billings. It was Marks. The handwriting was the way I
knew it would be. Rounded. Curly. Perfect.

309

I kept pretending I was home in California. Not here, not with this pain, facing the letter on Robert's desk. It wasn't sealed properly, only closed impatiently with a bit of tape. I picked it up.

When Robert came into the room at last, I was, I think, wonderful. I didn't want him to know anything was wrong. We went to our favorite restaurant for dinner. All through the salad, I made flippant remarks about Henrik Ibsen. All through the entrée, I talked about a funny history teacher I had once had. But I didn't order any dessert.

I couldn't bear being wonderful for that long.

Robert sat quiet.

I was in the hallway by my room now, saying good-night. But when I went inside, Robert didn't leave. "Aren't you going to offer me a bit of carpet?" he asked me, the way he had the first time ever he came to my room. And he sat down.

I didn't speak. I couldn't say a word.

"Didn't anyone ever tell you that there's a penalty for opening other people's mail?"

And then all of a sudden, I was crying, and out it all came. All of it. I told him about Rachel Billings, how I hated her, and all the times they had had together. So maybe I wasn't as exciting, gay, witty—but I loved him for himself—not the penthouse apartment. It was easy to talk. Robert looked impersonal, like a nineteenth-century silhouette. I finished and he didn't speak for a long time.

"You're right," he said finally. "No one in my life has been as dear to me as Rachel, or as loving or as wonderful."

I must have looked stricken to death, and he laughed.

"When I was in high school, I went out with a girl called Rachel Marks. You know, the one whose letter you were just looking at. I liked her. I liked her a lot. But that's not the Rachel I'm in love with. I'm in love with Rachel Billings who rides tricycles and makes plastic stained glass windows."

He pulled me to him, down onto the carpet.

"She's you, you idiot! You're Rachel Billings—I love *you!* Don't you see, you're such an arrogant little creature that you couldn't possibly conceive of a heroine who wasn't exactly like you are."

at me.

u know something? I was just coming to the conclusion Were somewhat perceptive, self-aware, and reasonably intel- ut I warn you—I am rapidly changing my opinion." And he my head and kissed me.

MARY – NOVELIST

*A*FTER the first semester of her sophomore year, Mary left Yale for Wellesley. Or to put it more accurately, Mary left Yale for Legal Mind, who had graduated from Yale the spring before and had gone on to Harvard Law School. She spent much of her time with Legal Mind in Cambridge, where they plied a life that was extraordinarily domestic for a couple so young. Mary wrote that when she wasn't studying or writing stories and adaptations for Hollywood (she was already a professional), she was "seeing foreign films and eating quiches and buying Lincoln rockers and learning how to quilt." No wild college years for Mary and Legal Mind. Such were not to their taste.

Mary didn't miss Yale a bit. She'd had a hard time her freshman year ("My roommate hated me and I hated my roommate") and the first term of her sophomore year was not much of an improvement. She found most of her fellow students "joyless and cold" and her time there an uphill struggle. Wellesley was more her cup of tea; it had "a beautiful library overlooking the lake and all the trees and nooky places that make me delude myself into thinking I'm a homespun country girl at heart." She much preferred Wellesley's English department to Yale's. In a real sense, she had returned to the English countryside where she had been so at ease. Her work blossomed; she became a quiet star among Wellesley's budding writers. And it was completely in character that she should write an honors thesis— *Children in Adult Literature*—from the perspective of a child surrounded by grown-ups.

But it was Legal Mind (since reading her story, I'm incapable of referring to him by any other name) who was pivotal in her life. He was her friend and staunch supporter during the lonely and awkward times; and he believed that she was talented beyond all others. Gradually, the shy but proud and determined girl was becoming, in her words, "so self-confident as to become quite obnoxious."

Both she and Legal Mind seemed to slide through their remaining college years quite effortlessly—or at least without agony—and both placed exceedingly high in their classes. In the hot New England spring of 1978, within a period of a few days, they attended each other's graduations and Legal Mind went off to New York to face the New York bar exams. A week after he'd completed them, they were reunited on "The Coast" and married quietly but elegantly in her parents' home in Beverly Hills.

Legal Mind was now well situated with a distinguished corporate law firm on Wall Street, and they found a lovely house on Long Island within easy commuting distance of New York. The study off the living room was designated as Mary's writing terrain, and by the time I stopped by for a short visit in the fall of 1980 it looked more like Mary than anything I could have imagined. A few favorite and imaginative cloth dolls and animals were tucked into the corners of small chairs, which were upholstered in pastel prints; her own needlepoint designs covered the small occasional pillows; a collection of Beatrix Potter figurines were arranged carefully on a shelf. On the walls, neatly framed, hung a few extraordinary examples of her work in collage and decoupage. I was sure there had been many others that had not met her high standards and had found their way— rather quickly—into the wastebasket. The mullioned window (which could just as well have been leaded) looked out over the front garden and the white picket fence that surrounded the tree-shaded house. Among all these delights, her main instrument of craft—the

313

typewriter—was hard to find. When I did spot it, it looked as mechanical and out of place as if I had come upon it in the corner of a little girl's bedroom in a nineteenth-century manor house.

I was, however, not in the least deceived. I knew many reams of paper had passed through her typewriter since I had last seen her; that she had completed her first novel; that she was under contract to Random House and was now busy rewriting the second half of it to meet her editors' requirements. Although she demurred to my congratulations, she was very pleased. And so was Legal Mind.

"Every word she writes is perfect," he told me with great pride. "Random House said it was one of the most brilliant things that they'd ever read."

"Aww," said Mary, smiling shyly in her characteristic way. "Don't believe him—but he is such a wonderful critic; he reads all my drafts and sets very high standards for me."

"Mary can never believe," Legal Mind replied soberly, "that what she writes is any good. I have to keep her from throwing things out."

"Well," said Mary, laughing, "some of what I write is pretty dreadful." Then, quite suddenly, both her expression and her voice changed and I could see the industrious writer emerge from behind the shy girl. "Whatever I write, I've got to be believing it every second. I never assume that I can write about something I don't know. At the beginning of this novel, I wasn't in control and what I wrote was not all that good. It got better as I came to know the characters better. It's about a fourteen-year-old girl, Effie, who falls in love with a rock star she's never met. And about what happens when they do meet—only for a few moments; it destroys them both. It's about obsession and the effect of media on family life.

"Also," she continued, "I'm a very slow writer—about five pages a day; this book's taken me almost five years. In this, I'm not my papa's daughter. He can write fifty to sixty pages a day." I asked her if her father also read her manuscripts. "Oh—yes," she replied. "He's read everything and helped a lot with suggestions, but he's also determined not to interfere. I must find my own solutions and my own command of the material. Puritan work ethic and all that."

With her enviable talent for finding powerful men to work on her behalf, Mary had searched out Mort Janklow—the tough lawyer-agent known for his entrepreneurial success in orchestrating lucrative book-film tie-ins—and persuaded him to become her literary agent. She then introduced Janklow to her father, who also became a client. "I was the one who found him first," she said, gleefully.

Before I left that evening, Legal Mind took me on a tour of the house, showing me the beginnings of their antique-furniture collection, which, bit by bit, they intended to augment over the years. There was the Lincoln rocker, bought in their Cambridge days, a fine eighteenth-century English highboy, and a whole bevy of tiny enamel-on-copper Battersea Boxes that were displayed neatly on a lovely English writing table. Returning to his protector's role, Legal Mind also requested that I not print any biographical material about Mary without showing it to her first. "After all," he said, "I think she's going to be one of the foremost writers of our time." Mary was not within hearing distance to protest his claim.

When I telephoned Mary in the spring of 1981, her novel *Perhaps I'll Dream of Darkness* was already in press and scheduled for October publication. She was somewhat disappointed by the cover (as what author isn't?); it was red instead of being "pale pastel French Impressionist." She also felt she had proved something of a letdown to Random House's public relations department. "I'm just not kinky enough for them," she said.

In the time since I had last seen her, the "slow writer" had almost finished her second novel, *The Success Story of Rosemary*, which was to be "all about a young girl growing up in California." Mary, I felt, was all set. I sensed she was living exactly the quiet and comfortable life the shy girl had always wanted—fully free to dream up from her inner experiences scenes and characters for whom she could create lives much woollier than her own. I admired her ability—but even more, I admired her astute insight into her own unique needs.

PORTRAIT OF BOB

Bob Simmons was a salesman, and I knew it even before I met him. On the night before I had to post the names of applicants admitted to my seminar, I stood staring at the papers that lay neatly piled around the floor of my study, trying to come to some decisions. Whichever way I turned, the title of Bob's story kept jumping out at me. "This is an ad man," I said to myself. "A one-liner type who'll never get down to anything real. I will not be hooked. I will not—absolutely not—read further."

The title staring at me was "I Am Married to the Woman I Hate," followed by the lead sentence "I will never understand how the delicate, soft, subordinate girl I met in high school turned out to be the bitch she is today." I was sure the young man was either putting me on with what he thought was cleverness or was a complete boor. Besides, any man who intimated that "soft" and "subordinate" were commendable adjectives for women, well . . .

But of course I did read on. And after passing through the melodrama of the early sentences, I discovered an underlying tenderness and the confusion of someone who had married before he was ready.

He seemed to have some insight into his current dilemma and was aware of his responsibility for it. He wanted to write about the preceding year—his sophomore year—in order to get some perspective on it. Moreover, he wrote well:

> Last year we lived together in one room . . . one room. We learned a lot of things about each other—most of them bad. We dressed, undressed, ate, studied, fought, and made love—all in that little room. We were always within a few feet of one another. At the end of the year, we knew each other as a prisoner knows a cell.

And so I was curious. What must it have been like to share—illegally—a tiny single room in Morse College with your girlfriend who was not a Yale student and was hundreds of miles from her home in Kansas City? And to be constantly on the alert so the authorities would not discover it? What was this like for him *and* for her? But the deciding factor for me was that his goal for the course was to learn how to rewrite—an activity I was most eager to teach students, who so rarely had that agonizing but necessary opportunity. "My biggest problem," he wrote, "is to make myself rewrite what I have written. I tend to get sick of my stories before I've finished the first draft. I'm afraid I may need to be forced to rewrite—at least once—so that I can learn how to hang in there." Perhaps this was part of his salesmanship; I had waxed rather eloquent on this issue when describing the course to the students. But if so, that part of his sales pitch worked. What I didn't know then was how accurate his assessment of himself would turn out to be.

When he arrived for the first class meeting, he was quite different from what I had expected. In my mind's eye, I must have had an image of the stereotypical Fuller Brush salesman—a live wire, short of stature, with nonstop patter and a perpetual grin. Bob was tall and lanky, and he moved slowly, with the gait of a traditional cowboy hero. He had curly brown hair and was quite handsome; his smile, which was beguiling, appeared only at moments of genuine appreciation. Although cheerily optimistic, he was rather shy and spoke infrequently; when he did, he was open and direct—almost naïvely so. "I have no qualms," he'd written, "about baring my soul to the reader's eye." There was an air of the small boy about him—and a

318

certain pathos, as if he were searching for answers he couldn't find. He was almost too open to suggestion. This trait emerged more clearly later when he wrote "An Address to the Group," which at first he showed only to me. There was an X on it with the penciled remark, "This is no good." Later he put it in the notebooks for everyone to read.

"I am like the rest of you," he wrote. "I am young. Many of the values of my family I have rejected as meaningless, only to find other values equally meaningless. This wonderful perception has put me away from the place where I began, but it has left me without a rock on which to anchor my soul. It is in this that I feel different from you, who may have rejected a meaningless world but still be able to embrace another." Bob urgently felt the need for some strong framework he could believe in and to which he could anchor some of his uncertain thoughts and feelings. His attempts to find God or "something else . . . I don't know what to call it now" emerged as a central theme to his long story.

Bob came from Kansas City, where he had graduated at the top of his high-school class. He was particularly strong in English and had written one very fine short story, "Clayton," about a young man returning to a fishing camp in search of an old guide who had befriended him and taught him how to fish when he was nine. It was a fond memory in a life that had not been filled with many fond memories. His father, who had been a professional gambler before Bob was born, decided at his son's birth that the child should not have a "disreputable father" and so went to work as an inspector of jet engines at Westinghouse's Kansas City plant. When Bob was nine, plant cutbacks eliminated his father's job and the family moved to Brigham City, Utah, so his father could work in the Thaikol Chemical Plant, which manufactured the first stage of Minute Man missiles. His half-sister—his mother's daughter by a former marriage—was much older and did not go with the family to Utah. His mother also soon found a job at Thaikol, but her resultant independence disturbed his rather conservative father and the couple were divorced a few years later. When that plant, too, began to close down, his mother followed Thaikol to Georgia, disappearing from Bob's life altogether. This was a great shock to Bob, who had been a close companion to his mother. At times they'd been secret

319

allies against his father's stringent rules and regulations. His father, now lonely and somewhat embittered, moved back with Bob to Kansas City, where he became a foreman in a bumper-plating factory. Bob was now twelve.

A shy child, Bob was inclined toward overweight and, as the new boy in town, had few friends at school. During his first two summers back in Kansas City he would spend his days at the public library, reading anything he could get his hands on. He particularly liked Hemingway and science fiction, which allowed him "to think in terms of the whole universe" and escape from his rather dreary daily life.

By his sophomore year in high school he had become a superior student and, having conquered that hurdle, decided that what he wanted more than anything else in life was to have a girlfriend. He quickly lost forty pounds at the height of his growth spurt, becoming tall, lanky, and popular. His last two years of high school were full of fun, friends, and good grades—but now his father became somewhat jealous of his new life and many friends. Bob lived uneasily with him, torn between trying to relieve his father's loneliness and rebelling against what Bob felt were unreasonable demands and strictures. When Bob fell in love with Ann in his senior year, things at home became even stickier. Neither his father nor Ann's parents approved of their relationship, and the opposition stiffened when they decided to become engaged. Bob's tale is about their struggle to work out their relationship during the difficult two years that followed—his freshman and sophomore years at Yale.

When he joined my seminar, Bob was a junior. Originally, he had asked if Ann might attend the class as an auditor so he could get her perspective on the story he was writing. I had told him that he would have to ask the class; it was a matter for the group to decide. He did this a few weeks later and Ann came the following week—sitting shyly behind him—but she must have felt quite out of place and didn't return a second time.

Although Bob's salesmanship wasn't apparent in class, he was not without his outside entrepreneurial endeavors. Nor could I ever imagine him being without some new enterprise—small or large. Whether he needed the money or not, his imaginative mind just kept leading him into new projects. What made him such a good salesman was not a slick patter but a boyish air of friendliness and innocent belief that attracted people to his projects. As a scholarship student, he had an ordinary bursary job clerking in the Yale psychology department offices, but he also had his own craft business and peddled his wares on Saturday. Pushing a small and rather snappy peddler's cart bearing a large Yale blue and white sign saying "The Little Store," he could be seen walking up and down Broadway near the Yale Co-op, selling candles and braided and macrame belts that he and Ann had made during the week. It brought in the badly needed extra money to live on.

With all this activity Bob had a hard time completing his story, particularly because it was a very long one. He delivered it on the last day of the semester with no time to rewrite—which I suspect he was avoiding like the plague in any case. The following year— his senior year—he asked if I would take him on for a tutorial, during which he would rewrite his story. He talked the dean into giving him the necessary permission, and this time I got tough: he rewrote, cut, and rewrote again, and we had a fine time together. "Forced," however, would be the right verb to describe the process.

Like Al-Noor Jiwan-Hirji, Bob chose another name for himself in the story—Billy; Ann is also a pseudonym. Otherwise, the story is exactly as he experienced it and of course bears a true Simmons title.

GOD AND ANN AT YALE
by Robert E. Thomsen-Simmons
Kansas City, Missouri

THIS is the story of myself, a girl, a friend, and something else. I don't know what to call it now. The three of us used to call it God.
. I never had the matter-of-fact belief in God that belongs to children whose families are devout. When I was a little boy, the only mention of His name came when my father would yell, or my mother would murmur, "God damn it." But I wasn't a fierce unbeliever either. If anything, I was fiercely confused. I prayed quite a bit when I first learned about death; and when I was unhappy, I prayed for things to get better. Things usually did get better, but it seemed that they did so more from the natural turn of events than from divine intervention. Being the kind who liked to hedge his bets, I began my prayers with "Dear God, if you're there . . ." But that made me feel insincere, so I attempted to resolve the problem by praying only rarely, when I was unhappy or afraid, and then with much self-consciousness. Eventually I decided to stop praying altogether and stick to dealing with the world I could see.

Two years ago, at the end of high school, I thought I was the master of my fate. I was leaving the Kansas City public schools for

Yale. I was leaving the sad little apartment where I lived with my father for a neo-Gothic dormitory and roommates. I was leaving the moral Midwest for the free and exciting East. Life looked good except for one thing. I was leaving Ann.

Ann and I had fallen in love. We met on a Friday afternoon in Latin club. We went out the next night, and in three weeks had become "engaged." She was quiet, pretty, and a bit shy. Her shyness with me disappeared in a few weeks, but she remained quiet when we were with people she didn't know.

Ann's parents were nice to me at first, but her mother didn't like to see us getting serious so quickly. I persuaded Ann to keep my ring, even though her mother told her to give it back. The closer Ann and I became, the further she withdrew from her parents and the more they worried. My father seemed more jealous of the time I spent with her than worried about me. He felt I cared more about Ann than I did about him, and his voice always grew tight when he talked to her on the telephone. By the end of my senior year both he and Ann's parents welcomed the fact that my going off to college would separate us. But Ann didn't. She still had a year of high school ahead of her and she didn't want to go through it alone. My father said she was possessive. Maybe, but I wasn't willing to give her up either. I wanted to believe that we could stretch a love affair across four years and fifteen hundred miles. My arguments sounded sensible to me, but Ann didn't like them. Despite her threats and pleading, September came and I left.

The first person I met at Yale was my roommate Paul. He arrived just after I'd finished putting my things in the single-bedded room of our three-room suite. He had blond-red hair and deep-set black eyes. I didn't quite know what to think of him. I helped him carry his things from his father's car up to our fourth-floor suite. Paul was all business. After his gear was brought up and he had established himself on the bottom bunk in the other bedroom, we left the room together. But just outside the entryway door, I turned left and he turned right, without a word.

Our other roommate, Bud, was the last to arrive and got the top bunk and the broken desk. But he didn't care. Bud was from Tennessee, lanky and easygoing, with a little bit of a drawl. He was much more approachable than Paul, and we became friends quickly.

I wrote Ann almost every day. It was an agreement we'd made. I told her I liked Yale, but she didn't want me to like it. I had come to Yale and left her alone with nothing to fill up the time we had previously spent together. She wasn't having much fun at high school. Although she was editor of the newspaper, she had forfeited her social life entirely. She wouldn't go out with anyone else, and I didn't want her to. She worked each night on the newspaper and wrote me a letter before going to bed. She spent almost no time on homework, and her grades were poor.

To make things worse, Ann's parents suspected that we had been making love, and they were constantly prying for information. By dropping subtle hints and talking matter-of-factly about the subject, they implied that they wouldn't really object but just wanted to talk it over with her. Ann and I both knew this was baloney. If she had told them the truth, there would have been a horrible row, and Ann didn't want to fight them alone.

Often in her letters she tried to explain her feelings to me. "When you said you wouldn't leave me, you said 'ever.' Billy, I feel so lost. I know I could help you. I could make lots of money and be a good wife. I really do try, but I can't understand why Yale is more important than me." In most of my letters, I tried to justify myself. I knew I was hurting Ann, but I didn't want to leave Yale.

I went to Kansas City for Thanksgiving vacation, even though it was only four days long. Both Ann and I had worked to pay the air fare. I reassured her that I loved her, but she wasn't happy with her situation and a four-day interlude didn't change it. She warned me that she wouldn't go through another year of it. Because I didn't want to lose her, I started looking for ways we could be together without my leaving Yale.

One possibility was to find a college for her in New Haven the next year. When I returned to Yale, I began investigating. But when the idea was broached to her parents, they adamantly opposed it. At the Christmas break Ann and I decided we would go ahead anyway; together we forged her parents' signatures on an application to the University of New Haven.

Just before I went home for spring vacation, Ann received her acceptance. That should have relieved some of our anxieties, but it didn't. Ann wanted to get married; she said she needed that kind of commitment from me after I had betrayed her by leaving. But I didn't want the responsibilities of being married, and I was sure my father would cut off all my money if I did. I told myself and Ann that her parents would never give their consent either. So, although it satisfied no one, the plan was for Ann to come east to school. The problem was that Ann had no place to live. The solution came to me one day during spring vacation, while Ann and I were sitting at the soda fountain in Woolworth's.

"You can live with me in my room at school," I blurted out.

"What?"

"Next year, next year. You can stay with me, right in the room."

"In whose closet? Yours or Paul's?"

"No, no." I began to gain enthusiasm. "Next year everyone will have a single room. You'd have to share the bathroom with all the guys on the hall but I'm sure they won't mind. I talk about you so much that most of them like you already."

"Billy, we can't do that. My parents won't let me leave if we're not married."

"They won't let me marry you either, will they? And since you're not eighteen we can't do a damn thing without their permission. How many times do we have to go over the same problem? Do you want to be with me or not?"

"Yes, I do."

"Do you think it's so wrong? Is getting married more important to you than our being together?"

"No," she said.

I watched her downcast eyes and thought I could see what was happening inside her. She was letting go of a belief. Ann had never been a rebel; now I was making her one.

"I love you, Billy. I'll live with you."

"I don't want things to be this way, Ann. I just don't see what else we can do."

After that afternoon we never questioned whether Ann should live in my room, only how we should go about it. We were sure that Ann's parents wouldn't forcibly stop her from going to college in New Haven. We would just have to concoct a discovery-proof story about her living arrangements that would sound respectable and plausible. But Ann didn't like lying to her parents, and every time

325

we'd try to work out a good cover for our activities Ann would break down and cry. I couldn't understand why it was so difficult for Ann to lie to her parents; I was able to lie quite glibly to my father—or so I thought. But then, I had never been close to my father. It was my mother I had been attached to, and she divorced my father and went away when I was twelve. After that I found it pretty easy to lie to anybody. Ann wasn't like me. Gradually, even I began to feel guilty about our deceptions—especially the ones that lay ahead. Our arguments intensified, and a wall went up between us. At the end of spring vacation, I was almost glad to leave.

The night I arrived in New Haven the campus was covered by a foot of new snow. Cars made muffled noises as they floundered in the streets. The buildings looked ghostly in the half-light of the evening, and the freshly shoveled sidewalks were empty. I was ready for spring, but it looked as if the snow would remain for a long time. I was depressed to be back at school—and confused. Ann and I would be together, but the fear of getting caught was robbing us of any security we might have felt, and the mechanics of deception were giving me ulcers. I felt alone; I wanted someone to talk to me and give me solutions. I wanted a fresh start, but there was no freshness in my frozen, snow-covered world.

The next week passed slowly. Drizzle and rain turned the snow to slush, and the grayness matched my mood. Most of the time I just lay around the room staring at my Russian book, hoping some of it would sink in. I had an exam coming up, but I couldn't work up much concern. I didn't even feel like writing Ann. I didn't care what I did.

The girl's name was Sylvia, and I still don't know where she came from. One of Bud's girlfriends brought her over. She spent Sunday afternoon on our couch, staring into the room where I was studying. No one talked to her except Bud's girlfriend. When I started to leave for dinner, Bud called after me to wait. He invited the two girls to come with us. His girlfriend was pretty, but Sylvia was chubby and pimply. I felt trapped as I sneaked a tray of food for her.

After dinner, while Bud brought his girlfriend back with him, Sylvia stuck to me all the way to my room. She sat down on my bed. I was angry, because I was lonely and she was no good to me. Then suddenly it didn't matter whether I was true to Ann, or that I didn't care for Sylvia. I sat down and began to kiss her.

When her shirt was off, I got up to turn out the light. The sky was twilight gray. When the light went off, the room turned gray, Sylvia and I turned gray, and we fumbled around in a world of grayness. I couldn't feel anything, not even the animal lust I had expected. I wished I was out of the room, even as I unhooked Sylvia's brassiere. When I saw her breasts, I thought of Ann's breasts. When Sylvia moaned I remembered Ann breathless and giggly.

Her picture sat on my desk, watching me. I kept thinking about her and her parents, about the unhappiness she was enduring. I got up and went to the window, staring out into the deserted street. Sylvia called me and asked me what was wrong. Instead of answering, I threw myself onto the bed and let out a cry of anguish.

"Aaaugh!"

"What's wrong? What's wrong?"

"Oh. Ohhhh." I was playing a game with her, to hide desperation I suddenly felt.

"What is it, Billy?" I winced when she said my name.

"Oh that God damned woman!" I cried, pointing to Ann's picture. "Why won't she set me free?"

In elaborate detail I told her both the truth and some lies about Ann and about my emotional inability to touch any other woman while her spell was over me. I said it was a deep psychological problem and that the doctors hadn't been able to help. The lies I told absolved Sylvia of any fear of inadequacy and also absolved me of the blame I deserved. More than once she offered to help me with my problem but I declined, nobly asserting my determination to win this fight alone. She didn't buy it entirely, but by the time her bus arrived her ego had been reinflated considerably and she was making a show of being angry. That made me feel a little better, but I didn't look up as the bus pulled away for fear I would find her eyes on me.

I trudged back toward the room feeling ashamed, mixed up, disgusted. The whole episode had been idiotic. I had betrayed Ann just as thoroughly as if I had finished what I had started, and I had hurt an innocent person's feelings as well. By the time I entered our suite, I had sunk even lower into my depression.

"How did it go?" Bud asked. He was sprawled out on the couch in the living room, wearing no shirt, exhibiting his lean muscles.

"Oh, shut up."

Bud laughed. "Come on," he said. "Tell me about it. Was she a good lay?"

"The best, Bud. The best." Then I did an unusual thing. Instead of making up a story, I told the truth. Bud thought the truth was very funny. I tried to laugh, too, but I didn't feel jolly; I was disgusted with myself.

I went downstairs, looking for someone to confide in. But no one would take me seriously. I ended up telling the story of Sylvia two more times to choruses of laughter. I walked outside into the snow, enjoying the sting of the cold. Voices of other people drifted across the campus—laughter, talk. There were friends there, but none of them were mine. The moon hung like a luminous face in the sky. I wallowed in loneliness.

When I came back in and threw myself on the couch, I thought about praying. Hell, even my prayers were selfish. It was always "help me," "save me," "give me." Maybe it was about time I prayed for something important, like forgiveness. I didn't know.

"Paul, do you ever pray?" He had come in from his bedroom and I shot my thoughts at him—sarcastically, bitterly—because I wanted to attack something. Paul was always rather good for an attack. The unenthusiastic relationship we had started on the first day of school had degenerated into a series of verbal fencing matches, usually enacted before an audience. Paul was a cynic, a mathematician. I was sure he never prayed. But he stopped and looked at me strangely.

"Yes, I do," he said in a straight voice. "Very often." Then he turned around and went back into his room and shut the door. I felt like an idiot. I wondered if *I* was the cynic. *I* was the one who attacked. *I* was the one who hurt people. Look at what I had done to Ann, to Sylvia for that matter. Suddenly my defenses fell away. I wanted to be Paul's friend. I wanted to talk to him, but his door was shut and I didn't dare intrude. I went back to my bedroom, sat down at my desk and began mouthing Russian words. After a few minutes I realized that I was just staring at my Russian book. I read the same sentence again and again: "Sauerkraut and oatmeal are on the menu." I was surprised when Paul knocked on my door.

"Come in," I said.

"Hey, Bill."

"Yeah?" I put down my book and looked at him as he stood in the doorway.

"What are you going to do for a final paper in psychology?"

"I don't know yet."

"Well, in my section we can pick a topic for a research paper or we can do a personality analysis of someone. I thought I would like to do one on you."

"What are you going to do? Try to prove I'm crazy?"

He gave me a searching look and said, "I don't see anything wrong with trying to understand the people you're living with."

He had a point. Did I understand anyone? I didn't even understand myself. "I'm sorry, Paul," I said. "You're right. If you want to do that, it's fine with me, any time."

"Okay," he said hastily. "I just wondered if you'd be interested. See you later." He closed the door softly as he left.

About an hour later Paul came back. This time he knocked and let himself in without waiting for me to answer. He looked nervous and uncomfortable. One hand was behind his back and I discovered that it held a bag of chocolate chip cookies. Paul had never shared his food from home with me or, to my knowledge, with anyone.

"I was getting pretty hungry," he said. "Would you like a cookie?" I noticed he had also brought in a notebook. "Are you busy?" he asked cautiously.

"No."

"I'm not quite sure how to go about formal personality research but if you feel like talking we could go over a few of the basic questions."

"What kind of questions?"

"Early dreams and family life, that kind of stuff. It's personal, I know, but everything you tell me will be confidential. I'm the only one who will know." I wasn't worrying about whether he would keep the information secret. The question was whether I should even give it to *him*. Exposing myself by answering those questions would mean that he would always have an advantage over me.

I decided to confide in Paul. I wanted his friendship; I wanted to be close to someone. "My first memory goes back almost to my infancy. It's hard to say if this is a memory or just something I've imagined or dreamed repeatedly. Anyway, I'm very small, still a baby really, and I'm sitting in my playpen. Pretty soon some older kids come to look at me and one of them takes a toy soda pop bottle out of the playpen. I become very upset and begin to cry, at which point my mother comes and retrieves the toy for me. She was like that; she always took care of me."

"Do you have any early memories of your father?"

"None that are very clear. He wasn't as close to me as my mother was. You see, I wasn't with him very much. He slept in the other room, so I never talked to him at night like I talked to Mother."

"Are you saying that you slept with your mother and your father slept in another room?"

"That's right. That's not the normal arrangement, is it?" I had never thought about it this way before.

"No, I don't think it is." I noticed a tiny hint of superiority in Paul's voice.

"Well, that's the way it was. There were twin beds in our room and a double bed in my father's. Sometimes when I woke up from a nightmare I would be so afraid that I would wake Mother up to tell her about it. She always listened to the whole story. She said that telling someone your dream kept you from dreaming it again."

"Did it work?"

"Yes, I think it did. It worked on all but the very worst."

"Try to think of things about your father. How do you remember him?"

"I remember him as a power figure, at a distance. He was the system my mother and I tried to beat. We bought real butter behind his back and served him margarine so he wouldn't know. We were both really afraid of making him mad. He hardly ever hit me; and I don't think he hit my mother; but the way he screamed and yelled was almost as bad. Sometimes he would yell at my mother until she cried. Other times he would sulk and brood for days and that was worse. Mother left him when I was twelve. I stayed with him, mainly because she didn't have any money. It still scares me when he yells."

"Uh, Bill, have you read anything about the Oedipus complex in your class?"

"You mean where the son wants to kill the father and make love

330

to the . . . mother? Oh, I don't think I ever really wanted to . . . well, I don't know . . ."

"Well, if it's any consolation, a lot of people have challenged that theory recently. Still, it's very interesting. I think now is a good time to talk about those recurrent dreams you mentioned."

"Oh, yeah. There was one in particular. It was a nightmare, worse than any of the others because it didn't seem to end when I woke up. It was a sequence of things, always the same. First there were the noises, two of them. One came from some kind of huge dark animal. It was in the shadows and I couldn't quite see it. Its noise reminded me of my father yelling. It was so loud and so deep, it could kill you. The other noise was like a tiny, tiny bell with a faint ring. I couldn't hear the noises so much as I could feel them. Anyway, the two noises were on opposite sides of me and they kept getting closer and closer, and I had to stop them because they were too loud for me to stand. Sometimes I would wake up then. Other times the scene would change. I would be outside, going down a flight of stairs to a neighbor's basement, and I'd almost get to the door when a white horse would materialize under me and carry me up into the air. There was something unearthly about the horse. The higher up we went, the bigger it became, until it was bigger than a house, until it stretched for miles like a cloud. It didn't have any hair or skin, just a smooth white surface. So smooth that I knew I would fall off. And then I would fall. I always fell. When I woke up, the dream would seem to go on. I couldn't bear to touch anything or to listen to anything—even the ticking of a clock. Everything was still too loud."

Paul looked up from his notebook. Notes were scribbled down the whole page. "You'd better calm down. Your hands are shaking."

I looked at them. They were shaking. "Well, you know, telling that dream is like reliving it."

I stood up and walked into the living room. It was dark except for a dim light reflecting off the snow outside. I went to the window, wondering how the pieces of my life fit together. The stars were bright. Only one cloud hung in the sky. It was quite a large cloud, floating solitary under the stars. I looked at it for several moments before I realized what it was. It was the cloud of my childhood dream.

I thought I was going to lose my mind. I saw every piece of my life, every thought in my head, coming down in one inexplicable, chaotic tailspin. I called Paul over to the window and showed him the cloud, still smooth against the winter sky. It was crazy. What was the cloud-horse from my dream doing in the real sky? Paul mentioned "a vision." I paced about the darkened room, nearly running. I kept returning to the window, and each time I looked out a shiver ran through my body. The whole room seemed to shiver. What was real? What was not? I stammered, "Oh, God. . . . Oh, my God. . . ."

As I said those words, a bright, flashing wave of love washed through my mind and everything was all right. I didn't know where it came from, but if I had had to describe it, I would have called it God.

Paul watched serenity spread over my face. He said, "What happened?" In answer, some kind of ecstatic sound came out of me, but I could find no words.

A few minutes later, in an excited conversation, I found out why Paul prayed. He said that he had become a Christian several years before through a vision of his own. Of course, he hadn't seen a horse in the sky. His vision had been "inner." My brain kept repeating how wonderful everything was, and I thought I must have been converted. We talked about things I can't remember now, and Paul told me how wonderful life would be now that I was with God. He said that everything would change; that handing control of my life over to God would make everything easy. Tests would be easier, people would smile, love would flow free. Faith, he said, could move mountains, but when I had that much faith, I would no longer care about moving them. He said that he could even make it thunder sometimes, and that God had once let him toss "heads" nine times in a row with a half-dollar, to show some unbeliever that He existed. Paul ran to his room and got the half-dollar out of his drawer and let me hold it. I was happy. I believed everything.

Later, Paul took a shower and I washed my face at the sink. The room was hot and steamy, in sharp contrast to the cold water I splashed on my face. The water seemed magical. The clean droplets caught the light from the bare bulbs above the sink and threw it back in rainbows. I immersed my face in it, and as I did, I thought I glimpsed the water's eternal meaning. "Paul!" I yelled. "Listen! Listen to this!" I went into the toilet stall, jumped up on the seat and looked down at Paul in the shower. In a rush of words, I babbled out the meaning of water, its eternal flow through all the world and everything that lives. My ecstasy carried our talk late into the night.

For more than a week Paul and I spent every evening in his room, talking religion. But I didn't just talk to Paul. I went around the dorm assuring anyone who would listen that God indeed existed and that He loved us all. God, with the assistance of Paul, seemed in some magic way to have solved the problems of my life.

I went on a weekend retreat with Paul in his hometown to meet his Christian friends. The retreat was led by the minister under whose guidance Paul had experienced his "inner" vision of God four years before. I told several of the people on the retreat about my experience. Although it surprised me that none of them had a similar story to tell, I enjoyed the support of the group.

On our bus ride back to school, Paul talked to me about becoming a minister. The way he talked, it sounded like the only occupation an enlightened man could undertake. Over the next week my enthusiasm grew. I wrote to Ann telling her I thought I had found the right profession, and asked her how she would feel about being a preacher's wife.

I waited anxiously for her reply, but when it came, she only alluded to my newfound calling in passing: "If you decide to become a minister, I will jump at the chance of becoming a minister's wife." I was hurt and thought she wasn't taking God very seriously. Over the phone I tried to convince her, as Paul had convinced me, that life was meaningless, impossible, until the overriding love of God entered it. I tried unsuccessfully to explain to her the despair of existentialism, the emptiness of materialism, the terrible loneliness of a godless world. But Ann was lonely for me, not for God. To her, the events of life had their own meaning. I told her she was wrong.

I prayed and looked for signs on Ann's behalf. Paul and I concentrated our nightly discussions on the problems of marriage to someone who had not seen the light. We agreed that prayer was not enough to make a real Christian. A revelation was necessary, some direct contact with God. I wasn't always sure that what had touched me was God, but Paul was sure, and my alternative to believing that

333

was believing nothing. Besides, these were Paul's deepest beliefs and to deny them meant losing his friendship. We agreed that if Ann and I continued to view the world from such vastly different positions, communication would become difficult. The only thing to do was to bring her to God.

So, for a while, God passed through the mail between Ann and me. She tried to go to God, probably to please me, possibly because she was unhappy and wanted her life to change. The magic, overriding love of God, as I described it, appealed to her. She prayed and looked for signs, as I suggested. One of her neighbors found a stray parakeet outdoors during a rainstorm. Ann took care of it, hoping that it was the sign she waited for. She looked to the clouds, as I had, for the symbols of her dreams. She tried, but revelation didn't come. Paul and I worried over this. We concluded that the trouble must be in Ann. Paul said that it probably would be necessary for her to be desperately unhappy before she could make the leap to faith. He said that both he and I had been at a breaking point when God had saved us. I agreed that I wouldn't have turned to God if I hadn't become totally unglued. God had been a safety net to catch me when there was nothing else below.

So I tried to push Ann over the cliff by telling her that our life together might be meaningless unless she found religion. I didn't make much headway. Finally, I gave up my attempts at long-distance conversion. Paul told me not to be discouraged; we would work on her next year.

After my conversion I had expected my life to change, had expected things to be easier. Paul had said they would be if I was sincere. But things went much the same as before, including my Russian test, which I failed. I had become fervently religious so quickly; I needed more miracles to keep the fire going. When Paul and I talked about this, he carefully explained why it was wrong to expect help from God every time. He said that help came in more subtle ways, such as a peace of mind that made studying easier. But when Paul said "subtle," I thought "vague." Such a God could be an illusion. Paul said true faith rewarded itself. I agreed with him, but I couldn't be faithful unless I was sure and I couldn't be sure unless I was reassured. I no longer mentioned God in my letters to Ann. We talked about my coming home and the "illicit" year ahead.

The word "illicit" was Ann's and she pretended to be joking when she used it. She had broken the news about the University of New Haven to her parents and they tried to accept her decision, although from time to time they vowed they'd never let her go. In the meantime, a Yale professor had agreed to pretend to offer Ann a room in his home, "in exchange for baby-sitting," and to cover for us in case of parental telephone calls or visits. Ann reported this arrangement to her parents, feeling guiltier than ever about our plans. I told my father nothing.

Summer came. I returned home and searched for a month before I could find a job. This delay was no help to our intentions to save for the coming year. When I did find work, it was as a clerk in a discount drugstore—two blocks from Ann's house, ten blocks from my house, and half a block from the pawnshop where Ann worked. We took our lunch hours together. Then she lost her job.

It was a lousy summer. Ann's mother and father were perpetually angry with us. We tried to ignore them. It hurt Ann to break with them and she blamed me for the break. If I had married her . . . if I had stood up to my father . . . she wouldn't have to betray her parents. Marriage was always at the center of our arguments. I argued again that since Ann was under eighteen, she couldn't marry without her parents' consent and they certainly wouldn't give it to her. But we never tested her parents on this issue, and Ann said I was just making excuses. To some extent she was right.

I had expected that getting Ann out of Kansas City would be difficult, but I hadn't foreseen the weight of the problems that were arising between us. We had never had prolonged arguments before. Once again, as in so many earlier emotional crises, I began to think of God.

One night we sat on the steps in front of Ann's house and didn't say anything. I think we both felt too desolate to speak. Finally, she said, "Bill, look at that light."

"Which one?"

"That porch light across the street. It's off now, but it was blinking on and off."

"Is someone just flipping the switch, or what?"

"I don't know. All the other lights in the house are off. . . . There it goes again."

A yellow bulb on the porch flashed on and off erratically. "Maybe it only makes contact when the wind blows or something." We watched the light blinking at us. The summer night was cool and breezy, as it rarely was. Few cars went by on the street. The bulb seemed to flash independently of the wind. "No, I don't know what it is."

We watched the light for several minutes. We were lonely for each other. I remembered the brightness that had flashed in my room the night Paul and I had talked of God. I tried out the idea. "I think it might be God."

Ann was silent. God was a subject we had both avoided. Quietly, she answered, "I think it might be too."

In my mind I addressed the light, "If it's you, flash." The light went on.

I told Ann what I had done and she tried it. It worked for her too. We spent the next hour playing twenty questions with God. For that evening, at least, it had helped us recover the closeness we had lost.

By the summer's end, Ann and I had collected a lot of housekeeping supplies for our new home at Yale. I kept them in the basement and shipped off our five hundred pounds of belongings a week before we were to leave. Ann's parents were still angry, but it didn't look as if they would try to stop her. They believed she would live with the professor's family. I was somewhat proud of that deception but Ann wasn't.

At five o'clock on the morning of September ninth I stood at the Kansas City airport with my father. We filled the time with trivial conversation. I hadn't told him about Ann's going east until a few days before we were to leave—too late for him to take any action. He was hurt and angry, but he tried to be civil. We talked about the airport. That was neutral. But by six o'clock we had exhausted the subject of the terminal. At five after, I said, "I have to make a phone call," and walked to the booths. Ann was overdue. The phone rang and rang, but no one answered.

"They must be on their way," I told my father. "There's no answer."

"Well, I'll go then. That's what you want me to do, isn't it?"

"No," I lied.

336

"Well, I'll go anyway. I don't want to see her mother."

He had never met Ann's parents. He hadn't wanted to and I hadn't encouraged it. He thought I was ashamed of him. That wasn't the point; I couldn't let them meet that morning; they might have joined forces against us. There were tears in my father's eyes when we shook hands good-bye, but I ignored them. It was too late to do anything else, and I wasn't sorry.

Ann and her mother arrived. Ann was nervous and her mother looked drained. She waited with us until we boarded the plane. It was a thirty-minute eternity of awkward silence. When the plane's departure was announced, Ann's mother burst into tears. Then Ann began to cry, and she cried all the way to New York.

We arrived at Yale in the early afternoon. No one I knew had yet returned to school. On that day we painted the room, broke a lamp, lost one of Ann's contact lenses, and brought five hundred pounds of boxes from the bus station. That night we opened the window to let out the smell of the paint and fell exhausted onto a bed that would have been cozy for one. I slept with one leg on an end table. Our year at Yale had begun.

Seeing Paul again was awkward. Although we had planned together for Ann's coming, I don't think he actually expected it to happen. The preceding spring I had been his disciple. Now I was filled with thoughts of money, material things, and Ann. When I introduced him to Ann, he was abrupt at first, as if he hadn't known of her or expected her. Ann was afraid he didn't like her. Several of the guys arrived the same day Paul did. They were all happy to meet her. After that, even Paul was cordial. I was relieved.

The first part of the term was hard for Ann. She had never lived away from home before and the situation she had moved into called for a lot of adaptation. To make things worse, Ann's parents made a number of attempts to check up on her. We used Paul's phone. The professor at whose home Ann was supposed to be living called Paul's room whenever Ann's parents called her at his house. Those were traumatic moments. We always thought up excuses for her not being at home at the professor's. One call would depress Ann for a week. Her mother was very suspicious. When Paul's phone rang late at night, Ann was terrified.

Ann's guilt feelings were reinforced by bad luck. When she registered for classes at the University of New Haven, she was required to declare her intended major. When she chose art, they informed her that the department was too crowded to admit out-of-state students, and that she had to major in either English or education. She nearly quit school then, but I talked her into staying on as an English major. Perhaps, I said, she could qualify as a resident next year and change her major. She didn't like the idea but she went along.

Then Ann received another blow. She had brought her portfolio of paintings to Yale and one day in early October, when we were rearranging the room to put up some shelves, I put it out in the hall. While we were working, a janitor came and took it away with the trash. By the time we found out what had happened, the trash truck had already left for the dump. We went there and searched, but it was useless. Ann didn't cry on the way back. She just sat on the car seat, staring straight ahead. She wouldn't talk. She didn't even move. Ann's portfolio had been more a part of her than anything else she had brought. Now it was gone.

I think that loss marked the point when a new wall started building between Ann and me. In late August and early September, when we had been fighting with Ann's parents, we had agreed that she would never go back to them. We had also made a pact to be married when school was over in the spring. But as things grew worse for Ann, with her college courses irrelevant to her ambitions and her portfolio lost, we stopped talking about our plans. I felt that she blamed me for her troubles. I drew this conclusion not from her words but from her silences, and at times, I scarcely cared what conclusions she drew from mine. I stopped bicycling with her to her morning class. Although she didn't say much about it, this hurt her deeply. We both took pride in hiding our pain from each other.

Except for me, Ann's only friend was Paul. As Ann and I grew apart, their friendship grew closer. I encouraged this friendship; at first I even enjoyed it. I could see that Ann needed more security and companionship than I could give her and I thought a friendship with Paul would help. Or perhaps I just wanted to shift some of the responsibility onto someone else. Whatever the reason, Paul gradually became included in everything we did. Whenever Ann and I went to a football game, Paul came with us. On Saturday nights, the three of us watched television together in his room. On weeknights after studying, we would all go out and share a pizza. When Ann and I bought a double mattress to replace the narrow dormitory bed, Paul came along to help us choose it. Then, little by little, Ann began to spend more time alone with Paul. Again I encouraged this, feeling that Ann needed someone to talk to besides me and that Paul might be bringing her to God. As he became more and more cordial with Ann, my conversations with Paul grew stilted and abrupt. He had once said that a close relationship with an unbeliever was impossible. Was there now something that overrode his bias?

As I worried, I began to think back. The year before, Paul had seemed to envy the daily letters I received from Ann. He had a girlfriend but not a lover. Then I remembered a conversation I had had with Paul a few months after Ann had come to Yale, about the trouble I was having communicating with Ann.

"I can understand it," Paul had said. "Ann and I have a lot more in common than the two of you do." That had angered me, but I said nothing. I thought he might well understand her better than I did. "You see," he had continued, "you are extroverted and relatively insensitive, whereas Ann and I are both introverted and probably more sensitive. This isn't to criticize you. You can't help being the way you are."

As the days passed and I remembered more incidents and watched them more closely, I came to the conclusion—slowly and reluctantly—that Paul was in love with Ann. I was shocked, but could not bring myself to confront either one of them. I could understand all too well that I was somewhat unsatisfying to Ann—especially after all the strain I had put on her. So I stood by and watched, feeling helpless and hoping against all reason that Paul would bring Ann to God and that that would solve everything.

By midwinter we had run out of money. We had made a little cash by selling Ann's handicrafts, and some more through my campus job, but we hadn't made enough to cover our expenses. We decided to make and sell candles. Every night Ann and I melted wax on a hot plate and poured it into molds. Paul often drifted in and out while we were working. Then, on Saturday, while I was out on the street selling the candles, Paul usually spent the afternoon in our room talking to Ann. He also kept her company while I worked weekday afternoons in the psychology department. If I was out of the dorm in the evenings, he would take Ann into his room and lock the door. Then he began "accidentally" barging into the bathroom when Ann was taking a shower. Whenever I was at home, I felt like an outsider. At the same time, I think Ann felt abandoned by me. The more I resented Paul and Ann's being with Paul, the less I talked to either one of them.

As Ann and I talked less, we made love more often. Although we had made love over the years, she had never had an orgasm and this had always troubled us. Now it possessed us, as if our bodies were trying to express the love our minds were stifling.

With no friends, no family, little expressed love, and even a poor sex life, Ann turned more and more to her "only friend," Paul, and I brooded more and more: Paul could now have Ann as a lover if he wanted her; but he was too cowardly; he wasn't man enough to have a girl live in his room. He was, however, *all* too ready to love a girl—*if* she were delivered up to him by the guy next door—his best friend! Although I said nothing, I blamed everything on Paul. I hated his guts. And by January, Ann and I, the couple with the undying love, were hardly speaking.

One April afternoon, after five days of rain, the clouds opened up and a watery sun sent feeble golden shafts toward the wet earth. As I walked to the dorm, I looked up toward the sun, smiling wanly at whatever might be there and hoping. When the elevator opened at our floor, I was surprised to find Paul in his room alone. We didn't speak. The door to my room was closed. I knocked. Ann opened the door and the scent of her perfume greeted me. The shutters were closed and the room was lit with candles. Ann wore the white ruffled blouse she had worn on our first date. She had almost finished cooking dinner. She was trying her best to revive our worn-out feelings.

"Sit down." Her voice was at once soothing and tense.

We went through dinner, both of us trying—oh, so hard—to feel romantic. I knew that I sounded artificial, but we continued. Later, as we made love, we communicated for a moment. Just once our eyes met unguarded and Ann let out a little of the flood that must have been inside her. "Billy, please make it happen this time or I won't want to again for so long . . ." I prayed silently for help.

Nothing happened.

Things continued much the same until the end of May. The school year was almost over and Ann and I had to decide what to do. I imagined that Ann might simply leave me and go away with Paul, but he didn't ask her. She couldn't go home to her parents; they might have taken her back but she didn't want to face the shame they would make her feel. Our marriage plans hadn't exactly fallen through but they hadn't materialized either. The uncertainty of our future weighed heavily on Ann but I shielded myself, doggedly refusing to deal with any problems other than final papers and exams.

One night I studied until midnight and went to bed. Ann was still in Paul's room. At about two, she came in, kissed me warmly, and climbed into bed. Early in the morning she got up and went off to her eight o'clock class. She had not done that in months. I was very surprised. When she came home that noon, she was cheerful, and she washed the dishes after lunch. It was miraculous how her mood had changed. I was suspicious that Ann might have been making love with Paul, but I quickly dismissed the thought. At dinner, Ann told me that Paul was helping her find God.

"Paul said that I should do something to show God I was sincere," she told me, "something that was really distasteful to me—so I went to that stupid earth science lab. And you know that jerk who says 'It's all a joke'? I let him copy my paper and I was really nice to him."

"Did he go after you again?"

"He followed me to the bus stop."

"How big is he? Maybe I'll beat him up."

"Don't bother, he's a jerk."

"Well, what did he say?"

"Nothing. He just followed me to the bus stop."

"How was the bus ride?"

"I didn't ride the bus home. Steve and Alice saw me waiting at the bus stop as they were driving by, so they gave me a ride. Isn't that neat? I think it's a sign that I did the right thing." She kissed me. I was looking for ways to feel better. I wanted to believe that God had never let me down, that all the pain had a purpose, a divine purpose. Once more I was ready to trust God and Paul, if only they would help me.

Later that day I went to Paul's room to talk to him. I felt ashamed of my jealousy. "Paul, we haven't been too close this year . . ."

"No." He was noncommittal.

"But I feel very bad about it. I mean, my own belief in God has been very confused. I feel kind of lost."

Paul, my old teacher and friend, smiled kindly at me. "Well, I've been waiting for the right moment to tell you something. Maybe it will help you." I felt relief. There was an answer after all. I waited.

"You remember last spring when God came to you?" I nodded. "Well, before that happened, my own belief was really lagging. I was having doubts. But when I saw what happened to you, it really changed my feelings. Now Ann is looking for God. She doesn't know how to ask Him yet, but she's trying. I think when God reaches her, it will help you a lot."

I waited for him to go on. "Is that all?" I asked.

"Isn't that enough?"

I nodded blankly. "Yeah, I guess it is, if it works. I just thought you'd have a better solution."

Paul looked at me haughtily. "Bill," he said, "I don't have any solutions. God has all of them. Let Him come to Ann."

I left Paul's room feeling extremely let down. Where was the magic? I wanted to believe in God again, but all I could see was Paul, qualifying statements, ducking questions, taking Ann away from me, talking to her late into the night. Had I known how to reach her, I think I would have tried to win Ann back; but as it was, I crawled inside my shell and continued to live from day to day.

A week passed and I grew angrier. Ann had stayed in Paul's room after midnight for six nights in a row. By the seventh night, I decided I had been betrayed and that I had asked for it. I had agreed to their privacy so tacitly that there was no way to object. Paul's door was always locked now. If they were sexually involved, I would never know. I could never ask.

All of a sudden, I had had it. I walked into the bathroom and threw my toothbrush against the wall. It broke in half. I muttered to myself as I picked up the pieces, intending to put them together with a piece of tape. As I was leaving the bathroom, I saw Paul standing in his doorway. The door was open and the room was dark. The only light came from a candle on his desk.

At that moment, Ann rushed out of our room. She held a small kitchen knife in her hand. She made some kind of noise in her throat as she dashed past me and started down the ten flights of stairs. I ran after her but I couldn't catch her. Sobbing hysterically and not seeming to care if she fell, she ran wildly, holding the knife above her head. When she reached the bottom of the stairs, she flung herself against the door and ran out into the college courtyard.

I caught her at the gate. She fell and hit her head on one of the flagstones, as the knife clattered away. I lunged over, picked it up, and stuffed it into the back pocket of my jeans. I had not let go of Ann, who was on her feet again. She was moaning.

"Let me go. Billy, what did you do with it? What did you do with it?"

"With what, Ann?" I was painstakingly calm. I was scared to death.

"The knife. I have to find it. Billy, what did you do with the knife?" She kept repeating, "Where is it? I have to find it."

Although she struggled violently, I held her as tightly as I could without hurting her. "Let me go. Let me go. Have to get away. Let me go."

Suddenly I could see the whole scene as if from a distance: under the moon—Ann and I—she trying to pull away while I slowly, dumbly, forced her back across the courtyard, step by step toward the dorm.

Then Paul arrived on the scene.

He came not as a specter or God. He had come down in the elevator and walked slowly toward us, very calm. With a sudden wrench, Ann broke away from me and ran to him. She buried herself against his body. He didn't kiss her; he just held her in his arms. Ann lifted her head to look at him and the two of them began to whisper to each other. I was once again irrelevant. I went to the bench in the courtyard. I knelt and prayed. "Dear God, you must be there. You have to be. Help her. Help me. Give us love. Wash us clean, as you washed me clean before. Give me one more chance." God was silent. I was silent.

Thirty feet away, Paul and Ann stood together, speaking in urgent whispers. He called to me, "Bill, let's go upstairs." Then Ann began to struggle again, but together Paul and I took her back inside.

The three of us sat together in my room until dawn. As the sun was coming up, Ann finally fell asleep on the mattress and Paul got up to go to his room. Before he left, he told me that she had been thinking of suicide for a couple of months, and recently had become quite desperate. He said that just after he had begun talking to her seriously about God, she had awakened while I was still asleep and prayed that she might be shown some sign to help her decide what to do. As she was getting dressed, she had seen a funeral procession pass by on the road below our window and had interpreted this to mean that her task was to die. When she told Paul about this, he made her promise to wait a week and see if things improved. Her week was now over.

When Paul told me this story I wanted to cry but I was too tired. I wanted to hit him for keeping such a secret but I was too weak. I went to sleep beside Ann. When we woke up, it was Sunday afternoon. I think Paul had been listening for us, because shortly after we awoke, he came in and suggested a walk to Ann. I volunteered to go along because I was afraid to let Ann out of my sight. I was also suspicious that Paul was trying to depress her even more so that he could push her to God.

It was a steamy spring day, too hot for us. After the rainy winter, we were not used to heat. We walked around the Grove Street cemetery across the street from our college, a favorite strolling place for Yalies. After a while we sat down on some graves and talked of trivial things. Then I wandered off to another part of the graveyard and saw Ann and Paul move closer together. In spite of everything that had happened, or because of it, I was jealous. They were lying on two adjoining graves, holding hands. Seeing them there, I imagined them dead. I wondered where they would bury us if we all three died at once. Probably in different family plots. What a ridiculous mistake—we belonged in a common grave.

It was an endless afternoon, yet the evening brought not relief but fear. The three of us sat together in Paul's room. Paul may have been trying to work, but I know that I was just pretending. Ann was restless. She paced about the room; she sat down next to Paul and began opening his desk drawers, looking through them. She kept muttering, "Now where *did* I leave that knife?" Finally she stood up and said, "Well, isn't this a fun evening?" Then she left the room. I started to get up, but Paul quickly leaned toward me, as if waiting for this moment.

"Bill." He looked at me judiciously. "This has gotten out of hand. I've done everything I can. I'm about ready to get professional help."

"What do you mean—a minister?"

"I mean a psychiatrist."

I was shocked but I said nothing. Paul had said that truly religious people were often regarded by society as insane, but he had said that that was society's problem. Now he was using society's "false" belief to get him off the hook. When God fails, call a psychiatrist.

"But what about God?" I said.

"I don't know. Maybe there are just some people that God doesn't come to. Or else she doesn't ask in the right way." He talked matter-of-factly. I could see him drawing into himself, bolstering himself. I could see him deserting Ann when she needed help. Even though I wished she'd never met him, I hated him for that.

Ann came in with a half-empty bottle of wine.

"Ann"—my voice was somewhat pleading—"don't do that."

Her eyes were wild. "Why not? What difference does it make?" She took a long pull at the bottle.

After Ann had nearly finished the bottle, Paul laid his work aside and turned to her. "You want to talk?"

"Sure." Ann gave me an adoring look. "Please don't be mad, Billy," she said.

Mad? How could I be mad? I had forfeited my right to anger long ago. I could be afraid, tense, full of despair, but I couldn't be mad at Ann. I winked at her and left Paul's room. I went to my room and sat down on the double mattress. I traced the pattern on the bedspread with my finger while I wept silently for my beautiful, miserable lover.

In a short time, I heard Ann's and Paul's voices in the hall. I ran to the door and opened it. Paul was holding Ann while she struggled to get away. There was dried blood on the back of her hand.

Paul yelled at me. "It's time to get help. Do you want to go, or shall I?" Her blood made my decision easy. I ran up two flights of stairs and knocked on the door of my college dean. As soon as I had told her the story, I was sorry I had. She called the campus police, who said they'd be right over with a psychiatrist. That wasn't what

I wanted. I knew psychiatrists didn't have any magic answers to life. I remembered how God had come to me during my first crisis, like a safety net catching me when I fell off the cliff. This time there was no net—not for me or for Ann or for anyone. I went back to our room. Paul was there; he was holding Ann on the bed. I told him someone was on the way.

"What did you do?" Ann asked incredulously. "What did you do? What did you *do?*"

Paul tried to explain to Ann. I looked around at our little room, our home. It looked horrible.

Ann's eyes stared at me in fury. "How dare you? How *dare* you?" About half an hour later, a man in a suit walked in. He looked out of place in our room. He sat cross-legged on the floor, exposing his hairy calves. Then, as if God had played a bad joke on us all, he announced his name.

"I'm Doctor Disciple."

Even now I find it difficult to write about what happened next. Ann refused to be calmed down, and Dr. Disciple got angry and threatened to put Ann in an asylum for a month. I wanted to back out, but I knew it was too late. Ann remembered her coat and purse as we all left. We drove over to the infirmary in Dr. Disciple's sickly orange Volkswagen. At the infirmary, the nurses were sweetly patronizing, especially with Ann. They put her to bed in a hospital gown and Paul and I stayed in the room with her. He looked relieved. Ann kept looking at me and whispering, "Get me out of here." I told her I would try, but when I did try the nurses just smiled and told me to wait. I fell asleep standing there in the room. The world became a dream in which the only task was to wait. Only Ann was wide awake, scared out of her wits. Finally, Dr. Disciple drove us to the Connecticut Mental Health Center.

The psychologists took us away, one by one, to talk. Someone asked me how I would label Ann's condition. I said I didn't know how to label it. Someone asked me if I wanted out of the relationship. I said I didn't know. Someone told me when visiting hours began. I went outside. Paul had already left. I walked home.

In our room I found my broken toothbrush and everything else we had left behind. On top of the refrigerator was the steak knife, Ann's blood dried on it. I held it in my hand and considered the possibilities. I thought of my own death and I felt my fear. I thought of God and of people, of how much we had depended on something that wasn't even there. We had placed our hopes on magic instead of on each other and ourselves. Some brains have safety mechanisms —some don't. Those that do, frequently call their own souls God, as if to deny that an overriding love could come from within them. I thought of Ann as a sixteen-year-old girl on a lawn with me one night. We had had a part of God right then. Love. The rest was there for atheists to laugh at, for psychiatrists to treat. I threw the knife in the trash and fell onto the bed. Finally there was time to rest.

And yet, it wasn't as simple as that. Ann returned and Paul soon disappeared for the summer vacation. Ann and I found summer jobs and rented a house in Connecticut so that we wouldn't have to go home. We never spoke about what had happened and we never mentioned God or anything connected with Him.

One summer Sunday at the beach I had to break the silence. I told her I had rejected God. I told her I was afraid of what might happen if I—or she—looked for God again. I told her I had to reject everything that had led to the rift between us, everything that had led to her suicide attempt. "God," I almost shouted, "doesn't exist!"

My words sounded hollow to me, and they didn't please Ann as I had expected. She smiled wanly and put her head down. I let my face fall into the wet, sandy towel and I closed my eyes. The surf pounded and the gulls cried overhead. The breeze smelled fresh and salty and the sun was warm on my back. I lay there for a long time, listening to my own silence.

BOB – JEWELRY SALESMAN

WHEN I tried to locate Bob in the fall of 1979, I telephoned all around the country—New Haven, Kansas City, Albuquerque, Augusta, San Francisco—finally tracking my favorite traveling salesman to a small jewelry shop in Newburyport, Massachusetts—just an hour away from where I was calling in Boston.

"Hey," he said, when I got him on the line, "come on out and stay with us. I've got this great old house built in Revolutionary times —lots of room—and you can see my jewelry shop and meet Jocelyn and everything."

"Jocelyn?"

"Yeah, we just got married a few months ago and . . ."

It sounded as if I had a bit of catching up to do. A few days later I found myself driving north on Route 1 along the coast, thinking about Bob. It seemed to me he'd been prey to many of the cultural upheavals of our time. On top of his classically conflicted—almost Kafkaesque—relationship with his parents, he'd experienced the breakdown of the family unit, leaving him virtually without a mother; the loss of community—through a family who moved frequently in search of employment; the breakdown of the church, which virtually was not in his life at all. And because he spent some of his early life in a town where the primary employment was manufacturing Minute Man missiles, he was exposed more than most to that consciousness—new to his generation—that the world could blow itself to bits at any moment. Much of the security and unconditional love so badly needed in the childhood years had passed him by. Yet somehow in spite of all that and his subsequent adolescent pitfalls, he remained cheery and seemingly resilient.

Was it any wonder that Bob longed for some magic—some absolute solution—something that would provide a simple answer in what looked like a confusing and apocalyptic world? And was Bob so different from many others in his generation? The flower children, tragically, had tried to recreate the bliss of infancy for themselves. The Moonies had capitalized on the longing, bringing disillusionment and pain to many young and their parents. As had the Hare Krishnas, the God Squad, the Jesus Freaks—not to mention the pseudoscientific cults of Scientology and the like. Now, trading on the hope for the same illusory goal, the born-again Christians, the Moral Majority, and God knows who else were coming over the hill to make political and financial hay in an age of uncertainty.

Bob's search had first led him into a very old-fashioned rebellion, living secretly with the "love" his father disapproved of or felt was premature. He and Ann set out to prove to their parents and themselves that they had a "real love" and a family unit, surpassing that of their elders. What had happened to their rather desperate attempt? When did Jocelyn come into the picture? What spiritual search—if any—was Bob pursuing now?

While mulling all this over, I suddenly found myself pulling up in front of Bob's store. A carved-oak sign hung out in front, reading "Jocelyn's." Bob bounced out of the door as cheery as ever and pulled me inside to show me around the airy and handsomely designed shop, filled with hanging plants and sporting a hexagonal carousel-counter in the center. His collection of silver and gold bracelets, pins, earrings, and necklaces were laid out artistically on bits of driftwood in glass-covered display boxes. He had designed the interior himself and was rightly very proud of it. I bought a pair of earrings, hardly able to make the choice because I was tempted by so many. He gave me an onyx pendant. "What's the point of being your own boss," he said, "if you can't give some of your merchandise away to the people you like?"

Bob's store was part of a complex of reconstructed buildings on Newburyport's old waterfront, and as we walked about I felt as if I were strolling through a stage set of whaling-ship New England. We stopped for a quick drink in one of the reconstructed "saloons," and then drove off to see the real Jocelyn and the "Revolutionary house." Jocelyn turned out to be an airline hostess who was lovely and welcoming. I had to inspect everything—the patterned tin ceiling added in the nineteenth century, the old sewing machine they had made into a bathroom washbasin, the antique wood-burning stoves, the porch with hanging grapevines, Jocelyn's extensive collection of ancient beer cans. The one touch of modern times was that there was no cooking stove, only a microwave oven.

After dinner the three of us settled into comfortable chairs in front of the Revolutionary fireplace. Bob brought out some excellent brandy and began almost immediately to talk about his further quests.

"You know," he said, "that horse-cloud experience in my freshman year made a tremendous impression on me. At that moment, suddenly, a complete peace came into my life; I felt there was something inside myself just loving me, telling me everything was okay and keeping me from falling to pieces. I experienced it inside, rather than something given to me from outside. Up to then—and later with Paul, who was a traditional Christian type—I was confused by the Christian concept of God the Father being something out there to pray to. Trying to invoke Him—or anything outside myself—was a big mistake. Since then, I've experimented with trying to recreate in myself the original feeling of peace and wholeness I had when I saw the horse-cloud."

"You tried to recreate *that*?" I asked, somewhat incredulous, remembering the painful experiences that had preceded it.

"Yeah," said Bob enthusiastically. "I've experimented with some psychedelics—especially psychedelic mushrooms—to see what I can learn from that. I've also tried John Lilly's Sensory Isolation Tank —you know where you float in a warm, shallow saline solution in a soundproof, lightproof tank and all external sound, sight, and touch are screened out so you can see what the brain will come up with if it doesn't have any stimuli." (And I had been worried that Bob might have joined the Moonies!) "But mostly I've been reading—Huxley, Lilly, Castaneda, Alan Watts, Robert Pirsig—and, from what I can gather, they are all saying that what we see as reality depends on how we look. We see the world through the filters of our beliefs—many of which are so embedded that we can perceive no alternative. To me, self-knowledge begins with seeing alternatives.

"I've just recently begun to read again," he continued. "There was a period when I just shut the door on all this self-awareness and God stuff—when I was breaking up with Ann."

"And what happened to Ann?" I asked, immensely curious and needing to get back to the earthy world of Kansas City. After pouring us another brandy, he began to unravel the tales of the intervening years. I will pick up Bob's life where he left off, just after the beach scene at the end of "God and Ann at Yale," the summer before he took my seminar.

Late that summer—1971—Bob and Ann decided to marry. This, they felt, would make everything all right for Ann's parents, about whom Ann was feeling guilty; she still blamed Bob for her "rebellious decision" to run off to New Haven and live with him. Bob also felt guilty, and he badly wanted the love affair to have a happy, familial ending to prove that it was "worth all the turmoil."

Ann's parents arrived the night before the wedding and stayed with Bob and Ann in the big house they were caretakers of in Stratford. Ann's mother helped Ann sew up her wedding dress and Bob made the refreshments for the next day's reception. The scene was not a jolly one. Ann's parents hadn't really forgiven the couple —particularly Bob. Bob's father, who did not approve of their marrying, and consequently had received only a halfhearted invitation, had decided not to attend. Everyone went to bed grumpy.

With a few close friends in attendance, Bob and Ann were married in the courtyard of Branford College at Yale by the Lutheran chaplain, Tom Chittick, whom Bob had been friends with since the day Tom had helped him save his peddler's cart from hoodlums in front of the Yale Co-op. Paul was best man and Bob to this day isn't

quite sure why. He hadn't felt too keen about Paul since the sophomore year crises, but Ann had wanted him around and the three still
hung out together.

The wedding was happy enough; refreshments buoyed everyone's
spirits and Ann's parents took everyone to dinner. After supper, Bob
and Ann drove Ann's girlfriend back to Smith, arriving home in
Stratford at 3:00 A.M.

"It's funny," he said, "but that drive is still a bitter pill to me.
After the reception I'd envisioned a honeymoonish situation, and
there I was driving all night."

"Why did you do it?" I asked.

"She had no one else to drive her back, and I guess I was still
playing the good guy—the martyr—just going along."

During the next two years, Ann and Bob's relationship did not
improve as Bob was torn between the demands of his studies—
psycho-linguistics—and Ann, who felt abandoned in whatever big
house they could "care-take." Ann continued making macrame belts
and leather goods for sale in the peddler's cart but this did not fill
her day, and in the mornings before Bob went off to school she felt
quite desperate. "You're going off to get your Yale education," she'd
say bitterly, "and I'm left at home with nothing." Bob now felt he
was caught in a double bind. "With the rules I'd set up for myself,"
he said, looking into his brandy glass, "there was simply nowhere to
go. If I left her, then all the vows that I'd made and all the love I'd
pledged was a lie. If I stayed, I would be living a lie because I wasn't
in love with her anymore. I blamed myself for what I had put her
through in my sophomore year, causing her to break down and then
putting her in an institution."

At graduation in the spring of 1973, Bob met Paul's father for the
first time and they instantly hit it off. A self-made businessman who
had worked his way through college and married his college sweetheart, Paul's father felt a special kinship with Bob and Ann and
offered to put up collateral for a bank loan to start them in a crafts
business in Kansas City. Bob and Ann looked forward to being
launched into a new life, where they hoped their relationship might
improve.

That October, with the backing of Paul's father, they opened the
Elephant's Trunk in Kansas City's Country Club Plaza. Ann made

quilts for it; Bob made jewelry, purchased additional merchandise, and minded the store. They lived in the basement of Ann's parents' house until they "fell into a great deal"—eleven thousand dollars for a run-down six-bedroom Victorian house across the street. They bought it and moved in.

"You seem to have a knack for finding great houses," I said, rather jealously, motioning toward the many lovely rooms of the "Revolutionary house."

"Yeah," said Bob. "I guess I've really got my antennae out. After the two of us lived in the single room at Yale, the thought of small spaces sends shivers through me. I've learned to appreciate space."

The next few years in Bob's life were a seesaw of financial and personal happenings that boggled my imagination. The ups and downs were peopled with sisters, fathers, old girlfriends, "best buddies from high-school days," all of whom were intertwined in a web of his business and home life and turned up in different guises on different days.

Initially, things did not go well on the business front. Ann and Bob were living on a hundred dollars a week and were down to their last four thousand dollars when they were given some Indian jewelry on consignment and it suddenly began to sell like hot cakes in the Elephant's Trunk. Very quickly, everything began to come up roses. Bob began taking buying trips around the country (principally to Albuquerque, the source of the Indian jewelry); he started a wholesale jewelry business and then, a year later, opened a second store, the Elephant's Tail, in another part of the city under the management of Charlie, "a macho-type friend from Yale and high-school days." A short time afterward, he started a jewelry manufacturing company, Starline, Inc., to make his own line of jewelry, and employed twelve more people. Bob promoted the retail enterprises with wildly original radio commercials, which he both wrote and recorded —complete with English accent. These made him rather famous in Kansas City.

Meanwhile, back at the Victorian, things were not so rosy. Jeff, Bob's "best friend from high school" had begun hanging out around the house, and a threesome, like the one with Paul, soon developed. Only this time God was not much in the picture, and it seemed completely obvious that Jeff and Ann were lovers. As with Paul, Bob didn't know quite what to do about it all, and "in all the turmoil" gained fifty pounds, returning to his fatty self. After a number of moves in and out of the house, support from friends, and a running-exercise regime instigated by Charlie, Bob finally was convinced that the marriage could not work. He moved out of the Victorian for the last time, gave Ann the house and a flat-fee settlement, and kept the Elephant's Trunk—their original joint enterprise. "I found the situation so much like the episodes with Paul," said Bob, shaking his head in retrospective amazement, "that I had to wonder about myself. I think I let it happen again for the same reason as before—I wanted a way out of my responsibilities. But of course it wasn't as simple as that. Yes, I wanted her to have an affair with someone else so I could leave, but when it actually happened, I was more jealous and hurt than I expected. So the whole thing would start over again. In the end, we were both too young to handle marriage, and we'd also given each other too much pain over the years."

Bob's relationship with his parents had also gone through some seesaws. He'd grown closer to his father, who had retired from the bumper-plating factory and had come to help Bob at the Elephant's Trunk, where his father also sold his own line of jewelry. Together they frequently traveled on buying trips to Albuquerque and, on one such visit, ate psychedelic mushrooms together. Bob was now calling his father by his first name, Frank. However, his father was still inclined to cause a stormy scene at the store if Bob did not treat him "as an authority" in front of the customers. Bob tried to laugh off these episodes, but they secretly bothered him. It would be some time still before Bob was no longer frightened of his father's outbursts and they could make real peace with each other.

His mother was another question altogether. In the action-packed summer of 1975, when Bob was breaking with Ann and expanding his business, his mother suddenly turned up for a visit almost out of nowhere. He hadn't seen her since he was twelve. He knew that his half sister had recently heard from her, but for Bob her arrival was a shock. He found her youthful for her fifty-four years and cordial —almost too cordial. She treated him more as a boyfriend than as a son, and he discovered she had recently married a twenty-eight-year-old soldier, just four years his senior. All this made Bob uncomfortable—and his discomfort was heightened by his sister's instigating an evening at a striptease show for the three of them. "When I was a little boy," Bob said, "I was often my mother's 'date,' but playing that role at twenty-four really made me nervous."

Around midnight, Bob interrupted his tale and looked at me quizzically. "Wow!" he said. "This is all beginning to sound like *Edge of Night*. Does everybody's life sound like a soap opera?"

"More than you'd suspect—if they're being honest," I responded. He grinned.

"Well," said Bob, plunging in again, "the activities of that summer left me somewhat exhausted, and since the business was doing great on its own, I decided to take a short sabbatical and get back to my real interest—alternative realities. I found another great buy in a house and then just stretched out on the sofa, ate some mushrooms, and read day and night—Lilly, Huxley, Gregory Bateson, and James Keyes. I had just discovered Bateson and Keyes."

Then the inevitable crash came—just a few months after Bob had launched his manufacturing business. First the Elephant's Tail was forced out of business because the minimart in which it was housed closed down. Then the Elephant's Trunk began to go downhill; Indian jewelry was going out of style. But Starline was the crusher. "Basically," said Bob, "we were trying to become a big-time company and weren't up to it—too many chiefs and too few Indians, and even they weren't kept busy. You know," he said, shaking his head quizzically, "it takes a lot of effort to actually lose twenty thousand dollars in one year."

Somewhere early in the boom-to-crash period, Jocelyn walked into Bob's life as a small investor in Starline, Inc. At first he didn't pay her much heed, but then one day when she walked into the shop to collect her long-overdue principal, she passed him a note that read "I need $200 to pay my car insurance. P.S. I have a gun." This made Bob stand up and take notice. He paid her the two hundred dollars and then, a week later, when he was tripping out on mushrooms with a friend in Chicago, he realized "in a flash" that he had to see more of Jocelyn. On his return to Kansas City he mustered up the rest of the money he owed her and made a date. "Right away," said Bob, "I knew she was special. I had all this book learning—all this intellectual stuff—but she had been to Europe on her own, hitching for nine months, and had the nerve to do a lot of real things. It seemed to me that I could learn from her how to make experience real instead of just in my head. I fell in love with her that night."

They were married four months later, in May 1977, and took each other's names, each becoming Thomsen-Simmons. This was just at the height (or depth) of Bob's crash period.

Then came the big Kansas City flood of September 1977, which washed away Bob's store. This turned out to be a piece of very good luck, because Bob now qualified for a federal disaster loan to rebuild his store elsewhere. He and Jocelyn moved to Amesbury, Massachusetts; found the Revolutionary house; and had the disaster loan to open up Jocelyn's in Newburyport. On the evening I spent in Amesbury, Bob was worried (he had a lot of money tied up in inventory) but determined. "I will either pull out or go under. I have a six-thousand-dollar bill and inventory worth twenty thousand dollars when it is sold. So it's just a question of do I sell it or let the bill eat me before I sell. So I will sell."

Jocelyn looked at her brandy glass, pensively. "I just wish we could get through this debt period," she said. For the moment, her airline salary was making a crucial difference. At the time, I was unaware that she was pregnant.

Bob told me that Ann had become a graphic artist and that he called her from time to time when he was in Kansas City. Paul, he said, was studying for the ministry "in a monastery, or what used to be a monastery—huge, dark German Gothic buildings deep in the Vermont woods." After he and Jocelyn were married, Bob had gone to visit him there to give him the good news and hoping "to talk to him about my mushroom trips and the new books I'd read." But Paul had received him coldly and hadn't wanted to talk about such things, which made Bob sad. "I guess," he said wistfully, "I was *still* looking for some ultimate answer—or approval—from Paul—just as I do from anyone I am reading seriously—Dr. Lilly, Huxley, Pirsig."

It was 3:00 A.M. when we stopped reminiscing and trudged upstairs. I was very happy to find that the guest room bed was not of Revolutionary design.

In June of 1980, Bob telephoned me in San Francisco to tell me, with great pride, that Jocelyn had given birth to a six-and-a-half-pound boy, who had made superior scores on his Apgar health test. Bob was bursting with paternal pride. They had named the child Moebius McCartney Simmons. Moebius after the Moebius strip, "because to me it's an analog of the cycle of life"; McCartney after Beatle Paul McCartney. Earlier in the year, Bob had pulled out of his debts during the gold and silver upsurge. He had bought up old spoons, rings, and candlesticks and had melted them down and sold the gold and silver on the market. Now he was concentrating on building his wholesale business.

When I stopped by to see them all again on my way back from Maine in September of 1981, the house suddenly looked very domestic. Bob had made a new family room out of a former porch in typical salesman-Bob fashion. He'd talked a local construction company out of some enormous old beams and one Friday had corralled enough manpower to install them by putting a sign in front of the house reading Free Beer. "That was a great day," said Bob. "The big truckers got right into the spirit of it."

Moeby—an engaging and energetic toddler of fifteen months— was running around in his diapers, touching base when he felt like it for a suck of milk from his mother's breast. Although Jocelyn had been back flying for some time, she was very proud that she had managed to keep breast feeding by using a breast pump when she was on a trip and freezing enough of her milk for Moebius while she was away. Both parents were sold on parenthood. "Moeby," said Bob, "has made all the difference in our lives."

Moeby had also done a lot for Bob's relationship with his own father. Bob had been able to confront his father directly in ways he'd never done before, and Moeby himself had become the delight of his grandfather.

Bob took me up to his attic office-workshop. Jewelry was strewn all around on tabletops. He was manufacturing his own design, which he sold wholesale. The silver and gold settings were cast elsewhere, but Bob spent much of his time setting the stones— amethyst, garnet, opal, onyx—in each piece. The rest he spent on the road selling to retail clients—"but not too far away. Because of Moeby, I don't want to be away from home for long." He was making a good living and, at last, was in control of his entire enterprise. He pointed to a large stack of tapes beside his work bench.

They were neatly labeled: Lilly . . . Bateson . . . Pirsig . . . "What's best of all," he said, "is that while I sit up here working on the jewelry, I can listen to all these tapes, reflect on the books, and try to understand how these people's concepts of self-awareness apply specifically to my own life. You have to keep practicing this stuff. That special night at Yale, I accidentally—and rather dramatically —broke down the rational separation between myself and the world and found the bliss of being whole. But I quickly reverted to my dualism, projecting God 'out there.' It's not an easy habit to break. But nowadays I don't push things. Thanks to the support of these books, the mushrooms of course, and the love I have for Jocelyn and Moeby, it's easier to accept my ignorance, live in the moment, and admit that I like the mystery of the search itself."

We left the mysterious attic and went downstairs, where Bob picked up Moebius and gave him a big kiss.

PORTRAIT OF PHYLLIS

*P*HYLLIS Orrick was a poet and I didn't know what to do about it. In the course catalogue and again in the first session of the class, I had stated dogmatically that students could write about their experiences in any form of fiction or nonfiction they wished: novels, short stories, articles, autobiography, biography, letters, journals—everything *except* plays and poetry. I knew too little about the latter two forms to teach anyone. As for poetry, I was completely in awe of it and what seemed to me its insoluble mystery: Just what elements turned it, often with a single word or only the juxtaposition of two words, from slush to divine resonance or vice versa? Not for me to teach the most inscrutable of the writing arts.

So, when I read the opening lines of Phyllis's first paper,

> Dreamwords for you were on my lips when I woke up,
> but they vanished in the silence
> before I knew you were gone.
> If I'd had spoken them to yourself, instead of to
> your dreamself
> What?
> Dreamwords.

I stopped her after class. "Phyllis," I said in a voice that suggested I'd caught her wearing a G-string and a feather boa at the Court of St. James's, "you're writing *poetry*!"

"Yeah," she said, with a sheepish twinkle in her eye, "I know, it just seems to come out that way." Laughing, she promised to mend her ways the following week. When she turned in her next assignment, I glanced at it quickly and was relieved to see the sentences all lined up on the page like proper prose. But when I sat down to read it, I found it was still poetry, now looking and sounding very peculiar because the phrases, which should have been given pauses by starting on a new line, were strung straight across the page with hardly any punctuation.

I nabbed her after class again. "Phyllis," I said with mock melodrama, "what am I going to *do*? Don't you think you should enroll in a poetry course where someone can give you proper instruction?" Both of us knew that my asking that question was distinctly dirty pool; the time period had passed when students could switch courses. She grinned at me with good humor.

At that moment, I realized Phyllis had a very special quality for someone so young. Her self-confidence was so firmly based that she could resist my mandates with playfulness; there wasn't a defensive bone in her body. Yet, in her quiet way, she was in a rebellious mood and there was something in her poetry that was extremely important to her—although I didn't yet know just what it was.

Except for her weekly offerings, there was nothing about Phyllis that suggested a poetic nature. She was of average height, athletic (she was on the field hockey team), handsome—on some days buxomly beautiful. Her long thick brown hair curled up naturally on her shoulders, usually covering the top of some out-of-shape sweater that was part of her daily uniform, along with baggy blue jeans and "sensible shoes"—the latter, leftovers from her prep school days at Roland Park Country School in Baltimore. Even with her slouchy attire and easygoing manner, she gave off a businesslike air, the no-nonsense assurance of a student who knows exactly what she's talking about, chapter and verse. Whenever she talked in class—which was not often—she spoke fluently, her arguments threaded with the scepticism and wit of a good critic. From her earliest years, she had read extensively—fiction, economics, politics, you name it

—and had the intellectual self-assurance of someone who had graduated at the top of her class from a scholastically rigorous girls' school. She hadn't suffered the slightest worry about being admitted to an Ivy League university; she had only had to decide which one it would be. But she had no pretenses. Her intellectual acumen fit her as comfortably as her old sweaters. She was, in fact, quite shy—so much so, that I was surprised by her sudden witticisms—sometimes teasing, sometimes wildly fanciful, and almost always delivered with the gentle grin that brought her whole face to life.

Phyllis was the youngest—by far—in a family of three children. She had lived all her life in the same large old house in Ruxton, Maryland, an elegant suburb of Baltimore. Although a "surprise" child, she was heartily welcomed and was known to her parents' friends as "The Child Phyllis." Her father, orphaned at an early age, was "raised by two maiden aunts to be a 'gentleman' in the southern tradition . . . with charm and courtesy as important aspects of his way of life." He was a prominent Baltimore lawyer—later head of the Maryland Bar Association. Her mother, who was also orphaned early, was the daughter of a U.S. senator—an Irish immigrant who had spent his early years as a labor organizer. At Vassar, she had studied labor issues and economics and was a devotee of Thorstein Veblen and Henry George. Both parents were active in the civil and social life of Baltimore. Her two brothers were eleven and fifteen years older, respectively, and so Phyllis's early experiences were very much those of an adored only child, surrounded by adults and the adult conversation of politics and literature that her parents and their friends loved to discuss. Because of these early years, she had the talent of feeling completely at home with people much older than she.

At Yale, Phyllis was embarrassed by her relatively affluent background (which was not *that* affluent) and was apt to discard her parents' endeavors in liberal causes. In this way, Phyllis—perhaps more than any other author in this book—typifies the classic, "radical" WASP student of the early seventies. Liberalism—especially as practiced by one's parents—was seen as a cop-out that did not reach the root of society's problems and was essentially paternalistic and patronizing, especially to the newly proud blacks. Charity was a *very dirty* word. In an early paper (prose!) describing her parents, Phyllis wrote with a mixture of pride, embarrassment, and disdain, "My parents come from families that have been near the top of our supposedly unstratified society . . . and in that sense, we are part of the leisure class." Just as Lynne Hall and Elías Aguilar focused on the ghetto side of their lives to conform to the black fashion of the times, Phyllis, as a "preppy WASP," felt guilty about her family's prominence in Baltimore society, her own private-school background, and the fact her mother had "planned for me to be a debutante" and "liked to have her silver polished." In the Yale of the seventies, owning silver—let alone polishing it—was altogether improper.

Her mother, however, was not just "polishing silver." In the fifties, she had monitored the House Un-American Activities hearings to record Joseph McCarthy's attacks on liberals and later had volunteered for the Job Corps, going into the ghetto to interview unemployed teen-agers for potential jobs. She took Phyllis to her first antiwar protest march when Phyllis was a high-school freshman. "In my high-school and college years," said Phyllis some years later, "my attitude, like that of many others, was, 'So what if you're going into the ghetto to interview kids? You are still a rich white person, patronizing the poor. If we whites can't change the situation entirely, then doing a little is just being hypocritical.' " She laughed. "Of course, I was right. But now I'm not so impatient or so tough on parents as I was in my rebellious days."

Nor was Phyllis without her own political activism. In her senior year of high school, she was elected head of the student body on a ticket that pledged to eradicate student government entirely. "We didn't manage to do that," she recalls, laughing, "but we did manage to institute independent studies and some coed seminars with the local boys' school—and that was viewed as a major triumph at the time." She and a group of ten high-school friends from both schools —"our two little Mafias"—went regularly to peace demonstrations and in 1969 formed a youth chapter of the Community for a Sane Society. Although she had always wanted to go to Radcliffe ("because of the Harvard education"), she decided on Yale when she visited a friend just before the Panther May Day demonstrations in the spring of 1970. "New Haven was teeming with political activity," she said, "and I thought, 'Jesus, this is great,' and decided then and there that was where I wanted to go. Of course, when I arrived the next fall, the SDS leaders were sipping sherry in their secret societies. But I stayed anyway." She was given two black roommates, who became her close friends throughout college and after, and almost immediately began to write for *The Yale Daily News*—even though she had to do so illegally for her first freshman semester.

So, on the surface, Phyllis was cheery and matter-of-fact, busy discussing politics and literary criticism—good solid, rational stuff, well distanced from tumultuous feelings. There was nothing at all to suggest the dark, brooding tenor of the material she was pouring out on paper:

> As I feel my face petrify every morning (what Medusa must exist around here!), I think of the silence I feel around me—not the fruitful kind, not the warm kind, not the soft kind. I feel a silence that drains my spirit, sucking until I am dry . . .

Something else was going on. The words seemed to well up from another part of her. Was she, as Ralph Ellison has said, putting in writing "all of what [the author] cannot understand and cannot say and cannot deal with and cannot even admit in any other way?"

I was soon to find out. One day, she handed in a paper that told —in bleak, hard-hitting prose—of her brother's accidental death two and a half years earlier. So that was it. In her quiet, unofficial, nonstudent moments, Phyllis was struggling with the tangled feelings—"pain, anger, love"—of unresolved grief. At the time of her brother's death, she had been only sixteen and, like many adolescents, had shoved away the conflicting emotions that beset everyone at the sudden loss of a family member. The funeral services had been brief, polite, and reserved in typical WASP fashion. No one talked much about what had happened. For an adolescent particularly, there had been little time and fewer vehicles to express feelings and absorb the tragedy. (Other religious groups, Catholics, Jews, black Baptists and, evidently, Ismaili Moslems—according to Al-Noor Hirji's account of his father's death—have kept their traditional mourning rituals more intact, providing invaluable time and structure for the bereaved to do their necessary grief-work.) Now, some two years later—triggered, perhaps, by a separation from her boy-

363

friend—all the painful feelings of grief had come bubbling to the surface, where Phyllis could only deal with them in sporadic bursts of descriptive words—"those nonexistent demons whose emptiness tugs at my sleeve."

She rarely discussed her brother's death with me directly, even in our private conferences. I urged her, however, not to give up writing about it, no matter how jumbled the outpourings seemed. For me, it was a personal as well as professional matter. My twin brother had fallen out of a window and been killed when we were eleven, and I did not come to grips with his loss until many years later when I married. I understood all too well the confusion of delayed grief and the importance of mourning as closely as possible to the time of death. One book that was required reading for all my classes—for both its content and style—was James Agee's *A Death in the Family.*

Agee had also written in a letter to Father Flye, "One thing I feel is this: that a great deal of poetry is the product of adolescence—or of an adolescent frame of mind: and that as this state of mind changes, poetry is apt to dry up. I think most people let it; and the one chance is to keep fighting and trying as hard as possible."

Well, Phyllis was fighting with a healthy, stubborn stamina—both for her poetry and for facing the tragedy with unsaccharine emotional honesty. But she did her grieving alone. During this period, although she was beset with bouts of intense loneliness (sometimes when she was alone in her room, sometimes when she was in the midst of student crowds in the dining hall or classroom) her distress was not noticeable to her friends. Nor did she mention it to her family. She found herself wandering in New Haven's nearby Grove Street Cemetery—a favorite student retreat from omnipresent "Yaleness." Grove Street was a place students went to be "alone" —either by themselves or with an intimate friend. Phyllis's walks there were, perhaps, more directly connected with the cemetery's central function than those of others, although many students claimed "it was a great place to go and cry."

Gradually, throughout the semester, Phyllis developed her piece —sometimes in prose, sometimes in poetry or poetic images, sometimes as a letter written directly to her dead brother or to her boyfriend. Her problem then became how to make it all hang together for the reader without losing its poetic density and emotional impact. The class debated the issue and came up with a dozen different ideas. Seldom had a paper drawn such intense feeling. For everyone, it evoked the special loneliness that comes when the rational world of Academia keeps making its incessant demands while the soul longs for emotional breathing space.

Some years later, when I was editing the student manuscripts for publication, I decided to cut Phyllis's piece, leaving only the prose narrative that described the Valentine's Day tragedy. In a superrational mood, I felt the rest was melodramatic and so did two other reader-friends from my generation. But, when I showed the edited piece to my son, Alex Gibney—also a Yale student and a great devotee of Phyllis's writing—he cried out in horror. "You're crazy," he said, with his usual polite deference to his mother. "You've ruined it." Ann Kennedy was equally shocked, though she put it somewhat more delicately.

Shortly after these two opinions were tendered, Tim Kenslea arrived on a week's vacation from his job at Little, Brown to help me do some editing. He had not been in Phyllis's class nor read anything of hers before. When I showed him both the cut and uncut versions, his reaction was just as vehement. Evidently, Phyllis had struck some deep chords in the hearts of the student generation that we elders were too flat-footed to appreciate.

I looked at the story again. This time, I thought I saw something else: Phyllis was not only saying *good-bye* to Jack, she was also saying *good-bye* to her safe, secure childhood. She was navigating that awesome adolescent passage when you realize—with terror and fury —that your parents aren't the gods and saviors you thought them to be (and why *aren't* they?); that neither they—nor anyone else— will experience life (or death) in exactly the way you do; or will understand exactly what you feel and take care of the hurt when it comes. You are alone in the world.

I didn't mention my thoughts to Tim. I thought he might feel they were melodramatic. But, while I was busy reading, Tim had written out a paragraph for me in order to make sure I would not tinker with Phyllis's story further. It said, "There is no better description of what it's like to be at college in the depths of the year, in the long, lonely, rainy-slushy season from mid-October to early April, than the third entry of Phyllis's journal. It's exactly right. It's her accomplishment that this deep sense of place comes out of a scene that's not just descriptive but very dramatic."

I defer.

*F*ROM A SPIRAL NOTEBOOK
by Phyllis Orrick,
Ruxton, Maryland

A girl sits down at her desk. It's an ordinary school desk. On it are
ordinary books: paperback books, textbooks, philosophy books, neatly
stacked and arranged by course. Beside her sits her typewriter, oiled
and cleaned, waiting for the new semester. She has spent the past few
days buying books, notebooks, paper, and pens. All neat and tidy. The
whole room is waiting for what will come in the next twelve weeks.
It's an ordinary college room, its number painted on the door—596.
For one year 596 is her number. When people write her, they put Box
596 on the envelope. When they want to talk to her on the telephone,
they dial 555-0596.

The girl slumps down in the armless chair and surveys the order
all about her. The cold moon watches through the window as she
touches the objects on her desk. Her hand passes lightly over each of
them, careful not to disturb their order. She pushes back the chair and
stares at the frozen face in the sky.

Tonight room 596 is not big enough to encompass what she is
looking for. Pain, anger, love. She is about to grapple with them for
the first time. They were originally taught to her as incidental givens

—things with which one must deal from time to time but never call one's own. Unavoidable, they were to be avoided. She knew them as problems, never feeling them, merely plotting her way around them. They got in the way of social strategies, formalities, graciousnesses, that guided her life. Pain, anger, love. The feelings frightened her. They implied attachment, dependence, need. She had met them in the pages of novels, plays, and poems, functioning within an author's artificial scheme. And she had left them there.

On the outside they tended to cause complications. And complications were to be avoided at all costs. At all costs. In high school she had perfected the practice of nonfeeling. How she felt hadn't seemed as important as the papers, the college applications, the tests, the school activities. She had never experienced the wrench of hurt or the kiss of gladness that might have come from within herself. There had been too little time, too much else that had to be done.

Now, as she sits at her desk, what must be done can't be done. She can't copy notes, write in the margins, underline Platonic truths. She can't do the things she has been so carefully trained to do. She picks a pen from the cluster on her desk and selects a spiral notebook from the stack of books and starts to write.

January 4

I can no longer do the things I'm expected to do. I can't afford the cost. Not this time. Tonight all I see under an arid moon are barren fields. Tonight may be their chance to start recovering from their blight. With my help, plants may begin to grow and claim their rightful ground.

I began to sow the seed two years ago, involuntarily, when a part of my life died on a rainy highway late one Saturday night. I realized that the emptiness I felt belonged to a part of me I had never known I had.

Now I want to travel back to the present of feelings, back two years, and tear away the veil from judgments deferred and feelings laid aside. I want to return to that morning, two years ago, when I awoke to grasp the emptiness—the nothing that death had dealt me.

It is the morning of February 14. I am in my senior year of high school. I am busy, overextended in all the school doings I got myself

368

into simply because I don't know how to say no. It is a senior year that will send me to Yale.

I live at home with my parents. My brother Jack lives here too. He has just turned twenty-eight. Home is a former farmhouse surrounded by two and a half acres of rolling lawns and miniforests which step their way around ivy banks and clusters of box bushes. In it my parents and my brothers, Jack and Chris, had spent many years before I joined them. They had lived here through World War II. Cats, dogs, turtles, and parakeets from two childhoods. Many pleasures and much happiness. I can only guess how the two teen-age boys felt at the arrival of this baby girl, me.

On this Sunday morning in February my parents woke me up at eight o'clock because it is St. Valentine's Day, and the three of us (Jack always sleeps late, even on Christmas) will exchange cards and small gifts over breakfast. It is odd to see my father in my room. He seldom comes in to wake me up. Then I notice how close he is standing to my mother, how frightened and frail and old they look in the cheery, morning-lit room. Something cold creeps into my warm lazy St. Valentine's morning.

"Jack's gone." My tall father blurts it out and turns his face so I won't see his tears. He explains briefly: accident, police, morgue. They tell me to come downstairs when I am ready. And they leave. Jack had gone out the night before to see some friends after he ate dinner with us. He aggravated my parents by hanging around during the day and not doing anything but drink their liquor and smoke their cigarettes. He hated being at home as much as my parents resented his hanging on to them. Our brother Chris was married and had a house and a job. But Jack couldn't seem to finish school or hold down a job or get along with anybody at home.

Most weekday evenings Jack would come in from night school at about nine and go to the kitchen to get some leftover dinner. Sometimes I would come in and watch him while he ate some cold pot roast in the kitchen. But he ate little. Mostly, he just sat and sipped glasses of red wine or Scotch and smoked cigarettes. He always left a lot of glasses lying around, containing the musty remains of cigarettes floating in melted ice cubes. My father used to pick these up with much disgust the next morning after reading the paper, while Jack was still asleep.

Sometimes he would come in later—around eleven—and go straight to the living room, where he would sit all alone. Our parents would have gone to bed before he arrived, and I would go soon after because I always had to get up early to go to school or to do some early-morning math problems. I remember him sitting there at night with his skinny legs crossed, listening to a sad French ballad. Edith Piaf would croon to him as he nursed his Scotch while the house cooled off. The big furnace silenced its roar for the night; the radiators grew quiet, gradually stifling their chuckling, hissing, comforting daytime conversation. Upstairs, the lights were out. He sat there, with his legs crossed, hearing words lifted out of the streets of Paris by the mouth of the lost sparrow.

As I climbed the stairs, I would peep back over the banister. I was still too young to understand what the music meant to him, what he was trying to find on those cold nights in our dark house. He was eleven years older than I. I was a child during most of his life. My world was neatly bound by my mother's guiding hand. Later on, it was shaped by the walls of school, by the playmates and games that were the center of social life.

I liked to get up early. Jack always slept late. He got out of bed long after I had gone to school, unless some bill collector was after him. They called very early in the morning. Even then, in the morning, my view of him was obscured by the Latin homework that ate breakfast with me or by his bleary eyes and the dingy terry cloth robe that he slept in, I think.

Sometimes he took me skiing, and I remember liking that. One day, when I was ten, I decided that I liked him better than my older brother. But most of the time, Jack's loose ease and nonchalance made me mad. I was a child. My world was peopled by goals and tasks easily touched, readily accessible. I viewed life as a delight to be savored and enjoyed, a series of challenges that were never too great, a plaything that never talked back or pinched the fingers.

Recently I had had things to say to him and he to me. Already —almost—I had begun to see him: a man fated to fail. Such a man can't call himself anything. He is meant to go out and do, yet somehow he wants to pause. Out of cowardice as likely as not. But there is no room for cowards in this world. There is no face for them to turn to. When they ask questions, they must seek their answers at the bottom of tall glasses—in amber liquid and tobacco smoke. In the dark and silent house. While the brave ones sleep and prepare for a new day, a renewed struggle.

I had just begun to realize that one could be afraid and be unable to hide the fear. Then Jack died. And the silence of the house on that last night had become the silence that rings in my ears tonight. Jack is the one whom I would like to talk to now, but now he is nothing. Death made him nothing. And now it is I who feel the fear, after two years of heroics, after two years of paying my dues in a world that denied feeling, while inside I was bleeding and crying.

I must free myself tonight so that I can talk to you, Jack. Even though you are nothing, I must speak. I must hear something.

This fall I found you in a graveyard. In the fall, when it started to turn cold and the sky began to rise up and turn blue, when the wind stopped rippling the grass and started whipping the dead leaves, I came to visit you. At school.

There is a cemetery right near my college where I walked among the stones to read them and sit on them and pretend I'd found yours. You had three or four very nice ones. The cemetery was designed like a little city. It was arranged in blocks, delineated by avenues and lanes—each with its own name. I was very methodical. I covered a square block every time I went.

Why did I look for you where you weren't? I had so many chances to see you in the graveyard at home; but I never could. I felt safer in a cemetery full of strangers.

Who are you? All fall that question bothered me. I knew you were "gone." That means you aren't talked about except in endearing saccharine tones. No one mentions how you used to visit your mysterious friends, or hung around the house smoking our parents' cigarettes, drinking their liquor, losing job after job, flunking one semester after another.

You didn't do that anymore. You weren't there. The last time I saw you, you were lying in a satiny box at the undertaker's. You looked very cold and still and waxy. I wondered what the car wreck had done to you, because your face looked different—you had false

371

eyelashes and false eyebrows and false lips. Maybe your head was crushed. I kept wanting to touch your forehead to see if you were hollow or stuffed with sawdust or straw.

And I remember wondering whether there was a wizard behind the curtain to give you a brain, because that was all you needed to be all right again. No one thought you were you. Your brother, our brother, said the only way he could tell was the hairline. I thought maybe it wasn't you, but just a dummy with your hairline painted on it. Tonight I am saying it *was* you. You are dead. You and I seem to be about the only ones who know. I think you might want to hear this so you can lodge a complaint. People die just like you died. In fact, you were noted down somewhere as Maryland highway death number 53 or something like that. People die, and when they're dead it's said, "They're dead. He's dead. She's dead. It's dead." But you're only "gone"—at least that's what they told me. They couldn't say "He's dead" to themselves so they couldn't say it to me.

Now I've found you. Found out where you've "gone." You're in that cemetery on that fall day with all those gravestones all perpendicular, all pointing straight up. So when I look at them from the side I can see all the spaces in between them: little patches of emptiness bounded by the stones.

But the day is golden and almost defeats the spaces. Yellow and red leaves fill the emptiness. I catch a gravestone unawares; it's tilting toward the leaves, seeming to want to join them in their rustling bed, in the warmth of all the summer days stored up in the flaming colors of their skins.

A groundskeeper may come along and set a stone straight. Until it leans over again. A fat squirrel, too busy gathering nuts to do anything but twitch and scrabble climbs the engraved facades. And there is the sunlight. It warms the stones so that they radiate the borrowed heat. Smells fill up the spaces. Even the stones breathe an organic damp breath that mingles with the earth scents and the humus. But stones should be cold. Like those they've replaced.

If this is where death lives, I am glad I found it. I didn't find death for a long time. For me, you had merely "gone." I didn't know that you had "left" for death.

You see, my sleep might as well as have not been disturbed, because you weren't really dead, just "gone."

FROM A SPIRAL NOTEBOOK

It has taken me two years to know that you are dead. Others knew right away. The visitors, the neighbors—they knew. They'd heard it on the radio before I woke up.

Even the minister knew you were dead. He came to help us through our grief. What grief? You weren't dead, just "gone." We might as well not have talked about it because we couldn't, we had no words with which to say that part of us had died. When the minister came in, I had to sit in the living room with him and weep into my fist, keep him entertained until our parents came down to meet his sympathy, parry his words, arrange the hymns, thank him very much, and send him away. My friends from school came and sat around all dressed up and very repressed, polite and kind, like the notes they wrote. They knew you were dead.

Do you remember in the church? The coffin was rolled in—that was where you were. I started to cry. Our brother took my hand and quickly released it. He started to say something to me, but not hard enough. All I could feel was that I was suffocating in the church in my fur coat, my brown dress, my black stockings.

The formalities were there. The pall bearers were bright, attractive young men. The hymns, the prayers, were all correct. If only you could have been there.

And you were. All these things were there and you besides. But death wasn't. How could I have recognized him in that crowd? He was never mentioned. If I had looked up to the dusty chandelier, to the wooden cross, maybe I would have caught a glimpse of him, the one whom religion has always sought to banish.

As it was, all I felt was the suffocation and our brother's hand. I heard the hymns and my eyes were cast down on the words on the page and he—death—made his escape and eluded me for almost two years.

You started coming to me in my dreams, alive, with a baby tucked under each arm. And I was so glad to see you, because you had been away so long. I saw you stepping out of your old gray Mercedes with your slightly jaundiced eyes and your cheap raincoat flapping around your skinny weak legs.

That dream was sent again and again by death. He was piqued that he should fail to show me you were dead. Until last night. For when I saw you in that dream last night, babies under your arms,

373

I awoke; and when I awoke I was grinning—at nothing—as you must be grinning now under the clay. I now know that in that darkness of yours, you see nothing; you know nothing; you are nothing.

So tonight, almost two years after you "left," I sit here talking to you. I want to tell you good-bye, because I have finally realized you are dead. I cherish your memory, Jack; you are not "gone"; you are dead and you are with me.

February 13

It will be two years tomorrow that you died.

It seems as if thousands of years have passed. Thousands of years and millions of miles. I have begun to journey out into other people. You are on my mind, Jack, because tonight is your anniversary and because you, in part, are what set me searching.

I found someone. I cherished him more than I will ever cherish you. Someone to trust, to cling to, to gain strength from, to accept my giving.

Nathan is the first person to whom I said "I love you" and to whom I said it again and again. He said the same to me. But a silence has grown up between us. The same silence I heard when I paused to look over the banister in that cold, dark house, and when I stood in my brown dress and black stockings in the crowded church.

It all started to go bad two weeks ago when we decided to go to Boston and visit Nathan's family for the weekend. Friday had finally come and we were off. On that cold midwinter day. Arm in arm we strode to the car, our knapsacks bumping against each other, carrying books that we never really intended to read. We had planned to hitchhike, but Nathan found a ride at the last minute with a friend of his father's who was doing research in New Haven and going home to Boston for the weekend.

Having a ride made our escape immediate. We smiled and laughed as we stashed our things in the trunk, knowing that we were leaving this place where we had felt smothered and listless. Here, we couldn't say the things we felt, surrounded as we were by the routines and places that we had seen so many times. Bounded by the paths, slate and brick, that we had tramped alone and together throughout the dreary winter, from room to class, from class to room.

Boston. Cambridge. The city. The scene. We would be able to go everywhere we wanted together with no one to see us, free to hold hands and just kiss.

We were dropped off in Boston, so Nathan could introduce the city to me. We wandered in the cold rain and nothing was said. All the famous buildings looked like their pictures, though I didn't know their names. As we walked on, some of them seemed to reappear, as if I were lost and going in circles. But I didn't stop Nathan and ask him what they were or where we were going. It was too cold, too wet.

Instead, I trudged after him through the traffic until we finally arrived at the Boston Museum of Fine Arts. Out of the rain and face to face with all those grand paintings. The museum's hush became our own.

By the time we caught the train to Cambridge, the glee I had felt in New Haven had turned to vertigo. Nathan's house—all weathered wood and skylights and marimeko curtains—was reassuring. So was his tall sandy-haired father in his soft clothes and his mother, who showed me to my room and gave me fresh towels.

They seemed glad to see us. But Nathan's glance told me nothing. He took me on a cursory tour of his brothers' rooms upstairs. We hugged for a moment beside a bunkbed. He showed me to the bathroom and left to go downstairs.

Downstairs, at the long table in the bright kitchen among the colorful offerings of food, we sat across from each other. Around us were his brothers, his mother, and his father. The talk babbled on about his high-school friends, about his old teachers that now were his brothers', about how the family dog was growing old. It was all foreign. I watched from inside a glass booth, as Nathan talked and looked and listened to them.

His glances toward me told me nothing. Jack, it was that same silence. The one you heard in our house. How can I break the silence, Jack? Break it as finally as I shattered the silence that cut me off from you?

Nathan, what happened that night in Cambridge? Where were you during that dinner? You, who had once looked into my eyes for

375

hours at a time, probing, loving, embracing. Those eyes I knew down to each brown fleck in their green irises. They had dealt me truth and love. Now they just shot glances. Family glances to make sure I was all right.

God damn it. I was all right, but where were you? Right now you could be at my elbow and I wouldn't care. I'd be afraid to care.

I want to think as I write this—What if we had been able to stop when we got to the car and had stood in that New Haven street and said, We can stay here and be together. Could we fight back this power that lives in the brick walls, the stone walls, trying to separate us from ourselves and each other? What if we had gone inside and grappled with each other?

Now when I sit in class away from you, I have this feeling, and I grow tired. I am becoming alienated by longing. Behind the hours of papers, tests, studying in the library, lurks this memory I have of hearing you speak to me in loving whispers, feeling you lie down beside me, spending hour after hour close to you.

I remember that and it hurts. It's hard to live with the thought that those tender moments are only scenes I play over and over in my mind—hoping for a sequel. They are no longer part of my life with you; they are memories of what has left and will remain gone.

Things got in the way. Experiments, papers, classes. You are compelled to go out and get what you want. Intellectually, at least, I know I crave those things too. It's just that when I have a spare hour or two, when something has disturbed me, when people seem too preoccupied, I want you. Oh hell. I want you any time of the day or night.

Only recently have I become able to let people enter my life. And you are the first to be allowed in. I have yet to learn how to let them out. How to let you out, to admit that I have lost you. I feel you've gone away because of your fear, a fear that I am just overcoming myself. Losing you adds to my old fear. Your fear has fed it. If only you had seen what I saw, if only you had lost someone through death, perhaps your fear of love would have grown as small as mine.

February 14

As I feel my face petrify every morning (what Medusa must exist around here!), I think of the silence I feel around me. Not the fruitful kind; not the warm kind; not the soft kind. I feel a silence that drains my spirit, sucking until I am dry.

This silence exists mostly in crowds of people. In the crowds I can't help but see the image of you, Jack, a solitary figure in a sleeping house.

I hear nothing directly from the people in the crowds. Instead, their words creep into my ears from somewhere else. But today starts differently as I step out of my cluttered empty room. The gray abandoned look that winter begins with has been covered by the white of new snow.

I cut across a courtyard-sized white wasteland to breakfast in the dining hall. There is a tremor behind the glassy cold, of a presence all around. When I step into the first yielding mound of flakes, I hear the voices: help me, save me, *SAVE* me. They are faint, but loud enough to send echoes of themselves throughout their brittle crystal brothers and sisters, which lie drifted into piles from their falling. The voices emanate from the hard-packed patches underfoot, but they die away as soon as I stop.

The physics lecture is finally over. Old Thompson dragged on about something or other. It has been another fifty-minute tête-à-tête with my physics binder. I look up at the bank of desks and see the faces of the people in the lecture. They wrap themselves in their woolens, protectors from the cold outside and keepers of the cold inside. They look like silent mockups of their prehistoric ancestors. Each one of us every minute girding for the battle against weakness and fear of weakness, denying the denial in order to power the torque that drives us. We prevent ourselves from seeing how close help lies —just inside a spiral-bound notebook, where the words unspoken unroll across the page.

We straggle out of the room and down the hall, down the steps past the other rooms, which are busily, mysteriously, discharging other participants in other ceremonies, all with the same end in mind. Knowledge, power, but most of all, silence.

I have almost forgotten the voices when I step outside into the white. As if it were not enough to sting my eyes with rays borrowed from the sun, the snow pierces my ears with its cries: Help me, save me.

I hear the voices as I walk within the silent crowds of people who

377

trample the snow underfoot, my comrades beating their way to another class. I must go too. So I join the silent ranks, still hearing the pleas for help.

At the intersection of the wet black streets, the persistent noise and stinging light of the snow have faded. I quickly forget its cries in the harum-scarum of cars and passing people. My ears are filled with the bustle of a snowy day: everyone is late; the plows are already at work.

By the time I get to the post office, most of the snow is piled out of the way. The post office is fuller than usual because of the wet everywhere, boots and overcoats, extra clothing, hats and scarves and mittens. All wet and sodden, swollen with the water they have drunk from the ground and out of the air. The people are clumsy. They crowd each other, jostling to postpone their exit into the realm of snow and crackling cold.

In the scramble I don't hear anything except the clink of post box keys. It is a glad time for the people who open the boxes and find something there. A letter deserves a private celebration, a reading of its contents in some secret corner. With a letter the little box speaks with a magic that no one else can hear. If only we could live our lives like a letter, full of the words we write down, fold up, and tuck into private containers. If only we could speak those words. Then the silence would be dispelled. The deathly pall would crack. And we would never again wake up dead.

My box has betrayed me. I open it just the same. The small glass door is my own confessional. Bless me father for I have sinned. No words of comfort today.

I step back into the snow. What do I hear? It sounds vaguely familiar. I look around trying to see what is making the noise. Nothing. No one. It's strange. The snow here is so clean, so untrampled, so full of those distinct cries. No mud, no wet, no black boots, no overcoats, have reached this place. I am alone. Where have I heard the cries before? Why are they calling to me? Are they warning or pleading?

I slip, but I must not fall, for the snow would deafen me if I were to lie in it. I pray for some Ulysses to hold me tightly to the mast so I will not succumb to their voices. I must hurry, I must get away.

I reach the safety of the watery, muddy street, shiny and black, where I find myself again with silence.

Lunch. The dining hall is more crowded today as people stay longer to rest their bones and warm themselves with cups of coffee. The hunters, the survivors, are resting from their daily tasks. They brood and talk a bit, keeping in the backs of their minds the struggle. They cannot forget what they must fight, yet they cannot talk about it. They must not allow themselves to turn away from their duty to win.

Someone has opened a window and I can see a tree outside. It's a pine tree with snow draping its branches. The dining room chatter does not cover the snow's cries—now so near that I hear nothing else. *Save* me. They have invaded even this place, where the walls should be too thick for their cries to penetrate. But I hear them. No one else does. What should I do? Should I turn to my neighbor and say, do you hear the calls for help? Do I stand on top of the table, knocking over trays and glasses and proclaim their plea for help? Would I be scorned? laughed at? Don't they hear the voices? Help me, *save* me. Are there others with the same thought?

The eaters have begun to disperse. I see them pushing themselves back from the tables. I haven't acted. I hear the voices still, coming from the open window, so loud now that I must say something to break the deafening roar in my head.

I must and yet I can't. The ritual of the meal is too powerful for me to destroy with words. The cries I hear have liberated me. But my liberation has left me alone, washed up gasping on an iceberg, temporarily safe from drowning; still I am exposed to ice that would freeze my skin, stick to it, and tear it from my body. The black waters, salt and cold, travel past.

I resist the urge to call out and I join the press toward the door and the wintry light. I pause, dazzled by the glare, while the others pass by.

The voices now are all around. It is as if the crowd has left behind invisible stragglers. The voices. The voices everywhere. Why must they talk to me? I can't help you. I can't save you. I'm no stronger than the rest. Damn it! Shut up. I must go to my class, with everyone else. Where is everyone?

Help me, *save* me. No. I can't. I won't. I have other things to do. What do you need to be saved from? Do you see any of us calling for help? We aren't weak, we're strong and silent. You should do as we do. It won't do any good, I tell you. There's no danger. I couldn't help you if there were. Where is everyone? Why don't they come back and help me answer these cries?

Help me, *save* me. What right do you have to cry for help? Tiny crystals from the clouds—that's all you are. Nothing ever happens to you. Why do you shriek so? What about us? Have you ever been truly alone? Have you ever needed to love someone? Help me. SAVE ME. Shut up and listen to my side of it, will you? How many times have you sat through just one of those classes or walked back to your room with only the moon for company, after spending all day running from place to place? You have no right to speak. You don't know what it's like to have a mouth to speak with and ears to hear with and yet say nothing, hear nothing—with all the things you want to say trapped within your mind, and heard only by your heart.

If you were one of us living here, wondering who everyone else was, wondering whether they loved or hated you when you knew they could do both, then you would have a right to cry out. To cry out with all your might for all the words never spoken, for all those hidden glances, for the cold hands never warmed by those of another. Then you should cry out.

The voices are silent.

I no longer hear them. Have they stopped speaking altogether, or have they merely stopped speaking to me?

I venture farther out, bend down, and hold my ear close to the snow. Earlier today I would have been deafened by their frenzy, by their pleas. Are you there? Are you all right? Why don't you speak to me anymore? Is there someone else who hears you now? Someone else for whom your words mean something? Are you silenced forever, like my fellows? Have you given up, too?

I explore every corner of the courtyard, checking for the faintest traces of sound. A whisper would do. Just so I know they are still there, still talking, still trying to get help. But now they are only mute particles that blow and scatter before the icy gusts, gradually hardening into stillness under the weight of pressing cold.

February 18

I've heard nothing for the past few days. The snow is gone, melted by the midwinter thaw. My feet have grown numb from standing in the cold and dark, waiting for signs of a storm that could bring one last snow before spring. I've decided that on that next snowy day, before anyone else is awake, I'll walk into the courtyard, put my ear to a drift of snowflakes. And listen.

If I hear nothing, I will go to the dining hall in time to get some breakfast before classes begin. And in the dining hall I will glance around and look for a worried face, a person who seems preoccupied, who steals a look at the tree just outside the open window. If I see that person, I will know the voices are still there. I will know that eventually everyone will hear them and that someday soon we will all take up the cry.

If it doesn't snow soon, I may just have to stand up in the middle of the dining hall and shout it myself. Or in front of the post office box I'll turn to my neighbor and say, Help me, SAVE me.

PHYLLIS – NEWSPAPERWOMAN

TOWARD the end of February that year, Phyllis decided she'd had her fill of "the unending New Haven slush, the same stinking cafeteria, the same people, the same rat pads, the same places." Sophomore and winter restlessness—both atmospheric and emotional— had set in with full vengeance.

During the spring break, she flew off "on a cheapie flight" to California for a week to visit a friend at Stanford, where the warm sun, "the tile roofs and one-story buildings," and the easy life-style felt awfully good. At almost the same time, she suddenly discovered from her Yale dean that she had a year's worth of credit because she had passed advanced placement exams her senior year in high school. The opportunity for a year's adventure in the sun had presented itself on a silver platter. South America beckoned. She dropped by my house one spring afternoon to announce the good news. "I called my father," she said, "and I said, 'Hey, by skipping a year, I'll be saving you seven grand. So how about giving me three thousand of it to travel for a year?' and he said, 'Okay.' " The normally calm Phyllis was leaping around the room.

After Yale let out for the summer, Phyllis flew straight to the University of Texas in Austin, where she took a six-week intensive Spanish course—"a special school for CIA agents"—and then, together with a woman friend from Yale, she explored Colombia, Mexico, Peru, and Panama—"staying in a spot or moving on just whenever we felt like it." The world was wondrous. "As a place of beauty, sunsets, clouds, hills, smells, flowers, sky, warmth, *sun*, Cuernavaca can't be beat," she wrote. At Christmas, she touched base with her family in Baltimore and then flew off to Europe—London, Edinburgh, Paris, Turkey, the Greek islands, where she spent two months "swimming, sunning, and exploring" and fell in love with the tiny island of Hydra: "The line of houses climbing up the natural amphitheatre of the hills is completely unspoiled . . . and the only bicycle, car, or motorcycle allowed on the island is the city garbage truck."

Phyllis's "year off" came exactly when she needed it most. As with many students, the seesaws of adolescence—almost always beset with some reliving of childhood traumas—had combined with the long years of formal schooling to produce exhaustion. A sense of deadness. A year away from all the old stuff—school, parents, hometown culture—left her free to explore "the real world out there" exactly when and how she pleased. Phyllis was lucky in that she had enough money to travel and investigate on her own; but working at a job can be just as valuable—in some cases, more so. She came back to Yale the following year with fresh energy and a new sense of herself. She was an almost perfect example of a remark made by McGeorge Bundy when he was Dean of the Faculty at Harvard: "Often the most valuable year a student has in college is the year he takes off."

After that year, I didn't hear from Phyllis for a long time. When she returned to New Haven for her senior year, I was away on sabbatical and after that I lost track of her altogether. Then one day in the early spring of 1977, while I was visiting my mother in upstate Connecticut, the telephone rang and it was Phyllis. She was in Gallup, New Mexico, and had just finished a novel that she wanted me to read. I was en route to San Francisco, where I was slated to put on a large conference for businessmen and -women at—of all places—a new conference center on a Zen Buddhist farm in Marin

383

County. The prospect filled me with apprehension because I had just heard that the new building had not been completed as promised and I sensed that the Roshi and other Zen people—in their larger Cosmic Scheme of Things—were not as worried as I about having the facility ready in time. I needed to get to the Coast posthaste and had not a breathing moment to read anything for at least two months. I envisioned myself engulfed in a crash "do-it-yourself" course on Zen and the Art of Carpentry.

I was about to explain all this to Phyllis over the long-lines to Gallup, when she told me that, during the years since I'd seen her, she had first worked on the political campaign of Timothy Wirth of Colorado and then, when (to everyone's surprise) he was elected, she had followed him to Capitol Hill to be one of his legislative assistants. Two years of Congressional politics—rife "with sexism and a lot of power tripping"—had left her hating "most of the people on Capitol Hill (but not Tim Wirth)" and burned out from eighteen- to twenty-hour working days.

Again, a golden opportunity had presented itself. Her senior year roommate, Frumi—who in the intervening years had been an editorial assistant at *Esquire*—called from Gallup saying she was "going crazy" in the wilds of New Mexico, where her new husband was a medical resident in a hospital for Indians. Why didn't Phyllis come out and join them? This gave Phyllis the chance, in a fine place and with good company, to return to her real interest—writing. She set herself the daring task of writing a novel.

As she was talking, it occurred to me that Phyllis, with all her Capitol Hill experience, was a godsend. She could help me organize the conference and handle the political machinations of the Zen Master—a confidante of Governor Jerry Brown and, as we were soon to discover, not without his own special skills in political gamesmanship.

"Phyllis," I said, "why don't you come to San Francisco and help me put on this 'Business and Right Livelihood' conference? Then when it's all over, we'll sit in the sun on a houseboat and I'll read your novel." I emphasized the word *sun*.

"This *what* conference?"

"You heard me—Business and Right Livelihood—a Zen concept."

"Yeah, sure," she laughed. She obviously thought I was pulling her leg.

"Look, Phyllis, you can sit Zazen on a black pillow at three thirty every morning, listen to gongs and learn to chant. All that meditation will clear your fuzzy head. You'll become centered and sane for life. How could you turn down such an opportunity?"

"You gotta be kidding. Do I have to shave my head?"

"Not until you become a priest."

Phyllis arrived in San Francisco just a week behind me and we set up a one-room temporary headquarters in the office building of Glide Memorial Church in San Francisco's Tenderloin district. We lived some miles away (on the other side of the Golden Gate) at the Zen Farm where we rented a small one-room hut with bunk beds, formerly a storehouse for garden equipment. But our hut was in the *sun*, which most of the Zen buildings in the damp, dark eucalyptus gulch were not.

In those frantic weeks, we lived half-time in Shangri-la and half-time in what can only be described as a combination of the Bowery and Madison Avenue. In Shangri-la:

When the deep gong rang out at 3:00 A.M., Phyllis would crawl out of the upper bunk—showering swallow droppings as she swung down off the rafters—to go meditate in lotus position in the barn-turned-Zendo. On the days that I felt strong enough to inhale the incense (an aroma that had made me squeamish ever since my contacts with the Catholic Church during my early married years), I would join her for the second sitting at 5:30, spending most of the period trying to get my legs to cross. Then, together with some fifty-odd Zen students, we would work silently in the lush fields of vegetables and fruits—weeding, tying up tomato plants, hoeing out strawberry patches—while the sun rose, slowly revealing the surrounding northern California hills and the blue Pacific beyond. Nothing was as beautiful. "And nothing," as Phyllis says, "ever tasted as good as the little cookies they gave us right after the hoeing and the big Zen breakfast that followed with its Tassajara bread fresh from the ovens." On those quiet, early mornings, infused as we were with the Grand, Glorious Scheme of Things, such petty agendas as conference preparations seemed wholly insignificant.

At eight we would return to our hut, don our city togs and drive up and over the tall hills, across the Gate to the Tenderloin, which was another world altogether. "The thing I remember best," said Phyllis recently, "was that after cleansing my soul with Zazen, I always had an incredibly vivid image of the whores and the pimps going to bed at eight A.M. as we drove to the office."

When we reached our little cubicle, the early morning bliss was blown away by the nitty-gritty of our immediate situation: 1) we were scheduled to put on a conference, now only a week and a half away; 2) the site for it—an elaborate Japanese-style building just one hundred yards from our swallow hut—was only half-finished. Two temple carpenters (imported from Kyoto) were hammering away at it in Zen fashion—quietly and unhurriedly—but only on those days when they weren't summoned to some mysterious "elsewhere"; 3) we couldn't make direct contact with the Zen Master, Richard Baker-Roshi—an all-American boy who had learned the entrepreneurial tricks of the Zen trade but must have missed out on some of its purported humility or compassion. We soon discovered that, behind an immaculate reputation for good works, dwelt a rather overriding worldly ambition that would have made the pros on Capitol Hill bow in deference—if not sit cross-legged; 4) we were women—which is not a wise thing to be at any Zen center, but particularly not at this one. Worse still, we were women without wealth or clout—a lethal combination. In short, we were being given the royal Zen runaround.

I was somewhat confused and discomfited by all this. But not Phyllis. She saw it all clearly and took it in stride. Although she enjoyed meditation and working in the fields, she was not much attracted—as many in her generation were—to any Shangri-la, even this beautiful, highly respectable "good works" Shangri-la. Phyllis was beyond the point where she could imagine giving up her adult self-reliance for a return to a safe, warm—but constricting—surrogate family. As for the mysterious Papa-figure, she had his number exactly. Throughout those crazy weeks, she was for me a witty bulwark who nudged me to laughter whenever she could, and calmly referred to our Zen friend as "that politician in monk's clothing."

The conference itself went off passably enough, after Phyllis and I located some extra beds in a beach motel a few miles up the coast.

I have little memory of the event—except for the moment when the Zen Master finally awarded us his presence in the conference room. He was preceded by a Zen student carrying a special straight-backed chair, which was ordinary enough except that it stood three or four inches higher than anyone else's chair. A few minutes later, he walked in—his shaved head and thin, handsome face topping an immaculate three-piece London tweed suit. He contributed intelligently and wittily to the discussions and then, at the end of the session, delivered a seemingly ingenuous and utterly charming request for donations to his new Japanese tea house, which he planned to have the temple carpenters build beside the still unfinished conference center.

When it was all over, Phyllis and I fell exhausted into a Sausalito houseboat and sat in the *sun*. While we recovered, I persuaded Phyllis to stay with me for a year, in which she would work half-time for me on a number of projects (none of them so eventful as the Zen conference) and have the rest of her time free to write. My work had a way of spilling over into her time but she did complete a number of short stories and devour all of Dos Passos—the author that seemed to fit best her particular interest in fusing personal stories with social concern.

But, with all the other things I was juggling, I never found time to read her novel! For which I felt bad for many months afterward. Only recently, I got up the nerve to ask her what it had been about. "Well," she said, "it was about this bunch of young people—all drop-outs from various professions—who are living in a Shangri-la spot in the mountains. Their Shangri-la gets threatened by the power company and the group has to decide whether or not to reenter the worldly fray to save their little piece of paradise. In the end, they decide to reenter the grubby world. The book leaves it uncertain about whether or not they win their battle, but the point is that they realize that they have to go back and confront reality and meet people on their own levels, if they want to keep their own place." No wonder Phyllis had understood the Zen Shangri-la! She'd already been there and back again. No wonder she had lost interest in her novel. She had "completed" that part of her life and grown beyond her subject.

As might well have been predicted, by the summer of 1978 Phyllis had tired of "living in strange happy-time places like California" and longed to return to "the good old grubby East Coast real world." Many of her old friends had returned to Baltimore after spending a few years away. She also realized her parents were growing older and she wanted to live nearby "in order to enjoy them." Phyllis's wandering years were over. She felt it was now time to develop her writing into an ongoing profession at which she could earn a living. And to do so in the place she most wanted to live—Baltimore.

The task was not altogether an easy one. Staying at first with her parents, she began by ferreting out free-lance and proofreading jobs with small publishing houses and newspapers. Then she found herself writing more and more for Baltimore's new alternative newspaper, *The City Paper*, which had begun publication just a year and a half before she returned home. In the beginning, she worked part-time and undertook any job that was needed, from writing movie reviews to delivering the papers to the stands. Today she is the "more-than-full-time" associate editor, and the paper has grown from a bi-monthly to a weekly and in circulation from twelve thousand to fifty thousand. Early in 1981, *The City Paper* staff launched a second paper, *1981*, in Washington, for which Phyllis is the contributing editor. One of the early editions was a parody of *The Washington Post* called *The Washington Past*.

"It's a lot of work but a lot of fun," Phyllis told me on the phone recently. "Not much money—and that's a bore, but I have the luxury of having work I enjoy. I can write what I want to write about —sometimes the least publicized side of things—and it's published exactly as I write it. It's fun to bring out stories that normally wouldn't be published, both because of their political content and their writing style. It's fun to write about the community—the real people and places that aren't sensationalized. It's great to go out and talk to people who know things and have experienced things I haven't and then try to put some of that across." I could see that the influence of Dos Passos was still very much with her.

"So you really like being a journalist?" I asked.

"I like that part of it. And I also like writing short stories when I can eke out the time, but my ear and my eye have changed a lot.

I'm now much more of a writer than when I wrote the novel or the story for your course."

Sometime in the middle of describing her work, Phyllis mentioned she was "living with a gentleman." "Oh?" I replied eagerly, waiting for more. As well as I knew her, Phyllis was not one to talk at length about her personal life or her relationships. She'd had a number of close male friends over the years but she hadn't seemed deeply involved with any of them.

"Well," she continued, "I met him one day when he came to see me about a story he wanted to write for the paper and I fell in love."

"Phyllis," I said, "as long as I've known you, I've never heard you use those words before. This must be serious."

She laughed, brushing my motherly remark aside, and told me that Jamie was a news reporter and had just taken a new job with *The Annapolis Capital*. At first, they had lived in a "student-type" apartment a few blocks from *The City Paper* in Baltimore, but when Jamie had switched papers, they had moved to a "great find—a big two-story flat behind a Toyota dealership and next to a warehouse in Annapolis."

"Tell him for me that you're the most wonderful person in the world," I said.

"I tell him that every night," she replied, laughing.

I asked Phyllis if she had yet shown her parents the Valentine's Day story.

"No," she said, quietly. "I will soon, I guess. I don't know. I won't make a big deal of it. In terms of my relationship to them, that story seems like eons ago. We know each other pretty well now, I think."

PORTRAIT OF ELÍAS

ALTHOUGH only nineteen and a freshman, Elías Aguilar (pseudonym) considered himself a man—a fully grown Puerto Rican whose sacred mission was to tell whites "the truth, man, the truth" and restore blacks and Puerto Ricans to their noble heritage and their proper place in a world "fucked up by the white race." From the first day, Elías made it clear to me that a writing course, although he loved to write, would always take second place to any black studies course or community work he became involved in.

Passion is the word that best describes Elías. His face, although covered by a full but immaculate beard, showed every flick of emotion. When he was in fighting trim, his tall athletic body radiated energy whenever he came into the room. Even his afro was electric. In class he rarely sat without squirming—especially if a middle-class white were speaking—and he would interrupt others regularly with bursts of enthusiastic rhetoric. When he was downcast—which was rare—he looked like a large damp rag and hardly spoke at all. The class was never quite in tune when Elías was out of sorts.

He asked that everyone use his full name—Elías. No nicknames for him. They lacked the respect that Puerto Rican adulthood demanded.

Although a superior high-school athlete—particularly in baseball and basketball—Elías had refused to play for Yale teams because he —like much of Yale's black community in this period—felt that his talents should not be co-opted for white establishment goals; nor should he waste time on these pursuits. After he graduated from college, he regretted his purist stance. "I am ashamed," he told me later, "that I didn't play. I lost a lot of joy. I could have played just for myself—for the fun of it—and not have done damage to anyone."

Elías arrived at Yale during the years when Yale's blacks and Puerto Ricans had consolidated to make a strong stand against any racist or patronizing tendencies within the university. The trial of Black Panther Bobby Seale and the march on New Haven had taken place in the spring of 1970, leaving well-organized and effective black community coalitions throughout the city. The Black Student Alliance of Yale was strong and laid down strict guidelines for behavior. This was the period when, in order to be considered authentically black by your youthful peers, you needed to put forth a stereotypical image: poor, a family on welfare, an absent or drunken father, a hardworking pure mother (usually employed as a domestic "bustin' suds" somewhere). In addition, it was a good idea to have suffered some demeaning experiences. Sometimes, the image was overdramatized, but it was important to maintain; being a middle-class black didn't help you qualify for "black is beautiful." Fraternization with whites was out of the question.

Such stances were unquestionably necessary to build up badly needed self-esteem—just as other stereotypical stances were necessary for the early phases of the women's movement. This period was particularly difficult for Yale students who were struggling with the problems of what it means to be black in a prestigious university, just as it was particularly difficult for the women who were struggling with what it meant to be female in an institution designed for males only. The seventies were not a simple time for minority students. On top of everything else, there was a lot of just plain culture shock. The awesome neo-Gothic Yale buildings and the traditional academic atmosphere (not to mention language) weren't designed to make many people feel at home—let alone those from urban ghettoes or tiny Puerto Rican villages. In reality, Elías qualified for the black image rather easily, but like many black students, he was caught in a conflict between taking political stands he believed in and enjoying the many advantages that Yale had to offer—such as athletic competition, social occasions at the college master's house, and—God forbid—singing clubs or the like. In my class, I felt he was frequently torn between expressing himself—especially his more vulnerable feelings—and his need to project an invulnerable political image. When other words failed, black rhetoric came in handy to keep the image in place and the art of drama was not unknown to him.

Elías lived the first three years of his life in Río Piedras, a small fishing village in Puerto Rico, and then moved to Harlem with his mother and his stepfather, Mario, who had dreams of a new and golden life. As a small boy in Harlem, Elías grew up in the midst of poverty and cockroaches. Later, the family moved to a Hispanic ghetto in Passaic, New Jersey, where he joined the street life of gangs, and was suitably blooded. At a moment's notice he would leap to his feet and show us his scars—knife wounds on his neck, stomach, and upper thigh. However, this same "gang member," when he was seventeen, applied for a scholarship and was admitted as a scholarship student to a private Episcopal day school in Paterson, to which he commuted each day during his last year and a half of high school. His stepfather had long since disappeared; his mother took in laundry to make a living for her three children. She exercised a considerable influence over her oldest son, who adored her.

At the Episcopal school Elías acquired a traditional education as well as some elongated social science jargon that he used with abandon. He used the same abandon with political rhetoric so that the liberal sprinkling of *motherfuckers* among phrases like "socioeconomic approaches to considerations of institutional identities" was sometimes devastating—if not unreadable.

When he was trying hard to be academic, he would back into a sentence in a way no reader could follow: "A growing consciousness to my existence and what it means in terms of Puerto Rican populace has probably been more the cause of my constantly moving thought process than the Yale community."

Yet after a few paragraphs of this, he would return—briefly—to

393

a simple place within himself and write with an undiluted Elías style: "I feel at home in Harlem. As soon as the train gets near 125th Street and Lexington, I begin to get loose; I'm ready to 'hang out.' I want to hear about the latest happenings—what people are rapping about now, what they're wearing, what steps they're dancing. It's hard to keep up with the latest dance steps."

Elías's original application for the course was one of his most dreadful efforts. It was a sentimental four-line poem about God called "Thine Is the Kingdom." I promptly put his application in the rejection pile. But early that afternoon he turned up on my doorstep, introduced himself, and persuaded me to reconsider him on the basis of another paper he would write by nightfall. At 8:00 P.M., he stood again at my door, this time with an eight-page paper (I had asked for one page) about the "house niggers" who had been co-opted by elitism. It exploded with terms like *white culture, marxism, capitalism, white supremacy, oppression.* But between the rhetorical paragraphs were two small jewels, anecdotes from his life in Puerto Rico. He had me. He was in. Besides, I liked his chutzpah.

As time went on, everyone—including myself—began to grow weary of Elías's ability to grab center stage in order to rap against "the whites" or to insist he was the only one who knew what it was to be poor. His hot arguments with Peter Werner became a ritual. But in spite of all his posturing, he was so passionately human that he was hard to resist. And behind the bombast was an enthusiasm for writing, and a genuine kindness, that was enormously appealing. He was usually the first to commend other people's writing in the notebooks and support them in their efforts to write. When Chun Shih, a Chinese computer scientist, was so embarrassed by what he felt was his awkward prose that he wouldn't allow any of his writing to appear in the notebooks, it was Elías who encouraged him: "Chun —everything I write about and the way I write it is embarrassing to me, too. I'm urging you to reconsider not *X*ing us out on what is undoubtedly very fine work because I know it's coming from your gut and is honest."

Moreover, by this time we had all come to realize that Elías was frequently reacting to his deep fear that he would be co-opted by Yale and become a "house nigger, kissing ass for a professor"—the greatest sin of all. He knew that if he was to be of any use to himself or to his fellow Puerto Ricans, he had to keep his base with them and not lose touch with his identity and his reality. He knew, too, that if he was lucky enough to get a college education, he would have to place that education at the service of his fellow Hispanics. In one piece he wrote with his usual vehemence, "I didn't come to this place for myself, man. I came here to prepare myself to deal with my people. The only way I can keep myself from being tarnished by the Yale environment is by keeping close ties with the Puerto Rican community. My summer jobs can't be in Washington earning two thousand dollars; they have to be in community organizing earning six hundred dollars." Then he charged himself, along with other Yale minority students: "Learn about yourself, nigger. The library is the greatest asset this place has. Use that, motherfucker. Read in print how your people have been degraded for four hundred years. It will set your mind straight. Do it now. Because when you graduate, whitey ain't never gonna accept you and you're going to have to come back to the community someday, and as Dick Gregory says, 'We gonna kick yo' ass.'"

As the class understood him more, they (and I) tried to persuade Elías that, if he wanted to convince us "whiteys" of his sincerity, he'd be a lot more effective if he stopped haranguing us and wrote directly about his experiences of being Puerto Rican. We all wanted some real stories from him and some honest descriptions.

Gradually he grew to trust the class a little more and his barking became less necessary. One day, he gave us a description of a terrifying episode he'd experienced in his first semester. He still blamed white Yale for the agony, but he was finally using "I" convincingly and most of the rhetoric was gone.

I went to my room and sulked for a while instead of doing my work. I began to reflect on my first semester at Yale and began to build up a great deal of tension as I remembered all the individual acts of racism and coldness that I had either witnessed or had been the victim of. The more I thought about it, the more disgusted I became. I began to think about home and mother and everything else that I associated with security and realized that none of it was here. I began to panic as I thought about the exam and the paper. My pulse quickened and my breathing came harder and my hands and armpits began to perspire. I called my dean at his house and explained my condition and asked for an extension on either the paper or the exam or both, preferably both. He said he couldn't do that; that I should have called him earlier.

After I hung up I began to cry uncontrollably and felt more helpless than I have ever felt in my life. I had always considered myself a sort of stoic until that happened. I then began to pound my palms into my forehead and yelled fuck this and fuck that and started kicking things all over the room. I built myself into a frenzy until I began to pound my fist into the wall and white dust began to fall to the floor from the plaster walls and blood began to streak down my knuckles. I can't remember anything after that except hearing the phone ring, first distantly, then closer, until I finally realized where I was. I picked up the receiver out of instinct and heard the monotonous buzz of the dial tone. They had hung up.

I looked around my room and began to recollect my thoughts. I realized what had happened and looked at the caked blood on my hands and the white dust on the floor and my things spread all over the room, some of them broken. I cried once more. . . . I cleared the mucus from my nose and lips and chin. After trying to straighten things out for a while, I finally cleaned off my hands and face and opened my Psych IIa textbook and began to study.

Elías had achieved a breakthrough, but he still had problems seeing through the eyes of other characters—although he was beginning to understand and accept as genuine some of the feelings of the "middle-class whites" in the class.

For his long paper, I urged Elías to write about something he really loved. I remembered his description of Harlem. I sensed that he would be able to turn his considerable imagination to storytelling if he were not throwing his anger around. Then, on the night before the paper was due, he wrote "Madre Puertorríqueña" in one sitting. "I just sat down with my typewriter," he told me later, "a meatball grinder from Yorkside, my coffee and a reefer and said to my roommate, 'When you wake up this is going to be done.' When he awoke, I was on page 27. He looked over at the typewriter and said, 'Twenty-seven? How did you do that?' I said, 'Man, this is not something you got to sit back and research or anything. It's the kind of thing that's gotta come out like that. Cause if you get up and come back to it, a whole lot of other stuff comes up and you lose the thread.' After it was over I was exhausted—thoroughly exhausted—because it was about all those things I hadn't thought about for a long time. I slept for two days. It was the kind of thing that when you get it out, it's like a catharsis. Even though it's painful, it turns out to be cool. It's all right."

*M*ADRE PUERTORRÍQUEÑA
by Elías Leonel Aguilar
New York, New York

*M*ama. *The scenes, Mama. The scenes of a childhood . . . they continue to toss back and forth in my mind, torturing me. I must face up to them, Mama. It's going to be difficult, but I have to do it, Mama, despite the pain that it will bring.*

Mama, you're so typical of Puerto Rican mothers. I can imagine how you felt when I was born—the way Aunt Filomena felt when my cousin Dolores was born. I asked her why she was so sad. She answered in a strange, almost crazy voice, "Porque mi hija a nacido para sufrir" (Because my daughter has been born to suffer). Seeing my bewilderment, she carefully explained how all Puerto Rican mothers feel guilty about bringing a child into this world, because the child faces extreme hardship. What's more, she said, the child's color and facial characteristics were so important that mothers in Puerto Rico would light candles to saints and pray for hours that their children would come out as white as possible. Barriers of language and culture hampered even the whitest Puerto Ricans, but the darkest and most phenotypically black in our race suffer the most. Not only are they spiks, they are also niggers. I was jolted by her talk. At that moment,

398

I began to see you, Mama, in a different light. I began to appreciate all you'd done for us. Only after listening to Aunt Filomena did I begin to understand why you would hold me in your arms or sit me on your lap and repeat over and over, "Mi pobre hombrecito, mi pobre hombrecito" *(My poor little man).*

I hope now I understand you better, Mama. If so, I understand myself better. What happens now, Mama? After all these realizations, what happens now?

I don't have the answers to my questions, Mama. However, I do know the result of those childhood scenes. What were some of those scenes like? Let's go back, Mama. Let's go back and look at them together.

Puerto Rico. Before I was born, Mama worked as a maid for an aristocratic white family in Río Piedras, a neighboring town to Carolina, where she lived. As far as I can tell, they were fairly nice. However, blacks who worked for whites were proud of their status and often covered up what really went on at their jobs. So I have no way of knowing how nice Mama's white employers really were. Mama was a novelty in the village; not many of our people worked inside the houses of whites. The entire village would crowd around Mama and ask her about the white people. The black people of Carolina, like those in the United States at that time, saw people as part of an intricate hierarchy according to the jobs people held. My mother was high on the hierarchy, and in order to maintain her honored status she would romanticize her situation.

While working in this house, my mother met Sebastian Aguilar, an orange vendor. One day, when driving by in his jalopy, he caught sight of my mother in a group of girls waiting for the bus. He pulled over and asked to speak with *la negrita* (an affectionate term for "the dark one"). My mother says that she was overwhelmed by this strikingly handsome man who asked her name.

Afterwards, he would go by every day to talk to *la negrita*. He filled her head with promises of love and marriage. My mother—a country girl who had never been approached by a man before—fell victim to the suave, shrewd, and enchanting rap of this man.

He seduced my mother with promises of a better life in a faraway and magic place called America. He told her that she was the only woman in his life and that they would soon be married. With perfect innocence, my mother believed all this; she had never before heard the sweet words of love, and her head spun.

Soon the inevitable happened: my mother became pregnant. Her family was outraged. The orange vendor refused to marry her. In self-defense, Mama finally told everyone who he was. He agreed to marry her only when my uncle Pablo threatened to castrate him with a machete.

My mother then went to live with my father in Río Piedras. At least, she thought she was going to live with him. She has confessed to me since that he was never home; he would be gone for days at a time, leaving fifty cents on the kitchen table before he went. When she went to the hospital to give birth to me, he never visited her there. As she watched all the other women happily showing off their babies when their husbands came to visit, she would look at me and say, *"Mi pobre hombrecito, nacido al mundo para sufrir."*

How horrible those days must have been for you, Mama! What did you answer the nurses when they asked you where your husband was? How desperately you must have waited for him; and still you loved him.

One of the harshest experiences that my mother had was the day she left the hospital with me. Sebastian didn't come to pick her up, so she took a taxi to the apartment. When she arrived home, she asked him to pay for the cab, but he started screaming and told her to take a taxi only when she had the money for it. He reluctantly paid the driver and then beat her, fresh out of the hospital, right out in the street, until a kindly neighbor had the nerve to ask him to stop. He kicked her one more time and walked off in a storm of anger.

Mama, you tell me that the day you named me was one of those sunny, tropical days that Puerto Rico is blessed with. The palms were swaying and the city of Río Piedras was filled with people going about their daily business. In singsong voices the vendors were hawking ice-cold coconut drinks, sweet guava juice, and oranges. In the park, everyone was in a festive mood, feeding the pigeons and passing a penny or two on to the drunks. You were caught up in this atmo-

sphere. You had your prize baby boy in your arms and you were going to give him a name.

I was named Prophet Elías Leonel Aguilar by the city clerk, a big strong black woman. My father wanted to name me Samuel, after his brother. My mother wanted to name me Leonel, after one of her brothers. The city clerk told my father that he had no right to name me. He started to protest but desisted after a look from Uncle Pablo. The clerk proceeded to denounce my father and his actions. She told him that he had a lot of gall even to think that she would allow him to name me. Between the clerk and Uncle Pablo, my father saw it was wise to give in.

Then the clerk turned to my mother and said, "For being a fool, you won't have the privilege of naming your son either." But on seeing my mother's face, she felt compassion for the innocent country girl and conceded that she could choose my middle name. But my first name was chosen by the clerk: Elías the Prophet. At that time in Puerto Rico it was common practice to give children a title.

Mama, I remember the tears running down your cheeks and the heaving of your chest and the pain in your eyes and the shame on your face when you told me the story of my first haircut.

I don't know how it is for white families, but one of the joyous moments for a Puerto Rican family is the day a son has his first haircut. Usually both parents—if not other relatives—witness the event. On the day of my haircut, my mother took me to the barber shop where my father normally had his hair cut. She was a proud and beaming mother showing off her firstborn child, a man, to the world. She told the barber that she was Sebastian Aguilar's wife. The jovial old barber picked me up with great gusto and said: "So you're the son of Don Sebastian." The barber was a jovial old man who joked and laughed the whole time we were there. My mother asked him to charge the haircut to my father's bill and the barber didn't hesitate to trim my not entirely cooperative head. The mere fact that my father wasn't there was embarrassing for mother; that she had to ask for credit was also embarrassing. But most embarrassing of all was, when she returned home, my father had a fit of anger and beat

401

her for using his name and presenting herself as his wife and me as his son—and, of course, charging the haircut to his name.

I wish I could have defended you, Mama.

It was during this time, when things were so rough, that mother met Nilsa and Pablo. Thank God for those neighbors; they were her salvation. They were very poor, but they kept her and me alive when my father went on his excursions.

Mama's eyes always warmed with appreciation and love when she told me about Nilsa and Pablo. Since they had no children, I was their pride and joy. They were an elderly couple, so Mama became a daughter to them, and I, of course, a grandson.

I remember the joy on your face when you told me about the day I was baptized.

Pablo was my godfather and Nilsa was my godmother: now she and they were official *compadres* (the relationship between the parents of the child and his godparents). It was a shame that Don Pablo and Doña Nilsa died before I knew them. They must have been the kindest souls to set foot on earth. Even though I was born under a cloud, they made life worthwhile. They never had enough to eat themselves, yet they had enough to feed Mama and me. They used to curse my father day and night. And Mama *(naïve little fool that you were)* defended him. She always received him. She never turned him away. There are those who say she accepted him out of fear, but Mama really loved him. He was the only man in her life.

She used to take care of me and my half brother Federico, my father's youngest son from a previous marriage—a marriage he had never told my mother about. Unlike me, Federico was well taken care of and always had enough to eat. He was my father's favorite son. My father had been shunned by his two older daughters and their mother, and he hated Mama and me, so Federico was his pride and joy. And yet Mama never resented Federico. She would always take care of him as if she had given birth to him herself. But I was always her *pobre hombrecito.*

And then one day my grandmother came from Carolina for her

first visit since Mama had married. It was quite a distance between Carolina and Río Piedras, and it wasn't easy to make the trip in those days. I was about a year and a half old when she came. I remember Mama telling me that the mixed emotions she felt at seeing her mother were enough to tear her soul into a thousand pieces. Evidently old Doña Carmen looked through all of the cupboards and in the closets and at everything in the apartment and said, "We're leaving this place, my daughter." Mama viciously told her that she wouldn't leave my father and that she had no right telling her to leave him. Doña Carmen slapped her again and again and asked her whether she loved him more than she loved her own son. *(Mama, when she took you away, she took you away from hell.)*

Doña Carmen wouldn't even allow Mama to say good-bye to Don Pablo and Doña Nilsa. She didn't see either of them again until five years later, when she attended their funerals, one just six months after the other. Mama never forgave her mother for that.

Back in her old village of Carolina, Mama felt the loss of her husband keenly. She would call out his name at night, murmuring over and over how much she loved him. And then she would look over at me and say out loud how much she hated him.

Everyone who knew Mama when she was young tells me she was a beautiful woman, with an angel's face and a heart to match; she was enchanting. They say that all the men in the area used to try to court her, but she wouldn't hear any of them. She was famous for her flat refusals of all men, young, gallant or not; she was a challenge to all. But they finally gave up on her—she was too busy thinking about Sebastian.

Until Mario came along.

Mario was a cowboy. He was a proud young man who would ride his chestnut mare up and down the streets of Carolina, claiming the attention and admiration of all the young ladies in the area. It was perhaps for this reason that he became attracted to Mama—she paid him no mind.

He saw her one day when she was washing me near the brook behind Doña Carmen's house. He rode up to her saying *"Buenos días, joven"* (Good day, young lady). She looked up and frowned at him. He said, "Why such a face? Don't you know that the beauty of an angelic face such as yours has no place for such frowns?" Still

403

she gave no answer. He waited a while, straightened in his saddle, sighed, gazed around. The only sounds were the clear water of the brook swirling over the large rocks that were used as stepping-stones, and the tropical birds singing from the mango and the pana trees. A breeze was blowing, cool and gentle, through the leaves of the tall palms in the distance.

Finally Mario lifted his hat and wiped his brow. He cleared his throat and asked about me. Still Mama did not answer. He dismounted and picked me up, tickling me and laughing an affectionate laugh. Mama jumped up, grabbing me from him. "Leave the child alone."

He answered confidently, "You look so enchanting when you are angry." She couldn't help but smile.

He watched Mama walk me back to the house and resolved to marry this enchanting woman. I was nearly two years old at the time.

The next day he appeared at our house to ask for Mama's hand. My grandfather was honored that Mario Del Valle wanted to marry his stepdaughter. My grandmother Carmen, however, had reservations. Since the woman is the one who really runs the household in Puerto Rican families—through the ages, it has been the woman who has held the family together when the man has run off—their decisions hold. Grandmother said no to Mario. Then my great-grandmother, the strongest woman I have ever known (and she's still going strong at ninety-seven), stepped into the picture and gave Mario permission to marry Mama. My grandmother protested feebly, saying, "But what about the opinion of Felicia?" My great-grandmother turned to Mama abruptly and asked, "What *is* your opinion?" Mama didn't hesitate to nod affirmatively. She was beginning to admire Mario, if not love him.

Mario immediately began building a house. When it was finished, Mama was married and we went to live there. Mario was the sweetest husband a woman could have. After having lived for all those long months with my father, Mama knew how to appreciate Mario. He would come home from working in the fields, pick both of us up at the same time, and give us a kiss. She was the happiest woman in the world in those days. And I had a papa, the only papa I had ever known. Mario was a big man (about six feet two), and strong. To a small child he was towering. Mama was beautiful in those days.

My only other memories are of Mario beating me for killing a
chicken, and of the dog that my great-grandmother used to have—
he was mean. The rest I know from your stories, Mama.

She told me that I was a bouncy little child, full of pep and that
I was my great-grandmother's darling. Great-grandmother would
play records for me, clap her hands and stamp her feet and sing *"A*
Leo le gusta el baile" (Little Leo likes to dance). So I would dance
for her. Holding my hands up in the air, thrusting my big belly
forward and spinning around, I would dance to the bomba beat of
my favorite song, Cortijo's *"El Bonbón de Elena."*

Just when everything was so happy and beautiful we received
some very exciting news: New York!

Mario had been talking about it for quite a while. He had been
told by friends about the financial opportunities that were there
simply for the asking. It was his dream to go to New York and give
my mother and me a better life. He was tired of the limitations of
Carolina. He was an intelligent man, with high aspirations and a
high-school diploma. In those days you could go far with a high-
school education.

Yes, Nuu Jork! The land of promise and freedom for all! The land
of opportunity for every man, black or white, rich or poor, weak or
strong. Mario believed it all, like a man whose life's ambition is the
fulfillment of the American dream: work hard and get ahead.

The day finally arrived when Mario left for Nuu Jork. He was at
his best that day, jovial, high-spirited, and loving. He left with a big
smile on his face and a tear that was suppressed: a man doesn't cry.

He would go ahead of us and work for a while, and when he was
established, we would follow. Meanwhile, there was tremendous
excitement in the village. Mario was already in Nuu Jork; we would
soon be there too. As I walked around the village, people would ask
me, *"Nene, a dónde vas?"* (Boy, where are you going?) and I would
answer, *"A joi con mimama"* (To New York with my mother), in
childish jibberish. Things didn't work out as smoothly as Mario
envisioned when he first told us of his plan. Although he slaved at
two jobs for several months, the object of his labor—getting us there
—didn't come for a long time. Weeks passed, then months, and still

405

we couldn't join Mario. At first he wrote almost daily, then weekly, then biweekly, then not at all.

It was destroying Mama.

She had been given the promise of a new life; instead, she once again knew pain and sorrow.

And then one day the letter arrived, neatly folded, with two Pan American Airlines tickets. We were going to New York! I was almost four years old. The blush returned to my mother's cheeks. Mario had come through after all.

Finally, on November 10, 1959, the town of Carolina sent us on our way to the San Juan airport. Tears ran down my mother's cheeks as she said good-bye to *las parsellas* (an affectionate term for the sugar cane fields).

Mama, it would have been much better if you had never left the security of those fields.

Papa should have told us it would be so cold. The icy November wind chilled my tropical bones as he put his cheap suit-jacket around me, his arm around Mama, and led us from the plane to the shelter of La Guardia Airport.

We had finally arrived. Mama was awed by the airport, the planes, the customs officers, and all the white people. She had never seen so many white people. I was frightened by it all.

We picked up our cardboard suitcases from a conveyor belt, met Papa's new friend Elías Zarzuela, and then went to the parking lot to find Elías's car. Elías was a handsome man, with a very light complexion. He was almost as tall as Papa and talked funny. He had been in the United States for over ten years and spoke a hybrid Spanish which he called Spanglish.

I was glad to see Papa, but I was unhappy in the unfamiliar surroundings. Elías noticed this and tried to make me laugh by making faces, which only made me cry harder. Finally he gave up trying to make me laugh and concentrated on my mother. My mother doubled over with laughter as I watched, and finally even I joined in the merriment. It was amazing how comfortable this man could make you feel. All four-year-olds should have someone around like Elías Zarzuela.

Papa looked different too. He had always had a clean, smooth face with a neat, trim mustache. Now he had a rough, scaly, unshaven face that made me squirm when he rubbed his cheek next to mine.

He wore a dark suit with a white shirt and a dark fedora. Elías wore something I had never seen before—a coat.

Even driving in the car it was cold. I thought the car would never stop, and I kept asking when we would get there. When we drove into Manhattan, I was stunned by everything around me. It must be shocking for anyone to be in New York for the first time; given my background, I was terrified. Mama remained awed.

Finally, we reached the apartment at 112th Street and Second Avenue. It was dark, and I felt the intense cold as soon as we stepped out of the car. We were rushed into the house, but it wasn't much warmer there.

The minute we entered, Mama shrieked, and I forgot about the cold momentarily. Elías laughed, Papa was flustered, I was puzzled, and Mama cried on Papa's shoulders. I asked Mama what was wrong and she didn't answer. I asked Papa what was wrong with Mama, and he didn't answer either. So I timidly asked Elías and he told me that it was a *ratón* (rat). I asked him what a *ratón* was and he said that I would find out for myself. I wasn't satisfied with his answer, but I dropped the subject since no one would explain.

Elías left the apartment and returned a little later with some white containers with metal handles. Inside: *cuchifritos y guineítos*—pork rind made in a sauce with boiled bananas. They tasted terrible.

That night was one of the most miserable nights of our lives. It was cold and dark. I was freezing and frightened. Mama says that Papa didn't sleep at all that night: he was watching over me with a baseball bat so the rats wouldn't come near.

After many nights like that we moved to a new apartment at East 106th Street and First Avenue. In the new apartment, Mama says that she and Papa would take turns watching over me at night because of the roaches. Sometimes she would doze off and find a blanket of roaches covering me. Then she would wake Papa in horror and Papa would take a casserole of water and throw it over me. Then he would dry and comfort me because I woke up scared and wet. I can't remember any of that, but Mama tells me it is true.

What I do remember is Christmas when I was five years old. My real father, who had been in New York for a few years, came over and brought me a red tricycle. I remember that he brought a box of chocolates for Mama and that Papa wasn't there. At the time I couldn't understand why Papa wasn't there but later I found out. I remember my real father beat me because I was "disrespectful." Even so, I loved that red tricycle. I played with it day and night. I was the envy of the neighborhood.

And so it was with the first five years of my life, Mama. For most of what I've related so far I've depended on your stories and those of friends and relatives. From this point forward, my own memory takes over.

Papa was a changed man from the gallant cowboy who had courted Mama in Puerto Rico. Mario had been full of high aspirations and hopes. Mama and I had to withstand the pain of watching the slow disintegration of a potentially great man. Like so many of our people, he came to the United States from the sugarcane fields of his native land looking for a better life for himself and his family. In this sense, Mario was no different from the majority of Puerto Rican immigrants.

Mario was also typical in another way. He gave up hope. After several years in this country, trying hard to become someone his family could be proud of, trying hard to fulfill his dream, he had gotten nowhere. He was still working in the same place where he had begun working, an Italian bakery.

Mario was the victim of the American myth—that anyone can do well in this, the land of the free and the home of the brave. This myth of opportunity is perpetuated by the very ones who become its victims. The man who comes here and has his dreams shattered will spend his money to buy clothes, gifts, and plane fare to Puerto Rico, where he will give his family and friends the impression that he is really making it big in the mystical land. Young men observe him closely, listen intently to his stories about Nuu Jork, dream, and wait for their chance to come too.

Mario was one of these young men. He came here to seek the promises offered by the American dream and was offered nothing but a nightmare. What happens to a man whose dreams have been shattered? What happens when he sees his family living in a cold apartment with rats and roaches? What happens when he hears his children cry because they are hungry? What is a man to do when his wife looks at him every day with hate, because her dreams, too, have been ruined? So many families have been torn apart this way, and ours was no exception. Mario tried and tried and then tired of trying.

Alcohol became his escape.

And Mama suffered.

O, Mama, how Papa made you suffer with his alcohol problem!

He would work all week (he couldn't stand it unless he was working), and then go to Johnny's Dover House and spend a good portion of his paycheck. Every street corner in every ghetto has a bar. Why? Because it takes advantage of the disillusionment of the many proud men who come to this country. Such men are led to believe that the only reason they can't become rich—or even President— is that they lack the will, that they are lazy good-for-nothings. The easy availability in the ghetto, first of alcohol, and now of drugs, feeds this disillusionment and also helps perpetuate it. With myths and alcohol, the establishment can maintain the status quo, but it also contributes to the ruin of many good families. If Mama had not been so strong, it would have destroyed ours.

Mama used to send me looking for Papa. I would always go to Johnny's Dover House first, but sometimes Papa wouldn't be there. Johnny impressed me as a kind man. He was short and pudgy, with no hair on his head and a deep bellow for a laugh. Both jolly and sensitive, he would feel sorry for Papa and tell him to stop drinking, that he had had too much. At the time I used to appreciate Johnny's saying that, but now I wonder: Why, if Johnny knew what his bar was doing to people's lives, didn't he close it?

Mama had a rough time with Papa. Do you know what it is to go to bed with a drunken man? Do you know what it is to watch him beat your son for no reason?

On payday, though, Papa would always bring home a five- or ten-pound sack of rice and some red kidney beans. Once or twice a week he would go to *el mercado* and buy fish, chicken, or beef. He instructed Mama that the meat was only for him, no one else was to touch it. "I'm a working man, I need it more than you do," he'd say. Little did he realize that Mama worked in the house just as hard as he did at the bakery. Yet Mama obeyed. A part of her was still the shy country girl, but another part was maturing into a strong woman. You learn fast in the ghetto or you don't survive.

Papa wasn't surviving.

Mama was.

I don't remember kindergarten very well; I simply remember that the teacher's name was Mrs. Pitman. She was a harmless creature —a small, round, pleasant black woman. She used to teach us to be proud of what we were. She would bring in pictures and slides which told of black people's history.

I remember first grade better. Mrs. Carney was the meanest white woman I've ever known. She was a big, square-jawed Irishwoman, with red hair and a nasty temper, who would pull my ears. One day when I arrived home from school, my ears were so red that Mama demanded to know what had happened. She finally made me tell her.

The next day Mama stormed into school and told that white woman to leave her son alone. I was deeply embarrassed when, in her broken English, she told old Mrs. Carney off in front of all the other kids. As I had anticipated, I never heard the end of it. It was at this point that I became a fighter. The very day Mama came to school to tell Mrs. Carney off, I had my first fight.

In the ghetto you have to fight to survive. If you don't kick somebody's ass every once in a while, you'll gain a reputation as a sissy. That day, Emilio, a tall, skinny Puerto Rican, had been riding me all day and I was pissed off. After school, in the large coat closet behind the classroom, we came face to face. He taunted me, called me a sissy, a mama's boy. He called my mother a *jibara* (country-woman) who hung out on the street corners as a whore. I grabbed him by his collar and picked him up with a strength I didn't know I possessed. Then I threw him against the wall and began punching his face. I drew back in horror. One of the coat hooks had stuck in his head. He fell to the floor unconscious with blood gushing like a running faucet out of the back of his head. All the kids started

410

screaming. Mrs. Carney came in and fainted, while I stood there just looking at him—terrified.

Soon the principal arrived and took him to the nurse's office for temporary care. The ambulance was called and the class was taken to the principal's office. I kept telling the principal that it was an accident, but all the kids accused me. My mother was called in and I stood there and watched this tall, gray-haired man with huge black-rimmed glasses tell my mother that it was her fault that her son was a delinquent.

Bless his soul, Emilio himself pulled me out of the bind, by insisting that it was an accident. The principal had been talking about sending me to a reform school. I was amazed listening to Emilio defend me. I remembered how scared I was when I had seen him fall. I had thought that I had killed him. Then, two days later, he defended me. It was a curious thing—that honor system we kids were loyal to. Emilio hated my guts, but he wouldn't break the rule that you don't rat on a brother. He wouldn't even rat on a brother who had nearly killed him. Emilio and I became great friends after that.

In December of my first-grade year, my little sister was born. You should have seen my mother. She had always wanted a girl and this one was her pride and joy: she had a light complexion with light brown hair and light eyes. My little sister's appearance was enough to blot out her guilt feelings about bringing a child into the world. She named her Milagros (miracle, named that because my mother considered her birth a miracle).

My mother spent a lot of money buying the baby dresses, toys, and a crib, and all the other things babies need. For the first time in her life she mismanaged money. Because of that, it was going to be an especially rough winter for all of us.

I had been an only child for seven years. In New York, I had lived in horrid conditions, but I had always had enough to eat. It wasn't very healthful food—I was always taking notes home from school saying I needed cod liver oil, vitamins, and protein and that I was anemic—but I was never really hungry. Of course, while we were in Puerto Rico I had eaten like a king, and it was healthful food too. But in the year following Milagros's birth, I was outright hungry.

Second grade brings much clearer memories for me than first. I remember the day that John F. Kennedy was shot. I was in Mrs. Runz's second-grade class. It was about one thirty or two o'clock in the afternoon. A young teacher came into the classroom in near hysteria and blurted out that President Kennedy had been killed. This set off further hysteria from Mrs. Runz and all the kids in the class. It was chaos. Kids were crying about something they didn't even understand. I cried too. I cried at the death of a president of the country that was destroying my father, putting my mother through hell, creating havoc in my mind, and keeping me hungry and cold. I cried at the death of the man who led this monster that was eating away our lives.

But it was the winter of that year that was so horrible. I will never forget it as long as I live. It was the winter that Benjie entered our lives and left just as abruptly.

Benjie was born in December—just a year after Milagros. A plump, jolly little nigger with a beautiful smile and dimples in his cheeks, Benjie was the most beautiful baby I had ever seen. But there were too many mouths to feed. Papa, Mama, me, Milagros, and now Benjie. And Benjie had a voracious appetite.

The apartment was incredibly cold. Benjie slept in the crib and my little sister would sleep with me. Mama kept Benjie's crib in the room reserved for her and Papa. But Mama always came to bed with me and Milagros because, as usual, Papa would be out drinking.

One morning Mama was frightened because Benjie, who always woke promptly at eight to holler for his food, had not awakened her. It was nine thirty and I had missed getting up for school.

I awoke as Mama stirred, then jumped out of bed at the sight of the clock and rushed from the room. Since I was still half asleep, I looked at the clock with one eye closed and was shocked at the time. I said "Ma—" but never completed the word. I heard wild screams coming from the next bedroom—and I'll continue to hear those screams forever. The screams of a mother who can't take any more; the screams of all ghetto mothers who have led a life like my mother's. I was so frightened I couldn't move from my bed.

A pounding on the front door and shouting from the hall outside brought me to my senses. I jumped out of bed and opened the front door. The neighbors all rushed in and picked up Mama, who was hysterical. She screamed uncontrollably and threw herself against the floor, calling for the devil to take her away. She cursed God and my father and my stepfather and the United States and everything that she could think of. Obscenities I had never heard before rolled off of her tongue. The neighbors tried to comfort her; they tried to find out what was the matter, they told her to think of her son who was standing there watching and her one-year-old daughter who was shrieking with terror and trying to hold on to her, but was being thrown around the room by the force of her anger. They tried to calm her by mentioning the baby. But each time Benjie was mentioned, Mama went into another fit. By this time I was so scared that I couldn't move.

It seemed strange that Benjie wasn't crying. Half of the neighborhood had crowded into the tiny three-room apartment and yet Benjie wasn't crying. One of the neighbors went into the baby's room, closely followed by others. Everyone else was either trying to control Mama or holding my little sister or saying something to me that I couldn't or didn't want to hear.

Suddenly, there were more screams from Benjie's room. The neighbors rushed out yelling: *"Está muerto, está muerto!"*

I couldn't take it at first. But gradually I realized what they were saying: "He's dead." I screamed and rushed into his room.

I'll never forget what I saw there. My little brother. Little Benjie. Healthy, bouncy, jovial, warm little Benjie. A hunk of ice. I kept thinking to myself, a hunk of ice. My little brother, killed by the cold, harsh winter of America. We live a winter in America all of our lives, and it slowly kills us all; but why so soon? Why Benjie? He died of pneumonia. A cold Harlem apartment killed my little brother.

I ran out of the room directly to Mama and began to kick all the neighbors who were trying to hold her. At the top of my lungs, with all the strength an eight-year-old could muster, I yelled, *"Maa-maa!! Maaaaaamaaaaaa!!!!!!!!!!!!!!!! !!!!!!!!!!!!!!!!!!!!!!!!!!!"* To this day I believe that those two screams of desperation from her eight-year-old son saved my mother from insanity.

She looked at me, a crazy look in her eyes, then brought my head to her bosom and cried silently as I wept uncontrollably. Then my little sister curled up under the other arm. From that moment on, Mama became a Rock of Gibraltar for my sister and me. From that moment on, Mama became the Mama that I know.

But where was Papa?

As usual, he was nowhere to be found.

Mama told Papa to leave after that. She told him never to come back. She blamed him for Benjie's death. And he blamed himself. It's the victim who's taught to take the blame in America.

With Papa gone, it was just me, Mama, Milagros, and Mama's growing belly, testimony to Roberto, who would be arriving in a few months.

From then on in our life, it was all Mama. No longer the shy country girl from Carolina who had been seduced by the orange vendor; she was a ghetto mother now, complete with all the pain and heartache that being a ghetto mother brings. She was ready for anything now.

ELÍAS–POLITICAL SCIENTIST

*W*HEN Elías jumped off the train at Bedford Hills, I could see that he'd lost none of his old energy and bounce. He looked as trim and happy as a basketball player stepping out of the locker room after a winning game. Very kindly, he had come out from New York to meet me because I didn't have time to drive into the city. He approached with a big smile. It was August 1979.

"Well, how ya doin', Mrs. Coffin?" (He was always very formal in addressing me.) "How ya doin'?"

"I'm fine, Elías. And you?"

"Great, man, great!" Then he paused and looked at me, turning temporarily serious. "You know, I've been through a lot, but I'm getting wiser. I'm not as crazy as I was." He smiled again; this time his face relaxed and his eyes spoke with a gentleness I hadn't seen before. I'm not sure I could have predicted the stories he would tell during the rest of the evening but I did realize, right at that moment, that Elías was no longer frightened of being co-opted by "whites" as a "house nigger" and that his basic values and tenderheartedness had held strong. Nothing could have given me greater pleasure. I

415

thought for a moment of other young activists I'd known and some of the routes they had taken—violence, Indian gurus, California space-outs, or an about-face to ultra-conservatism. Elías had navigated the revolutionary seas and was standing steady, still determined to make the world a better place.

As we walked across the station parking lot to the restaurant, he told me he had taken a year off from his graduate studies in political science at Yale and was now working as an administrator for the Youth Employment Program of the A. Philip Randolph Institute in New York, helping high-school dropouts get their diplomas and training them for a career.

"And you like working with these kids?"

"Yeah, I love my job. I worked with kids more directly when I was in New Haven. Now I'm an administrator—hah!—so I don't work with kids that closely, but it's still exciting. Mostly because I believe, at least at a practical level, in what the Randolph Institute believes in. They're socialist, but they believe in America and working within the political framework—voter registration, lobbying, union organizing, all that stuff. They've got a hundred and eighty chapters in eighty-nine different cities."

He gave me a sidelong glance. Elías, I knew, was warming up to his subject. "You know, as Che Guevara once said, 'A true revolutionary is motivated by intense feelings of love.' That's true, but we've got to be smarter in our love. In the sixties a lot of people were out screaming and protesting. We've got to move from protest to politics, as Randolph would say, and become a lot more mature in the way we view things. At one moment the pendulum is way over here and you go along with all the injustices because you don't know any better—you're an Uncle Tom. At the next moment, the pendulum has shifted to the other side and all you can do is hate the oppressor. Then the pendulum finally settles and you begin to understand things for what they are. It's so easy for me as a man, growing up in the time I grew up, to judge Uncle Toms and all that bullshit. Maybe, if I had lived in that time, I would've acted that way too. Not everybody's an A. Philip Randolph. Not everybody's got that kind of balls."

After a year at the Randolph Institute, Elías was planning to complete his Ph.D. at Yale and then teach, he hoped, at City

College in New York, where there were more Puerto Rican students than at any other college in the country. "I was never taught by a Puerto Rican," he said, "and I think it would have made things a lot easier if I'd had someone who understood what I was going through—socially, psychologically, and academically. There are still very few of our people who can act as resources to our students, and I'd like to be one of them.

"You know," he continued, "people are a lot smarter than you think—they know what's wrong with the political and economic system. It's just that they've got this *Ay Bendito* complex—the leave-it-alone attitude. They say *'Que sea lo que Dios quiera'*—let things be as God willed—what can we do about it? Well, we've got to *do*. We've got to dream up something better. In *Don Quixote* it is said, *'Los sueños, sueños son'*—dreams are dreams. I don't believe that. Shit, man, that's precisely what distinguishes man from animals—he can take what's in his head and make it real. As Gramsci says, 'The active politician thinks about what ought to be.' " He was now back in full form—quotes and all. But now they were beginning to sound less like the Panthers and more like footnotes to a thesis.

It was not until we had almost finished dinner that Elías spoke about his marriage and divorce . . . and his son. Even then, he backed into the subject by saying that he felt that the pressure cooker of graduate school forced students to become dehumanized and develop survival tactics that were inimicable to personal relations. "It's no good if you're working all the time and have no time for feelings—especially if you have a situation at home you gotta deal with." Elías was not the only one I'd heard from on this problem. "Or you're in love."

"In love?"

"Yeh." he laughed, somewhat embarrassed. Then turned serious. "Yeh, I was married and everything was fine until I went to graduate school."

Elías married Maria, a fellow Yale student, just after he graduated in June 1978. They had a small ceremony and lively reception at St. Thomas More, the Catholic chapel at Yale. Maria was six months pregnant. They had discussed the possibility of abortion—neither was opposed to it on religious grounds—but they had decided

417

against it. They were very much in love. Maria's family, however, had opposed the marriage. Her Japanese mother and Filipino father had emigrated to Los Angeles shortly after they were married—under similar conditions—in Japan in 1953. They now lived in Orange county, where Maria's father, formerly a sailor, worked as boilermaker for a university and her mother ran a chain of prosperous beauty shops. "You know," said Elías, "I wasn't exactly what her family had in mind for their youngest child and only daughter. I was Puerto Rican and I was poor. Her mother had a vision of Maria marrying a good Japanese boy from a wealthy family and living near her in Orange county. I think she might have been willing to accept most of the rest—everything except the fact that her daughter wouldn't be living in California."

Elías worked that summer for the Randolph Institute in New Haven and both eagerly prepared for the baby, who was born after a difficult labor on August 26. "Boy—did I get into my son," he recalled. "I saw him born. I cut his umbilical cord. Maria had forty hours of labor and I was there every minute."

"And what did you name him?" I asked.

Elías laughed sheepishly. "Junior," he said.

Big Elías sectioned a part of a room in their student housing apartment for little Elías. He painted it light blue with white trim and bought him white furniture and a blue rug and blue curtains. He was very proud of it. He was happy with his wife and baby, and his life was great.

In the fall Elías started graduate school, and in late December Maria and the baby went to visit her parents in Los Angeles while Elías prepared for midterm exams. On January 9, the day they were scheduled to return, Maria called and said they were not coming back. He has not seen them since.

It was taking Elías some time to recover from this loss, and he was trying hard to understand what had happened. "I try to look at it from her point of view. My mother was against the marriage too. She wanted me to marry a Puerto Rican, and I guess Maria sensed that. Then graduate school—I was working from nine to midnight six days a week and didn't have much energy left over. I could be pretty insensitive. I can see how she was unhappy—between her family, my

418

school, lack of money, and a lot of inexperience and lack of maturity on both our parts."

He took out his wallet and showed me a picture of a handsome plump baby. He smiled. Then suddenly his face clouded over as only Elías's face could cloud over. "Oh shit—man—I loved my wife and I love my son. I miss them both. I had my whole life figured out. I was a student, I was going to be a teacher, I had this scholarship. Everything was cool. It's like a nice long album—it's real mellow and it's just beginning and you're five minutes into it and you're really cooled out. Then all of a sudden somebody scratches it all the way across. I have to sit back and think about things now. You see, my motivation for graduate school was my son—I had to make a future for him. Without him, I wasn't sure it made sense for me."

That's when Elías decided to take a year off to work in New York. He was now living in a three-room apartment on Mott Street in New York's Chinatown. He felt at home "back with my people" and was doing things he couldn't do at Yale. He played basketball in the neighborhood park, and in the evenings he played the drums— bongos, congas, and timbales—in local street bands. "They are really good—high quality music. It's very exciting. I take lessons every Wednesday night with two of the best drummers in the world." Elías drummed on the table with his hands and grinned broadly. "You know," he said, "I couldn't live without music. It always cures me when I think I can't make it."

Elías's main worry now was money. "Man, I'm twenty-five. I should be out there working consistently and contributing to my family—not going back to graduate school." When he returns to Yale, a fellowship from the Danforth Foundation will support him and allow a small stipend for his son. He was grateful for this. "I send him what I can. I think that's very important. When he's older I never want him to say what I said about my father—'Damn, man, where were you when I was a little kid?' " But his sparse funds were not sufficient to allow him to visit his son in California or have his son visit him—even if his wife and her family would permit him to. "Right now, I simply can't afford to do anything about seeing my son," he said sadly.

He was even more concerned about his mother, who had developed diabetes and high blood pressure. She was living in the same

419

house in Passaic and had remarried, but her third husband suffered heavily from asthma and neither could work regular hours any longer. They were having a hard time making ends meet, and it would be some time still before Elías's younger sister and brother could contribute. His sister had another year of high school before entering Rutgers Nursing School and his brother was still only a high-school sophomore. "I can contribute something this year, but when I go back to Yale, then . . ." What seemed to keep Elías in graduate school, in spite of his tough economics, was his desire to teach. "Perhaps I can instill in my people the idea that it's possible to change things through organization," he said.

Elías had never shown his story to his mother because he felt it might be too painful for her to relive those memories. But he was reluctant to publish it without her reading it. "She cried," he said. "She was surprised I remembered so much about our early life. But she was relieved that it was all okay. We're very close." She helped him change names and places so that it wouldn't hurt anyone else —particularly his father and Mario.

I asked him if he ever saw his father or Mario. "Not Mario—but my real father, yes. I still feel he was wrong in the period I wrote about," Elías said, "but I'm a human being and he's a human being. All right, he did some fucked-up things. But now he looks at me and he's proud of me—Yale and all that. My first reaction to that was, 'Damn, man, I needed you when I was a baby. Now I'm a man and I can take care of myself!' But he's become very active in the labor movement in New York and I've come to respect some of the things he does."

As we walked back to the station in the night, I told him I was glad to see him so well and happy in spite of his troubles.

"Yes," he replied, "things are looking up again."

Things were still looking up in summer of 1981. He was back at Yale and had just completed his master's thesis and was planning his Ph.D. dissertation on political and economic life in Puerto Rico. He was in love again—this time with a Puerto Rican student from Marymount College in New York, who was "beautiful and very calm —just what I need." They see each other on weekends and are thinking—just possibly—of being married when she graduates. "Everything's pretty cool for me—except for money, and that's always depressing."

Elías's year in New York had shocked him. After a brief honeymoon with the city, he found the inner city completely disintegrating—especially for the poor. Around Mott Street, where he lived, the city had decided to renovate and upgrade an eight-block area, installing new street lighting and electricity lines to the apartment buildings, most of which had been rent-controlled. With city backing, the landlords began evicting the tenants, many of whom were elderly. They raised their rents in some cases by four hundred percent.

"I saw how shopping-bag ladies are made," said Elías. "An old woman who lived on the floor below me was so weak that sometimes she couldn't open her door, which used to stick in its frame, especially in hot weather. I used to help her out—go to the store and things like that. One day I came home from work and there she was on the street with her few belongings in a shopping bag and the landlord was just standing around, smiling. I lost my temper and went after the landlord, but a black cop stepped in and got me to cool it. I'm glad he did. It wouldn't have done any good. They evicted everyone on the block. I was evicted the same day. I never got any notice. By law, the landlord has to give you notice, but not necessarily in writing; if it comes to a court case, he can always claim he told you, and it's your word against his. I just returned home and all my belongings had been taken in boxes to the Sanitation Department, where I had to go and pick them up. I had paid $175 a month in rent. They planned to raise it to $700. If I teach at City College, I guess I'll have to live in the suburbs."

Elías wanted to add a postscript to his story, which I was reluctant to have him do, but I told him I would include some of it in his biography. It read, in part, "In spite of the harshness of some of my life, I feel I am very lucky, for I grew up with a great deal of love and retain the spiritual intuitiveness that my mother imparted. I now have a rewarding relationship with my father. I no longer am bitter about my early years but I *have* been left with a deep commitment to do all within my power to change the conditions which create stories like 'Madre Puertorríqueña.'"

HARRIET HARVEY

A graduate of Vassar, Harriet Harvey started her career as a journalist in Japan, China, and Hong Kong, where she became the chief feature writer for the *Hong Kong Telegraph*. Following her return to the United States, she worked in television and hosted her own interview program, *It's a Wonderful World*, for WJZ-TV, ABC's New York Station. She then began to develop her specialty: translating scientific and medical research into popular books, articles, and films, working first at the American Geographical Society and, in subsequent years at Harvard and MIT. In 1961, at the Boston Children's Medical Center, she founded a unique publishing program, Publications for Parents, and developed some thirteen books and films, including such standard works as *The Child Health Encyclopedia* and such perennial favorites as *What to Do When "There's Nothing to Do."* From 1971 to 1976 she taught writing at Yale University. She then returned to television to produce documentaries and acted simultaneously as an editorial consultant for Norman Lear's Tandem/TAT Productions to create books from their situation comedies. She is currently working on a TV documentary on the quality of working life with California Newsreel and the National Film Board of Canada.

She has published short stories and articles in *The New Yorker, The New York Times, Vogue,* and *Parents Magazine.*

She is the mother of two children and presently lives in California.

DATE DUE

JUN 1 3 83			
NOV 9 1987			
MAY 2 2 2002			